CONFLIC

ONE WEEK
LOAN

This book is due for return on or before the last date shown below.

Conflict: Human Needs Theory

Edited by

John Burton
Center for Conflict Analysis and Resolution
George Mason University, Virginia, USA

palgrave
macmillan

First published in Great Britain 1990 by
THE MACMILLAN PRESS LTD
Houndmills, Basingstoke, Hampshire RG21 2XS
and London
Companies and representatives
throughout the world

A catalogue record for this book is available
from the British Library.

ISBN 10: 0-333-52141-7 hardcover
ISBN 13: 978-0-333-52141-7 hardcover
ISBN 10: 0-333-52148-X paperback
ISBN 13: 978-0-333-52148-9 paperback

This book is printed on paper suitable for recycling and made from fully
managed and sustained forest sources. Logging, pulping and manufacturing
processes are expected to conform to the environmental regulations of the
country of origin.

First published in the United States of America 1990 by
Scholarly and Reference Division,
ST. MARTIN'S PRESS, INC.,
175 Fifth Avenue,
New York, N.Y. 10010

ISBN 0-312-04034-2 (cloth)
ISBN 0-312-10618-1 (paper)

Library of Congress Cataloging-in-Publication Data
Burton, John W. (John Wear), 1915–
Conflict: human needs theory/ John Burton.
p. cm.
ISBN 0-312-04034-2. — ISBN 0-312-10618-1 (paper)
1. Social conflict. 2. Conflict management. I. Title.
HM136.B785 1990
303.6'9—dc20 89-10965
CIP

Printed and bound in Great Britain by
CPI Antony Rowe, Chippenham and Eastbourne

The Conflict Series

1. CONFLICT: RESOLUTION AND PROVENTION,* by *John Burton*

2. CONFLICT: HUMAN NEEDS THEORY, *edited by John Burton*

3. CONFLICT: READINGS IN MANAGEMENT AND RESOLUTION, *edited by John Burton and Frank Dukes*

4. CONFLICT: PRACTICES IN MANAGEMENT, SETTLEMENT AND RESOLUTION, *by John Burton and Frank Dukes*

*Provention
The term *prevention* has the connotation of containment. The term *provention* has been introduced to signify taking steps to remove sources of conflict, and more positively to promote conditions in which collaborative and valued relationships control behaviors.

Foreword to the Series

Samuel W. Lewis
President, United States Institute of Peace

We seem to know much more about how wars and other violent international conflicts get started than we do about how to end them. Nor do we understand very well how to transform settlements that terminate immediate hostilities into enduring peaceful relationships through which nations can continue to work out their differences without violence. The lack of attention to these questions, at least with regard to relations among sovereign governments, is due in some degree to the way international relations as an academic subject has traditionally been studied. By and large, more academic theory and analysis have been devoted to patterns and causes in international behavior with an eye to perfecting explanatory theory than to effective, usable remedies to international conflicts. We have assumed the remedies would become plain once the correct theory was found.

That imbalance is now being corrected. Interest is now growing in the theory and practice of "conflict resolution," a new field concerned specifically with the nature of conflict as a generic human problem and with techniques or initiatives that might be applied productively in addressing conflicts. This new emphasis is reflected in the emergence of alternative dispute resolution methods in the law profession, of peace studies or conflict resolution programs in many of the nation's colleges and universities, of research journals devoted specifically to conflict and its resolution, and of community mediation or problem-solving strategies at the local level and "second-track diplomacy" at the international level.

Providing much of the conceptual foundation for an explicit focus on conflict itself has been a small but growing group of interdisciplinary scholars engaged in a search for formulas and processes that seem to work in ending conflicts among nations and groups. They are seeking to identify those institutional and societal structures that have the best chance of ensuring a lasting and just peace among conflicting interests. Unfortunately, the work of these scholars has not reached the widest circles of policy makers, professionals, students, and researchers who could benefit from the stimulating explorations of the conflict resolution school of thought.

The United States Institute of Peace wishes to commend the four book Conflict Series: an effort by one of the acknowledged founding fathers of the conflict resolution field to summarize the main insights of the field to date for a wider readership. In these books, John Burton, with the assistance of other major contributors, delineates the distinctive scope of the conflict resolution field, defines its key concepts, explains how the field emerged out of existing approaches to conflict and peace and how it differs from them, summarizes the field's leading substantive insights about conflict and its resolutions, collects some of the best readings produced by the field, and probes where the field needs to go in the future to strengthen its theory and applicability to real problems. The series also surveys extant practical techniques for conflict management such as mediation, adjudication, ombudsmen, interactive management, and problem-solving workshops and explores their utility for different types of conflict situations. Of course, the views expressed in these volumes are those of the authors alone and do not necessarily reflect views of the Institute of Peace.

Impressively, John Burton and Frank Dukes completed this broad examination of the conflict resolution field during Burton's year as a Distinguished Fellow of the United States Institute of Peace in 1988–89 while he was also a Distinguished Visiting Professor at the Center for Conflict Resolution at George Mason University in Virginia. No one in the world is better qualified to present the conflict resolution field's distinctive perspectives and unique contributions than is Burton, whom many in the field regard as its first leading explorer and one of its most ardent spokesmen before students, scholars, and governments since its beginnings in the late 1950s. In preparing this series, Burton has drawn on the wealth of his extensive academic training in economics and international relations and his 25 years of research and teaching at universities in three countries, as reflected in his previous ten books and numerous articles. He also has applied the lessons of his practical experience as a diplomat for the Australian government and as a third party facilitator in efforts to end such conflicts as Lebanon, Cyprus, Northern Ireland, and Sri Lanka.

The United States Institute of Peace is a non-partisan, independent institution created and funded by the United States Congress to strengthen the nation's capacity to understand and deal more effectively with international conflict through peaceful means. It serves this purpose by supporting research and education projects that will expand and disseminate available knowledge about the nature of international conflict and the full range of ways it can be resolved within a framework that maximizes freedom and justice. Within this challenging mandate, one of our tasks is to identify serious, innovative, but less well known approaches that may bear further examination and to bring the insights from these approaches to wider circles so that fruitful dialogue among different perspectives is fostered.

John Burton's work complements another Institute project that is mapping all the major "roads to peace" – e.g., international law, diplomacy and negotiations, transnationalism, deterrence theory, non-violence traditions, and international organizations – that have been emphasized in the scholarly literature and world of practice as important methods and tools for achieving international peace. The conflict resolution method and outlook is one of the approaches the Institute wishes to see more widely understood so their respective strengths and limitations can be sorted out and constructive syntheses can be developed. In short, we seek to stimulate much faster dissemination of ideas and cross-fertilization than normally would occur across the barriers of different academic disciplines, professions, governmental spheres, and private organizations that are concerned in various ways with international conflict and its resolution, although they may not necessarily describe their concerns in exactly these terms.

By supporting John Burton's work, the United States Institute of Peace hopes that the perspectives, insights, and new directions for analysis of this relatively new field of conflict resolution will be brought before, and enrich the work of, a wider readership of international relations and conflict resolution students; practitioners in fields such as law, government, labor and industrial management, and social work; policy makers at all levels; as well as scholars concerned with conflict issues.

Washington, D.C.

Preface to the Series

It is not easy for those who are seeking new approaches to move from deterrence theories and practices of conflict *settlement* and *management* to conflict *resolution* theory and practice. The jump to prevention and the predictive capabilities that prevention requires, is even more challenging. These are different fields with different assumptions. While they exist concurrently they are in different conceptual worlds. Some practitioners and theorists seek more effective institutional and management constraints, power negotiating techniques and peace through technologies of mutual threat. There are consensus seekers who employ more sophisticated socialization processes largely within existing systems. Problem-solving advocates pursue more analysis of human behaviors and seek to deduce processes of conflict resolution and prevention. There cannot be communication between different approaches, or with policy makers and the public generally, until there is a precisely defined language, appropriate concepts that enable a clear differentiation of the various approaches, and an adequate and agreed theory of human behaviors at all social levels. This is the purpose of these four books concerned with the study of Conflict.

There are four books in this Conflict Series. They are:

1. *Conflict: Resolution and Provention.* This book seeks to provide an historical and theoretical perspective, and a framework for consideration of theory and practice in conflict resolution and provention. It is in five parts: Part I defines the approach; Part II deals with the political context of conflict provention; Part III is concerned with the theory of decision making, and with conflict resolution processes; Part IV is concerned with the longer-term policy implications of provention; and Part V draws together some conclusions.

2. *Conflict: Human Needs Theory.* An adequate theory of behavior is required to provide a basis for the analysis and resolution of conflict, and particularly for prediction of conflict and a guide to conflict prevention. "Needs theory" is put forward as this foundation. The chapters contributed in this book were written as a result of an international conference convened in July 1988 for that purpose.

3. *Conflict: Readings in Management and Resolution.* A new subject has origins in many fields, and this is an attempt to bring

together some earlier contributions from a broad spectrum of disciplines. A newly developing subject also has gaps requiring attention, and this book includes contributions requested to fill some of these gaps. It also contains an extensive annotated bibliography.

4. *Conflict: Practices in Management, Settlement and Resolution.* It is useful to survey practices generally, even those that proceed from contradictory theories. This book is a general survey of management, settlement and conflict resolution practices.

Conflict, its resolution and provention, comprises an *a-disciplinary* study, that is, a synthesis that goes beyond separate disciplines, beyond interaction between separate disciplines, and beyond any synthesis of approaches from several disciplines. An a-disciplinary approach accepts no boundaries of knowledge. Consequently, it has as yet no shelf in any discipline-based library. These four books seek to make a start.

JOHN BURTON

CONFLICT: HUMAN NEEDS THEORY

Acknowledgements

Human Needs, edited by Katrin Lederer, was published in 1980 as a result of a seminar in Berlin in the previous year. The participants were interested in human needs as a theory of development. Some years later, after much applied work in the areas of community and international conflict, and after observing major powers being defeated in wars with small nations and central authorities failing to control religious and ethnic conflicts within their boundaries, it became clear to me that conflicts of this kind were not generated primarily – or even at all – by shortages of material goods, or even by claims to territory. There were fundamental issues in all cases, issues touching on personal and group security, identity and recognition, and especially a sense of control over political processes that affected security, identity and recognition. The power of human needs was a greater power than military might. The conditions that explained conflict and, therefore, suggested means toward its resolution were frustrated human needs, not human lawlessness or character deformities. Needs theory moved the focus away from the individual as a miscreant and aimed it at the absence of legitimization of structures, institutions and policies as the primary source of conflict.

A general or generic theory of this order would obviously be a challenge to scholars accustomed to working with their own disciplinary concepts. With the help of the German Marshall Fund of the United States a preliminary conference was held at the Center for Conflict Analysis and Resolution at George Mason University, Virginia, in January 1988 to discuss needs theory with sociologists, anthropologists, political scientists and scholars who had taken a particular interest in conflict and its resolution. I submitted a general statement describing a needs theory approach to conflict resolution that included definitions of terms and elaboration of concepts.

This exploratory discussion justified an international conference of scholars interested in conflict resolution, and those who had given special attention to needs theory. It seemed to me that it would be useful to bring together a number of scholars who had contributed to the Berlin conference, others from the United States and elsewhere whose field was conflict resolution, and my colleagues at the Center at George Mason University. In this way the needs theory group and conflict resolution researchers and practitioners would be able to interact, possibly to the benefit of all concerned.

With the support once again of the German Marshall Fund of the United States, a conference took place in July, 1988. Both groups were surprised at the added perspectives which the interaction promoted. Papers, submitted in advance were discussed and subsequently reconsidered. The chapters in this book are a result of that meeting.

It will be at once obvious to the reader that there are still differences in the use of terms, and differences in conceptual frameworks. Nonetheless, the reader will have a sense that fundamental a-disciplinary issues are at last being addressed.

Professional conferences tend to throw scholars together who already know each other's work. In any event they meet in panels for a few hours only. It is true that barriers which separate disciplines are gradually breaking down, but this seems to lead to further barriers between those in the same field who adopt different approaches. There is little meaningful interaction, for example, between those in management studies and those in conflict resolution, yet the fields adjoin. The open-mindedness that is required for seminal communication seems to be promoted far more by small seminar interactions lasting for some days than by the ordinary conference interactions of professional societies.

It is for this reason that my colleagues and I are greatly indebted to the German Marshall Fund of the United States for making possible these two valuable conferences, and for the improved quality of thinking that has been a result. I hope other foundations will follow its example.

I have acknowledged in *Conflict: Resolution and Provention* my debt to the United States Institute of Peace, and to my colleagues at the Center for Conflict Analysis and Resolution, and to others who have contributed to this project. I wish to express my appreciation for the cooperation of Pam Tribino, whose responsibility it was to organize the July conference, and of Gertrude Wetherall, who edited the contributions in this book, both of whom were involved in the Center academic program.

The editor and publishers also acknowledge with thanks permission from the following to reproduce copyright material: The Free Press, for the quotation from John C. Eccles and Daniel N. Robinson, *The Wonder of Being Human* (1984) in Chapter 9; Cambridge University

Press, for Figure 8.1, from N. R. Hanson, *Patterns of Discovery* (1965); Oelgeschlager, Gunn & Hain, for Table 5.1, from Katrin Lederer (ed.), *Human Needs: A Contribution to the Current Debate*; Springer-Verlag Publishers, for extracts from Ronald Fisher, *The Social Psychology of Intergroup and International Conflict Resolution* (1990).

Contents

PART III   NEEDS THEORY AND BEHAVIORS

Notes on the Contributors

Christian Bay received his LL.B in 1934 and his Ph.D. in 1959 from the University of Oslo, Norway. He has had appointments at the University of California, Berkeley; Stanford University; the University of Alberta, Edmonton; and has been a Professor of Political Economy at the University of Toronto since 1972. He received the Woodrow Wilson Award of the American Political Science Association in 1959 for his *Structure of Freedom*. His areas of research have included problems of freedom, justice, personality development and political orientations.

Mary E. Clark was born in California and received her undergraduate and masters degrees at the University of California, Berkeley where in 1960 she received her Ph.D. in zoology. She is a professor at San Diego State University, California where she teaches biology and has carried out research on the biochemical adaptations of organisms to conditions of water stress, particularly high salinities. She has been dedicated to making the living world understandable to non-specialist students and wrote the first major textbook, *Contemporary Biology*, which incorporated not only "facts" but applications of those facts in everyday life. She has just published *Ariadne's Thread: The Search for New Modes of Thinking*, which addresses limits to growth, human nature, the development of the Western worldview and affecting change (St. Martin's Press, 1989).

Ronald J. Fisher is Professor of Psychology and Coordinator of the Applied Social Psychology Graduate Program at the University of Saskatchewan, Saskatoon, Canada where he received his undergraduate and master's degrees. He earned his Ph.D. from the University of Michigan. During 1989–90 he has held an appointment as Research Fellow at the Canadian Institute for International Peace and Security and in 1990–91 was a Visiting Professor at Carleton University, Ottawa, Canada. His primary interests include the development of theory, research and practice in applied social psychology and the resolution of intergroup and international conflict through third-party consultation.

Yona Friedman, an architect by profession until 1957, turned to related sociological activities and other scientific interests and applied his findings to practice. He has taught at several of the large American Universities, including Harvard, MIT, and Princeton. Friedman is a consultant to the Council of Europe, UNESCO, and UNEP, among other institutions.

Johan Galtung studied at the Universities of Oslo and Bergen and received the equivalents of the Ph.D. in mathematics in 1956 and in sociology in 1957. He has taught at Columbia University and the University of Oslo and has been visiting professor and researcher at numerous universities throughout the world. He founded the International Peace Research Institute in Oslo and the *Journal of Peace Research*. He is a consultant to a large number of international organizations and served as director general of the Inter-University Centre in Dubrovnik. He has been the research coordinator of the United Nations University Project on Goals, Processes, and Indicators of Development.

Katrin Gillwald received her degree in sociology in 1971 from the University of Hamburg. From 1971 to 1973 she was a member of a city and regional planning consulting office in Berlin, and from 1973 to 1975 she worked with the Berlin Center for Future Studies. Between 1976 and 1983, she was with the International Institute for Environment and Society, Science Center Berlin, involved with the further development and application of environment-related needs research and with the theory, methodology and strategies of socially relevant environmental research and policy. From 1983 to 1988, she worked as a deputy managing director for the same institute. Since 1988, she has gone back to active research, joining the President's Working Group Social Reporting at the Wissenschaftszentrum Berlin für Sozialforschung (formerly Science Center Berlin).

Herbert C. Kelman is the Richard Clarke Cabot Professor of Social Ethics at Harvard University and Chair of the Middle East Seminar at the Harvard Center for International Affairs. In 1989–90, he was a Jennings Randolph Distinguished Fellow at the US Institute of Peace in Washington. He is past president of the International Studies Association, the International Society of Political Psychology, and several other professional associations. He is recipient of a number of awards, including the American Psychological Association's Award for Distinguished Contributions to Psychology in the Public Interest

(1981). His many publications include *International Behavior: A Social-Psychological Analysis* (editor, 1965); *A Time to Speak: On Human Values and Social Research* (1968); and *Crimes of Obedience: Toward a Social Psychology of Authority and Responsibility* (with V. Lee Hamilton, 1989).

Christopher Mitchell is currently Professor of International Relations and Conflict Resolution at the Center for Conflict Analysis and Resolution at George Mason University, Virginia. Prior to that he was Professor of International Relations at the City University in London. His main fields of interest have always been international conflict and its mediation, but he is also interested in the development of mediation skills for use within the community and between individuals. To this end he set up the Conflict Management Research Group at City University and helped to launch the community mediation movement in the UK by holding conferences, courses and training workshops on the theme of alternative dispute resolution. He has acted as an informal facilitator in a number of international and intercommunal disputes and has written books and journal articles on the theme of mediation and conflict management, most notably *The Structure of International Conflict* and *Peacemaking and the Consultant's Role.*

Oscar Nudler is Project Coordinator of the United Nations University (Costa Rica) and Senior Fellow of the Bariloche Foundation, a not-for-profit organization devoted to research and postgraduate training in the development problematique. He has published many articles and co-edited *Human Development in its Social Context* and *Time, Culture and Development.* He has developed an epistemological approach to conflicts involving alternative frameworks or "worlds."

William R. Potapchuk is Associate Director of the Conflict Clinic, Inc., a private not-for-profit organization created to improve the practice of conflict resolution in disputes of public significance. He received his M.A. in Political Science from the University of Missouri in 1988. He serves as a Board Member of the National Conference on Peacemaking and Conflict Resolution and has chaired the Board of Directors for the Lentz Peace Research Laboratory. He has been an author of many articles in the field including "Using Conflict Analysis to Determine Intervention Techniques" and "Getting to the Table: Three Paths" both for the *Mediation Quarterly.*

Victoria Rader is Professor of Sociology at George Mason University. She received her Ph.D. at the University of Chicago and is a past president of the Association for Humanist Sociology. The focus of her work has been the study of social conflict and social change. She has published articles about dramaturgical sociology, sociology of knowledge and social change. In 1986 she published *Signal through Flames* after her research on the homeless movement in the US. From that fieldwork experience she became sensitized to the elite domination of social science knowledge and has taken seriously the conceptions which emerge from ordinary people struggling for their liberation.

Ramashray Roy, a Senior Fellow at the Centre for the Study of Developing Societies, Delhi, India, is a political scientist by training. Through his work on the Indian political system and its linkages with socio-cultural dimensions of Indian society, he came to examine the concept of development, particularly man's relationship with his external environment. Finding Western approaches to development inadequate, he is currently exploring the nature of traditional Indian thinking for understanding what development involves. Two of his books, *Self and Society: A Study in Gandhian Thought* and *Dialogues on Development: The Individual, Society, and Political Order* (with R. K. Srivastava), both published by Sage of Delhi, are the result of this exploration.

Richard E. Rubenstein is Professor of Conflict Resolution and Public Affairs at George Mason University and a core faculty member and Director of the Center for Conflict Analysis and Resolution. He is the author of *Rebels in Eden: Mass Political Violence in the United States* (1970); *Left Turn: Origins of the Next American Revolution* (1973); and *Alchemists of Revolution: Terrorism in the Modern World* (1987). Rubenstein was educated at Harvard College, Oxford University and Harvard Law School. Before joining the faculty at George Mason University, he had been a practicing attorney, Professor of Political Science at Roosevelt University in Chicago and Professor of Law at Antioch School of Law in Washington, D.C. He has been an advisory consultant to the National Commission on the Causes and Prevention of Violence and assistant director of the Adlai Stevenson Institute of International Affairs.

Dennis J. D. Sandole received his Ph.D. in Political Science from the

University of Strathclyde in Glasgow, Scotland and is presently Associate Professor of Conflict Resolution and International Relations at George Mason University. He has taught at the University of London (University College), Garnett College, Kingston Polytechnic and the City University, all in London, England. He has also taught for the University of Southern California Graduate Programs in International Relations in both England and Germany. His research interests, in which he has published, include international relations theory and methodology, conflict analysis and management/resolution, attitude change and paradigm shifts.

Joseph A. Scimecca received his Ph.D. from New York University. He is Professor of Conflict Resolution and Sociology at George Mason University where he has been Chair of the Department of Sociology and Anthropology and Director of the Center for Conflict Analysis and Resolution. He is the author of *Crisis at St John's: Strike and Revolution on the Catholic Campus* (1968); *The Sociological Theory of C. Wright Mills* (1977); *Education and Society* (1980); *Society and Freedom: an Introduction to Humanist Sociology* (1981); and co-editor of the forthcoming *Conflict Resolution: Cross Cultural Perspectives*.

Paul Sites has served as Chair of the Department of Sociology and Anthropology and is now Emeritus Professor at Kent State University. He is the author of *Lee Harvey Oswald and the American Dream; Control: The Basis of Social Order; Control and Constraint* and many professional papers and articles. He has a special interest in seeing Human Needs Theory being accepted as part of social theory.

Introduction

The majority of readers of this Conflict Series, and of this Volume in particular, will understandably be surprised at the emphasis on "human needs" and that human needs theory is the framework of the Series. Is this some special religious approach, a narrow psychological approach, perhaps an interest focus like that of the Greens, or perhaps some other orientation designed to bring to attention some particular concern or belief?

It is none of these. Social and political sciences, and the philosophical traditions from which they emerged, were structured within societies that were hierarchical, subject in many cases to revolts and revolutions, and almost universally defensive of existing structures, institutions and roles. The focus of interest was the institutions that had to be protected at all costs. From this frame were deduced the rights and obligations of members of society. It was society that was supreme, not its rank and file members. Within this frame the social good as interpreted by elites was the measure of legitimacy, not the development of individuals in society.

A reason why the individual was so relegated to this subservient status was that there was no understanding of the power of human needs and, therefore, the role of the individual in political processes. There was (and still is in most societies) wishful thinking on the part of ruling elites. The assumption was that the person was what they would like "it" to be: a wholly malleable tool. As psychology and psychiatry emerged as separate disciplines they were, understandably, not greatly interested in the human person as a unit of analysis or an entity; their interest was and has remained the normal or abnormal responses of persons to their social environments. If the individual could not cope, then help might be given. The remedy was never the changing of the institutions of society. Sociology was until recent years largely concerned with the processes whereby groups were socialized and adapted to social environments. With the added incentive of trying to be "scientific" economics invented a special construct, economic man, whose behaviors could be predicted, thus validating economic theories and policies.

The interest in human needs in this Series is to point to this traditional failing of social sciences and to incorporate the individual and the identity groups of the individual as the units of analysis and,

1

furthermore, to treat this individual as a real person. There could have been a hypothesis that economic man is the reality, and a quite different theory would have emerged from which would have been deduced quite different settlement processes. With such a construct all disputes could be settled by one side or the other paying the necessary price. Indeed, there are those in the dispute field who seem to work on this assumption: disputes are settled by bargaining and by compromise. We have chosen, however, to deal with the real person, regardless of complexities. This has made necessary more consideration of that person than is generally the case. If there were no other variables at all, then a *dispute* between two persons over the price of an article could possibly be settled in a predictable way by reference to the human construct within this economic frame. But once we start trying to understand the nature of *conflict* – that is, a situation involving not just interests (as disputes do), but human needs, and the processes parties must go through in order to move from an aggressive frame to a problem solving one – we have to try to deal with the real person.

This study of conflict pays attention to human characteristics that are ontological and universal. The approach removes the study from any one separate discipline, and removes it also from the bulk of past thinking and past research.

It could well be that human needs theory as presently conceived is as wide of the mark as the constructs of the past. Certainly, as these contributions will demonstrate, we are at a very early stage in discovering the real human person; but they do recognize that there is a real person involved. Furthermore, they recognize that whether conflict be within the family or within the international system, the person is the same one in all cases; the person in the family is also the person in the market place, as well as the person who as head of state declares war, and the person who is the terrorist, and the person who runs risks and makes a sacrifice for others. Once we try to understand conflict we are in the world of political and social realities. Introducing some tamed construct that conforms, that can be deterred or incorporated by compromise, tells us little about the nature of conflict and even less about what it takes to resolve it. This is why human needs theory is our starting point.

Let us recall that at the week-long conference at which the authors of these papers were present, there were two groups, those from needs theory and those from conflict resolution. The frames of reference were accordingly different. The needs theorists were oriented toward human development. The conflict theorists and practitioners focused on explanations of conflict and the conditions required to prevent or to resolve it. At the outset it was clear that there was not effective communication between the two groups, but it was not clear why this was so.

The conflict resolvers saw the provision of institutional and structural conditions that made possible the full development of the person as an important means of avoiding and resolving conflict. Without such development there would not be the full satisfaction of needs of recognition and identity. There was something worrying the needs theorists about this assumption that individual development would lead to conflict resolution. On the contrary, they felt that it could be conflict making and, furthermore, conflict resolution might prejudice human development.

The needs theorists, concerned with conflict arising out of the development process, had focused on "satisfiers," that is, the means people and groups adopt to pursue their needs. They related certain satisfiers to the pursuit of certain needs – for example, the need for recognition could relate directly to role seeking. Role seeking, being competition for scarce resources, could be conflict making. In one contribution (Chapter 13), reference was made to the dark side of human satisfactions meaning that the satisfiers were conflict making, as when a powerful group employs role positions and resources to pursue developmental needs, at the expense of others.

Those from conflict resolution had no problem with this aspect of needs theory. The purpose of problem-solving conflict resolution was to discover options that make possible the satisfaction of the needs of all concerned. These, they had assumed, could be discovered once those concerned had made a thorough analysis of problems in their relationships and had costed the longer-term consequences of their satisfiers, including the probable responses of others. In an ethnic conflict the dominant group seeks to maintain its role position by force if necessary, for its identity rests on this. The weaker community seeks its identity through role acquisition, even at the expense of lives and the destruction of the system. The conflict resolution process is, however, one that encourages an informed costing process and the search for options (satisfiers), even separation of communities if necessary.

All participants went home and redrafted their papers, and in some cases quite different contributions emerged. As editor I attempted to write an introductory summary, but soon discovered that I could not do justice to them. They all deserve to be read in full, and with care.

I have, however, tried to place them in some order beginning with those that dwell on human needs as ontological or biological (Chapters 1–4). There follow those that examine the link between needs theory and conflict resolution (Chapters 5–8), then those concerned with needs theory as explanation of behaviors and situations (Chapters 9–14). Finally there are two (Chapters 15 and 16) which can be regarded as assessments.

One cannot help wishing that a discussion such as this were a recognized part of any course in the behavioral sciences, especially in economics and politics. Policies might then achieve their declared goals.

I

Human Needs

1 Needs as Analogues of Emotions
Paul Sites

It is becoming increasingly evident that if needs theory is to prevail as a viable part of social theory it must have an ontological grounding which hopefully will provide a basis for agreement among scholars and help silence the critics.

Such a grounding now appears possible given the large amount of scholarly work that has been and is being done on emotions in both animals and humans. This chapter is an attempt to show that human needs can be tied realistically to human emotions, thereby giving needs a grounding in the very nature of the human species. I will attempt to show that human needs can be seen as analogues of primary emotions, thus giving needs a naturalistic basis. If this is the case most of the criticisms leveled at needs theory as a basis for general social theory fall by the wayside.

ANIMAL AND HUMAN EMOTIONS

Scholars have identified over 400 different emotions in the human species. Such a large number obviously presents problems for a serious science seeking parsimonious explanations. Scholarship in this area over the past two decades or so has shown, however, that most emotions are secondary having their basis in a relatively few primary emotions. Kemper[1] posits only four primary emotions – fear, anger, depression and satisfaction (happiness, joy). In doing this, he shows that many scholars, using a variety of different approaches, have isolated nearly the same primary emotions even though some add a very few others and/or use different terms in naming the same ones. In any case, there is now widespread agreement that there are a relatively few primary emotions. Kemper makes a convincing case for the existence of his four primaries in terms of evolutionary value, ontogenetic primacy, cross-cultural universality and differentiated autonomic patterns. His argument is thus that primary emotions in animals came into existence because they were adaptive thereby

7

having evolutionary value, that expressions of the *same* primary emotions appear very early in human infants and that these emotions are the ones most often identified in cross-cultural research. In addition, as Funkenstein[2] and Kemper, have argued:

> fear is associated with the autonomic processes indicating the action of epinephrine (E) and anger with the action of norepinephrine (NE). Both these neurochemicals activate the sympathetic nervous system (SNS), although in different ways. Satisfaction and depression, which appear to depend on variable activation of the parasympathetic nervous system (PNS) have been associated with the action of acetylcholine (ACh) which is the neurotransmitter of the PNS.[3]

Even though it is too early to say we can with certainty conclude there are four and only four primary emotions (I will suggest the possible addition of one more emotion below) and that these can be directly tied to specific autonomic patterns, the evidence presented by Kemper is highly suggestive. The counter-argument to specificity was presented by Schachter and Singer[4] and even though some scholars support this counter view, Kemper's[5] critique of this view and the research supporting it are convincing.

Kemper goes on to show that during the socialization process, people learn to identify secondary emotions by being taught to name more specific feeling states thereby producing an array of these. Secondary emotions can thus be traced to either one or a combination of the primary emotions. For example, Kemper sees guilt as a form of fear, shame as based on anger, hate, jealousy and envy as derived from a combination of fear and anger etc. In summary, the argument is "that there is an autonomic ground – among others – for judging which emotions are primary and that secondary emotions are socially constructed but attain their emotional tone by virtue of their linkage, in the course of socialization, with primary emotions."[6] Thus, even though the social constructionist view of emotions[7] applies in the formation and learning of secondary emotions, this view does not apply to the formation of the primaries even though it does have limited application in their expression.

Kemper is not arguing, nor am I, that the manner in which primary emotions are, at times, *evoked and expressed* is biologically determined. Few, if any, scholars would disagree that the same stimuli in different societies produce different emotions (or no emotion at all) and that the same emotion might be expressed in different ways in different societies in terms of what Ekman[8] calls display rules. Concerning the first point, many people in the American society, for example, experience the emotion of fear when walking outside at night but this is not true in all societies. Concerning the second point, all societies have display rules concerning how, when and where different emotions may be expressed. Even though this is the case, however, there appears to be considerable, if not complete universality, in the ability to recognize the expression of the primary emotions in the absence of social control agents. As Ekman, Friesen and Ancoli[9] have shown, with very sophisticated methodology, a naturalistic expression of an emotion overrides socialization in the absence of agents of social control lending evidence for the pervasiveness even of the *expression* of the primary emotions.

EMOTIONS AND NEEDS IN ANIMALS

The human species, like other species inhabiting the earth, is a product of evolutionary forces. As Leachy[10] points out, there is no reason to believe the human species is anything more than just one more bud on the bush representing all species. Futhermore, there is every reason to believe that this bud, classified as *homo sapiens*, contains much within it that is shared with other creatures whose mutations over time brought it to fruition. Given this, it seems reasonable to agree with Kemper and others that humans share the physiological basis of the primary emotions with the higher animals. Animals, for example, experience fear, anger, depression and satisfaction as do humans.[11] There is little doubt that emotions came into existence in the evolutionary scheme of things because they enhanced survival value.[12] If the logic of the analysis presented here is to hold, it follows that since animals have the same primary emotions as humans, a case must be made that animals like humans *can be said to have* a corresponding set of needs.

Such a case can be made in the sense that just as animals need food for survival, they also have other needs which can be seen as analogues of the primary emotions named above. An animal cannot survive in a constant state of heightened fear, anger or depression and some degree of satisfaction can be seen as essential for rest and recuperation. Thus, it can be said that animals have needs for conditions or states of existence which will reduce the three negative emotional states of fear, anger and depression and thereby permit the positive emotional state of satisfaction. From this it seems reasonable to say animals have "needs" for at least security, the need analogue of the fear emotion and a predictable environment, the need analogue of anger. For the latter, Homans[13] and others have shown that when animals do not receive what they have been conditioned to receive following certain behavior, the emotion of anger is displayed. The need analogue of the depression emotion in animals is difficult to name (it will be named for humans below) but it probably has to do with the absence and/or confusion of relationships with other animals in the same species group. For example, young animals seem to experience depression when they are rejected by their mothers. The same is true when an animal seeking dominance in animal groups having dominance hierarchies loses in the struggle; the animal becomes "moody" and silent as it goes off by itself, depressed and sulky. The need analogue of the satisfaction emotion will be called latency, in the sense that periods of rest and recuperation are necessary for survival and the satisfaction emotion enhances this possibility. It can thus be said that animals below the level of humans have needs in the sense that they must have conditions which enhance the possibility of survival.

My argument is that these same emotions and corresponding needs are present in humans even though in humans they become intertwined and extremely complex as they become related to *the survival of the self* as well as survival of the physical organism. Of course, no one has ever "seen" an emotion. Emotions are inferred from such things as facial expressions, action patterns and, in humans, verbal reports.

Because needs cannot be directly observed, all we can do is to conceptualize a need as existing when certain emotions are observed or reported since, as indicated, needs are tied to emotions. Given that emotions are survival mechanisms and that we can infer needs from emotional states, rather than come up with one more definition, I will use Masini's[14] definition of need which is consistent with what is being said here: "Needs can be understood abstractly to refer to those human requirements calling for a response that makes human survival and development possible in a given society." This definition is close to that of Galtung and Mallman and Marcus but rejects those of Roy and Rist all discussed in Lederer.[15] To this point we have given needs a naturalistic basis by tying them to emotions and survival. People cannot be tied too closely to animals, however, since human have "added dimensions."

Humans share with lower animals a physical body and thus share similar needs with animals as these relate to the survival of the physical organism. In addition to the physical organism, the human has a self which, once established, also has a survival problem. I argue that the same emotions that serve to enhance the survival of the physical organism also serve in the human to enhance the survival of the self. Given this, a brief discussion of the nature of self is in order. Along with this I want to discuss the importance of control in the human as this relates to the creation and maintenance of self. Even though there seem to be some limited exceptions, animals merely adapt to their environments. Humans, on the other hand, have the capacity to construct (and thus control and change) their physical and social environments because they have an ability to use language in conceptualization, which produces the possibility of interpretation and reinterpretation.

SELF AND CONTROL

Before beginning the discussion of self and control it should be said that there is a tendency on the part of lay people and even some social scientists to overemphasize the uniqueness of the human in the sense that a self (or soul) in all its uniqueness is present at birth and continues to live on after the death of the body. This leads to mystification and a belief that there is something about the self that is other than a result of biology and social interaction.[16] This type of thinking is very difficult to break down even for social scientists since each of us likes to see ourselves as something other than the result of our biology and social interaction. A belief in some kind of pre-given "entity' which we then develop permits us to take what is perhaps undue credit for our accomplishments. At the same time, we blame others for their lack of similar accomplishments, disregarding their biological structure and past and present interaction patterns. It is evident that this type of thinking leads to a variety of problems concerned with conflict resolution, especially that of some persons thinking they are in some manner better or special. This is another reason a more naturalistic theory is necessary.

I hasten to add that this does not make me a social biologist. The self cannot be seen totally as part of nature, as this is typically interpreted, even though its possibility is obviously embedded in nature. One reason the self cannot be so interpreted is that evolutionary forces alone could not produce the nearly infinite number of solutions necessary for life in modern societies: these must be rapidly and continuously constructed. Evolutionary forces are far too slow, and this is one reason I argue that individual control, based on the above considerations, is basic to social life. Biology is not complete destiny.

The work of George H. Mead[17] comes as close as any to being a naturalistic theory of the self while at the same time including the importance of the social dimension. Mead was primarily influenced by the work of James, Dewey, Whitehead and Watson. His work on the nature of the self is thus a combination of pragmatism, process philosophy and behaviorism. It is a given that the human infant is a rather helpless creature and remains dependent on others for a considerable length of time compared with other animals. This forces parents to care for the infant during the dependency period and it is during this period that the essential components of self begin their development.

Since there is no self at birth, only potential, the infant engages only in what Mead calls impulsive acts. He refers to these as being lodged in the "I," or non-social component of the self even though these impulsive acts become progressively influenced by past experiences. As these impulsive acts are rewarded or punished, memory traces are stored in the brain which permit the infant "to know" through memory how to act in the future in order to minimize punishment and maximize rewards. Mead refers to the product of rewards and punishment as the "me" component of self. It is this "me" that becomes lodged in memory and influences future impulsive acts. In this, following Whitehead, Mead insists that the self is not a substance or an entity. Self is a process, as it must be, to cope with changing environmental circumstances, including changes in the behavior of others over time. The self should thus not be reified as a thing. Like a component of any system, the self must be as dynamic as other parts of the system in which it is embedded if it is to survive. In sum, the self is pragmatic in the sense that it seeks the "best" immediate solution based upon past conditioning, lodged in memory, along with interpretation as this become possible through maturation.[18] And the self is part of a process, as it must be if it is to be pragmatic. How then is a control orientation built into the self?

When the new infant acts impulsively, *it produces effects* on others. As the new infant "takes note" of these effects in experiencing the responses of others to these impulsive acts the dynamics of self-construction are set in motion. That is, the effects produced by individual acts set the infant apart from others as the unique entity that produces these effects. At a very early age, the infant thus comes to recognize that she/he is set apart from the surrounding environment and soon comes "to know" that what she/he does has an effect on the behavior of others. I am, therefore, arguing that what in essence happens is that infants learn that what they do controls (produces effects on) the behavior of others toward them. If an infant's behavior produces pleasant effects on others, they provide rewarding behavior in turn. Conversely, if infant's acts have unpleasant effects on others, they react with behavior which is punishing. As the individual grows older she/he "takes the role of the other," in Mead's terms, in order to gain reward and avoid punishment. A consciousness of self and a control orientation towards the world and others are developed as a result of the same dynamics, and they remained intertwined.

Mead's use of pragmatism and behaviorism are evident but even though he was aware of these dynamics, he failed, as most others have failed, to draw out the implications of the importance of the control orientation taken by the individual and the implications of this for social life and social theory. I do not want to press this too far, however, since Mead does discuss such things as the importance of the prehensile hand in the manipulation (control) of objects. In addition, he sees the essence of mind as the manipulation of linguistic symbols so that acts and their possible effects on others can be rehearsed in the mind before acts are carried out. Humans are oriented toward the future as they must be if they are to attempt control. Thus, even though he seldom speaks directly of the individual taking a control orientation, it is evident that he would not object to this usage. Indeed, as indicated above, this is precisely what taking the role of the other is all about: controlling one's behavior in order to control the responses of others.

The individual is not totally a piece of plastic that can be completely molded by others. Nuances in learning and different genetic structures produce different manipulations of symbols in the mind so individuals become unique and act differently.

Mead did not ignore the importance of mind and interpretation as do some behaviorists. In any case, there is good reason to suggest that all individuals come to take a control orientation toward the world and others. Just as individuals attempt to control the physical world to gratify their biological needs, they attempt to control others, either alone or in coalition(s) to gratify needs related to the self. All this is why I titled my earlier work[19] *Control: The Basis of Social Order*.

In that work, because the importance of individual acts producing effects was not clearly seen, I depended too heavily on the principle of conditioning. The case made, however, is still worth noting: even if the individual did not recognize the importance of control in the manner outlined above, she/he would still come to know that control through conditioning is the essence of social life and later cognitive learning, because the socialization agent's orientation toward the infant is and must be that of controlling the child's behavior. Without this orientation, socialization could not and would not be successful. Impulsive acts are, at first, random and must therefore be directed by the socialization agent into a somewhat consistent pattern if an "ordered" personality is to develop. The necessity to consistency in controlling the impulsive acts of infants over time is well documented.

The importance of the individual having control or at least a sense of control is now being documented by research. Seligman's[20] book on helplessness documents this from a variety of animal and human experiments and other types of studies. He says, "a person or animal is helpless with respect to outcomes when the outcome occurs independently of all his voluntary responses."[21] He goes on to report, for example, that an infant's not producing effects on others in the very early years has disastrous effects in later life. Old people placed in nursing homes against their wills lose a sense of control over their lives and die earlier than those who admit themselves voluntarily. Seligman thus finds that control is important not only for humans but also for animals so the necessity of producing effects may have roots in the biological organism. If this is the case, the fact that humans are *conscious* of an inability to produce effects makes the absence of control even more disastrous.

Langer[22] also presents considerable evidence that control or a sense of control is of critical importance for the psychological and even physical health of individuals. She presents evidence from a broad variety of settings: with mental illness therapeutic situations, crowding, and among the aged, for example. In addition, she finds a fall in self-esteem is associated with a decline in control, a matter discussed below. Studies by medical sociologists also find that physically ill people return to health more rapidly if physicians permit them a higher degree of control in the healing process. There is thus increasing evidence that having control over situations is of critical importance.

It is also interesting to note that the study of *social* control is one of the central concerns among social scientists. That is, society is seen as possible, in large part, because individual behavior is controlled by a variety of social control mechanisms, from socialization to the passage and enforcement of laws. But "the social" in this can be only individuals acting in coalitions of one type or another. The point is that even though this is the case, most social scientists still do not typically see the *individuals*-in-coalition nature of this. Therefore they do not see that all single individuals attempt to control the behavior of others in the same sense as coalitions, even though the former typically cannot produce such great effects as the latter, thereby making this evident. But, on reflection, the dynamics and the reasons are the same. Coalitions attempt control to further their own interests (interpreted here as largely the gratification of needs), and this is true of individuals as well. If one accepts the former, one should also accept the latter.

I am often criticized for this point of view since on the surface it appears to be a very "cold" and critical view of humans, negating any possibility that humans may be altruistic in their actions. But this is not necessarily the case if adequately understood. People who claim altruistic values as the basis of their self-identity can be expected to attempt control of the responses of others based upon activities that reflect these values. It is clearly the case that Jesus and Socrates, along with many other martyrs, based their self-conceptions on what most would call altruistic values. They attempted to control other people through their teachings by attempting to convince these others to accept their values. Of course, they failed, at least in the short run, and were thereby forced to die in order to save their (conception of) selves. People thus attempt to control others based upon a certain conception of self which it is hoped will produce certain effects on others in terms of others' estimates of them and/or others' responses toward them. Martyrdom and its opposite, the use of raw force to kill others, are perhaps the ultimate control strategies. In the former case, the physical body is lost but the self (the value) is "saved." In the latter case, the physical body may be saved but the self is in real danger of being damaged.

Having established the importance of self and control in human life and the connection of emotions and needs in animals, I now turn to a more specific discussion of the connection of emotions and needs in humans.

EMOTIONS AND NEEDS IN HUMANS

Again, what I am arguing is that human needs are ontologically grounded in emotions and that negative emotions are triggered in humans when there is a threat to the survival of either the physical organism or the developing self. People can thus be said to have needs for those conditions or state of existence which will alleviate the suffering caused by negative emotions and which will enhance the possibility of satisfaction which, as interpreted here, is also necessary for healthy survival.

Few would disagree that people, under certain social conditions, do indeed suffer emotional distress and that emotional distress is unpleasant just as physical pain or real hunger is unpleasant. People are driven by this distress and/or anticipated distress to act in particular ways to produce conditions of relief and/or to produce social conditions that will provide insurance against distress occurring in the future. In the case of satisfaction, since the feeling is pleasant, no action is needed short of that which will guarantee the continuance of this emotional state. In short, people attempt to reduce feelings of fear, anger, depression since these are unpleasant and increase feelings of satisfaction. It should be emphasized, however, that at least the *anticipation* of these feeling states is typically present. *This is why it can be said that people* have *needs.* As indicated, futures can be expected greatly to influence present behaviors. For example, young people spend a long time in college and some of this is no doubt seen by many as highly punishing. Yet, their anticipation of a college degree and a future position with high prestige, both of which tend to give high self-esteem, keeps them at the task.

Now we need to discuss primary emotions in humans and their need analogues.

THE EMOTION OF FEAR AND THE NEED FOR SECURITY

The connection of the fear emotion with threats to physical security is well established in the human dialogue, both popularly and in scholarship. But there are as well many potential threats to the self and I am merely arguing that real or imagined threats to the self evoke the same physiologically-based emotion of fear evoked when physical security is threatened. Imagined threats may, of course, be actually experienced as a secondary emotion based on the primary emotion of fear. The emotion of fear is often "masked," for example, in the derived learned emotion of guilt, as Kemper points out. This masking of fear under the name of guilt has important implications for social control as discussed in my earlier work,[23] but that does little to relieve the pain of the emotion experienced by the individual. Indeed, it probably makes it worse since, by naming it guilt, individuals blame themselves rather than others or social conditions which may have led to the behavior producing the feeling in the first place.

The emotion of fear, based upon real or imagined threats to the self, is pervasive in social life. The extreme, in terms of imagined threats, is paranoia where people imagine others are out to destroy either the self and/or the physical body – an extremely painful condition. The source may be imagined, but the fear is real. Even though relatively few people are paranoid to the degree that they are completely debilitated, most of us experience a mixture of real and imagined threats to self in our daily lives. Many people probably work harder because of real or imagined fear of being fired and/or not receiving a hoped-for promotion or pay raise than they would do otherwise. Children often obey their parents, at least in part, because they fear bodily harm or damage to the self and its future. Often battered wives remain with their husbands because these women fear the alternatives open to them.

Many people have irrational phobias; pervasive fears of almost everything that can be imagined. If Gazzaniga[24] is correct, phobias have their basis in the attempt on the part of the individual to interpret a mental state that by chance happened to coincided with an experience. Again, even though irrational, the feelings of fear are real. This is enough to show that fear is pervasive in social life and at the same time to make the case that it can be said that people have a need for security. Again, as is the case with the other needs, saying that people have a need for security is a shorthand way of saying that people need conditions that will alleviate unpleasant mental states just as food is needed to alleviate the unpleasant feelings that occur when people are hungry.

THE EMOTION OF ANGER AND THE NEED FOR MEANING

In the brief discussion of animal emotions and needs, the need analogue of the anger emotion was called predictable order. For humans this is called a need for meaning. Based upon past interaction, people experience anger when others treat them in a non-rewarding or punishing manner contrary to what might have been predicted. As Homans[25] says: "When a person's action does not receive the reward he expected, or receives punishment he did not expect, he will be angry." When the actions of others are unpredictable, and especially when that unpredictability produces harm, the world is rendered "senseless."

As Eliade[26] has pointed out, primitive people, perhaps more than anything else, feared chaos. Because of this they constructed myths and corresponding rituals in an attempt to order this chaos and prevent if from reoccurring. Modern people do the same with their various constructions of social reality.[27] When these socially constructed realities are threatened, anger occurs; indeed "righteous anger" often occurs. Since people base their selves and interactions on these constructions, if these are threatened by others, the world and self-constructions no longer make sense and people become angry: meaning is lost. This has been demonstrated many times by ethnomethodologists[28] with their breaching experiments. When people's socially constructed worlds are breached, they become angry, and for good reason. If social reality is threatened, selves and meaning systems are threatened since these are constructed and perpetuated within a reality which tends to be taken for granted.

A brief discussion of values and their relationship to needs may help clarify not only what is being said concerning meaning but other needs as well. Sociologists typically see socially constructed worlds as based on values of one kind or another. That is, among humans, values are important in terms of organizing predictable social worlds which provide meaning. Kluckhohn writes, "A value is a conception, explicit or implict, distinctive of an individual or characteristic of a group, of the desirable which influences the selection from available modes, means and ends of action."[29] Needs are related to values in the sense, following Becker,[30] that *people value what they need.* Values are thus related, in one way or another, not only to meaning but to the other needs as well. Hungry people value food, threatened · people value "havens" that provide security; and, as I am arguing, social values are created not only to "organize the world" to provide meaning (much of Weber's work on rationalization[31] is precisely this) but also to provide concurrently a basis for the evaluation of self on a scale which is seen by others as legitimate. Thus, following Becker, what Emerson[32] calls "value domains" can be related to human needs.[33] This is not to say that all people can have their needs gratified by pursuing existing values in a given society. Indeed, the fact that existing values may not serve the needs of many in a society is the cause of a great deal of conflict, as we shall see.

Now back to the emotion of anger and its need analogue.

Kemper[34] also sees the secondary emotion of shame as based in the anger emotion. Scheff,[35] along with Kemper, sees shame as caused by the perception of negative evaluations of self. As with guilt, a secondary emotion masks a primary emotion and, as Scheff points out, the experiencing of this emotion or the anticipation of it produces conformity. Furthermore, since shame is recursive[36] it may lead to a pathological condition, as may guilt. Again, the individual takes the blame for an act over which she/he may have little control and, rather than being permitted by others to express anger, only shame may be expressed. Sennet and Cobb[37] have shown the negative consequences of shame among members of the working class in the United States. The lives of people in this class are rendered meaningless because of the lack of control in the workplace, and they are thereby forced to experience shame rather than react with outright anger for fear of losing their jobs when no other alternatives are present. There is little doubt, based on this and other evidence, that people have a need for meaning, but gratifying this need is possible in any complete sense only when they have at least some control over the world in which they live. It is difficult, if not impossible, to make complete sense of a world that has been completely constructed by others since the lives of individuals are unique and may not "fit" within a world they did not help construct and to which they therefore do not relate in a meaningful manner.

THE EMOTION OF DEPRESSION AND THE NEED FOR SELF-ESTEEM

The need analogue for the depression emotion in animals was not named. For humans this is called a need for self-esteem, and this need is perhaps the most pervasive of any of the needs in humans.

The self is what sets each of us apart from others as unique entities. If the self is evaluated in a negative manner continuously and over time, all individual hope for "the salvation" of self may be lost. The importance of the self is also indicated by all of the defense mechanisms which are used to "defend" it. For example, people project negative evaluations on to others, use a variety of rationalizations in defense of the self and, in severe cases, regress to an earlier stage of life. In the psychoanalytic tradition, these are called ego defense mechanisms since Freud was not clear in terms of the meaning of the concept of self. I like to call these control mechanisms to be consistent with other formulations relating to the control orientation of the individual.[38]

The major basis of self-esteem is approval by others and thus depression is likely to occur when approval by others is not forthcoming or threatened and/or actual disapproval of a person occurs. In short, a feeling of depression occurs when a person's self-esteem is in some manner threatened or damaged. Depression may occur, for example, when a family member or close friend dies. These are the people most likely to provide approval behavior and their death negates this. Or, people may become depressed when they retire or lose a job which has for years been a source of self-esteem. In short, any event or happening which disturbs a source of approval is likely to produce the emotion of depression. This may, of course, apply to a change in value orientations in the general society. Since people base their self-esteem on the rewards they receive from living out certain values in the presence of others, if these values change and people cannot "relate" to new values, depression is likely to occur. Hundreds of treatises have been written on depression and self-esteem so I will not belabor the point here. It is interesting, however, to compare the basis of depression in humans with what was suggested earlier concerning depression in animals. Both appear to experience depression when rejected by others and this may be an area worth exploring in comparative research.

THE EMOTION OF SATISFACTION (HAPPINESS, JOY) AND THE NEED FOR LATENCY

The production of the satisfaction emotion and therefore the gratification of the need for latency in lower animals is easier than this process is with humans because of the existence of the self in the latter. This may be true in capitalist societies, in large part, because of what Marx called the fetishism of commodities which comes into existence in these societies as an ever-increasing number of needs (interpreted here as wants and desires) are produced in order to extend markets. In short, people want more and more before they are satisfied (happy). And/or, in Simmel's[39] terms, many more stimuli must be dealt with in urban societies before satisfaction is possible. Therefore, as he point's out, people in the metropolis attempt to control these contingencies by taking a blasé attitude.

What is referred to as stress is pervasive in modern societies making the need for latency difficult to gratify. It is well known that prolonged stress is likely to damage both the physiological organism as well as the self, indicating there is a need for latency. Recent research on stress and the immune system is highly instructive in this regard.[40] Many stressors[41] such as the death of a loved one, high dissatisfaction in the workplace or many which threaten the physical organism have been identified. Even though emotional arousal has been seen by some scholars[42] as the cause of stress no one seems to have isolated *in definitive and specific terms* why stress is produced under the force of these stressors – that is, why stressors affect people in a negative manner particularly when they are excessive and prolonged.

It seems reasonable to suggest that people feel stress when the needs we have discussed in relationship to the physical organism as well as the self are not gratified and/or if they feel a threat to the continued gratification of these needs. (See the earlier discussion concerning shame in the workplace and depression when a loved one dies.) When people are experiencing stress the latency need obviously cannot be gratified, and this is perhaps why continuous stress may produce physiological as well as psychological damage. Indeed, some now believe that the body has great capacity to heal itself, but this seems most likely to happen only when individuals have their need, for what we are calling latency, gratified. If we look at the many relationships people in complex societies experience which may produce threats to security, meaning and self-esteem, along with the difficulty of having a sense of control, it is easy to see why these societies are so "stressful" and thus why the need for latency is difficult to gratify.

Before going on it should be said that there is no intention of underplaying the importance of cognition as this relates either to emotion or to stress.[43] Cognitive appraisal of an environment and/or interpretations of "vague feelings" of one kind or another[44] may arouse any or all the emotions we have considered either alone or in combination. Indeed, aside from sudden occurrences which may produce such emotions as fear and anger, cognitive appraisal and interpretation are, without doubt, heavily involved in triggering emotional states in humans. How an event is appraised and interpreted, correctly or incorrectly, has a great deal to do with emotional states and thus whether or not a person feels a sense of need gratification.

As discussed above, the paranoid may misinterpret the behavior of others and feel fear when this has no grounds in anyone's reality but her/his own. Or, all of us may, at times, gratify our self-esteem by "kidding ourselves" that others approve of our behavior when this is not called for in more objective terms. In short, there is little doubt that misappraisals and misinterpretations gratify needs as well as triggering negative emotional states that are not called for from others' points of view.

Gazzaniga's[45] modular model of the mind which attempts to show the interaction of emotions and interpretation seems to be a step in the right direction in understanding the complex interplay of feelings and cognitions. In this view of mind, feelings are filtered through interpretation and interpretation through feelings so that the individual arrives at "theories" of what is going on not only externally but also internally. People are both feeling and interpretative animals as they must be to cope with the complexity of social life and internal "states of mind." This brings us to a brief discussion of the interconnection of emotions and needs.

THE INTERCONNECTION OF NEEDS, AND POSSIBLY AN ADDITIONAL NEED

Even though, in an attempt to arrive at a realistic listing of needs, I have separated the various emotions and needs for the purpose of analysis, in real life this type of separation cannot be clearly made. For example, people may have fears that self-esteem will be damaged or meaning systems destroyed. By the same token, people may become angry when self-esteem is threatened. Or, people may become depressed if they are forced to live under constant fear. Other examples could be given but this is enough to make the case: primary emotions and their need analogues are intertwined. If this were not the case, such things as mental illness and irrational behavior would probably be much more easy to understand. Needs theory, in a sense, may be seen as a major refinement of Freudian theory in that needs replace Freud's undifferentiated libido and thus provide a more sophisticated theory of motivation. By the same token it should increase our ability to understand the problems that people face in a complex world and facilitate treatment of individuals *as well as the groups and societies* that help to produce individual problems. Individuals have *taken all the blame* for far too long. In short, specificity, as this relates to particular emotions and needs, gives us something more concrete to look for in the "haystack" of complexity.

At the risk of losing the parsimony necessary if needs theory is to be widely accepted and useful, it may be necessary to add one more emotion and its need analogue in order to complete the primaries in both cases. The emotion is boredom, and the need analogue is stimulation.[46] Ethologists tell us that animals continue to engage in activity, playful and otherwise, when they are not searching for food or protecting their territories. It thus seems that even animals might experience the emotion we are calling boredom and thereby have a "need" for stimulation. The same appears to be universal in human societies. People seek stimulation to overcome a feeling of boredom when all necessary work is done (and sometimes when it isn't) and when the other needs are gratified.

Having introduced the possibility of a need for stimulation based on the emotion of boredom, I want to equivocate a bit. It may be that if other needs are being adequately gratified at high levels this need would not exist. That is, if people have high security, a vibrant meaning system and high self-esteem, all leading to a high satisfaction, boredom would not be present. I say this because so far as I know there has been no physiological basis found for this need (perhaps adrenalin?). If such a basis cannot be found, it would have to be concluded that the emotion of boredom and its need analogue, stimulation, do not fit the model. It is simply that more work needs to be done in order to ascertain whether or not this is the case.

CLEARING UP SOME MISCONCEPTIONS

There are a variety of misconceptions in the discussions on needs theory in addition to the confusion of needs with culturally specific interests, wants and desires which others have discussed.[47] I will deal briefly with only three prominent examples. Many authors, following

Maslow[48] and others, believe there is a need to belong to a group,[49] and others believe there is a need for freedom[50] or list various needs under the rubric of freedom needs.[51] In my opinion neither of these should be classified as needs. These two "needs" are better seen as *necessary conditions* for the gratification of needs. That is, if the basic needs are to be gratified at optimum levels, persons must be *meaningfully* included in groups and live under conditions of freedom. Note, for example, that many persons who belong to groups do not have their needs gratified. Indeed, just the opposite may be the case: belonging to a group may damage self-esteem, destroy meaning and threaten security. Thus, it is not belonging to a group that gratifies needs but what goes on in the group in a positive sense for the individuals that gratifies needs. Thus, even though belonging to a group is a necessary condition, specific types of interaction must occur with others in groups if needs are to be gratified.

In addition, there was much talk at the Conference about the need for identity. I have never been exactly sure of what this means since all people have an identity of one kind or another and there are, of course, many groups that may provide a basis for identity. It is true that some people have a "spoiled identity" as Garfinkel[52] treats it in his discussion of degradation ceremonies, but they have an identity nevertheless. Or, it may be identity as Erikson[53] treats it, but what he calls identity comes very close to being what others call the core self. People who have an "identity problem" are people who are not meaningfully included within the framework of a group and thereby suffer because they have low self-esteem and perhaps little meaning in their lives. And identity (self), by definition, can be established only in relationship to others. And, most of us want an identity (self) that is held in high esteem by at least some others.

It all comes down to this: if we are to establish a listing of needs as a viable basis for theory and subsequent social policy, we must be very careful in the use of language. Otherwise we revert back to what might be called the MacDougall problem; positing a need for everything people do or "want."

Before discussing needs theory in relation to conflict resolution, I want briefly to discuss the connection of needs to individual control since this has implications for the discussion that follows.

CONTROL AND NEEDS

The possibility of gratifying each of the needs discussed depends, in large part, upon the degree of control people have over their environments. If people cannot control the responses of others, they can be expected to be in constant fear that the actions and/or words of others directed toward them will damage either their physical bodies and/or their selves. They have little security. It is obvious that people with more power can and do control the responses of people with less power. Few people will tell the emperor he has no clothes, so the emperor feels no threat to security of self. The school bully controls the responses of others toward himself and, at the same time, makes derogatory remarks to the school weakling. By doing so he damages the latter's self-esteem. The school weakling, because he has little control over others, is constantly obsessed with the need for security since others can easily damage both his physical being and/or his self. People with little control over various situations are constantly in fear of others making derogatory remarks about them in terms of such things as how they dress, how they talk, how they act, etc. Control over the responses of others is important if people are to feel secure.

Goffman[54] shows that there tend to be tacit agreements among people that each will not expose another as each attempts to "present a self." Thus, in the typical primary group people do not constantly fear the responses of others. Others' responses are controlled because these others also fear the possibility of retaliatory exposure. The fact that this subtle agreement exists adds additional evidence for much which had been said above. If people did not have needs, these agreements would hardly be present. Ethnomethodology literature[55] makes essentially the same point. For example, we tend to "let things pass" in potentially embarrassing situations with the agreement that others will do the same. All this permits mutual control of each other is many group situations so that people are not afraid to enter into known group relationships. Following Collins's[56] idea of interaction ritual chains, people often ritualize interaction in order to guarantee mutual and continued gratification of needs.

If the need for meaning is to be gratified, people must have at least some control over the construction of social reality. The so-called rebelliousness during the adolescent years is a good example of the attempt to assert control in the construction of social reality for the purpose of gratifying the need for meaning. Young people, by definition, inherit a world they did not help construct and to which they may not be able to relate in a meaningful manner. They are alienated because they can make no sense of that which is required of them. Marx[57] was well aware of this and saw that in capitalist societies workers are alienated because they have no control in the work place. The USSR and China, however, have not improved on this. The party apparatuses usurp power in the revolutions and remain reluctant to share power with workers. Democracy, at least ideally, is a system which permits the possibility of individual control but democratic countries that permit participation (and many times even this is a farce) only in the political arena and not in other areas such as the school and the work place have a long way to go if the need for meaning is to be gratified for all citizens.[58]

Individual control is obviously necessary if the need for self-esteem is to be gratified. If people cannot produce meaningful effects on their environments and receive credit for the effects produced self-esteem in any meaningful sense is not possible. People in high prestige positions in modern industrial societies attempt to gratify their needs for self-esteem from their positions rather than from their creativity. In this, careers are substituted for contributions and in C. Wright Mills's[59] terms intellectuals become experts living *off* rather than *for* ideas. Those in lower positions feel only a sense of shame (see above). Marx[60] had something to say about this as well. In his discussion of the human species, he saw the uniqueness of the human as that of a creative animal. If creativity is not possible because there is no control, there is little possibility of gratifying the need for self-esteem or the need for meaning. Marx and Engels[61] wanted to abolish all social categories that reduced people to the status of objects. In short, they wanted a world where every individual would be the subject of her/his own existence – a world in which every individual would be in control of his/her own life rather than being only an object of someone else's control.

People can be controlled *only* because they have needs, and for the same reason they can control others. *This is the basic reason sanctions work!* People control each other by providing rewards that gratify needs or threaten punishments which would deny such gratification. In this, rewards which gratify one need are often exchanged for rewards which gratify another; approval behavior, for example, may be exchanged for behavior which provides a sense of security. As Homans[62] shows, if a person is not being rewarded, she/he cannot be controlled unless punishment or threat of punishment is used which is, of course, often the case.[63]

CONFLICT PREVENTION AND/OR RESOLUTION

A recognition of the importance of individuals having control for the maintenance of the self and the gratification of needs may help to explain why such ideals as individual freedom,[64] justice and equality have been valued at least in Western societies, since the time of the Old Testament prophets and still remain a dream even in modern democratic societies. If the acts of individuals are restricted, they are not so free to control effects, and this damages the possibility of gratifying the need for self-esteem. If people do not get what they deserve, based on their relatively unrestricted pursuit of values, meaning and a sense of well being are not possible and justice is a farce. Inequality produces unequal effects as individuals compare themselves with others. Lack of freedom, injustice and inequality can be said to destroy the ontological grounding of the human self and the possibility of adequately gratifying needs, at least for the masses. Those with great power can obviously produce effects, and they typically get more than they deserve. One basis of conflict, if the above discussion has any merit, is the unequal distribution of power. Those with great power, of course, control the means of intellectual and emotional production.[65] In short, those persons tend either to create a systems of values or to take over an existing system which protects their interests in terms of need gratification.[66] People who cannot relate to these values are alienated. People who can and do relate, perhaps because of the lack of alternatives, may be willing to fight and die for these values in an attempt to gratify their needs – e.g., become a hero in war and thereby increase self-esteem and meaning. The latter might be called "The Rambo Solution" to the problem of self-esteem and meaning.

The difficulty of preventing or resolving conflict in all this becomes evident. People need at least some control in social relationships if self is to be perpetuated and needs gratified. People are driven by emotions which are tied to needs. Because of this, appeals to reason are not likely to be effective. To ask persons with great power to share this power is to ask them to give up the possibility of gratifying needs as they see or feel them from their immediate perspective. Also, since the possibility of gratifying needs tends to be connected to existing values, many persons will fight and die to protect these values rather than change them since change threatens security and present values may provide at least some degree of need gratification. At the macro-level most, if not all, present or potential conflicts among nations are based upon the attempt to perpetuate certain values and the possibility of the gratification of needs based upon these values (e.g., USSR versus the USA, Israel versus the Palestinians). Political parties struggle to protect and/or promote their respective values. The same is also true at the more micro-level. Family conflicts are, at base, power struggles over which partner is to realize his/her respective values and thereby gratify needs. If a property owner highly values holding property as a basis for need gratification, she/he will fight with a neighbor over the placement of a fence. Some people engage in deviant behavior in an attempt to realize some value which will provide gratification of needs,[67] and/or deviant behavior may result from pure rage because existing value systems and their implementation does not provide the possibility of need gratification. On the other hand, the only thing that keeps even more conflict from occurring in terms of the use of raw force is that people must abide by certain values, which are validated and supported by others, if the needs for meaning and self-esteem are to be gratified even at minimum levels.

As has been indicated above, the masking of primary emotions with secondary emotions, which prevents the expression of the former, no doubt produces the possibility of conflict over time. Emotions become "bottled up" in one situation only to "explode" in another. For example, the male blue-collar worker, who has learned to feel shame rather than anger, does not show anger in confronting the boss in the workplace for fear of losing his job. He may, however, go home and abuse his wife or children to relieve the real anger that shame has masked. Or, the person who is taught to feel the secondary emotion of guilt (masked fear) from an act over which she/he had little control may, over time, become frustrated and engage in aggressive behavior which, in turn, produces more guilt and more aggression. Structural conditions may affect entire nations if basic needs are not gratified. For example, the emotions of fear and anger combine to produce hate or jealousy, and this may be a prime cause of nations going to war, even though the real reason may be masked in religious or nationalist ideals. The lesson learned from Hitler's rise to power and the subsequent destruction of millions of Jews, along with others, in the course of the Second World War should not be forgotten. The German people had lost a basis for meaning, and the security of many was threatened by economic depression. Rather than place blame on the real source, they vented their anger and fear by hating and killing the innocent. People are not so far removed from animals in terms of emotional make up that the "fight or flight" syndrome produced by these two emotions can be controlled by reason, even though it may be the self rather than the physical organism which is being threatened. The basis of most conflict can hardly be said to be rational. Until we learn that human needs demand gratification, evil produced largely by emotional responses to the lack of such gratification will without doubt continue.

I am increasingly convinced that the only long-term solution to conflict is to establish a hegemony of thought, based upon different values, that permits equality in the gratification of human needs, just as the powerful have established a hegemony of values based upon their interests in gratifying their own needs. An over-arching value, of course, would have to be that all people have the right to pursue any value they wish so long as this does not interfere with the realization of like or unlike values by others. This would create a truly pluralistic world: a world in which individuals would feel free to switch from value to value depending upon needs and abilities at a given time. No prestige system would exist, only esteem systems. Persons would be judged by others on the basis of what they do and are, not who they are, based on the position they hold. People could always change what they do and are in order to optimize the gratification of needs. In short, we must get "behind" present distributions of power in order to change them, and this is best accomplished by changing values since those who presently have great power depend upon existing values for the gratification of their own needs. A refusal to abide by existing values, even though risky, also undermines existing values. If what has been said is correct, an arrangement such as this can be the only truly legitimate world system, since it is grounded in the very nature of the species.[68]

All this, of course, is easier said than done. Most people like to think they are presently pursuing ultimate values, be they religious values or the invisible law of supply and demand, as though "God" had created these for human creatures and disregarding human suffering. But, if we want to talk about an ultimate in any manner, it seems to be the case that this "ultimate" must have a naturalistic basis since there is no scientific reason to believe that human beings are anything but a bud on the evolutionary bush. I have tried to make the case of this "ultimate" by showing that the characteristics of individual species members who "inhabit this bud" are of a certain nature, given their biology, and by showing the necessity of living in social groups and all this implies. Since part of this nature is the ability to reason and anticipate alternative futures, the choice concerning what the actual future will be is collectively ours.

A FINAL NOTE

In case the above is rejected, and I am sure it will be by some and perhaps many, I write this final note for those who reject the possibility of needs theory on the grounds that it is essentially political in nature. Soper[69] makes two points at the beginning of her discussion of needs: "Every actual or possible form of social organization is value based. It is underwritten, that is to say, by some 'theory of human needs' " and "a second point I would want to make is that if the very attempt to deny the politics of need is itself a form of politics, then perhaps we can distinguish between a politics of need that exists in the form of suppression of that politics, and a politics that explicitly recognizes itself to be involved in that politics." In these two statements she sums up both sides of the case very well.

In addition, Schattschneider[70] has pointed out in much the same vein that all social organization is the mobilization of bias. This is the case from the social organization of science to the social organiz-ation of state politics and the military, and it is also true for organizations whose goal is the abolition of human conflict. Monies spent in these areas, for example, could be spent in other ways. But as Soper and Schattschneider indicate, those who oppose organiz-ations for conflict resolutions and/or the attempts to formulate a needs theory merely have different political orientations. My bias merely says that the attempt to arrive at a theory of human needs, which may help to reduce conflict and alleviate human suffering, is the better way to go based on the additional assumption that human suffering is, at base, an evil. Some people may enjoy causing others to suffer, but few normal people seek suffering for its intrinsic enjoyment.

NOTES AND REFERENCES

1. Theodore D. Kemper, "How Many Emotions Are There? Wedding the Social and the Autonomic Components," *American Journal of Sociology*, 93 (1987): 263–89.
2. David Funkenstein, "The Physiology of Fear and Anger," *Scientific American*, 192 (1955): 78–80.
3. Kemper, "How Many Emotions": 272.
4. Stanley Schachter and Jerome Singer, "Cognitive, Social and Physiological Determinants of Emotional State," *Psychological Review*, 69 (1962): 379–99.
5. Theodore D. Kemper, *A Social Interactional Theory of Emotions* (New York: Wiley, 1978).
6. Kemper, "How Many Emotions": 282.
7. Rom Harre (ed.), *The Social Construction of Emotion* (New York: Blackwell, 1986); Theodore D. Kemper, "Social Constructionist and Positivist Approaches to the Sociology of Emotions," *American Journal of Sociology*, 87 (1981): 336–62.
8. Paul Ekman, "Expression and the Nature of Emotions," in Klaus R. Scherer and Paul Ekman (eds), *Approaches to Emotions* (Hillsdale, N.J.: Lawrence Erlbaum, 1984).
9. Paul Ekman, W. V. Friesen and S. Ancoli, "Facial Expressions of Emotional Experiences," *Journal of Personal and Social Psychology*, 39 (1980): 1125–34.
10. M. E. Leachy, symposium held at Kent State University (1988).
11. Kemper, "How Many Emotions;" Ekman, "Expression and the Nature of Emotions."
12. Charles Darwin, *The Expression of Emotion in Man and Animals* (New York: Philosophical Library, 1955).
13. George Casper Homans, *Social Behavior: Its Elementary Forms* (New York: Harcourt Brace Jovanovich, 1974).
14. Eleanora Masini, "Needs and Dynamics," in Katrin Lederer (ed.) with Johan Galtung and David Antal, *Human Needs: A Contribution to the Current Debate* (Cambridge, MA: Oelgeschlager, Gunn & Hain, 1980): 227.
15. See Johan Galtung, Carlos A. Mallmann and Solomon Marcus, "Logical Clarifications in the Study of Needs;" Ramashray Roy, "Human Needs and Freedom: Liberal, Marxist, and Gandhian Perspectives;" Gilbert Rist, "Basic Questions about Basic Human Needs," all in Lederer (ed.), *Human Needs*.
16. For this view see Karl R. Popper and John C. Eccles, *The Self and Its Brain* (New York: Springer, 1977).
17. George H. Mead, *Mind, Self and Society* (Chicago: University of Chicago Press, 1934).
18. Michael S. Gazzaniga, *Mind Matters* (New York: Houghton Mifflin, 1988).
19. Paul Sites, *Control: The Basis of Social Order* (New York: Dunellen, 1973).
20. Martin Seligmann, *Helplessness* (San Francisco: W. H. Freeman, 1975).

21. Seligmann, *Helplessness*: 17.
22. Ellen J. Langer, *The Psychology of Control* (Beverley Hills, CA: Gunn & Hain, 1983).
23. Sites, *Basis of Order*.
24. Gazzaniga, *Mind Matters*.
25. Homans, *Social Behavior*: 37.
26. Mircea Eliade, *A History of Religious Ideas*, vol. 1 (Chicago: The University of Chicago Press, 1978).
27. Peter Berger and Thomas Luckman, *The Social Construction of Reality* (Garden City, N.Y.: Doubleday, 1967).
28. Such as Harold Garfinkel, *Studies in Ethnomethodology* (Garden City, N.J.: Prentice-Hall, 1967).
29. Clyde Kluckhohn, "Values and Value Orientations in the Theory of Action," in T. Parsons and E. A. Shils (eds), *Towards a General Theory of Action* (Cambridge, MA: 40 Harvard University Press, 1951).
30. Howard, P. Becker, *Through Values to Social Interpretation* (Durham, NC: Duke University Press, 1950).
31. As in much of Weber's work. See Max Weber, *Economy and Society*, Guenther Roth and Claus Wittich (eds) (Berkeley: University of California Press, 1968).
32. Richard Emerson, "Toward a Theory of Value in Social Exchange," in Karen J. Cook (ed.), *Social Exchange Theory* (Beverley Hills, CA: Sage, 1987).
33. Turner is in agreement with this formulation. See Jonathan H. Turner *A Theory of Social Interaction* (Stanford, CA: Stanford University Press, 1988).
34. Kemper, "How Many Emotions."
35. Thomas Scheff, "Shame and Conformity: The Deference Emotion System," *American Sociological Review*, 53 (1988): 395–406.
36. Thomas Scheff, "The Shame/Rage Spiral Case Study of an Interminable Quarrel," in H. B. Lewis (ed.), *The Role of Shame in Sympton Formation*, (Hillsdale, N.J.: Lawrence Erlbaum, 1987).
37. Richard Sennett and Jonathan Cobb, *The Hidden Injuries of Class* (New York: Vintage, 1972).
38. Sites, *Control*.
39. Georg Simmel, "Mental Health in the Metropolis," in Kurt Wolff (ed.), *The Sociology of Georg Simmel* (Glencoe, IL: The Free Press, 1950).
40. R. Ader, "Psychosomatic and Psychoimmunological Research," *Psychosomatic Medicine*, 42 (1980): 307–21.
41. H. Selye, *The Stress of Life* (New York: Van Nostrand Reinhold, 1979).
42. Selye, *The Stress of Life*.
43. See Richard Lazarus and Susan Folkman, *Stress, Appraisal and Coping* (New York: Springer, 1984).
44. See Michael S. Gazzaniga, *Social Brain* (New York: Basic Books, 1985); Gazzaniga, *Mind Matters* (1988).
45. Ibid.
46. New experience, see W. I. Thomas, *The Unadjusted Girl* (Boston: Little, Brown & Co., 1923).
47. See selected essays in Lederer (ed.), *Human Needs* and Ross Fitzgerald

(ed.), *Human Needs and Politics* (Oxford: New York: Pergamon, 1977).
48. A. H. Maslow, *Motivation and Personality* (New York: Harper & Row, 1954).
49. See Turner, *A Theory of Social Interaction*.
50. See Scimecca and Bay, Chapters 9 and 11 in this Volume.
51. See Galtung, Chapter 15 in this Volume.
52. Garfinkel, *Ethnomethodology*.
53. E. H. Erikson, *Childhood and Society* (New York: Norton, 1963).
54. Erving Goffman, *The Presentation of Self in Everyday Life* (Garden City, N.Y.: Doubleday, 1959); Erving Goffman, *Interaction Ritual* (New York: Doubleday, 1967); Erving Goffman, *Strategic Interaction* (Philadelphia: University of Pennsylvania Press, 1969).
55. See John Heritage, in Garfinkel, *Ethnomethodology*.
56. Randall Collins, "The Microfoundations of Macrosociology," *American Journal of Sociology*, 86 (1981): 984–1014; Randall Collins, *Theoretical Sociology* (New York: Harcourt Brace Jovanovich, 1988).
57. Karl Marx, *Economic and Philosophical Manuscripts of 1844*, M. Milligam (trans.) (New York: International Publishers, 1964).
58. See C. B. Macpherson, *The Real World of Democracy* (Toronto: Canadian Broadcasting Co., 1965).
59. C. Wright Mills, *White Collar* (New York: Oxford University Press, 1953).
60. Marx, *Economic and Philosophical Manuscripts of 1844*.
61. Karl Marx and Frederick Engels, *The Holy Family* (Moscow: Progress Publishers, 1975).
62. Homans, *Social Behavior*.
63. Also, see Richard Emerson, "Power–Dependence Relationships," *American Sociological Review*, 27 (1962): 31–4.
64. See Christian Bay, *The Structure of Freedom* (Stanford, CA: Stanford University Press, 1958).
65. Randall Collins, *Conflict Sociology* (New York: Academic Press, 1975).
66. Gerhard E. Lenski, *Power and Privilege: A Theory of Social Stratification* (New York: McGraw-Hill, 1966).
67. John W. Burton, *Deviance, Terrorism, and War: The Process of Solving Unsolved Social and Political Problems* (New York: St Martin's Press, 1979).
68. See Christian Bay, "Needs, Wants and Political Legitimacy," *Canadian Journal of Political Science*, 1 (1968): 241–60.
69. Kate Soper, *On Human Needs* (Atlantic Heights, N.J.: Humanities Press, 1981): 2 and 4.
70. E. E. Schattschneider, *The Semi-Sovereign People* (New York: Holt, Rinehart & Winston, 1960).

2 Meaningful Social Bonding as a Universal Human Need
Mary E. Clark

Human needs theory, if it is to be universally applicable – and hence useful in resolving the broadest spectrum of human conflicts – must carefully avoid becoming merely a description of the self-perceived "needs" of the particular group that is developing the theory. Yet it is just this trap into which, I believe, the development of human needs theory in the West has largely fallen. And because Western thought – by which I mean Eastern European, Western European and North American intellectual traditions – dominates so much of the international scene at this moment in history, the failure to perceive our own narrowness could well have unfortunate consequences globally. What is needed, then, is for those of us in the West not only to seek understanding from others outside our own traditions, but also conscientiously to identify and critique as many of the assumptions underlying our own thinking as we possibly can.

In preparing this chapter, however, I do not wish to dwell on the gaps – and therefore the limitations – of human needs theory as it has so far been developed. Suffice it to say that, in my view, it has taken for its model of "human nature" the individual of Western thought. Hobbesian man, at odds with both his fellows and with Nature, was endowed in the primal past with reason for the sole purposes of conquering an unruly Nature and negotiating tit-for-tat social contracts with otherwise unfriendly fellow humans.

This idea of the isolated individual had made fleeting appearances in the ancient world. The scions of the noble families of Periclean Attica must have thought themselves "somebody;" and in Judaea, a century or so later, tribalism was giving way to concerns for individual redemption, which paved the way for the flowering of Christianity.[1] But for over a millennium, "individualism" was postponed until the next life, and in *this* life a strong social order based on the Church obtained. Post-Enlightenment thinkers, displaying their new-found distaste for the enslavement of the human spirit by the chains of

34

social custom, labeled this the Dark Age.

Since the intellectual ferment of the fifteenth, sixteenth and seventeenth centuries the West has never looked back. The individual was placed on a pinnacle – Locke gave him the right to possess personal property; the American revolution created a polity in which cultural meaning was deliberately set aside, and social relations were defined solely by Hobbesian parameters. The right of individuals to be free from the injustices formerly experienced at the hands of powerful demagogues slowly (yet in retrospect, perhaps logically) evolved into a competitive, possessive individualism: a "human nature" seemingly endowed by Providence with intrinsic selfish needs.

It was in this context that modern Western social theory, aided and abetted by scientific notions of logical positivism and temporal "progress," evolved. Political science developed theories to explain the new tensions between "government" and the "individual;" and economic theory, following suit, invented "laws" of economic behavior that assumed a society of isolated, self-centered individuals rationally calculating what was best for Number One.[2] These were later followed by psychology, the earliest days of which as an experimental science began by studying not the behavior of colonies of rats, but that of far more scientifically "controllable" individual rats, often reared in isolation; it then transposed the intellectual argument implicit in this methodological approach to its study of human behavior.[3]

Even Darwin was affected by this emphasis on the individual, and from his day forward the primary argument of evolutionary adaptation has been couched from the perspective of an isolated individual organism concerned only with its own survival in an external and separate "environment" and with leaving more offspring than its competing siblings. Most contemporary ecological studies tend implicitly to assume an adversarial relationship between the organism and its environment and the organism and its relatives. Nature has taken on the trappings of a competitive commercialism, with "efficiency" as the primary means for offsetting "scarcity."[4]

Similarly, cultural anthropologists during the first half or more of this century often viewed their "subject" peoples from an individualistic perspective. They looked for and reported on those aspects of life that held most intrinsic interest for the Western mind – the perspective of the individual: how do people "feel" towards others? It was much more difficult for them to report coherently on the cosmic vision and social meaning of the societies they studied. Among earlier anthropologists Ruth Benedict perhaps came closest,[5] and more recently, from a different perspective, so did Joseph Campbell.[6] Yet we are still only at the beginning of developing the skills needed for understanding the role of *social* meaning in creating "sane" societies – societies wherein the sacred social vision invites the bonding of the creative individual with the social enterprise, thus fulfilling the deepest, most human of all our needs: those for social attachment and psychological purpose.

THE ORIGINS OF SOCIAL BONDING

I am a biologist by training, and so professionally I regard *homo sapiens* as but one more biological species, which happened to evolve a particular strategy for surviving that other species had not yet tried, namely the ability to accumulate information that enabled it to manipulate its environment. Now every species, whatever its survival strategy, has certain constraints placed upon it as it evolves. Evolution is contingent – it can use only the materials already present in the ancestral organism to shape and modify them into divergent forms. Nature does not create traits *de novo*. Furthermore, such traits in humans as big brains or binocular vision or backbones (to extend things back in time) do not evolve independently of the rest of the organism. Multiple traits are changing in interactive ways that constantly result in a functioning whole. This means that complex sets of adaptations are co-evolving. In the case of humans, big brains were accompanied by – indeed, had as their prerequisite – bipedalism, an opposable thumb, and most especially, *an extraordinary degree of social bonding*. It is this latter aspect of "human nature" that I wish to stress in this chapter, and I shall return in more detail to its origins below. Here I simply point out that our current fission of the concepts of "the individual" and "society" into separate, often warring, compartments blinds us to the fact that these are *one* thing. To the extent that a society is dysfunctional, then so are its individual members: for every person is inescapably a social being, formed by and forming others within his or her circle of contacts. This statement, a near tautology, seems conceptually to escape most modern social thinkers.

There is a corollary problem in contemporary Western thought, namely the notion of linear "progress." This, too, gets in the way of clear thinking. For example, it is almost uniformly denied that prehistoric societies could have been more humane than were the civilizations that emerged between 4000 and 2000 years ago. Indeed, it is a measure of just how far "civilized" society has fallen from being "sane" that its thinkers repeatedly fail to perceive the unfulfilled *social* needs of humans living in the thinkers' own societies, and those thinkers instead regularly ascribe others' anti-social behaviors to some intrinsic barbarity from our supposedly bestial origins still lurking inside us. For such thinkers, the present problems of human-kind arise from primitive – and hence "bad" – hypothalamic and limbic system urges, rather than from a set of inhumane institutions that have evolved slowly with the growth of large, highly organized societies. Thus Hobbes, Locke, Darwin and many others (Adam Smith, Hegel, Marx, Freud, Fromm, to name but a few) regard present society as a distinct improvement on the past. Failures in human social behavior – violence, alienation and injustice – are seen as a burden from our animal origins that civilized society is still learning to cope with, through education, bribery or coercion. With but few exceptions, writers argue that humankind has yet to invent the social institutions that will conquer, once and for all, this shady side of our evolutionary past. Almost never is the problem cast in terms of a failure of the institution of civilized society to meet intrinsic needs of the human organism.

I shall argue here that the present approach to our obvious difficulties as a species is doomed to failure. The problem does not lie in some biological deficiency that can be overcome only by either genetic or social engineering. Rather, the problem lies in having become blind to the *kind* of society that satisfies our deepest human needs, and in having constructed, through a long series of deficient social visions, institutions that deny rather than satisfy those needs. Suffice it to say that humankind, given the institutions characterizing modern civilizations, could never have evolved!

DEFINING "HUMAN" NEEDS

Before tackling human origins in relation to human needs, it is necessary to define what one means by *human* needs. The abstract word, needs, is never clearcut. We can, for example, state the obvious: all people need nutrients and water to survive; they need habitats that protect them from the elements. Yet these are not specifically "human" needs; they are shared by other life forms. At the other end of the needs spectrum are those that are defined by a particular culture: southern Californians "need" cars. Cars, however, are not a "human" need; they are a cultural need. Critical though such cultural "needs" often are to individuals living within a particular culture (and hence their importance to understanding that culture), they are *derived* needs – that is, they are needs that stem from one's membership in a particular society, and not from one's universal need for membership in *a* society. To that extent, such needs, which are so often met at the expense of the environment or through exploitation of others, do not require suppression of a part of our intrinsic selves or some form of eugenics to overcome. Rather, they require cultural modification. It is our *other* needs – those that are *specifically* and *universally* human – that I wish to address.

What is it that makes the human animal distinct? Western Biblical tradition, which places man closer to God and the angels than to the rest of Creation, was a gigantic departure from the animistic universe of primal peoples, in which humans were but one actor on the stage of life. And it has been only in the past century that the Darwinian argument, now supported by abundant paleontological finds, has presented us with a picture of our biological origins. Yet Western thought, while accepting the *fact* of evolution, has still not absorbed what evolution *means* for our self-understanding. In most academic circles, the notion of the original Hobbesian man – self-centered, aggressive, selfish – has simply, even enthusiastically, been pushed back in time on to "sub-human" (hence "inferior") apes, from whom we have progressed enormously, although still retaining some nasty remnants of our bestial origins. "Human" traits are seen to "progress" through a sequence of individual fossil specimens: "Lucy," the diminutive Australopithecine with a tiny brain but an upright gait; *homo habilis*, a 2 million-year-old "real" human, with a bit bigger brain; the much more recent thick-browed Neanderthalers, who are still mostly thought of, especially in comic strips, as bumbling mental defectives. This imagery – of a "progression" of individual human ancestors, striding from left to right across the page of a textbook as they escape our apelike past – is carefully nurtured in each new generation. This parade of a series of anatomical changes shows man (they are *always* males) "learning" gradually to walk upright, acquiring an opposable thumb that permits grasping a tool (inevitably a club), and growing a bigger and bigger head, bedecked with flowing hair and a beard, all that remains of the original fur. The implicit statement is this: becoming human consisted of acquiring bipedalism, tools (especially weapons), and a brain with which to have "rational" thoughts. These anatomical "advantages" permitted humans to "succeed" as a species, to "outcompete" less "advanced" forms, and to manipulate nature to their own advantage. These Hobbesian images permeate almost every textbook, encyclopedia, and high-school teacher's lectures. And they are utterly misleading, for they leave out the most fundamental aspect of our biological origins – namely, our social nature. Indeed, there is no doubt that our ancestors were social *before* they were human, and consequently the greatest human need that we all have is for social bonding.

THE MAGNITUDE OF THE HOBBESIAN ERROR

Today, much of Western social thought – despite considerable theoretical argument to the contrary and the on-going evidence of daily existence, even in the most alienating of modern societies – still treats human social institutions as something distinct from the lives of individual people. The individual is our central focus, and she or he out of constraining necessity is embedded in an external "thing" called "society." The two concepts are considered separately, and frequently treated as at odds. "Culture" is merely the backdrop against which the individual actor's life is lived out. As Ramashray Roy says, people in the West, especially liberals, "believe that the individual is prior to society, that society is created by individuals and that society exists to serve individual purposes. They believe that man is, therefore society is."[7]

Our Western vision of society – as a Hobbesian contract, consciously entered into primarily to ensure harmony – offers no way of explaining the existence of family bonds, of lifelong friendships, of the sense of cultural membership afforded by shared language, and a thousand other precious things. Indeed, it totally misses and even denies the deepest requirement that characterizes our species – the need for social identity. Hobbes's notion that without society, humans would be at each other's throats in a grand free-for-all is totally right, but for completely the wrong reasons. He assumed that isolated human beings "in a state of nature" would naturally destroy one another because their supposedly innate competitive drives would lead them to do so. What Hobbes failed to realize – and many still do today – is that humans evolved with a desire to *belong*, not to *compete*. Biologically, we are obligatory social animals, wholly dependent on a supportive social structure, and it is in the *absence* of such a support system that destructive, "inhuman" behaviors occur.

The so-called "civilized" societies that have existed since the dawn of the historic era have all been less than supportive of great numbers of their members, and hence history has been largely a record of unhappy peoples. It is perhaps not surprising that Hobbes misread the problem, for in his time the West was still largely ignorant of the evidence that would show that social institutions were failing to meet human needs, rather than that humankind suffers from some intrinsic behavioral maladaptation. Only now are the pieces accumulating from a number of disciplines that permit insight into the kinds of social relations human beings require, but this information has yet to find its way into mainstream social thought.

THE BIOLOGICAL EVIDENCE

What follows is a brief sketch of the evidence that the primary human need – in order to live a humane existence – is for a supportive society.

The evolutionary split between the ancestors of humans and of our nearest extant relatives now seems to have been quite recent – around 5 or 6 million years ago.[8] Every few years, new evidence suggests an ever shorter time-frame. Studies of the great apes, particularly gorillas and chimpanzees, have yielded considerable insight into traits that our forebears must have possessed during the early days of our emergence as a species. (To the extent that *any* species's behavior is determined by its genes, we can note that the identity of the genes coding for proteins in chimpanzees and humans is greater than 99 per cent.[9]) Of particular value are the three decades of observations of chimpanzees by Jane Goodall, which have yielded a far clearer understanding of the lifelong bonds that are formed, not just between females and their offspring, but among siblings and even among unrelated childhood playmates. Goodall records joyous embraces between unrelated males reunited after long periods of separation. Personal pleasure in social interaction is constantly evident, in infant play, adult grooming, and spontaneous sliding by all down steep hills on leafy branches. And the withdrawal of a social bond can create psychic havoc, especially when an infant is separated from its mother.[10]

This profoundly strong bonding, exhibited not only among the

great apes, but also among many monkeys, no doubt also characterized early human societies. Indeed, there are biological reasons for
believing that social bonding became even stronger during human
evolution. For one thing, as Stephen Jay Gould has pointed out, the
evolution of large brains – that particularly human evolutionary
adaptation – surely required the most absolute degree of social
bonding. As the human head became relatively larger and larger,
babies had to be born in an increasingly premature and helpless state
if they were to make their way successfully through the mother's
birth canal.[11] Hence, the original bonding was between mothers and
their increasingly dependent offspring. (If you are going to be very
big-brained as an adult, you must begin with a *relatively* big brain at
birth.)

These increasingly helpless infants demanded a whole panoply of
biological and behavioral adaptations in the adults that cared for
them if they were to survive. For a helpless infant to become a
"smart" adult, it must have parents and other adults around who
are "smart" enough to look after it. And this entailed not only
"intelligence" but – even more importantly – emotional bonding that
lasted not just for a few weeks or months, or even until weaning
occurred after several years, but virtually throughout life. Some of
these bonds had a primarily anatomical or physiological basis. The
enlarged human breast, which other primates do not share, ensured
eye-to-eye contact between child and mother.[12] The evolution of
facial expressions and other signals of emotional states conveyed
much social information. Established initially between infant and
mother, these signals were also understood by others, so parent–offspring bonds expanded through shared signals to create the "extended
family" – all those individuals of the same troop, whether genetically
closely related or not, who had experienced similar social signals.

Meantime, frequent nursing by the infant went beyond establishing
permanent bonds. It effectively spaced our births by postponing
ovulation, giving the parent more time to raise each offspring,
and decreasing opportunities for direct sibling rivalry.[13] Among
chimpanzees, older siblings, especially the prepubertal females,
regularly assist in the care of younger brothers and sisters. And of
course, other adults, both male and female, extend attention to – or
at least tolerate the presence of – all youngsters belonging to the
group.[14] As infants, our ancestors very likely also received enormous
social attention. Furthermore, the degree to which emotional information was exchanged grew far beyond what other apes could

manage. Laughing, crying, pouting, flirting – the whole spectrum of moods – became far more conspicuous in humans.[15] Evidently, many of our thalamically and hypothalamically controlled social drives, far from being merely an "unfortunate" remnant of our animal instincts, in fact evolved as the biologically grounded basis of all human relations. Hobbes was quite wrong. Our earliest ancestors did *not* evolve as calculating individuals, assessing how others might forward their own interests, but as entities programed to seek out and enjoy the company of others of their own kind. The earliest humans were biologically designed to trust one another, and to become an intimate member of a group.

The evolutionary driving force of this entire process must surely have been the expanded social bonding – beyond parent and offspring – needed to protect the helpless human infants – a job that mothers alone could no longer accomplish. This included not only looking after the infants and their mothers, warding off predators and even "strangers" of the same species; it meant sharing food, often carrying it long distances back to the troop.[16] It also came to mean a lifelong *need* to be among known others of one's own kind, and at this stage, "kind" meant not just any member of one's own species, but recognizable individuals who shared the same social signals.[17] Social bonding to one's group ultimately became an inescapable biological necessity.

Such close bonding has had a second and integrally related purpose. Helpless infants not only need protecting after birth but, if their large brains are to fulfill their adaptational purpose of processing complex information, they also need to acquire information – far more of it than, by chance, they might learn on their own. Furthermore, they need to know how to interpret that information, to fit it all together, to become, in short, *wise*. Each new generation must thus not only be protected *by* society: it serves, as it matures, as a living receptacle for society's accumulated wisdom, and hence ensures the continuance of society itself. The integrity of social bonds is thus *doubly* essential to the survival of knowledge-dependent social animals. Is it any wonder that social bonding has become such a deeply emotional part of our biological programing? How, one is forced to ask, can modern Western societies possibly expect that individuals can somehow successfully create themselves?

Turning to the evolution of the human brain, we can ask: what properties have evolved that promote the survival of a knowledge-dependent social species? The enormous growth in thickness of the cerebral cortex is widely heralded as the basis for human "intelligence" – a hugely expanded memory capacity. But additionally there must have been some "hard-wiring" (some heritable organizations of neurones) that led to at least two universal human behavioral propensities.

One of these was the propensity to form attachments. As British neurobiologist, J. Z. Young, states: "It may be that a large part if not the whole of later cerebral organization is arranged to some extent around various human features . . . The evidence from childhood certainly shows that humans are born with a propensity to pay special attention to the sights and sound of each other." He continues: "Outside the family adults very often become attached to groups or institutions, sometimes focusing only too readily on its leader, president, or king. Attachments to stars of stage, ring, or football fields are commonplace. This very characteristic human feature of attachment must have a specific basis in the brain. Indeed, it must have a common basis in all mankind."[18]

The second area of probable "hard-wiring" of the human brain has to do with language. The major proponent of this idea is the linguist, Noam Chomsky. Again quoting from Young: "Chomsky . . . has argued that language is a structured system with an independent existence. We are indeed saying that the programs of the brain constitute a structured system written in a 'language'."[19] Not only does this internal property of our brain permit us to communicate useful information through mutually understood abstract sounds; it also permits us to draw upon our vast memory stores to create imagined worlds – think about the future.

With the onset of self-consciousness, which presumably accompanied the development of language, even deeper avenues for bonding occurred. The ability to share together questions about the meaning of events, about where the first humans came from, and about what happens after death led to a set of shared explanations that satisfied the newly experienced *need* for meaning. The symbols embedded in each language thus created a cultural bond through which an individual attained self-identity. (We shall return to this idea below.)

SOCIAL BONDING AS AN ABSOLUTE PHYSIOLOGICAL AND PSYCHOLOGICAL NEED

Genie, a girl who had been locked away by her parents all her life, was discovered at age thirteen by Los Angeles authorities, some years ago; she was mute and incontinent, crawled on all fours, and understood nothing that was said to her, a primitive creature without any evidence of mind. But it was not because of gross brain defectiveness; within four years, in foster care, she had developed some language ability, many social skills, and the mental capacity of an eight-year old.[20]

Genie's story underscores what we all already know. Human beings have an absolute need for social intercourse from the first moments of life. Without social contact, babies fail to become people. They may not die, but they do not become fully human; their pre-programed brains fail to develop normally. (In fact, this realization has led to the introduction of a bill in Montgomery County, Maryland granting four months' paid leave to county employees, both men and women, for bonding with their newborn offspring. Officials are convinced that in the absence of such bonding, too many children are growing up to become social "problems.")

We now know that socialization begins in the womb, and newborns are able differentially to respond to their mother's voice. Further-more, we know that brain development, both pre- and post-natally, is dependent upon a rich variety of sensory inputs. Among mammals the size of, and the number of, neuronal connections in the cerebral cortex are directly correlated with the richness of environmental inputs. Rats raised alone, without companions or a complex environment to explore, have underdeveloped brains and are slower learners than are their siblings raised in a group and provided with ladders, tunnels, swings and wheels. But rats that were merely permitted passively to watch other rats playing in enriched environments remained underdeveloped – a potent warning to parents whose children spend long hours passively watching television.[21]

Young primates raised in isolation from parents experience even more serious consequences. In the 1950s and 1960s, H. F. Harlow and his colleagues deprived baby rhesus monkeys of all social contacts, creating in them a desperate and permanent autism, with symptoms not unlike those of many autistic human children.[22] Nobel prize-winning ethologist Nicholaas Tinbergen and his wife Elisabeth found that many autistic children could be helped greatly by gently re-establishing human social contacts; slowly, trusting bonds could be formed.[23]

In the opposite direction, there is the true physiological depression that occurs following the breaking of long-established bonds. This can occur when isolated immigrants are immersed in a new culture, or more notably, when a person loses a parent or spouse. This is not only a matter of "psychological" grieving. The entire body suffers, and particularly the immune system.[24] The incidence of death among surviving spouses is significantly higher during the months immediately following the loss. Even the seemingly non-traumatic act of retirement – with its attendant social deprivation – can be accompanied by measurable physiological symptoms.[25]

Finally we can mention the permanent psychic damage that afflicts a tragic number of young men and women exposed for weeks and months on end to the inhumane horrors of violent combat. It was nearly a decade after the end of the war in Vietnam before there was any significant understanding of the psychic damage done to tens of thousands of apparently "healthy" veterans, who had lived through the most terrible atrocities – experiences that denied the very existence of human bonding – and found themselves unable to escape from the effects of those experiences. Phrases like: "It don't mean nothin'" and "Fighting for peace is like fucking for virginity" indicated the depths of their disillusionment. Post-traumatic stress disorder, as their symptoms came to be called, cannot be cured, but it can be made tolerable after long months of angry grieving and catharsis, especially in the presence of fellow sufferers.[26] Recently Americans, who had either been to Vietnam themselves or who assisted those who had, have traveled to Russia to help the veterans returning from Afghanistan, many of whom are suffering identical symptoms.

Separation, alienation, ostracism, humiliation – all are denials of human bonding, of acceptance within a circle, a group, a family, a support system, a community within which one can find not only companionship but also a sense that life really *does* have a purpose. If denial of bonding creates distress, marked healing is effected by a supporting community. Before the modern age of pharmaceuticals for every ailment tribal peoples, while applying their repertoire of (sometimes very effective) medicines, would also offer continuous attention and support to the ailing person. Long labelled as no more than "superstition," this attentive behavior has recently been found to have considerable efficacy.[27] Group therapy – an almost unknown idea a few decades ago – is now used to treat a wide variety of problems from obesity and alcoholism to depression and bereavement.

This role of bonding in primate and especially in human behavior has, however, received almost no serious analytical attention. What attention *has* been paid to it has focused not on its positive functions but on the consequences of its absence, as in the Harlows' study of infant monkeys deprived of companions, and in studies of aggression. The indexes in books on primate ethology or the biological origins of human behavior have twenty or thirty times as many entries under "aggression" as under "love" and "altruism." Of course, bonding behaviors such as grooming, playing, teaching the young and so forth are described, but their role in establishing and maintaining the entire social structure is all but ignored. Aggression, dominance, hierarchy and appeasement – the skills presumably needed to get along in a competitive and unfriendly world – are tacitly assumed to be the critical traits for survival. Evolutionists, ethologists and sociobiologists have all taken the same tack, unconsciously accepting the Hobbesian vision of human origins – bolstered up as it is by the behavior of modern industrial man – as the correct one. Only recently have we begun to prove "scientifically" what was there to be seen all along: that meaningful social bonds are an absolute need of the human organism, and that rupture of these bonds is – as novelists and playwrights have been telling us for centuries – a tragedy.

THE ADDITIONAL NEED FOR MEANING

So far, I have adduced some of the accumulating evidence that bonds – strong interpersonal relationships – are a biologically, physiologically, and psychologically based human need. I have argued that when those bonds fail, human beings suffer and often exhibit a wide range of pathological and self-destructive behaviors. I have further noted the universal need for acceptance *within* the social group. But what can we say of the nature of the shared bond? Is it enough for humans – as it seems to be for chimpanzees – simply to recognize another individual as a familiar "someone" encountered on a regular basis? Or for human individuals is something more needed to forge a satisfying bond of acceptance?

This question is an enormous one – indeed, it may be *the* central question of human existence. What is the quality of the relationship we humans need to live a satisfying life? It is far too big a question to tackle here in depth. All I shall try to do is hint at the components of the answer. It should, I think, be obvious that while humans certainly need something like the level of social bonding required by other primates, especially the great apes, our requirements are at once more flexible and more demanding. For example, modern-day humans can move far more freely than can chimpanzees from societies where they are known to societies where they are total strangers. With but few exceptions, chimpanzees may find themselves in mortal danger in attempting to move between groups. Clearly, humans are far more able to send and receive the signals needed for non-violent acceptance.

On the other hand, once a chimpanzee is accepted in a new group, it flourishes. This is far from true for transplanted humans. Although they may experience a superficial acceptance, a tolerance, that permits physical survival, it may be many years before they are able to establish the quality of bonds needed for satisfactory human existence. It is not simply language, *per se*, that matters. It is shared goals, values, customs, traditions; it is the shared worldview, the shared jokes, taboos, social niceties, sacred objects and ideas; it is the sense of a people reciprocally sharing a common fate that extends across not just a lifetime but across generations. All of these things provide what I call "sacred meaning" to human life. Without such meaning, life, despite one's being surrounded by multitudes of people, becomes lonely, and all too often leads to physiological deterioration, psychological depression or frequently to both.[28]

Such despair can obviulsy occur when isolated individuals transfer from one culture to another, as when wave after wave of immigrants arrived in America. As Peter Martin has pointed out, America is composed of the descendants of transplanted men and women, and it became the responsibility of those children to try to create, *de novo*, a quality culture of a sort different from that of their parents.[29]

This is an extraordinarily difficult task, one that has seldom been wholly successful in human history. The Manus, a tribe on the Admiralty Islands near New Guinea that was studied by Margaret Mead, attempted to do just this: to move in a single generation from the stone age into the twentieth century. Although briefly "successful," the tribe began to disintegrate in the absence of the deeper meaning and ritual of their old, traditional way of life.[30] In a less sudden yet still evolutionarily brief period, America itself has attempted to create a "new society" based not on long-term cultural traditions but upon a recently invented philosophy of an "ideal human society" that emphasizes individual freedom, defines individual rights, explicitly precludes any shared religious goals, and reduces other shared societal goals to providing an arena where isolated individuals may freely compete with one another for the materialistic prizes of life. This central goal of society is, by definition, destructive of a life of shared sacred meaning. That life, if it is to occur at all, takes place in private.

A number of recent books have documented aspects of this American problem, which is increasingly shared by many other of the more "advanced" societies.[31] One recent book in particular records with remarkable frankness the materialistic impasse of the globe's "cutting-edge" societies. It deals with the reflections of blue-collar American laborers in a Ford Motor Company factory on the shallowness of their own materially well-rewarded lives.[32]

For example, Al Commons says: "We're all competing with each other materialistically so much that people have gotten withdrawn. They are more conscious of how their home compares with your home, their car with your car. That tends to destroy the free-and-easy relationships between people."[33]

Unlike chimpanzees, humans require more than simple personal familiarity in order to feel "comfortable" with one another and accepted in a deeply meaningful social group. They require a sense of *shared* social goals – goals that extend far beyond tomorrow's breakfast, lunch and dinner to the lives of their children and grandchildren. The historically remembered past extends through the brief present into an indefinite future. Perhaps one of the greatest human needs of all is this sense of temporal continuity between an unexperienced yet culturally present past and a never to be experienced yet personally significant future. Chimpanzees and other great apes can only vaguely grasp in their consciousness this immortal connectedness which, for us, is so explicitly evident. Somewhere in this temporal expansion of the individual human lifespan the necessity for a culturally significant existence must be understood. Chimpanzees and gorillas may, like us, need to feel comfortable with their known contemporaries – but unlike us, they have no need to be anchored in both a knowable past and a hoped-for future. The world, when they evolved, did not yet demand that level of conscious meaning.

I think we can therefore conclude that social bonds are *not* temporary contracts, entered into simply for the convenience of the individual, but are absolute requirements for human existence.

Society is *not* a take-it-or-leave-it affair. Social embeddedness *is* the essence of our nature. It is simply wrong to claim that human nature is basically individualistic, competitive and aggressive: biologically, we are designed to be precisely the opposite. When conflict arises *within* a society, it is almost always because this biologically-based need for bonding among its members is being thwarted by one or another social arrangement. When conflict arises *between* societies the threat is to the integrity of the group either through deprivation of its resources, which is what observers most commonly look for and expect to find, or through threat to its symbolic bonds, which is far commoner than is generally realized. It is the latter that accounts for religious and other "ideological" conflicts. Because religious beliefs are often tied to survival activities such as planting and harvest, conflict over resources has often involved submission of one set of religious beliefs to those of the conquerors.

SOCIAL CONSEQUENCES OF A FAILURE OF SOCIAL BONDING

While everyone agrees that babies need care and that "love" is generally a good thing there is, I believe, a widespread tendency in the West to presume that, unlike animals, human beings can adapt themselves to almost any set of circumstances. Moreover "emotions," particularly among males, generally are regarded as weakness and sentimentality when affection or concern are displayed and as bestial residues when anger or violence are displayed. All affective behaviors are suspect, especially when "practical" decisions are being made. Public life thus tends to be not only unemotional but anti-emotional. Decisions are based on "logical" arguments "rationally" carried out. Furthermore, these rational arguments are constructed from the point of view of an isolated individual who ought to be as *free as possible from* social constraints. Social discussions almost totally fail to ask why institutions of society are in fact acting against or even actively preventing social bonding, which leads to social disorder.

Pieces of the problem are easily found in any large industrial society, particularly those of the capitalist West. First is the decline of an extended social support system – the extended family, lifelong friends and neighbors. Personal conflict is no longer a social matter but a very private one, confined to the nuclear family closeted in its box-like residence. Nuclear families, moreover, are growing smaller –

often reduced today to only a single parent and one or perhaps two children. They become ever more isolated in their self-sufficient privacy; and they are less stable in time (divorces continue to rise) and in place (the average American family moves every few years).[34] Social cohesion is thus superficial and tenuous. The individual has almost no psychic social security. As psychologist Paul Wachtel observes: "Our view of the self is that it is 'portable,' it can be carried around from place to place, fully intact, and then plugged in whenever necessary."[35]

Another social institution that tears at social bonding is competition. Whereas in almost all hunting-gathering societies that have been studied, competition is actively suppressed,[36] in the West it has been put on a pedestal. It is the most "efficient" means to produce wealth and allocate resources; it is taught from earliest childhood; it is converted, by means of gigantic sports stadia and televised spectacles, into the national pastime. This continues to happen, with widespread social approval, despite ample documentation of its social destructiveness. The institution of competitive individualism which we worship has been linked to many forms of alienation – crimes, homelessness, drug abuse, alcoholism, suicide, anxiety, stress diseases, child abuse, and so on.[37]

A third, more subtle cause of alienation in many large, pluralistic, technically "advanced" societies is the disappearance of shared sacred meaning. There are many components here. One is the alienation of modern work — better called "labor." Rather than being one's gift to society, the product of one's efforts today seldom has direct social meaning, and the receiver of one's efforts is an unknown stranger in the mass marketplace. Only professionals actually meet those on whose behalf they work, but "efficiency" dictates that even that personal contact be minimized. Doctors and nurses spend less and less time per patient; social workers case loads go ever upward; teachers are asked to take bigger classes and do more extracurricular work, and so on. Work, once imbued with sacred social meaning, is now "labor," the value of which is measured in purely monetary terms.[38] One's social worth is no longer understood in terms of reciprocal personal relations, but in terms of impersonal wages and bank balances.

Sacred meaning has likewise disappeared from public discourse, especially in America. In the name of "freedom of conscience" almost all formerly shared myths and values that people's ancestors used to pass to their offspring have been "privatized." True, there are still churches and ethnic centers, but these are fragmented and scattered throughout the sea of mundane uniformity, and those who struggle to maintain their ethnic ties must become adept at moving between two such disparate worlds, constantly performing psychological "quick change acts" – a difficult task, at best. To those without such ties, the larger society offers little in the way of shared meaning and values, leaving the sharing for each individual to invent for herself or himself. It is a task that is well-nigh impossible, and hence people must search about them for substitutes as best they can – something to which "loyalty can cling," as Simone Weil has put it.[39]

SUBSTITUTE "BONDS"

It was Lewis Mumford who pointed out that when human societies first grew from small, personal neolithic villages into large, impersonal fortified cities, they may have gained in economic productivity, but they rapidly lost the ability to meet humankind's deepest need – the need for social bonds and shared meaning.[40] Without reiterating here all the consequent forms of suffering that civilization has brought, it is possible to identify a variety of substitute institutions to which peoples have clung – and still cling to today.

The major religions of the world, of course, come first to mind. It is no accident that they arose in parallel with the earliest civilizations, largely to ameliorate some of their worst excesses, and even today they represent important sources of sacred social meaning for tens of millions of people. Islam is perhaps the chief contemporary example.[41]

Secular religions have also emerged in more recent times. Sometimes called "nations," modern political entities – or states – have had to create new myths, a new form of sacred meaning, in order that their people's loyalty should have something to cling to, thus maintaining a cohesive social unit. This sort of "nationalism," says Isaiah Berlin, is a new phenomenon, the self-conscious creation of a sacred society arising out of a historical vacuum. The Enlightenment had raised the individual to the forefront of social thought, weakening traditional religious, tribal, and feudal ties, while simultaneously industrial technology had created an impersonal, bureaucratic social structure, with built-in exploitation and injustice. Under such conditions, Berlin argues, "meaning" had to be recreated, often through dangerous assertions of national superiority and a perfected set of values.[42]

Under such conditions, sacred symbols are newly invented. "Liberators" and "Founding Fathers" take the place of the god-kings of ancient Egypt and Nippon; national flags, military heroes, and winners of Olympic medals are revered; there is a national anthem that charges citizens' breasts with patriotic emotion, a national slogan, and always a national day. History is rewritten to suit changing national needs. Politicians become particularly skilled at nationalist rhetoric: Adolf Hitler and Ronald Reagan were both outstanding practitioners, and excerpts from their speeches are remarkably similar. Both claimed to be leading a nation favored by God and threatened by an evil empire. The equivalent virtues of American apple pie and motherhood are present in Hitler's speeches, as well as in those of Churchill, Stalin, and so on.

When nationalism is not enough, other mass substitutes for social bonding flourish. Sometimes the state encourages these, as when the United States post office sells "LOVE" stamps, exhorting the public to a sense of bondedness. At other times, perceptive entrepreneurs fill the gap. Madison Avenue long ago recognized the desperate need of American consumers for social acceptance, and designed their advertising pitches accordingly.[43] The most dominant mass substitutes, perhaps, are "sports" – a major money-making endeavor that allows literally millions to feel a sense of loyalty to "local" teams. Millions of utter strangers become unified behind a city's football or baseball or hockey team, even though they share nothing else in life and the players seldom if ever are "home-town" boys. A championship team does wonders for "community pride." The search for social status through money, wealth and power is perhaps the commonest, yet most unsatisfactory, attempted substitute for social bondedness and meaning. At least since the time of Confucius in the East and Plato in the West, the quest for this kind of social recognition has created enormous and still unresolved social problems. Since, even for the "successful," the need for meaningful social bonding remains largely unfulfilled, the search becomes endless. Each fulfilled "need" is no more satisfying than cotton candy. Indeed, these are not true "needs" but are "wants" generated in the absence of a socially satisfying existence.[44] And the greater the failure of true social bonding, the greater the number of unfulfilled "wants" – a fact that advertisers have turned to their lucrative advantage.

Another attempt to create a sense of social bonding is the advent of socialism – a kind of re-creation of social meaning through conscious and directed communal effort. In some instances this has seemingly worked rather well. Sweden is the shining example.[45] Without denigrating the Swedes' accomplishments, however, it should be noted that Sweden is a small country, comprising a narrow ethnic range, with a single language, shared culture, and common history; many of the underlying qualities needed for social identification were already in place. Socialism in Sweden has surely helped, however, to cure or offset many of the alienating effects of modern industrial society.

By contrast, the Soviet attempt to impose, top-down, a single socialist ideology on dozens of ethnic groups from Europe across northern Asia has not worked. The whole system required massive coercion. Socialism did not unify – instead, seen as Russian imperialism, it became a threat to the cultural bondedness of ethnic minorities. Nor did the Marxist dream of an internationally unified working class ever materialize. Marx, misunderstanding the fundamental need of all human beings for sacred cultural roots, saw the world purely in economic terms.

SOCIAL CORRECTIVES AS SOCIAL OVERHEADS

Why societies become larger and more impersonal is not altogether clear, but throughout written history this coalescence has recurred. (Economic "efficiency" is often tendered as the benefit, but this is not likely to be the whole answer.) As Joseph Tainter has shown, such expanding polities repeatedly face a concomitant growth in overheads of social management that leads ultimately to collapse.[46] The cost of maintaining the system sooner or later outruns its resource base. Although Tainter focuses mainly on the economic overheads of complex societies, surely social overheads also play a role.

In his book, *The Rise and Fall of the Great Powers*, Paul Kennedy has shown how the history of giant states has been a sequence of technological leapfrogging, punctuated by wars, as each new power outruns an earlier one.[47] Today we see all the industrial powers engaged in a technological race to outcompete one another economically. The cost of the race itself is wearing out those same economies, as well as putting an increasing strain upon their social institutions. And as societies become strained and less stable, they seek alternative means for maintaining political cohesion. In his book, *Global Conflict*, John Burton presents a convincing argument for the ability of an external threat to hold together an otherwise unstable social system. Indeed, he argues that this has been, if not the conscious cause of, at least a politically convenient consequence of, the East–West arms race. Both Soviet and American leaders have maintained among their peoples a kind of national loyalty as the result of their continuing Cold War.[48] The spiralling costs of this ongoing build-up, however, now threatened the internal economic integrity of both superpowers. Indeed, for almost every country that has used externally directed militarism as a means for maintaining internal cohesiveness, it now appears that the costs of increasingly expensive modern weapons are cancelling any political benefits.[49]

Meantime, as cohesion from fear fades, and the substitutes for social meaning increasingly fail to satisfy that central human need, the cost of managing the growing internal unrest escalates. This can be seen in the rising needs for social welfare; for more police, more courtrooms, more prisons; for a "war" on drugs; and for more social workers and psychiatrists. All these are overhead costs of a society in which peoples need for a satisfying, meaningful, and socially engaging life are being less and less met.

USES OF THIS THEORY

If the above argument is correct – that human beings have a biologically-based need for identity within a social group that imparts sacred meaning to their lives – then a number of avenues for further inquiry are opened up.

1. We can begin to seek out the components of sacred meaning in various cultures, and try to grasp the manner in which they provide satisfaction to the peoples of each culture.
2. We can begin to make cross-cultural comparisons, not only of the variety of beliefs, rituals, and social institutions that provide sacred meaning, but also, in a semi-quantitative way, of their summed ability to satisfy that need.
3. We can ask if there are correlations between the apparent sufficiency in sacred meaning within various societies and their cultural homogeneity, or recent disruption thereof.
4. We can examine what appear to be contrived substitutes for actual social bondedness in various societies, and assess how effectively they appear to function in satisfying the need for

meaning.[50]

And in terms of conflict resolution:

1. We can seek means for evaluating the sources of internal conflicts within societies: which are due to social injustice and which to a failure of compelling social values? Which are due to ethnic divergence within a pluralistic system, and which to a long history of external interference?
2. In conflict situations, we can ask: what are the (perhaps few and tenuous) sacred remnants of social identity that the antagonists desperately cling to and will not compromise? How are they perceived to be threatened?
3. We can ask whether threats to social bonding are correlated with terrorists and guerrilla movements – which are surely socially conservative in nature.[51] Also, do the proclaimed grievances of terrorists appear to contain elements of concern for sacred social patterns?

And in terms of prediction:

1. We can contrast the degree of social bondedness and sacred meaning that exists among Western capitalist societies, among the Soviet oblasts, and in Japan, and ask: what level of social stability would exist in face of a major breakdown in their industrial economies? To what extent is there a reserve of social bondedness to ward off chaos during a period of severe institutional dislocation?
2. Does history offer us ways of correlating the degree of sacred meaning in a society with its ability to retain its cohesiveness in the face of severe social stress? What evidence have we, in this respect, about the American black slave experience; about post– First World War Germany and the Weimar Republic; about the social structure of contemporary Iran and Tibet?
3. Can we, from studies of past and contemporary societies undergoing rapid technological change, discover the following: what processes of change will help most to maintain social cohesion through preservation of sacred social meaning and social bonding? If and when these happen to have been weakened or destroyed, how successful have societies been at consciously recreating *new* social meaning? (Here many examples are available for study,

such as the largely failed efforts of the Manus, mentioned earlier, or contemporary China, Korea, Japan and Europe.) To bend an old aphorism: how much of the baby of social meaning can safely be thrown out with the bathwater of social change? Or, put another way, how adept *are* human societies at creating social meaning from scratch?

Learning to perceive the sources of shared social meaning through which individual human beings discover satisfaction in life and so generate stable societies may well help us not only as we seek to reduce human conflict at all levels, but also as we seek to improve the wellbeing of humankind by developing less socially destructive – as well as less environmentally destructive – technologies.

NOTES AND REFERENCES

1. See discussion in R. Cavendish, *The Great Religions* (New York: Arco, 1980): 149.
2. See discussion of "Rational Economic Man," in M. Clark, *Ariadne's Thread: The Search for New Modes of Thinking* (New York: St. Martin's Press, 1989): 276–7.
3. S. B. Sarason, *Psychology Misdirected* (New York: The Free Press, Macmillan, 1981): 173.
4. See discussion in M. Clark, *Ariadne's Thread*: 122–4.
5. See, for example, R. Benedict, *Patterns of Culture* (Boston: Houghton Mifflin, 1934).
6. See J. Campbell, *The Masks of God* (New York: Viking Press, 1959–1968) 4 vols.
7. R. Roy, "Three Visions of Needs and the Future: Liberalism, Marxism and Gandhism," Chapter 4 in R. A. Coate and J. A. Rosati (eds.), *The Power of Human Needs in World Society* (Boulder, CO: Lynne Rienner, 1988): 74.
8. S. J. Gould, "Our Greatest Evolutionary Step," in Gould, *The Panda's Thumb* (New York: W. W. Norton, 1980): 124–33.
9. Gould, "Our Greatest Evolutionary Step": 130.
10. All these – along with many other examples of strong social bonding among chimpanzees – are described in Jane Goodall's two major works: *In the Shadow of Man* (Boston: Houghton Mifflin, 1971) and *The Chimpanzees of Gombe: Patterns of Behavior* (Cambridge, MA: Belknap Press, Harvard, 1986).
11. See S. J. Gould, "Homage to Mickey Mouse," in Gould, *The Panda's Thumb*: 95–107 and "The Child as Man's Real Father": 63–9 and "Human Babies as Embryos": 70–5 in Gould, *Ever Since Darwin* (New

York: W. W. Norton, 1977).
12. R. Hinde, *Biological Bases of Human Social Behavior* (New York: McGraw-Hill, 1974): 181.
13. R. V. Short, "The Evolution of Human Reproduction," in *The Proceedings of the Royal Society, London*, 195 (1976): 17.
14. In *The Chimpanzees of Gombe*, Goodall repeatedly documents observations of these kinds of interactions among the members of the troop she studied.
15. The range of facial expressions of chimpanzees is shown in Goodall, *The Chimpanzees of Gombe*: 120. Theories of the origin and evolution of human facial expressions are found in Hinde, *Biological Bases of Human Social Behaviour*: 125–39.
16. J. B. Lancaster, "Carrying and Sharing in Human Evolution," *Human Nature* (February 1978): 82–9.
17. The importance of group identity is also highly developed in chimpanzees. As documented by Goodall in *The Chimpanzees of Gombe*, outsiders of either sex that wander within the group's territory will be attacked by all adults, although males are generally most active. Only young nulliparous female strangers are accepted into the troop, and even they may temporarily experience aggression from the group's adult females. Furthermore males who split off from their group and form a new one become "strangers" open to attack. See Chapter 17, "Territoriality": 488–534.
18. J. Z. Young, *Programs of the Brain* (Oxford: Oxford University Press, 1978): 148.
19. Young, *Programs of the Brain*: 175.
20. M. Hunt, *The Universe Within* (New York: Simon & Schuster, 1982): 228. Similar cases are documented in V. Reynolds, *The Biology of Human Action* (San Francisco: W. H. Freeman, 1976): 158.
21. M. C. Diamond, *Enriching Heredity: The Impact of the Environment on the Anatomy of the Brain* (New York: The Free Press; Macmillan, 1988). The failure of passively watching the activity of others to cause changes in brain size is described on 165.
22. H. F. Harlow, "Love in Infant Monkeys," *Scientific American* (July 1959); H. F. Harlow and M. K. Harlow, "Social Deprivation in Monkeys," *Scientific American* (November 1962): 331.
23. E. A. Tinbergen and N. Tinbergen, "Early Childhood Autism – an Ethological Approach," *Tierpsychologie*, Beiheft 10 (1972): 1–53; N. Tinbergen, "Ethology and Stress Diseases," *Science*, 185 (1974): 20–7. See also, L. I. Gardner, "Deprivation Dwarfism," *Scientific American* (July 1972) for developmental disorders in humans resulting from parental deprivation.
24. James R. Averill, "Grief: Its Nature and Significance," *Psychological Bulletin* 70 (1968) pp. 721–48; Mary F. Asterita, *The Physiology of Stress* (New York: Human Sciences Press, 1985). That psychological stress can increase susceptibility to disease has been suspected for millenia and has been directly demonstrated many times over the past three decades. The central reference in this area is R. Ader (ed.), *Psychoneuroimmunology* (New York: Academic Press, 1981). See especially S. M. Plaut and

S. B. Friedman, "Psychosocial Factors in Infectious Disease": 3–30; and J. Palmblad, "Stress and Immunologic Competence: Studies in Man": 229–57.

25. J. S. House, K. R. Landis, and D. Umberson, "Social Relationships and Health," *Science*, 241 (1988): 540–5.

26. W. P. Mahedy, *Out of the Night: the Spiritual Journey of the Vietnam Vets* (New York: Ballantine, 1986).

27. For example, see the description of psychosocial medicine in Africa in C. M. Good, *Ethnomedical Systems in Africa* (New York: Guilford Press, 1987): 13–15. Details are given in J. M. Janzen, *The Quest for Therapy in Lower Zaire* (Berkeley: University of California Press, 1978) and M. L. Swantz, "Community and Healing among the Zaramo in Tanzania," *Social Science and Medicine* 13B (1979): 169–173. For the *absence* of group and community support in America, see J. Veroff, R. A. Kulka, and E. Douvan, *Mental Health in America: Patterns of Help-Seeking from 1957 to 1976* (New York: Basic Books, 1981): 6–7.

28. See Hans Selye, *Stress in Health and Disease* (Boston: Butterworth, 1976) pp. 240–4: "Separation of infants from their mothers, and all types of relocation of people into strange environments which leave few possibilities for interpersonal contacts, are very common forms of sensory deprivation; they may become major factors in psychosomatic disease." Psychic health, long thought by psychologists (but hardly by novelists and propagandists) to be internally determined, has at last been experimentally demonstrated to be largely externally determined and reinforced. For example, see W. B. Swan, Jr. and S. C. Predmore, "Intimates as Agents of Social Support: Sources of Consolation or Despair?", *Journal of Personality and Social Psychology*, 49 (1985): 1609–17. Writing about stability of self-conception, which is vital for survival and sanity, they state "[O]ur findings suggest self-concept stability emanates from forces *outside* the person, from continuity in the manner in which people's *social relationships* are organized . . . For better or worse, [the] activities [of those around us] may often be the single most potent determinant of the survival of [people's] self-conceptions": 1616–17. Being among those who share our visions, hopes, beliefs and values, who daily reconfirm our *own* view of ourselves in society and in the universe, is critical to psyche stability.

29. P. Marin, "Toward Something American," *Harper's* (July 1988): 17–18.

30. See Clark, *Ariadne's Thread*: 177–8.

31. Alienation in American society has been demonstrated repeatedly: in D. Yankelovich, *New Rules: Searching for Self-Fulfillment in a World Turned Upside Down* (New York: Random House, 1981); in P. Wachtel, *The Poverty of Affluence* (New York: The Free Press; Macmillan, 1983); in R. N. Bellah, R. Madsen, W. M. Sullivan, A. Swidler and S. M. Tipton, *Habits of the Heart* (Berkeley: University of California Press, 1985) – to mention a few recent popular accounts.

32. R. Feldman and M. Betzold (eds.), *End of the Line: Autoworkers and the American Dream* (New York: Weidenfeld & Nicolson, 1988).

33. Feldman and Betzold (eds.), *End of the Line*: 101.

34. P. H. Rossi, *Why Families Move* (Beverley Hills: Sage Publications,

1980). Since the 1930s, approximately one in five Americans has moved each year: 28–30.

35. Wachtel, *The Poverty of Affluence*: 120.
36. See, for example, R. B. Lee, "Eating Christmas in the Kalahari," *Natural History* (December 1969): 14–22, 60–3.
37. The social consequences of competition are well documented in A. Kohn, *No Contest: The Case Against Competition* (Boston: Houghton, Mifflin, 1986). For specific comments on alienation see 63–5, 115, 120–5, 161.
38. See discussion in Clark, *Ariadne's Thread*: 279–81.
39. S. Weil, *The Need for Roots*, A. Wills (trans.) (New York: Putnam, 1952): 12, 127.
40. L. Mumford, *The Myth of the Machine*, vol. 1 of *Technics and Human Development* (1967) and vol. 2, *The Pentagon of Power* (1970) (New York: Harcourt, Brace Jovanovich).
41. For origins of major religions, see Clark, *Ariadne's Thread*: 185–204. Islam, with nearly a billion followers around the world, remains closest to its original inspiration.
42. I. Berlin, "Nationalism: Past Neglect and Present Power," in Henry Hardy (ed.), *Against the Current: Essays in the History of Ideas* (New York: Viking Press, 1980): 333–55.
43. J. Mander, *Four Arguments for the Elimination of Television* (New York: William Morrow, 1978): 131.
44. See discussion in D. Yankelovich, *New Rules*, Chapter 5.
45. See, for example, F. M. Lappe, "Sweden's Third Way to Worker Ownership," *The Nation* (19 February 1983): 203–4; H. M. Christman, "Swedish Buyout," *The Nation* (4 February 1984): 117. For a description of the history of socialism in Sweden see S. Koblik, *Sweden's Development from Poverty to Affluence, 1750–1970* (Minneapolis: University of Minnesota Press, 1975); M. Forsberg, *The Evolution of Social Welfare Policy in Sweden* (Stockholm: the Swedish Institute, 1986).
46. J. A. Tainter, *The Collapse of Complex Societies* (Cambridge: Cambridge University Press, 1988).
47. P. Kennedy, *The Rise and Fall of the Great Powers* (New York: Vintage Books, Random House, 1987). Historian Leften Stavrianos has called this the "Law of the Retarding Lead" in his book *The Promise of the Coming Dark Age* (San Francisco: W. H. Freeman, 1976): 181–5.
48. J. W. Burton, *Global Conflict: The Domestic Sources of International Crisis* (Brighton, England: Wheatsheaf Books, 1984).
49. See, for example, L. J. Dumas, *The Overburdened Economy* (Berkeley: University of California Press, 1986).
50. See Feldman and Betzold (eds.), *The End of the Line* as an example of such a study.
51. See R. Rubenstein, *Alchemists of Revolution: Terrorism in the Modern World* (New York: Basic Books, 1987).

3 The Biological Basis of Needs in World Society: The Ultimate Micro–Macro Nexus
Dennis J. D. Sandole

INTRODUCTION

The purpose of this Chapter is to explore whether there are any *biological* constraints to systemic integration, to explore the "ultimate micro–macro nexus": the link between biology and the international system.

An examination of possible biological constraints to transcending the nation-state is particularly important for at least four reasons: (1) there is a common assumption (which I share) that our biology influences and pervades our behavior, often in insidious ways; (2) the biological dimension of human behavior – what we might call the "Biological Imperative" – is not often subjected to analysis because it is not readily "see-able;" (3) the biological dimension is not often subject to analysis also because of a "skunk"-like resistance which seems to repel efforts to contemplate or explore the assumption that biology influences *human* behavior; and (4) rooted in biology but influenced by environment are *basic human needs*: necessary conditions to basic survival and further physical and psychological development. Whether or not human socio-political organization can transcend the nation-state may depend, in part, upon the nature of "needs" and the extent to which they are violated or fulfilled.

BASIC HUMAN NEEDS: NATURE AND "REALITY"

"Needs," according to Katrin Lederer,[1] is an "ambiguous concept," one of many which concerns social scientists. A major reason for this ambiguity is the conceptual/empirical distance between the concept and its corresponding "realities."

Apropos concepts and realities, Abraham Kaplan[2] tells us that there are (1) *observational terms*, where the reality of a concept can be observed directly (for instance, a table); (2) *indirect observables*, where the reality can be observed indirectly (e.g., inferring a dream from a dream report); (3) *constructs*, where the reality of a concept can be observed in terms of bits and pieces of conceptually "distant," but otherwise relevant empirical sightings (e.g., "observing" government or a nation-state by visiting a legislative body, voting, paying taxes, travelling internationally, etc.); and (4) *theoretical terms*, where reality can be observed only within the context of some theoretical framework (e.g., Jung's "collective unconscious," Freud's "superego").

Where we assign concepts depends, to a large extent, on the *paradigms*[3] or *images*[4] we hold. What for one observer might be exceedingly theoretical, might for someone else border on the observational: "However the lines are drawn, . . . drawing them is to a significant degree arbitrary."[5]

All that said, where does "needs" fit in here? According to Lederer,[6] "needs are theoretical constructions . . . [i.e.] the existence of an individual's needs, or, stronger, the 'truth' of those needs, cannot be proven in a direct physical way." This I take to mean that, in terms of Kaplan's scheme, needs lie somewhere between indirect observables and theoretical terms. I agree. Accordingly, "perhaps the most challenging – and still unsolved problem of needs research is how to [*operationally*] define a need."[7]

The ambiguous nature of needs notwithstanding, there is evidence that they exist. D. M. Davis for example, studied self-selection of diet by two-year old children and "found that infant self-selection corresponded . . . with nutritive requirements [thereby indicating] that organisms can 'know' their needs and, left alone, can act appropriately in response to them."[8] Other examples of the "rationality of the body" include sweating or shivering to return an organism to an equilibrium temperature, the repelling of diseases by "natural killer" (NK) cells, the reduction of pain by natural painkillers (endorphins), etc.

Harry Harlow[9] demonstrated the disintegrative consequences of depriving infant monkeys of normal maternal care, while John Bowlby[10] and René Spitz[11] observed the same phenomenon in very young children. According to James Chowning Davies[12] "frustration of the . . . *need for affection*, . . . is so crucial as to produce, sooner or later, a rage reaction" (emphasis added).

In addition to needs for physical maintenance and affection, there is evidence of a need for self-esteem, violation of which could also lead to "deviant" behavior. Courtland Milloy,[13] for example, in his discussion of the Sasha Bruce House, the only shelter for runaway children in Washington, D.C., notes that 96 per cent of the roughly 3000 runaways "who have lived at the facility since it opened in 1976 . . . have been returned home to a positive, stable living arrangement." A major factor underlying this success is that the children, during their temporary residence at the House, "are told what is good about themselves, thus improving their *self-esteem*" (emphasis added).

Similarly, in his review of Fred Harris and Roger Wilkins' *Quiet Riots: Race and Poverty in the United States*, Milloy[14] reports that, according to the editors and contributors, the major reason why "many low-income blacks turn their anger and frustration on themselves, their families and their neighbors," is:

> the *sense of self*, or lack of, that forms an open wound from which most of the major ills affecting the black community ooze forth . . . At the crux of the matter is a *lack of self-esteem* among black youths (emphasis added).

Self-esteem implies a need for recognition, for an identity which one can feel good about. Identity also relates to a need for security: a need for one's identity to be protected. This may explain, in part, the profound sense of outrage among Moslems regarding the publication of Salman Rushdie's *The Satanic Verses*[15] which, according to reviewer Jonathan Yardley,[16] "contains . . . a stinging depiction of Islamic fundamentalism."

In his analysis of ethnic and religious conflict in 25 countries during 1987, Don Podestra[17] tells us that "These simmering conflicts [are] rooted in the most basic forms of human identity," reflecting "the *need* to assert *group identity*" (emphasis added), and originating in one particular emotion: a fear of group extinction. Podestra also mentions that the need to express one's group identity is particularly acute among those who have been disenfranchised through a prior colonial relationship. In this regard, Frantz Fanon[18] argued that violent conflict between European colonizers and native peoples was inevitable "because the *human need* for *dignity* and *self-respect* could never be satisfied under colonial rule."[19] Hence, a rise in self-esteem could follow a violent response to the vestiges of colonialism.[20]

Barbara Harff and Ted Robert Gurr[21] have examined instances of massive state repression leading precisely to group extinction: forty-four episodes of genocide and politicide that have occurred in all world regions since 1945, with estimated casualties ranging from seven to sixteen million people: "at least as many who died in all international and civil wars in the period."[22] Genocides and politicides are brutal efforts to maintain the security of one's "identity group" at the total expense of other groups. Concerning the likelihood of such extreme acts occurring in the future, Gurr and James Scarritt[23] have estimated that there are 246 minority groups at risk in ninety-five countries:

> many of the groups . . . are now or have been victimized by selective discrimination and repression in recent decades. And those which have not been victimized share some essential characteristics of those which have.

Clearly, the pool of potential victims of mass murder is rather large.

Looking at external as well as internal wars (with a minimum of 1000 fatalities), Ruth Leger Sivard[24] reports that the most frequent causes of the 471 wars fought worldwide between 1700 and 1987 (with a total of 101 550 000 casualties) were territory (which is suggestive of the *security* need) and independence (which suggests the *identity* and *self-esteem* needs).

Distressing though it may be that just as many people may be killed in violent conflict *within* nations as well as between them, it is still the case that international warfare ranks first in terms of potential scale of destructiveness. The nuclear, biological, chemical, and "conventional" arms stockpiles and races are also extreme efforts to protect threatened needs for security, identity, and self-esteem. Indeed, France and Great Britain apparently decided to become nuclear powers, in part, to retain the "Great Power" status they enjoyed when they presided over intact, far-flung empires.[25]

Implicit in the discussion thus far are most of the items from Abraham Maslow's[26] Hierarchy of Needs: needs for (1) physiological maintenance, (2) safety and security, (3) love and belongingness, and (4) self-esteem. I have said nothing directly about evidence pertaining to the most "theoretical" item of Maslow's list: (5) self-actualization needs. Ross Fitzgerald[27] maintains that, although there is some "evidence bearing on innate needs [in general] in Maslow's sense . . . There has been no unequivocal empirical verification of the existence of Maslow's 'higher' needs[:] the distinctly *human* needs."

Nevertheless, for me, the overall evidentiary record, sketchy though it may be, is sufficient reason for examining the potential role of needs in moving beyond the nation-state and into regional and global, collaborative problem-solving systems. As Peirce[28] has said, "there is only one place from which we can ever start . . . and that is from where we are."[29]

Maslow's Hierarchy of Needs implies a vertical structure of ranked prepotencies – i.e., each level of needs, beginning with the physiological, is more prepotent than those which follow. Hence each level must be "fairly well satisfied" before one can move on to the "next prepotent ('higher') need."[30] Although I am not completely comfortable with the hierarchy of prepotency (which has, in any case, received "at least partial support"[31]), I accept Maslow's sense of what the important categories of needs are. Maslow, then, is a fruitful point of departure for examining the role of needs in moving beyond the nation-state. In this regard, I am also comfortable with Davies's[32] modification of Maslow such that "there are four substantive needs in descending order of prepotency: the physical, social-affectional, self-esteem, and self-actualization needs," plus "three closely interrelated implemental needs" – security, knowledge, and power – which are pursued primarily (though not exclusively) as means to achieve the four substantive needs. I also share Davies's[33] sense that "violence becomes increasingly likely when *any* kind of basic needs which has come to be routinely gratified suddenly becomes deprived."[34]

John Burton[35] also hypothesizes a link between deprivation/violation of basic needs and violent conflict, although instead of Maslow's he employs Paul Sites's[36] system: needs for response, security, recognition, stimulation, distributive justice, meaning, rationality [including the need to be seen as rational], and control.

I share with Davies, Burton, Maslow, Sites, and others[37] the assumption "that all these basic needs are organically genetically programmed predispositions,"[38] that needs are universal, common to all Humankind across time and space, although the means or "satisfiers" by which these ontological needs are met can differ across time and space. I also agree that actors will aspire to fulfill their needs one way or another: within the mainstream or in "deviant" ways, sometimes at great cost to themselves.

John Burton and I[39] have argued that, although the universal/objective view of needs implies "genetic" and therefore, *biological*, it does not imply biological reductionism. (For a lively

debate on this point, see Avruch and Black and Burton and Sandole.[40])
In any case, given this assumed, intimate connection between needs
and biology, it is important to explore the biological basis of needs,
in order to have a better sense of what they are, what they are
"meant" to do, and how they may facilitate or inhibit moving beyond
the nation-state into collaborative problem-solving systems.

THE BIOLOGICAL IMPERATIVE: SOME BACKGROUND

The argument that biological factors shape human behaviour has
been around for hundreds of years. Kenneth Waltz[41] indicates that
the argument paints either a pessimistic or optimistic portrait of the
human condition. Among the pessimists there are philosophers and
political scientists such as Benedict de Spinoza and Hans Morgenthau,
and theologians such as St. Augustine and Reinhold Niebuhr. For St.
Augustine[42] and Niebuhr,[43] violence was due to a flawed human
nature, to original sin; for Morgenthau,[44] it was not an evil human
nature as such but a *power need* which was just as biologically
determined; and for Spinoza,[45] violence was due to a human nature
which allowed the passions to triumph over reason.

The pessimists tend to be identified with one of the oldest schools,
traditionally the dominant school of thought in both the study and
practice of politics: Political Realism (*Realpolitik*), or as it is often
called, Power Politics (*Machtpolitik*). That Realism paints a very bleak
picture of the human condition can be seen by noting Thucydides'[46]
account of the destruction by Athens of the civilization of Melos
during the 16th year of the Peloponnesian War (415 BC); in the
advice given by Kautilya[47] to the rulers of ancient India (Fourth
Century BC) for maintaining themselves in power abroad as well as
at home; or in that given some 1800 years later by Machiavelli[48] to
his Prince; or a bit later, in the exceedingly bleak picture painted by
Hobbes[49] of Humankind in its state of nature.

That Political Realism, with its bleakness, appears to be very much
a part of the contemporary world – in North–South as well as East–
West relations, but also at less "cosmic" levels such as Beirut, Belfast,
Gaza, Los Angeles, Washington, D.C., and elsewhere – is testimony
to the power, the endurance of the Biological Imperative as a *negative*
explanation of human behavior.

Sigmund Freud[50] added a psychoanalytical dimension to
philosophical/theological pessimism by characterizing human experi-

ence as a great drama which is played out in every one of us by a spontaneously aroused death instinct (*Thanatos*) whose proclivities toward destruction of the Self are kept in constant check by an aggression-externalizing life force (*Eros*). Konrad Lorenz[51] added the ethological view that there is an aggressive instinct in all animals, including humans, that is no different from other instincts (e.g., sexual, hunger); it is not, however, necessarily lethal. Indeed, except in humans, where it has gone awry, the aggressive instinct within species tends to be *functional* (for example, by warding off intruders into one's space).

The views of the pessimists/Realists, though dominant for centuries, have generated a good deal of controversy among optimists and others who are associated with Political Idealism or Marxism – those who tend to believe that human nature, and therefore human behavior, is *changeable*. The controversy is aptly, though perhaps simplistically, known as the "nature/nurture" debate. Waltz,[52] for instance, though tending toward Realism, does not allow the pessimist view to go unchallenged:

> Do such evidences of man's behavior as rapes, murders, and thefts prove that he is bad? What about the counterevidence provided by acts of charity, love and self-sacrifices? . . . [clearly,] what we make of the evidence depends on the theory we hold.

As might be expected, scholars espousing Idealism such as Erich Fromm, have also been critical of the "instinctivists" (or neo-instinctivists) such as Freud and Lorenz (the latter more so than the former) for scientific and also political reasons: "Both, by different routes, arrive at a picture of man in which aggressive-destructive energy is continuously produced, and very difficult, if not impossible in the long run, to control."[53]

If human beings are really this way – and we have behavioral scientists and not just theologians and philosophers saying so – then why should any concerned person attempt to improve situations that are crying out for change? This question implies an argument that could be used to justify a whole range of behaviors from "benign neglect" to outright genocidal repression on the part of those who govern. The ruling elites of states could, following such an argument, justifiably incorporate in their policies the advice of Kautilya, Machiavelli, and others[54] in their efforts to maintain, in a Hobbesian-like world, the survival of their states (and their own roles). Against the background of this argument, the perpetrators of the horrors of the twentieth century – Stalin, Hitler, Pol Pot – are not madmen but "rational" beings. Clearly, those who are perceived to be identified with such views could be labelled fascist, authoritarian, racist or, at minimum, seen as lending implicit support to repressive political regimes.

This particular debate goes back far into antiquity and, early in the twentieth century, probably received its most intense expression in the great exchanges between William McDougall[55] ("instinct of pugnacity") and J. B. Watson,[56] the father of behaviorism.[57] It has certainly not been laid to rest with the various responses, such as Fromm's or the work of Freud and Lorenz. (For specific critiques of Lorenz and also Robert Ardrey, see Montagu.[58]) Indeed, the debate has been energized by Edward Wilson's[59] work in "sociobiology." Wilson argues that much of human social behavior (e.g., aggression, altruism, religion, equality/inequality) can be explained by evolutionary theory as a function of Darwinian natural selection.

I should be explicit here about what was probably implicit in Waltz's criticism of pessimism; namely, that the nature/nurture debate, whether waged ideologically or scientifically, is not necessarily a zero-sum, either-or affair. For instance, although Fromm does not accept the thesis that "man is innately endowed with a spontaneous and self-propelling aggressive drive,"[60] he does accept that biological factors nevertheless play a role in the expression of aggressive behaviors: "Defensive aggressiveness is 'built in' the animal and human brain and serves the function of defence against threats to vital interests."[61] This he refers to as *benign aggression*, because it is "biologically adaptive, life-serving" in contrast to *malignant aggression*, which is "biologically non-adaptive."[62] While benign aggression is "phylogentically programmed" in animals and men, this is not the case with malignant aggression. And though Fromm is also critical of the strict environmental theorists such as Watson and Skinner, he believes that malignant aggression, which is unique to humans, results from the "interaction of various social conditions with man's existential *needs*."[63]

Fromm is not, therefore, against the Biological Imperative in all its forms, just as he is not against the Environmental Imperative in all its forms: he is critical of both while simultaneously holding views which are compatible with both. Such "position complexity" also applies to Wilson's critics. Somit[64] for instance, has been working in "biopolitics" for nearly two decades, and shares "Wilson's underlying conviction that human social (and political) behavior *is* to a significant degree influenced by our genetic makeup."[65] And Eysenck[66] whose views on genetic determination have resulted in him being physically assaulted, argues that:

> Fundamentally we all know that nature and nurture are but the opposite sides of one and the same coin, and that neither could exist without the other. The only real problem is a quantitative one; for particular groups and situations, what is the relative contribution of either?

For Eysenck, Wilson's work overlooks some important evidence in support of his own position and for Somit[67] Wilson does not answer the "how much of each?" question nor shed much "new light on how we might more successfully attack that question."

Wilson's own arguments are reflective of "position complexity". Although he argues[68] that "human beings have a marked hereditary predisposition to aggressive behavior," he is also critical of Freud, Lorenz, and even Fromm:[69]

> human aggression cannot be explained as either a dark-angelic flaw or a bestial instinct. Nor is it the pathological symptom of upbringing in a cruel environment.

Accordingly, the nature/nurture debate is still very much alive, and it still "raises emotion in political ideologues of all stripes."[70] But it is important that we notice that it is not only a simple debate between the "goody nurturists" and the "baddy naturists," but also involves complex combinations of differences and similarities. It is also important to note that, these complex combinations notwithstanding, one major hypothesis emerges from an examination of the various positions discussed above: *it is not a question of nature or nurture but the extent to which each plays a role in the expression of particular kinds of human behavior*, including behavior which facilitates functional or dysfunctional conflict, systemic integration or disintegration.

The general purposes of this Chapter – exploring the link between biology and the international system – will be pursued against the background of this hypothesis, keeping in mind that, as suggested earlier by Waltz, whether we accept or reject any particular "evidence" will depend upon our mood, our preference, "the theory we hold."

THE BIOLOGICAL IMPERATIVE IN HUMAN BEHAVIOR

Before proceeding, we should sketch out a framework that could be helpful in examining the link between biology and the international system. One framework that comes to mind is that which inheres in Waltz's classic study, *Man, The State, and War.*[71] Here biological factors would join physiological and psychological ones at the level of "man" while cultural, religious, social, political, economic, military, and other factors would apply to the "state" as well as the international system. Other possibilities are suggested by Rosenau's[72] pre-theory of foreign policy; Snyder, Bruck and Sapin's[73] grand decision making model; and Singer's developmental model of world politics plus scheme for guiding the Correlates-of-War project.[74] Whichever one an analyst prefers, it should be such that he/she will "not forget that in any real situation behavior will be the result of factors from all levels,"[75] and that the Biological Imperative is not only one of a number of factors but probably *interacts* with them in complex ways to facilitate functional or dysfunctional conflict, systemic integration or disintegration.

I have developed a "four-worlds'" model of human behavior[76] which incorporates many of the elements from the above perspectives, plus the influence of Sir Karl Popper.[77] The model reflects the assumption that, for any decision making actor, at any level, there are two *internal* and two *external* sources of influence on the actor's behavior. The external is comprised of the "world of nature" plus the human-made world. The internal consists of the psychological plus the biological/physiological worlds.

The biological/physiological world, with which we are primarily concerned here, is comprised of all things innate (senses, neurons, brain, muscles) plus various processes linked to the functioning and maintenance of the organism, and of course, the overall ontological character of the organism, including basic human needs. "Ontological character" is the stuff that excites and exercises the minds, logical systems and reconstructions of philosophers and theologians, but it is not, as indicated earlier, subject to direct or even indirect observation. The brain and other things innate, plus various processes, on the other hand, excite the minds of physiologists and students of sociobiology,[78] psychobiology,[79] and biopolitics,[80] precisely because they *are*, to some extent, observable. Among the relevant processes are those associated with *homeostasis*[81] which are concerned with the maintenance of certain key factors (body temperature, heart rate, blood pressure) within a crucial range of values. When the equilibrium value range of any one of these factors is disturbed homeostasis, which is controlled by the *hypothalamus*, involves the activation of counter-measures to restore the factor to its proper level.

Homeostasis is built into the organism and can operate quite independently of the consciousness and will of the actor. It is a programed, autonomous survival mechanism and hence, as implied earlier, relevant to the most "basic" of the basic human needs: physiological maintenance. There are other innate mechanisms relevant to actor survival, although actors tend to be aware of their operation, and can influence them to some extent. Anxiety, for instance, alerts us to possible dangers while anger may brace us for possible confrontations. The hypothalamus part of the brain regulates these (and other emotions) as well. The hypothalamus clearly plays a role in survival-relevant mechanisms at different levels of the organism. And with particular regard to the emotions, the hypothalamus operates in conjunction with what has been called the "emotional brain," the *limbic system*.

Thus far we have looked at only a few aspects of the biological/physiological world, but already we seem to have a basis for a "biological theory of rationality," in the sense that, ultimately, any action that is relevant to survival must be rational. The hypothalamus governs homeostasis and "fights" disruptions to the equilibrium of key bodily factors; together with the limbic system (with which it is closely interconnected), it responds to various dangers by "fight or flight." It is this latter aspect of "biological rationality" that concerns me here: the innate predisposition to fight or flee. To what extent are our brains "pre-wired" for such behaviors?

Paul MacLean[82] tells us that "we are the possessors of a *triune brain* – not one brain but three, each with its own way of perceiving and responding to the world."[83] In ascending order on the phylogenetic scale, they are: (1) *reptilian* (central core), (2) *paleomammalian* (limbic system), and (3) *neomammalian* (cerebral cortex). The first of these, the reptilian, is the most primitive; MacLean has also labelled this the "R-complex." It is comparable to much of the brain found in reptiles. And it includes the hypothalamus. Surrounding the reptilian R-complex is the next level, the limbic system which is associated with the brain found in early mammals. It is interesting that "both the reptilian and limbic brain are concerned primarily with self- and species-preservation;"[84] hence, our "biological theory of rationality." It is also interesting that MacLean feels that by studying reptiles and subhuman mammals, we can uncover *paleo-psychic processes* – i.e., ancient forms of behavior that we have inherited from our reptilian and mammalian ancestors.[85]

In effect, we appear to have been "pre-wired", at least partially, by the reptilian brain to be ritualistic, to be in awe of authority, to develop social pecking orders, and perhaps even to develop obsessive-compulsive neuroses.[86] That the reptilian brain has certain authority and pecking-order functions was demonstrated by MacLean when he ablated parts of the R-complex of (gothic) squirrel monkeys with the result that the programed tendency to "display" among such monkeys stopped.[87]

Needless to say, such experimentation has not been carried out on human subjects. Nevertheless, the awe-for-authority phenomenon has been noted among humans with regard to Nazi war criminals and others who "obeyed orders" to commit atrocities and other crimes,[88] and also in the laboratory in the classic but ethically problematic experiments on "obedience to authority" conducted by Milgram[89] and others.[90]

We appear to have been pre-wired in the case of the limbic system as well, to respond *emotionally* to threats to self- or species-preservation. Restak[91] tells us that, in the last 25 years, experiments on various animal species have shown that alterations (stimulation or destruction) in the limbic system can bring about profound changes in "feeding, fighting, fleeing, and sexual behavior." The electrical stimulation of the *amygdala* (a part of the limbic system) in a cat, for example, will produce hissing, pupil dilation, salivation, arching of the back, and general preparation for attack.[92] Hilgard, *et al.*,[93] report similar findings from experiments involving stimulation of the hypothalamus (the reptilian brain) in various animals.

To what extent does this apply to human beings? One tragic anecdote provides part, but not the whole, of an answer: in 1966, Charles Whitman, the "Texas Sniper," shot and killed his mother and wife, and then subsequently shot 49 other people before he was gunned down. His autopsy revealed that a tumor "the size of a walnut" was pressing against a part of his brain involved in the control of aggression.[94] In animal research, the critical experiment demonstrating conclusively that the "limbic system is the area of the brain most concerned with emotion," was carried out in 1939 by Kluver and Bucey who severed one of the two amygdala in a monkey. The result was, among other things, "extreme docility."[95]

It appears, therefore, that humans share with reptiles and subhuman mammals certain brain components which are relevant to self- and species-preservation, that would appear to be the main "functions" of ontological needs and, clearly, not just in humans: "Even one-celled life forms, lacking a distinct nervous system, 'want' to survive."[96] But humans are also characterized by MacLean's third and highest brain type. Given that the neomammalian brain or cerebral cortext "is more highly developed in human beings than in any other organism,"[97] and that the higher the cortical development and phylogenetic location of a species, the more complex its behavior,[98] we might expect that human behavior would be governed more by MacLean's third brain type than by the reptilian and limbic brains. Even in other mammals aggression is not automatically aroused by stimulating, for example, the hypothalamus.[99]

> The hypothalamus may send a message to the cortex indicating that its "aggression center" has been activated, but the cortex, in choosing the response it will initiate, considers what is going on in the environment and its memory of past experiences.

The message here is clear: if monkeys can exercise "cognitive control" over their reptilian and limbic brains, then surely humans can do the same, and more of it!

It might be tempting to stop our discussion at this point on the assumption that there is nothing more to be said on the issue of the biological underpinnings of human behavior. This assumption would imply that the "biological rationality" of the reptilian and limbic brains is somehow synchronized with or regulated by the rationality of the cerebral cortex. The appeal of this assumption notwithstanding, there is concern that the "higher" forms of rationality are not really in control.

John Pfeiffer,[100] for example, maintains that our brains are repositories for the collective experiences of our genus, experiences in the sense of "successful survival strategies evolved over millions of years." Providing structure for these experiences are partial, simple models of reality "that have been inherited from times past and wired in from birth." Pfeiffer also states that "these models control, even dictate, action." This is significant, given MacLean's thesis that humans are characterized by the reptilian and limbic brains as well as by the cerebral brain; that in any particular social situation, "all three brains would be experiencing the same thing [but] each in a different way,"[101] and that the experiences mediated by one or two of these brains might be in conflict with those mediated by the remaining brain(s). MacLean has developed the term, *schizophysiol-ogy* to refer to the conflict between *feelings* (limbic brain) and *thinking* (cerebral cortex). If the limbic brain gains the ascendancy in such conflicts and starts to control and dictate behavior, then actors may "feel" strongly about something but be completely wrong! When feelings are so powerful that they begin to control and dictate, then, according to MacLean, "this may be the basis for some forms of paranoid psychosis: a schizophysiology where believing is seeing rather than seeing is believing."[102]

"Paranoid psychosis" sounds a bit strong, but seems to reflect, in part, a phenomenon that William Graham Sumner,[103] among others, thought was a universal human trait: *ethnocentrism*, in which "each group nourishes its own pride and vanity, boasts itself superior, exalts its own divinities, and looks with contempt on outsiders." Ethnocentric behavior is clearly implicit in many attempts to fulfill needs for security, belongingness, identity, and self-esteem. Funda-mental to ethnocentrism is the view that domestic tranquility (*ingroup* peace) is a function of hostile relationships with other groups (*outgroups*). Various theories in the social sciences disagree about the nature of the internal–external conflict nexus,[104] and empirical studies of the relationship conducted by Rummel,[105] Tanter,[106] and Wilkenfeld[107] have led to "ambiguous and controversial results;" however, Dougherty and Pfaltzgraff[108] maintain that the internal–external conflict link will continue to warrant careful attention and research because, in part, "the mind of the social theorist is recurringly intrigued by the appearance of evidence which generally seems to validate the connection." (During October 1983, for example, the militarily successful US invasion of Grenada which occurred a few days after some 240 US Marines and others were killed in Beirut, did appear to inhibit the development of any significant domestic outcry against the Reagan Administration.)

Some sense of evidence regarding the internal–external conflict link seems to have intrigued the mind of Wilson,[109] who has said that "Our brains do appear to be programmed to the following extent: we are inclined to partition other people into friends and aliens, . . . [and] we tend to fear deeply the actions of strangers and to solve conflict by aggression." Pfeiffer[110] says about this programming that "the problem is that our built-in universe was formed largely in prehistoric . . . times [when] the sight of a stranger . . . meant real trouble – and triggered swift, generally violent, action." He also maintains that "large-scale violence may be a throwback," something that made sense in earlier times, but not in the modern era.

This notion that what was "rational" or "logical" in one set of circumstances may not be rational or logical in other circumstances has also been put forward by David Hamburg. He indicates that there is a human tendency to justify the "slaughter of outside groups" by the *need* to protect one's own; that the "human tendency to react with fear and hostility to strangers has roots in our prehuman past," and that the survival-relevant behaviors that humans learned in ancient times are now proving risky against the background of modern weapons and social complexity.[111]

Once again, reptilian and limbic "rationality" does not appear to be under the control of cerebral "rationality." This is certainly the view of Arthur Koestler,[112] whose explanation of human aggression, although biological, is at odds with the other biological theories of aggression we have discussed. Implicit in Koestler's analysis are basic human needs – e.g., the need for belongingness: the "excessive capacity and urge" among humans "to become identified with a tribe, nation, church, or cause."[113] Koestler identifies these integrative, self-transcending tendencies, rather than the self-assertive ones, as major factors underlying violence in human history.[114]

> the crimes of violence committed for selfish, personal motives are historically insignificant compared to those committed . . . out of a self-sacrificing devotion to a flag, a leader, a religious faith or a political conviction.

Specifically addressing the most destructive level of human violence, he says[115]: "War is a ritual, a deadly ritual, *not the result of aggressive self-assertion, but of self-transcending identification*."

Accordingly, in the process of transcending the Self, one *identifies* with a tribe, church, flag, or ideal; and subsequently, one may experience "vicarious . . . violent emotions on behalf of the entity."[116] One also surrenders responsibility for one's behavior to the entity, thereby facilitating acting "with ruthless cruelty towards the enemy or victim of the [entity]."[117] Personal hating is *not* a part of this process: "The individual victim . . . is punished not as an individual, but as a symbolic representation of [the 'enemy']."[118]

For Koestler,[119] this is all evidence "that there is a flaw, some potentially fatal engineering error built into . . . the circuits of our nervous system." Such "would account for the streak of paranoia running through our history." "The Ghost in the Machine" that drives all this for Koestler is MacLean's schizophysiology between the limbic and neocortical systems.[120]

> evolution *superimposed a new, superior structure on an old one*, with partly overlapping functions, and *without providing the new with a clearcut, hierarchic control over the old* – thus inviting confusion and conflict.

If Koestler[121] is right, in that the cerebral cortex "did not become properly integrated and coordinated with the ancient emotion-bound structures on which it was superimposed," and if the "excessive capacity for fanatical devotion" among humans tends, with some exceptions, to stop at the level of the nation-state, then:

(a) Is it the case that we can only escape the Hobbesian state of nature *nationally* (domestically)?
(b) And if so, is it the case that we can do so only if the Hobbesian state of nature continues to exist *internationally*?
(c) Are ethnocentrism, racism, genocide, and war *necessary* parts of the price we pay for internal peace?

In effect, are we stuck with a war-prone system?

APPLICATIONS TO SYSTEMIC INTEGRATION AND DISINTEGRATION

Some scholars of the Realist persuasion in international relations come to mind here regarding tentative answers to these questions. Raymond Aron,[122] for instance, has argued that "states have not emerged, in their mutual relations, from the state of nature." Martin Wight[123] has put forward the classic Realist view that, given the anarchic nature of the international system, mutual suspicions are a basic feature and no nation can ever feel assured that other nations are not "out to get it." In such a situation no country, even with the best of intentions, can yield any part of its security and liberty to another country: "This is the situation of 'Hobbesian fear' which Herbert Butterfield[124] has called " 'the absolute predicament and the irreducible dilemma' of international politics."[125]

"Hobbesian fear" is a key feature of Political Realism, and fear is controlled by the reptilian and limbic brains. Realist theory, therefore, is essentially a cerebral reconstruction and explanation of processes determined in part by the more instinct- and emotion-based parts of the brain. Fear, under certain circumstances, can give way to anger that is also controlled by the reptilian and limbic brains. One circumstance under which this might occur is when an anticipated negative event actually comes to pass. For instance, "once security is destroyed, all the higher objects of politics are swallowed up in the struggle for self-preservation, a tendency seen in every war."[126] Though Realist theorists talk rarely in any terms but "national interest," "power," "sovereignty," etc. Wight here is hinting that these macro-phenomena may relate to experiences at the personal level. This micro–macro connection is made more clear by Waltz[127] in his discussion of the relative ease that governments experience in securing almost unanimous backing for their foreign policies in crises leading to war: "The united front is enforced by the feelings of individuals, by their conviction that their *own* security depends on the security of the state" (emphasis added).

Both Wight and Waltz are referring here to "level (2)" needs in Maslow's hierarchy: safety and security (see p. 63). Depending upon where an actor is in relation to fulfillment of these needs – in terms of stability of position or direction and pace of movement – she/he can be characterized by competitive *or* cooperative processes of conflict resolution,[128] by power bargaining ("track one"), *or* problem-solving ("track two") approaches to conflict resolution.[129] To paraphrase Wight's comment above, "once the *needs for safety and security* are violated, all the *higher level needs* are swallowed up in the *struggle for self-preservation*, a tendency seen in every war."

Let us hypothesize that the reptilian brain (specifically the hypothalamus, which controls homeostasis) plays the dominant role in fulfilling the physiological needs; that the reptilian and limbic brains combine in various ways to fulfill the safety and security, love and belongingness, identity, and self-esteem needs; and that the cerebral cortex plays the dominant role in fulfilling the self-actualization needs. Let us also hypothesize that the competitive power bargaining processes of conflict resolution are related primarily to the reptilian and limbic brains, and that the cooperative problem-solving processes relate primarily to the cerebral cortex. Finally, let us hypothesize that, with regard to *both* or *all* parties to any conflict situation, competitive power bargaining is related primarily to dysfunctional conflict and disintegrative processes, while cooperative problem-solving relates primarily to functional conflict and integrative processes.

Now, let us return to Wight's statement above, "once security is destroyed . . .," as a point of departure for imagining what might happen to a relatively sophisticated policy once it has experienced a violent, protracted, costly conflict. As the actors in the society either compare themselves to others or actually begin to move down the needs' ladder, from self-esteem to somewhere below a comfortable position on the safety and security level, they might begin to experience *rank disequilibrium*,[130] the *J-curve* of rising expectations followed by an acute reversal in gratification,[131] *relative deprivation*,[132] and, lest we forget, *frustration*.[133]

As the feelings associated with these manifestations of "cognitive dissonance"[134] begin to translate into epiphenomenal emotional states such as fear or anger, or some combination thereof, something like MacLean's schizophysiological phenomenon (Koestler's "Ghost in the Machine") begins to dig its heels in, and the actors in the society, including the decision makers, may ignore cautions associated with the cerebral cortex and give in to the demands of the limbic system: "Violence . . . is produced when certain innate needs or demands are deeply frustrated."[135]

As Holsti, North, and Brody[136] uncovered in their analysis of the outbreak of the First World War: "If perceptions of anxiety, fear, threat, or injury are great enough, even the perception of one's own inferior capability will fail to deter a national from going to war." Under such circumstances, the actors would probably engage in competitive power bargaining processes of conflict management, including the use of violence and, beyond some critical threshold of escalation, would enter into the insidious "bite-counterbite" world of the negative self-fulfilling prophecy where all actors' worst fears are realized: a world where Political Realism, because of its inherent, self-reinforcing nature, makes more and more "sense."[137]

As Restak[138] tells us, "from here it may be just a step to understanding how behavior based on intensely felt emotion can stir large numbers of people into irrational, even destructive, behavior." This applies to the obvious cases such as the Nazi phenomenon in Germany as well as to the less obvious cases such as the Watergate and Iran-Contra experiences in the United States. As the strategic arms race begins to assume extraterrestrial dimensions, it may apply not just to superpower or East–West relations, but to relationships at all levels worldwide. In any case, dysfunctional conflict and disintegrative processes would seem to be key characteristics of those relationships.

CONCLUSION

We have merely scratched the surface of a vaguely-defined but apparently important source of influence on human behavior at all levels. So, what can we conclude, at least tentatively, about the role of biology in human affairs in general? "Proof" surely lies in the eyes of the beholder, *even* in the natural sciences, but lest we forget the seminal work of Thomas Kuhn,[139] there is, as Eysenck[140] puts it, "impressive . . . evidence for strong genetic determination of differences in intelligence, personality, social and sexual behavior, criminality, mental disorder, and many other aspects of human sociality." There are also the studies conducted at the University of Minnesota, comparing the personalities of twins (both fraternal and identical) reared together with those of twins *reared apart*, showing that *genetic influence accounts for about fifty percent of the variance in personality traits*, such as well-being, alienation, aggression, control, and risk avoidance.[141]

There also appears to be increasing evidence to support MacLean's schizophysiological and Koestler's "Ghost in the Machine" thesis, of a discordant relationship between the limbic system and cerebral cortex, between *feelings* and *thinking*, such that, "in nonroutinized acts, notably those involving the [threatened or actual] use of physical force and violence, the neocortex becomes the servant of the limbic system."[142] The evidence concerns a social problem which, in the United States, is increasing in duration as well as frequency. At the individual level, it has resulted in depression, alcohol and drug abuse, destroyed family relationships, caused heart disease, suicide and homicide. A the societal level, it may be costing the economy as much as "$150 billion a year – almost the size of the federal deficit" – in reduced productivity, absenteeism, and escalating medical costs. The social problem is *stress*.[143]

> At one level the phenomenon is purely physiological. It's an outgrowth of what scientists call the "fight or flight" response, a primitive reflex that prepares humans for conflict. When confronted with possible danger – or a testy co-worker – the body secretes adrenaline and hydrocortisone. The hormones help the body turn off some functions – including parts of the immune system – and turn on short-term energy reserves. In today's . . . world, that can be a problem.

The "short-term energy reserves" are increases in oxygen consump-

tion, heart rate, blood pressure, respiratory rate, and in the blood
flowing to the skeletal structure. In the modern world, the range of
possible cues that can activate fight or flight is greater than it was in
prehistoric times. The "problem" is that many of these do not lend
themselves to simple "fleeing" or "fighting" – e.g., threatened marital
dissolution, job loss, war or environmental decay. According to
Herbert Benson,[144] our inability to flee from or fight these situations
can lead to hypertension, chronic pain, and anxiety. Also, the decline
in the body's immune system increases our susceptibility to infectious
disease. Finally, fight or flight also exacerbates various problems:

> for example, chronic back pain or repeated headaches cause
> anxiety, which worsens the pain, further activating the fight-or-
> flight response in a vicious self-sustaining cycle.

Again, what is "rational" or "logical" in one set of circumstances
may, in other circumstances, run counter to self- and species-
preservation. This sounds remarkably similar to what goes on in the
international system. Indeed – what about the link between biology
and the international system?

We have sketched an outline of a general multi-level theory in which
biological factors play a part, and which suggests that, depending on
"circumstances," we may or may not be able to move beyond the
nation-state. If "Hobbesian fear," the "absolute predicament and
the irreducible dilemma of international politics," were to subside; if
negative self-fulfilling mechanisms were to be "nipped in the bud;"
and if the needs for safety and security, love and belongingness,
identity, and self-esteem could be satisfied for *all parties* to relationships, as a prerequisite to mutual satisfaction of the self-actualization
needs, realization of these factors would perhaps stimulate for future
generations further growth of the cerebral cortex which apparently
responds to an enriched human-made world.[145] Then cooperative
problem-solving approaches to conflict management could be the
order of the day, with profound implications for transcending the
nation-state. In that event, Puchala's[146] "concordance system," Burton's[147] "conflict resolution as a political system," and Davies's[148]
"civilized anarchy," could become, at the global level, more than
interesting ideas.

This is not to say that the nation-state could or should be completely
eclipsed by some other form of organization or that it will "wither
away." According to Joseph Frankel's[149] model of a "mixed" international system, which may be in the process of developing, states

will continue their status as dominant actors, while shifting their authority in different directions:

> delegating it both to some broader bodies – global and regional – to deal with problems with which the state on its own is helpless, and downwards, where minorities feel dissatisfied and press for devolution.

Though there may be some evidence that the present international system may be moving in the direction of combining functional integration and political decentralization, there is also evidence that the "security dilemma"[150] is worsening, and that by the year 2000 there will be a *minimum* of fourteen nuclear powers in the world[151] – a condition very close to Morton Kaplan's[152] *unit veto* system where all actors have the capacity to destroy everyone else. We could go in either direction (integration or disintegration), both at once for a time. However, nuclear proliferation and the extension of the arms race into space, especially against the background of other global problems (the greenhouse effect, overpopulation, hunger), would probably stimulate the ascendancy of the reptilian and limbic brains. The resulting heavy emphasis on *zero-sum* satisfaction of the safety and security needs would give rise to the competitive bargaining modes of conflict management but socio-economic integration would not be sufficient to stimulate the cerebral cortex for *positive-sum* satisfaction of needs in general, and the use of cooperative problem-solving. "It all depends": perhaps in part on the success of *Glasnost* and *Perestroika*.

In the meantime, however, that "most people in the world . . . share with lower animals a nearly exclusive concern with self-survival and species-survival,"[153] and that the international environment is closer to "primitive" than to "civilized anarchy,"[154] make it exceedingly likely that the nation-state will retain its Hegelian identity as the highest form of socio-political organization. Assuming a continuous, reciprocal relationship between human nature and the (national and international) political environment,[155] such that a stunted human nature leads to a stunted political environment, and vice versa, then the chances are "excellent" for the maintenance of an international system where state, security needs, *Realpolitik*, and the reptilian/limbic systems not only dominate but interact to reinforce each other and strengthen the system of which they are all a part until the system changes. And it will, one way or another.

Against this uncertainty one thing seems clear: there *is* a *non-*

deterministic Biological Imperative underlying human behavior in general and at the international level in particular. While it may be impossible directly, indirectly, or even at a "distance," to perceive needs, it should not be surprising that, *at minimum*, security and survival, love and belongingness, identity, and self-esteem needs, are part of this Imperative. There are those of us who are convinced that it is the *phenotypic* violation of these *genotypic* needs that underlies much of the violence in the world today and our inability, thus far, to transcend the nation-state and a war-prone international system; and we face the theoretical as well as methodological problem of discovering how better to define what those needs and their *alternative* "satisfiers" might be and how to use *observable*, potential satisfiers to fulfill those needs.[156] In effect, for needs to be ultimately relevant to the practice *as well as* the theory of moving beyond the nation-state into regional and global collaborative problem-solving systems, we must have some agreed-upon sense of what needs are. But, perhaps more importantly, we need some sense of how, in the observable world, to *fulfill* them. We clearly have our work cut out!

NOTES AND REFERENCES

1. Katrin Lederer, "Introduction," in Katrin Lederer (ed.) with Johan Galtung and David Antal, *Human Needs: A Contribution to the Current Debate* (Cambridge, MA: Oelgeschlager, Gunn & Hain, 1980).
2. Abraham Kaplan, *The Conduct of Inquiry: Methodology for Behavioral Sciences* (New York, London: Chandler (Harper & Row), 1964) Chapter 2.
3. Thomas S. Kuhn, *The Structure of Scientific Revolutions* (Chicago, London: University of Chicago Press, 1970) 2nd edn.
4. Kenneth E. Boulding, *The Image: Knowledge in Life and Society* (Ann Arbor: University of Michigan Press, 1956).
5. Kaplan, *The Conduct of Inquiry*: 57.
6. Lederer, "Introduction" in Lederer (ed.): 3.
7. Lederer, "Introduction."
8. Ross Fitzgerald, "Abraham Maslow's Hierarchy of Needs – An Exposition and Evaluation," in Ross Fitzgerald (ed.), *Human Needs and Politics* (Oxford; New York: Pergamon Press, 1977): 44.
9. Harry F. Harlow, "Mice, Monkeys, Men and Motives," *Psychological Review*, 60 (1953): 23–32; Harry F. Harlow and S. J. Suomi, "Social Recovery by Isolation-Reared Monkeys," *Proceedings of the National Academy of Science*, 68 (1971): 1534–8; Harry F. Harlow and C. Mears, *The Human Model: Primate Perspectives* (New York: John Wiley,

1979).

10. John Bowlby, *Attachment* (New York: Basic Books, 1969); John Bowlby, *Separation* (New York: Basic Books, 1973).

11. René A. Spitz, "The Role of Ecological Factors in Emotional Development in Infancy," *Child Development*, 20 (1949): 145–55.

12. James Chowning Davies, "Aggression, Violence, Revolution, and War," in Jeanne N. Knutson (ed.), *Handbook of Political Psychology* (San Francisco; London: Jossey-Bass, 1973): 255–6.

13. Courtland Milloy, "For Runaways, an Island of Stability," *The Washington Post*, 29 January 1989, section C: 3.

14. Courtland Milloy, "Ending the 'Quiet Riots' in Cities Across America," *The Washington Post*, 6 November 1988, section B: 3.

15. Salman Rushdie, *The Satanic Verses* (New York: Viking, 1988). Russell Watson with Donna Foote, Ray Wilkinson and Jane Whitmore. "A 'Satanic' Fury," *Newsweek*, 27 February 1989: 34–9.

16. Jonathan Yardley, "Wrestling with the Angel," *The Washington Post Book World*, 29 January 1989: 3.

17. Don Podestra, "The Terrible Toll of Human Hatred: Wars May Come and Go, but Ethnic Rivalries Are Forever," *The Washington Post National Weekly Edition*, 8 June 1987: 9–10.

18. Frantz Fanon. *The Wretched of the Earth* (New York: Grove Press, 1968).

19. Theodore A. Couloumbis and James H. Wolfe, *Introduction to International Relations: Power and Justice* (Englewood Cliffs; London: Prentice-Hall, 1986): 214–15, 3rd edn, emphasis added.

20. Davies, "Aggression, Violence," in Knutson (ed.), *Handbook*: 245.

21. Barbara Harff and Ted Robert Gurr, "Toward Empirical Theory of Genocides and Politicides: Identification and Measurement of Cases Since 1945," *International Studies Quarterly*, 32 (3) (September 1988): 359–71.

22. Harff and Gurr, "Toward Empirical Theory": 359.

23. Ted Robert Gurr and James R. Scarritt, "Minorities' Rights at Risk: A Global Survey," *Human Rights Quarterly* (August 1989).

24. Ruth Leger Sivard, *World Military and Social Expenditure, 1987–88* (Washington, D.C.: World Priorities, 1987); 28–31, 12th edn.

25. *War and Peace in the Nuclear Age*, a television course and public television series. Unit Four, "Europe Goes Nuclear," Boston: WGBH, 1989.

26. Abraham H. Maslow, "A Theory of Human Motivation", *Psychological Review*, 50 (1943): 370–96; Abraham H. Maslow, *Motivation and Personality* (New York, London: Harper & Row, 1987) 3rd edn.

27. Fitzgerald, "Abraham Maslow's Hierarchy of Needs."

28. Charles Sanders Peirce, *Collected Papers*, vols 2 and 4 (Cambridge, MA: Harvard University Press, 1934).

29. Kaplan, *The Conduct of Inquiry*: 86.

30. Maslow, "A Theory of Human Motivation": 394; Fitzgerald, "Abraham Maslow's Hierarchy of Needs": 36.

31. Fitzgerald, "Abraham Maslow's Hierarchy of Needs": 44.

32. Davies, "Aggression, Violence," in Knutson (ed.), *Handbook*; James

Chowning Davies, "Roots of Political Behavior," in Margaret G. Hermann (ed.), *Political Psychology: Contemporary Problems and Issues* (San Francisco; London: Jossey-Bass, 1986).

33. James Chowning Davies, "Toward a Theory of Revolution," *American Sociological Review*, 27 (1962): 5–19; James Chowning Davies, "The J-Curve of Rising and Declining Satisfactions as a Cause of Some Great Revolutions and a Contained Rebellion," in Hugh Davies Graham and Ted Robert Gurr (eds), *The History of Violence in America*, (New York: Bantam, 1969).
34. Davies, "Aggression, Violence," in Knutson (ed.), *Handbook*: 247.
35. John W. Burton, *Deviance, Terrorism and War: The Process of Solving Unsolved Social and Political Problems* (Oxford: Martin Robertson; New York: St. Martin's Press, 1979); John W. Burton, *Global Conflict: The Domestic Sources of International Crisis* (Brighton, England: Wheatsheaf; College Park, University of Maryland, Center for International Development and Conflict Management, 1984); John W. Burton, *Resolving Deep-Rooted Conflict: A Handbook* (Lanham, Md., London: University Press of America, 1987).
36. Paul Sites, *Control: The Basis of Social Order* (New York: Dunellen, 1973).
37. Johan Galtung, "The Basic Needs Approach," in Lederer (ed.), *Human Needs*.
38. James Chowning Davies, "The Existence of Human Needs," in R. A. Coate and J. A. Rosati (eds), *The Power of Human Needs in World Society* (Boulder, CO: Lynne Reinner, 1988).
39. John W. Burton and Dennis J. D. Sandole, "Generic Theory: The Basis of Conflict Resolution," *Negotiation Journal*, 2 (4) (October 1986): 333–44.
40. Kevin Avruch and Peter W. Black, "A Generic Theory of Conflict Resolution: A Critique," *Negotiation Journal*, 3 (1) (January 1987): 87–96; John W. Burton and Dennis J. D. Sandole, "Expanding the Debate on Generic Theory of Conflict Resolution: A Response to a Critique," *Negotiation Journal*, 3 (1) (January 1987): 97–9.
41. Kenneth N. Waltz, *Man, the State, and War: A Theoretical Analysis* (New York, London: Columbia University Press, 1959).
42. Saint Augustine, *The City of God*, Marcus Dods (trans.) (New York: Hafner, 1948).
43. Reinhold Niebuhr, *Christianity and Power Politics* (New York: Charles Scribner's Sons, 1940); Reinhold Niebuhr, *Christian Realism and Political Problems* (New York: Charles Scribner's Sons, 1953).
44. Hans J. Morgenthau, *Politics Among Nations: The Struggle for Power and Peace*, Kenneth W. Thompson (rev.) (New York: Alfred A. Knopf, 1985) 6th edn.
45. Benedict de Spinoza, *The Chief Works of Benedict de Spinoza*, R. H. M. Elwes (trans.) (New York: Dover, 1951).
46. Thucydides, *The Peloponnesian War*, Richard Crawley (trans.) (New York: The Modern Library (Random House), 1951).
47. Kautilya, *Arthasastra*, R. Shamasastry (trans.) (Mysore: Mysore Printing and Publishing House, 1967) 4th edn.

48. Niccolo Machiavelli, *The Prince*, W. K. Marriott (trans.) (New York: E. P. Dutton; London. J. M. Dent, 1958).
49. Thomas Hobbes, *Leviathan* (New York: E. P. Dutton; London: J. M. Dent, 1950).
50. Sigmund Freud, *Beyond the Pleasure Principle* (London: Hogarth Press, 1922); Sigmund Freud, "Why War?," a letter from Freud to Albert Einstein, written 1932 in *The Collected Papers of Sigmund Freud*, vol. 5, Ernest Jones (ed.) (New York: Basic Books, 1959); Sigmund Freud, *Civilization and Its Discontents* (New York: W. W. Norton, 1961).
51. Konrad Lorenz, *On Aggression* (New York: Bantam Books, 1967).
52. Waltz, *Man, the State, and War:* 27–8.
53. Erich Fromm, *The Anatomy of Human Destructiveness* (Harmondsworth, Middlesex, New York: Penguin Books, 1977).
54. Heinrich von Treitschke, *Politics*, Blanche Dugdale and Torben de Bille (trans.) (London: Constable, 1916).
55. William McDougall, *Social Psychology* (New York: G. P. Putnam's Sons, 1908).
56. John B. Watson, "Psychology as a Behaviorist Views It," *Psychological Review*, 20 (1913): 158–77.
57. Hans J. Eysenck, "Man as a Biosocial Animal: Comments on the Sociobiology Debate," *Political Psychology*, 2 (1) (Spring 1980): 43–51.
58. Robert Ardrey, *African Genesis: A Personal Investigation into the Animal Origins and Nature of Man* (New York: Atheneum, 1961); Robert Ardrey *The Territorial Imperative: A Personal Inquiry into the Animal Origins and Nature of Man* (New York: Atheneum, 1966); Ashley Montagu (ed.), *Man and Aggression* (Oxford; New York: Oxford University Press, 1973) 2nd edn.
59. Edward O. Wilson, *Sociobiology : The New Synthesis* (Cambridge MA; London: Harvard University Press, 1975); Edward O. Wilson, *On Human Nature* (New York: Bantam Books, 1979).
60. Fromm, *The Anatomy of Destructiveness*: 131.
61. Fromm, *The Anatomy of Destructiveness*: 251.
62. Fromm, *The Anatomy of Destructiveness*: 253.
63. Fromm, *The Anatomy of Destructiveness*: 294, emphasis added.
64. Albert Somit, "Wilson's *On Human Nature*," *Political Psychology*, 2 (1) (Spring 1980): 59–63.
65. Somit, "Wilson's *On Human Nature*": 62.
66. Eysenck, "Man as Animal": 49.
67. Somit, "Wilson's *On Human Nature*": 63.
68. Wilson, *On Human Nature*: 102.
69. Wilson, *On Human Nature*: 122.
70. Wilson, *On Human Nature*: 101.
71. Waltz, *Man, the State, and War*.
72. James N. Rosenau, "Pre-Theories and Theories of Foreign Policy," in Barry Farrell (ed.), *Approaches to Comparative and International Politics*, (Evanston Ill: Northwestern University Press, 1966).
73. Richard Snyder, H. W. Bruck and Burton Sapin, "Decision-Making as an Approach to the Study of International Politics," in Richard Snyder, H. W. Bruck and Burton Sapin (eds), *Foreign Policy Decision-Making:*

An Approach to the Study of International Politics (New York: Free Press, 1962).

74. J. David Singer, "The Global System and Its Subsystems: A Developmental View," in James N. Rosenau (ed.), *Linkage Politics: Essays on the Convergence of National and International Systems* (New York: Free Press; London: Collier-Macmillan, 1969); J. David Singer and Melvin Small, "Alliance Aggregation and the Onset of War, 1815–1945," in J. David Singer (ed.), *Quantitative International Politics: Insights and Evidence* (New York: Free Press; London: Collier-Macmillan, 1968).

75. John Paul Scott, *Aggression* (Chicago; London: University of Chicago Press, 1958).

76. Dennis J. D. Sandole, "The Subjectivity of Theories and Actions in World Society," in Michael Banks (ed.), *Conflict in World Society: A New Perspective on International Relations* (Brighton, England: Wheatsheaf; New York: St. Martin's Press, 1984); Dennis J. D. Sandole, "Conflict Management: Elements of Generic Theory and Process," in Dennis J. D. Sandole and Ingrid Sandole-Staroste (eds), *Conflict Management and Problem Solving: Interpersonal to International Applications* (London: Frances Pinter; New York: New York University Press, 1987).

77. Sir Karl R. Popper, *Objective Knowledge: An Evolutionary Approach* (Oxford: Oxford University Press, 1972).

78. Wilson, *Sociobiology*; and Wilson, *On Human Nature*.

79. Richard M. Restak, *The Brain: The Last Frontier* (Garden City, N.Y.: Doubleday, 1979).

80. Thomas C. Wiegele, "The Life Sciences and International Relations: A Bibliographic Essay," *International Studies Notes* 11 (2) (Winter 1984–85): 1–7.

81. W. B. Cannon, *The Wisdom of the Body* (New York: W. W. Norton, 1939) revised edn.

82. Paul MacLean, "On the Evolution of Three Mentalities," in Silvano Arieti and Gerard Chrzanowski (eds), *New Dimensions in Psychiatry: A World View*, vol. 2 (New York: John Wiley, 1975); Paul MacLean, "A Mind of Three Minds: Educating the Triune Brain," in *Education and the Brain*, 77th Yearbook of the National Society for the Study of Education, Part II (Chicago: University of Chicago Press, 1978).

83. Restak, *The Brain*: 35–6, emphasis added.

84. Restak, *The Brain*: 41.

85. Restak, *The Brain*: 36.

86. Restak, *The Brain*: 37.

87. Restak, *The Brain*: 37–8.

88. Herbert C. Kelman and V. Lee Hamilton, *Crimes of Obedience: Toward a Social Psychology of Authority and Responsibility* (New Haven; London: Yale University Press, 1988).

89. Stanley Milgram, *Obedience to Authority: An Experimental View* (New York; London: Harper & Row, 1974).

90. David M. Mantell and Robert Panzarella, "Perspectives on Obedience to Authority in Germany;" paper presented at the Congress of the

International Political Science Association (IPSA), Edinburgh, Scotland (16–21 August 1976).
91. Restak, *The Brain*: 49.
92. Restak, *The Brain*: 46.
93. Ernest R. Hilgard, Rita L. Atkinson and Richard C. Atkinson, *Introduction to Psychology* (New York: Harcourt Brace Jovanovich, 1979): 321, 7th edn.
94. *Understanding Human Behavior*, a television course and public television series. Lesson Five: "Functions of the Brain" (Fountain Valley CA: Coast Community College, 1980).
95. Restak, *The Brain*: 46–7.
96. Davies, "Roots of Behavior," in Hermann, *Political Psychology*: 48.
97. Hilgard, *et al.*, *Introduction*: 42.
98. Hilgard, *et al.*, *Introduction*: 42.
99. Hilgard, *et al.*, *Introduction*: 321.
100. John Pfeiffer, "Human Nature: The Universe Inside Your Skull," *Science Digest*, 92 (2) (March 1984): 92.
101. Restak, *The Brain*: 51.
102. Restak, *The Brain*: 52.
103. William Graham Sumner, *Folkways* (New York: Ginn, 1906): 12–13; R. A. LeVine and D. T. Campbell, *Ethnocentrism: Theories of Conflict, Ethnic Attitudes and Group Behavior* (New York: Wiley, 1972): 8.
104. LeVine and Campbell, *Ethnocentrism*: 213–14.
105. Rudolph J. Rummel, "Dimensions of Conflict Behavior Within and Between Nations," *General Systems*, 8 (1963): 1–50.
106. Raymond Tanter, "Dimensions of Conflict Behavior Within and between Nations, 1958–60," *Journal of Conflict Resolution*, 10 (March 1966): 41–64.
107. Jonathan Wilkenfeld, "Domestic and Foreign Conflict," in Jonathan Wilkenfeld (ed.), *Conflict Behavior and Linkage Politics* (New York: McKay, 1973).
108. James E. Dougherty and Robert L. Pfaltzgraff, Jr, *Contending Theories of International Relations: A Comprehensive Survey* (New York, London: Harper & Row, 1981) 2nd edn.
109. Wilson, *On Human Nature*: 122–3.
110. Pfeiffer, "Human Nature": 92.
111. Bryce Nelson, "Old Behavior Traits Pose Danger Today, Researcher Declares," *The New York Times*, 20 January 1983, section A: 17.
112. Arthur Koestler, *The Ghost in the Machine* (New York: Macmillan, 1967); Arthur Koestler, *Janus* (London: Hutchinson, 1978).
113. Arthur Koestler, "The Brain Explosion," *The Observer* (London) 15 January 1978: 25.
114. Koestler, *The Ghost in the Machine*: 234.
115. Koestler, *The Ghost in the Machine*: 253.
116. Koestler, *The Ghost in the Machine*: 244, 245.
117. Koestler, *The Ghost in the Machine*: 248, 251.
118. Koestler, *The Ghost in the Machine*: 252, 253.
119. Koestler, "The Brain Explosion."
120. Koestler, *The Ghost in the Machine*: 281–2.

121. Koestler, "The Brain Explosion."

122. Raymond Aron, *Peace and War: A Theory of International Relations* (Garden City, N.Y.: Doubleday, 1966): 7.

123. Martin Wight, *Power Politics*, Hedley Bull and Carsten Holbraad (eds), (Harmondsworth, Middlesex; New York: Penguin Books, 1979): 101–2, 2nd edn.

124. Herbert Butterfield, *Christianity and History* (London: G. Bell, 1949): 89–90; Herbert Butterfield, *History and Human Relations* (London: Collins, 1951): 19.

125. Wight, *Power Politics*: 102.

126. Wight, *Power Politics*: 292.

127. Waltz, *Man, the State, and War*: 179.

128. Morton Deutsch, *The Resolution of Conflict: Constructive and Destructive Processes* (New Haven, London: Yale University Press, 1973).

129. Burton, *Deviance, Terrorism*; Burton, *Global Conflict*; Burton, *Resolving Deep-Rooted Conflict*; John W. McDonald, Jr and Diane B. Bendahmane (eds), *Conflict Resolution: Track Two Diplomacy* (Washington, D.C.: Center for the Study of Foreign Affairs, Foreign Service Institute, US Department of State, 1987).

130. Johan Galtung, "A Structural Theory of Aggression," *Journal of Peace Research*, 1 (1964): 95–119.

131. Davies, "Toward a Theory of Revolution."

132. Ted Robert Gurr, *Why Men Rebel* (Princeton: Princeton University Press, 1970).

133. John Dollard, L. W. Doob, N. E. Miller, O. H. Mowrer and R. R. Sears, *Frustration and Aggression* (New Haven, London: Yale University Press, 1939).

134. Leon Festinger, *A Theory of Cognitive Dissonance* (Stanford: Stanford University Press, 1962).

135. Davies, "Aggression, Violence": 251.

136. Ole Holsti, Robert North and Richard Brody, "Perception and Action in the 1914 Crisis," in David Singer (ed.), *Quantitative International Politics*: 136.

137. Sandole, "The Subjectivity of Theories;" Sandole, "Traditional Approaches to Conflict Management: Short-Term Gains vs. Long-Term Costs," *Current Research on Peace and Violence*, 9 (3) (1986): 119–24; Sandole, "Conflict Management."

138. Restak, *The Brain*: 53.

139. Kuhn, *The Structure of Scientific Revolutions*.

140. Eysenck, "Man as a Biosocial Animal": 45.

141. John Leo, "Exploring the Traits of Twins: A New Study Shows that Key Characteristics May Be Inherited," *Time*, 12 January 1987: 39: Auke Tellegen, Thomas J. Bouchard, Jr., Kimberly J. Wilcox, Nancy L. Segal, David T. Lykken and Stephen Rich, "Personality Similarity in Twins Reared Apart and Together," *Journal of Personality and Social Psychology*, 54 (6) (June 1988): 1031–9.

142. James Chowning Davies, "The Proper Biological Study of Politics," *Political Psychology*, 4 (4) (December 1983): 731–43.

143. Annetta Miller with Karen Springen, Jeanne Gordon, Andrew Murr,

Bob Cohn, Linda Drew and Todd Barrett, "Stress on the Job," *Newsweek*, 25 April 1988: 40–5.

144. Herbert Benson, "The Relaxation Response: A Bridge between Medicine and Religion," *The Harvard Medical School Mental Health Letter*, 4 (9) (March 1988): 4–6.

145. Hilgard, *et al.*, *Introduction to Psychology*: 42.

146. Donald J. Puchala, "Of Blind Men, Elephants and International Integration," *Journal of Common Market Studies*, 10 (3) (1972): 267, 284.

147. John W. Burton, *Conflict Resolution as a Political System*, Working Paper 1 (Fairfax, VA: George Mason University Center for Conflict Analysis and Resolution, February 1988).

148. James Chowning Davies, "The Development of Individuals and the Development of Politics," in Ross Fitzgerald (ed.), *Human Needs and Politics*, (1977); Davies, "Roots of Political Behavior."

149. Jospeh Frankel, *International Relations in a Changing World* (Oxford; New York: Oxford University Press, 1979) 3rd edn.

150. John H. Herz, *International Politics in the Atomic Age* (New York; London: Columbia University Press, 1959); Robert Jervis, *Perception and Misperception in International Politics* (Princeton; Guildford, Surrey, England: Princeton University Press, 1976) Chapter 3.

151. Leonard S. Spector, *Going Nuclear* (Cambridge, MA: Ballinger, 1987).

152. Morton A. Kaplan, *System and Process in International Politics* (New York: John Wiley, 1957).

153. Davies, "Roots of Political Behavior,": 44.

154. Davies, "The Development of Individuals;" Davies, "Roots of Political Behavior."

155. Davies, "Roots of Political Behavior."

156. Katrin Lederer (ed.), with Johan Galtung and David Antal, *Human Needs: A Contribution to the Current Debate* (Cambridge, MA.: Oelgeschlager, Gunn & Hain, 1980).

4 Needs Theory, Social Identity and an Eclectic Model of Conflict*
Ronald J. Fisher

INTRODUCTION

The appeal of Needs Theory is that it offers additional support and a fresh perspective for the appropriateness and utility of the problem-solving approach to conflict resolution.

In terms of conceptualization, Needs Theory is of course not a completely new collection of ideas. In the fields of humanistic psychology and applied social psychology there are numerous concepts and principles that are complementary to Needs Theory. In particular, the concept of identity in terms of its implications for intergroup relations has a unique potential for linking Needs Theory to conflict resolution. In addition, an eclectic model of intergroup conflict, based primarily in social-psychological theorizing, provides a context for Needs Theory and a broader framework for understanding and ultimately resolving protracted conflict. Humanism and humanistic psychology provide a starting point for the value base and the conception of human beings which underlie applied social psychology and which permeate the study of intergroup relations and the policy implications for multiculturalism derived therefrom. Additionally, an eclectic model of conflict draws on understandings of intergroup relations and points toward approaches to resolution that are consistent with the humanistic value base. The understanding and acknowledgement of basic human needs, as asserted by Needs Theory and as promulgated by humanism, is thus seen as essential to the improvement of intergroup relations and the resolution of protracted social conflict.

SOURCES OF COMPLEMENTARY IDEAS: HUMANISTIC PSYCHOLOGY

The philosophy of humanism contends that the basis for moral values should be found in human experience and human needs as opposed to religious dogma.[1] The human capacity for critical reasoning and scientific inquiry should be used in constructing moral values and solving social problems in humanitarian directions. Thus, in searching for social justice, humanism is committed to democracy and social equality. The principle of equality requires that all people are equal in dignity and value and are deserving of equality of opportunity and treatment.[2] In minimal terms, this means meeting the basic economic and cultural needs of all people. An essential mechanism for effecting humanism is participatory democracy, in which individuals have involvement in decisions which directly affect them. Humanism thus calls for the democratization of all institutions in order that they become responsive to the views and needs of those within them. Finally, humanism calls for individuals to exercise freedom with responsibility in order to develop their full potential and to use their competence in the pursuit of human welfare.

In the social sciences, humanism finds clear expression in the subdiscipline of humanistic psychology, which is concerned with the full development of the human potential, individually and collectively.[3] The ultimate goal of humanistic psychology is to produce a complete description of what it means to be alive and its methods are thereby subjective, descriptive and holistic. In the search for full potential, humanistic psychology advises that individuals take responsibility for their own lives, adopt a here-and-now perspective, accept expression of the full range of human emotions, search for mutuality and authenticity in social relationships, and adopt a growth orientation to their experiencing of life.[4] This orientation of course places individuals on a collision course with the norms of contemporary society, and the manner in which people typically deal with conflict! That is, humanistic psychology prescribes an open, collaborative approach for dealing with differences, as opposed to the typical strategies of dominance, suppression or avoidance.

Within the context of humanistic psychology, conceptualizations regarding the essential needs of human beings have been developed. The best known of these is Maslow's Hierarchy of Needs, which specifies the basic positive motives that underlie human behavior.[5] From his experience as a clinical psychologist, Maslow identified and organized these needs into a hierarchy in which lower order needs must be satisfied before the individual becomes concerned with higher order needs. Unfortunately, little research has been done to examine the nature of the needs specified or the ordering of the hierarchy. Nonetheless, Maslow's model has had considerable influence in the fields of clinical and organizational psychology, and in the development of Needs Theory. The hierarchy, including the addition of cognitive and aesthetic needs identified later by Maslow, is as follows:

– *Self-actualization needs*: the ultimate motivation, involving the need to fulfill one's unique potential.
– *Esteem needs*: the need for achievement, competence and mastery, as well as motives for recognition, prestige and status.
– *Aesthetic needs*: the craving for beauty, symmetry and order.
– *Cognitive needs*: the desire to know, to understand, and to satisfy one's curiosity.
– *Belongingness and Love needs*: needs that are satisfied by social relationships.
– *Safety needs*: needs that must be met to protect the individual from danger.
– *Physiological needs*: basic internal deficit conditions that must be satisfied to maintain bodily processes.

The ordering of the hierarchy is perhaps not so important as the supposition that the needs represent the basic requirements of human beings for survival and development in both physical and social terms. The major commonality between Maslow's ideas and later expressions of Needs Theory is therefore clearly evident. There are, however, a number of sticking points that have been expressed as criticisms of Maslow's model by several contributors to Needs Theory. Lederer,[6] for example, in introducing a collection of seminal contributions on Needs Theory, notes that Maslow's hierarchy suggests a distinction between more basic and less basic needs with respect to the urgency of satisfaction. In addition, more basic needs are equated with material satisfiers while less basic needs are related to non-material satisfiers, thus creating a set of potentially confused priorities for international development, and parenthetically, conflict resolution. Similarly, Galtung[7] sees the hierarchical conception of needs as dangerous since it limits the range of theoretical possibilities and could be used to legitimize the superior position of intellectuals or ascetics who specialize in dealing with the higher non-material needs.

In addition, the normative specification that lower needs must be satisfied before attention is given to higher needs could be used to justify deliberate inattention to non-material needs and for preserving an unacceptable status quo. Furthermore, Galtung[8] points out that Maslow's theory, along with much other work on needs, demonstrates a strong Western imprint. He discusses this contention in relation to certain characteristics of Western society including a unilinear conception of time, an analytic conception of epistemology, a man-over-nature stance, and a vertical division of labor. Setting the hierarchical nature of Maslow's model aside would satisfy many of these criticisms and would leave a list of needs that bears considerable resemblance to those identified in many other statements of Needs Theory.

It should be noted that Maslow is not the first psychologist to construct a list of human needs, as Klineberg[9] discusses. The earlier conception of instincts in social psychology was a forerunner to numerous lists of human motives, wants and needs, one of the most notable of which, under Murray's construction, distinguished between viscerogenic and psychogenic needs. Klineberg[10] points out that Murray posited many leads, such as affiliation, dominance, nurturance, etc. which have important social implications, including ramifications for intergroup relations and conflict resolution. In addition, the need for achievement, made popular in social research by the work of McClelland and his colleagues, has received much attention in relation to economic and social development. As with Maslow's model, this construct has been criticized as embodying a Western bias and therefore of having limits in relation to the development of a theory of universal human needs.

A broad though not well known statement of needs by a humanistic social psychologist, Hadley Cantril, represents a holistic attempt to specify universal elements of the human design which do transcend particular cultures, societies, or political systems. Listed below in slightly paraphrased form are the eleven characteristics which Cantril believes represent the essential elements of the human experience:[11]

- Humans require the satisfaction of survival needs.
- Humans want security in both its physical and psychological meaning.
- Humans need sufficient order and certainty to be able to predict the effects of their actions.
- Humans continuously seek to enlarge the range and enrich the

quality of their satisfactions.
- Humans are creatures of hope and are not genetically designed to resign themselves.
- Humans have the capacity to make choices and the desire to exercise this capacity.
- Humans require freedom to exercise the choices they are capable of making.
- Humans want to experience their own identity and integrity.
- Humans want to experience a sense of their own worthwhileness.
- Humans seek some value or system of beliefs to which they can commit themselves.
- Humans want a sense of confidence that their society holds a fair degree of hope that their aspirations will be fulfilled.

After stating these fundamentals, Cantril[12] briefly considers the interplay between the individual and society in terms of meeting basic needs. It is clear that a viable society must provide for survival needs, security and the achievement of satisfactions. In addition, an effective society enables individuals to develop loyalties and aspirations compatible with social values while at the same time taking account of individual differences. In this sense, every social and political system is an experiment which will eventually have to accommodate to the fundamentals of the human design. The assertions of Cantril, Maslow and other psychologists thus help to set the agenda for attempts to understand the dynamics of social change and within that the resolution of conflict.

APPLIED SOCIAL PSYCHOLOGY

Applied social psychology moves the concerns of humanistic psychologists into the social sphere in an explicit and systemic manner. This emerging field can be defined as social-psychological research and practice in real world settings, directed toward the understanding of human social behavior and the solution of social problems.[13] The emphasis on the role of social science in the pursuit of human welfare requires that the field be based on a clear conception of what it means to be human and on a clear articulation of the humanistic value base. Applied social psychology thus assumes that individuals and social groups have undeniable needs and rights for dignity, respect, security, and a "place in the sun" in both physical and psychological terms – that is, identity, participation and adequate control over their own destiny.[14] Through the active interplay of theory, research and practice at several levels of analysis, applied social psychology provides direction as to how group and intergroup relations should be ordered to successfully meet human needs and how social change should progress in order effectively to resolve social problems. The underlying rationale is that all human problems have social components and that in fact the most serious human problems are primarily social. A social science is thus required that is both humanistic and scientific and that is seen within the context of humanistic values and societal needs.[15] A crucial element in this approach is the manner in which social conflict is conceptualized and approached in terms of methods of resolution that are compatible with the value base and rationale of applied social psychology.[16]

SOCIAL IDENTITY, INTERGROUP RELATIONS AND MULTICULTURALISM

The concept of identity, in particular social identity, has the potential of providing the key linkage between Needs Theory and intergroup and international conflict resolution. The need for identity is regarded by several contemporary needs theorists as a fundamental requirement for constructive human development. Foremost among these is Nudler,[17] who proposes that the need for identity is the first and most fundamental need of the person since the alternative is disorganization and death. Following an open systems approach, Nudler[18] contends that identity is developed and maintained through a process of exchange with the environment, which parallels the classic notion of Mead that personal identity is formed through social interaction. Galtung[19] gives prominence to identity needs as one of four categories in his comprehensive typology that sees identity as primarily dependent on the social structure – that is, the level of satisfaction of the need for identity is determined more by the nature of the social structure than by the motivations and capabilities of particular actors. This immediately connects the identity needs to the level of intergroup relations within and between societies. In his social-psychological approach to understanding human needs, Klineberg[20] links the need to belong and identify with a group to the need for affiliation which Murray postulated. The importance of the individual having a group identity is based on Erikson's classic and well accepted contention that identity is expressed both in the core of the individual and in the core of a communal culture in a simultaneous fashion. Although Klineberg[21] is reluctant to distinguish between needs that are fundamental to human well-being versus those that are less important, he concludes that the need to belong and identify with a group is almost universal. Finally, he implies through examples a point that Galtung[22] and others have made directly: human beings are willing to suffer immeasurably and to sacrifice – and in some cases take – their own lives in the struggle for and the protection of their identity. Such dramatic occurrences underline the more general point that identity is a fundamental need that influences a great deal of social interaction at the group, intergroup and international levels.

Social psychologists have generally accepted Sherif's[23] definition that intergroup behavior involves individuals interacting in terms of their group identifications. A contemporary line of investigation known as *social identity theory* has re-emphasized the importance of group or social identity as it affects relations between groups. This framework combines the concepts of self-esteem and social identity with social comparison theory in order to explain intergroup discrimination.[24] In this way, the theory provides useful linkages among the individual, group and intergroup levels of analysis.

The initial research supporting the theory involves laboratory experiments demonstrating that the mere perception of belonging to an artificially created group was sufficient to produce intergroup discrimination favoring the ingroup in the distribution of small rewards. Intergroup discrimination was thus created without any real conflict of interest being present and without any history of interaction. The researchers thus looked for explanations by which the simple occurrence of social categorization into groups leads to discrimination between groups. The key explanatory concept was seen to be *social identity* – that is, those aspects of an individual's self-image that derive from the social categories to which he or she belongs and the emotional and value significance of such membership. Social identity is seen as an important contributor to an individual's self-esteem or positive self-concept, a quality that it is assumed people are generally motivated to increase or maintain.

These considerations lead to four basic propositions of social identity theory: (1) individuals strive to maintain a positive self-concept and social identity, (2) membership in groups contributes to an individual's social identity, (3) evaluation of one's own group is based on social comparison with other groups, and (4) a positive social identity is based on favorable comparisons. The central hypothesis is that pressures to gain distinctiveness and to evaluate the ingroup positively lead to intergroup discrimination in the ingroup's favor. The theory thus underscores the central importance of group identity in both individual and intergroup functioning. In a sense, the basic need for social identity fuels the comparative process that is part of ethnocentric discrimination among groups. It is important to note, however, that the discrimination found in the research consists of only one side of the ethnocentric reaction, that is, ingroup favoritism. Outgroup rejection and hostility, the other side of ethnocentrism, does not commonly occur in this line of investigation.[25] Nonetheless, work on social identity theory does demonstrate the potential influence of self-esteem and social identity on intergroup relations and thereby on intergroup conflict. The striving to acquire and maintain a positive social identity through intergroup interaction is compatible with the statements of needs theorists that see recognition of identity as an essential requirement for human development. The possibility that the quest for identity can have negative as well as positive ramifications for intergroup relations will be given further attention in discussing the eclectic model of conflict.

The history of social psychology is permeated with a continuing interest in topics related to understanding and improving intergroup relations, from the early work on attitudes and ethnic stereotypes, through the studies on persuasive communication and propaganda, to an abiding interest in prejudice and discrimination. More directly, a number of theories of intergroup relations, focusing primarily on majority–minority issues, have been developed in an attempt to deal with fundamental questions, particularly the causation, escalation and resolution of intergroup conflict.[26] On the practical side, social psychologists have contributed to the development of principles of positive intergroup relations which attempt to specify the conditions under which different groups should be able to interrelate effectively in the societal, and presumably international, context. These principles emphasize the importance of each group having sufficient *identity*, autonomy and power in order to enter into an interdependent relationship in a secure, respectful and meaningful fashion.[27] A lack of sufficient identity and power on the part of the minority group results in ghettos if the groups remain separate or in mere desegregation with limited intergroup acceptance if the groups attempt to interrelate. When the minority group possesses adequate identity and power, separation maintains segregation and fuels competition while interrelation should lead to true integration and interdependence. The latter situation is seen as the ideal in which each group maintains its identity, autonomy and independence while at the same time participating in social and institutional interactions of an equal and cooperative nature. To move in this direction in the context of majority–minority relations, Pettigrew[28] and others propose a mixed enrichment and integration strategy, whereby minority ingroup development is fostered at the same time as meaningful interdependence is encouraged.

In terms of actual interaction between members of different groups, social psychologists have proposed a set of facilitative conditions for intergroup contact, based on a wide variety of studies from laboratory experiments to community surveys covering a diversity of intergroup relationships. These conditions specify the parameters within which intergroup interaction is more likely to lead to a reduction in prejudice and hostility among members of groups, usually from a majority–minority relationship, with the potential that intergroup conflict may ultimately be reduced. Reviews of research bolstered by social-psychological theorizing on attitudes and attitude change have led to a generally accepted set of conditions which represent the best distillation of wisdom that the field has to offer.[29] On-going theorizing and research in the area continues to support and refine the conditions and to demonstrate the wide variety of group relationships to which they apply.[30] In brief, the conditions which promote positive intergroup contact include:

1. High acquaintance potential which allows for members of different groups to come to know each other as persons and to break down stereotypes and barriers to interaction.
2. Equal status of participants or higher status of minority group members so that mutual respect is likely.
3. Supportive social norms and institutional expectations that influence participants toward positive qualities of interaction including friendliness, openness and trust.
4. A cooperative task and reward structure that involves participants in functionally important activities directed toward common goals.

To a degree, the facilitative conditions can be seen as congruent with individual and group needs which are seen as essential to viable intergroup relations and the resolution of intergroup conflict. The conditions are compatible with each group receiving the recognition and having the security it requires to support its unique *identity* and to place it in a position of equality within interdependent relationships with other groups.

The principles of intergroup relations and the facilitative conditions of intergroup contact have proved useful in understanding and providing policy recommendations for improving majority–minority relations in Canada and in New Zealand. Fisher and McNabb[31] documented and evaluated the work of a local committee charged with the task of improving Native/non-Native relations in a small Western Canadian city. Through a combination of participant observation and of interviews, a report was produced which described the functioning of the committee and provided a model for other municipalities interested in addressing Native/non-Native relations. Strong support was found for the basic approach of the committee – that is, integration that involved activities and programing wherein each group could maintain its unique identity and independence and yet come together to interrelate and collaborate on matters of common concern. The committee thus held intercultural dialogue conferences involving Native and non-Native participants in mutual sharing and analysis of identified problem areas. The committee then formed task forces with members of both groups working together on action research projects designed to increase Native security and autonomy and to reduce non-Native ignorance and prejudice. Pilot programs were initiated for Native participants and followed a strategy of independence and enrichment in order to foster their unique cultural identity; the ultimate goal was integration on the basis of equality. The principles of positive intergroup relations and contact drawn from social psychology appeared to make good sense, particularly to the Native members of the committee and its task forces.

Underlying principles from the social psychology of intergroup relations also proved useful in developing policy implications from an interview study of Maori–Pakeha relations in New Zealand.[32] Personal interviews with a select sample of concerned and knowledgeable bicultural individuals covered perceptions of the history of relations, of present and future relations and of an ideal relationship. The modal view of an ideal relationship involved self-determination for each group, intercultural understanding, equality, and biculturalism. Blending in the principles of intergroup relations and the facilitative conditions of intergroup contact led to a set of four interrelated policy implications. Significant and continuing support for

Maori self-determination was suggested as a means of ensuring autonomy and power over cultural affairs in educational, economic and political terms. Intercultural understanding should be increased through well-planned and well-executed intercultural education and training programs for all sectors of society based on the facilitative conditions of intergroup contact. A comprehensive and integrated policy of bilingualism, biculturalism and multiculturalism should be developed to make te reo Maori an official language, to integrate Maori cultural values into existing institutions, and to encourage the development of a multicultural society. Finally, efforts should be made toward the equitable distribution of societal resources so that group identity does not become fused with economic and thereby political status, thus compromising social justice and sowing the seeds for destructive and protracted conflict. Hence, the policy implications, while stressing interaction at the intergroup level, were also cognizant of the wider conditions in society that affect group identity, autonomy and security. In both of these cases, a strong theme was the recognition, protection and enhancement of the minority group's social and cultural identity in order to assure satisfactory intergroup relations and to work against escalation of the conflict.

Ethnically diverse societies are increasingly looking to policies of multiculturalism to prevent intergroup conflict and to enhance the cultural quality of life of citizens. In the early 1970s, the government of Canada, embarked on some innovative policy developments in multiculturalism, motivated partly by the need to place official French–English bilingualism in a wider and more acceptable context, Berry[33] provides a social-psychological analysis of Canadian multicultural policy by identifying issues and assumptions and by reviewing theory and research that is relevant to the policy. According to Berry, the policy

> seeks to improve intergroup harmony by encouraging all ethnic groups in Canada to develop themselves as vital communities, and by further encouraging their mutual interaction and sharing; the assumption, which is quite explicit in the policy, is that such group development will lead to a personal and collective sense of confidence, and this in turn will lead to greater ethnic tolerance.[34]

Multiculturalism is seen as a mechanism for reducing ethnic discrimination and for ultimately fostering equality, cultural richness, and unity at the national level.

Berry's analysis identifies four major elements of the policy and the interrelationships among them: own group maintenance and development, other group acceptance and tolerance, intergroup contact and sharing, and the learning of official languages. The policy eschews assimilation and actively encourages groups to maintain their unique cultural identity which in combination with intergroup sharing, will foster acceptance of other groups, that is, integration. At a societal level, full participation is facilitated by the learning of the official languages by all ethnic groups. When own group confidence is defined as a sense of security rather than ethnocentric self-glorification, it appears to be related to ethnic tolerance, thus supporting a key assumption of the policy. Furthermore, research generally demonstrates that the policy has a basis in the preferences and attitudes of Canadians and that the intergroup contact hypothesis generally holds true. There is thus a reasonable amount of congruence between multiculturalism policy and the social-psychological principles and evidence that exists. On the side of practical affairs, the government has committed considerable resources to the implementation of the policy through the Secretary of State for Multiculturalism and has recently brought forward new legislation to strengthen its commitment to positive intergroup relations within a national context.

AN ECLECTIC MODEL OF CONFLICT AS A CONTEXT FOR NEEDS THEORY

The work in humanistic and applied social psychology outlined above provides a number of supportive complements to the basic tenets of Needs Theory as it applies to intergroup conflict. These complements identify useful ideas and principles at the individual, group and intergroup levels of analysis. However, what is required to understand intergroup conflict is an initial focus directly at the intergroup level of analysis followed by the selective integration of relevant variables from other levels. This is the strategy followed by Fisher[35] in developing an eclectic model of intergroup conflict, which it is suggested, can provide a context for Needs Theory as one explanation of the etiology of intractable conflict.

The eclectic model of intergroup conflict has been developed by drawing on classic and contemporary contributions from the social sciences, particularly social psychology. The model is dynamic and process orientated and is based most strongly in Realistic Group Conflict Theory,[36] the field experiments and theorizing of Sherif,[37] and the phenomenological approach of Deutsch.[38]

Development of the model follows the approach to theory building proposed by Dubin[39] which is tailored to developing applied theories that have utility for the practitioner as well as the scholar. The approach also uses the philosophy of science on theory construction and involves a healthy combination of induction and deduction. It encompasses seven features of a theoretical model which are also the steps that a theoretician goes through in constructing a model. Simply put, the process of theory building moves from specifying the basic variables to the laws of interaction, the boundaries and system states, the propositions and empirical indicators, and finally moves to the hypotheses to be tested by research.

The initial model (see Figure 4.1) organizes the variables of interest by level of analysis (individual, group and intergroup) and by the point in time where the variable is formed or takes prominence (antecedents, orientations, processes and outcomes). Variables have been selected by their inclusion in previous theories or by their having stood the test of time in terms of being related to important elements of intergroup conflict. To capture the essence of intergroup conflict from a social-psychological perspective the three levels of analysis are seen as minimal. Antecedent variables exist prior to the manifest expression of conflict and are characteristics of the individuals, groups or intergroup relationship. Orientations are predispositions, perceptions, attitudes, or approaches that are expressed in the early stages of the conflict in ways that have a critical influence on its form and intensity. Processes are individual styles, group behaviors or intergroup interactions which both feed into and express the manifest conflict. Outcome variables are the effects of products of the conflict at the different levels of analysis. While the identification and placement of the variables is selective and somewhat arbitrary, it is suggested that by and large they capture a good deal of the essence of intergroup conflict.

Relationships among the variables (laws of interaction or principles) are represented in Figure 4.1 by lines and arrows connecting the variables. In the process of model building, principles are statements of general relationship that are deemed to hold for the entire range of values of the variables involved. Many of the principles specified in the model can be found in previous theories of intergroup conflict. However, the utility of the model lies in the attempt to integrate these statements into a more comprehensive, cohesive and yet concise whole. Thus, the principles that are included are seen as primary

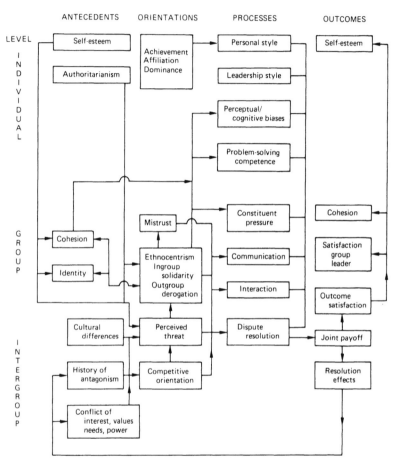

Figure 4.1   The eclectic model of intergroup conflict

rather than secondary, and the resulting model is seen as core rather than comprehensive. Principles are organized by level of analysis, and the model gives prominence to those principles at the intergroup level which deal most centrally with the causation, escalation and resolution of conflict.

PRINCIPLES OF RELEVANCE TO NEEDS THEORY AND SOCIAL IDENTITY

The first principle of the model is stated at the intergroup level and deals specifically yet broadly with the major sources of conflict between groups:

1. Real conflict of interests, values, needs, or power causes intergroup conflict.

This principle is initially rooted in Realistic Group Conflict Theory and the objective approach to conflict, but this is immediately complemented by the subjective sources of incompatible values and unmet needs. Conflict over material needs is encompassed in competing interests which most often relate to resource and/or position scarcity. Then, following the reasoning of Burton and Azar,[40] the model acknowledges that all social groups have fundamental needs for recognition, identity, security and participation which, when frustrated, result in an inexorable push for redress and satisfaction. This dynamic is seen as particularly useful in explaining the large number of communal and international conflicts in the world that are protracted and apparently unsolvable. In addition, a need for power, either as part of the maximization dynamic of social systems[41] or as the mechanism by which interests, values or needs are obtained, is a further source in the etiology of conflict. All of these sources can be summed up under the concept of incompatible goals.

Additional principles at the intergroup level which emphasize the role of perceived threat and ethnocentrism explicate the manner in which the initial differences escalate into a destructive social interaction.

2. Real conflict causes a mutually competitive orientation and reciprocal competition interaction.
3. Real conflict, cultural differences, a history of antagonism and competitive orientation and interaction cause perceived threat.
4. Perceived threat causes ethnocentrism including ingroup solidarity and outgroup hostility.
5. Competitive orientation, perceived threat, and ethnocentrism escalate conflict through ineffective communication, inadequate coordination, contentious tactics and reduced productivity.

In relation to essential needs for recognition, identity and security, any actions of the other group that are seen to limit or deny these basic rights will be interpreted as particularly threatening. Such threats will fuel ethnocentrism in the sense of ingroup loyalty and glorification with a concurrent increase in outgroup derogation and hostility. The intergroup interaction will further deteriorate and the likelihood of addressing basic needs will be further reduced: the more the conflict escalates, the more intractable it will become.

At the group and individual levels, two principles specifically relate the concept of identity to perceived threat and ethnocentrism, which are essential elements of the escalatory process, and to self-esteem, which is a widely acknowledged component of personality.

6. Group identity and group cohesion are positively and reciprocally related to ethnocentrism.

7. Self-esteem is positively related to group identity and cohesion, and negatively related to perceived threat.

The first principle at the group level is the competitor to the ethic of multiculturalism noted earlier. If group identity is assured – for example, by government policy – then confidence in identity and a sense of security can lead to respect for other groups. However, in the absence of assurances, group identity may begin to feed ingroup glorification and solidarity which tends to be related to more negative attitudes toward other groups. Especially when group security is threatened, this type of ethnocentric reaction is likely. The second principle, stated at the individual level, ties in part of the work on social identity theory in that group identity is linked to individual self-esteem. Group identity is seen as supportive of self-esteem in that when the group is threatened, the members are threatened in a personal sense. Threat toward the fundamental need for identity is thus seen to be operative at both the individual and group levels, thereby increasing the power of this dynamic in situations of intergroup conflict.

These considerations lead to a perplexing possibility for Needs Theory in relation to conflict resolution: the need for identity may have a "dark side" which in seeking satisfaction escalates and perpetuates conflict rather than helping to resolve it. According to social identity theory, individuals will strive to enhance their self-esteem and enhance their social identity through invidious comparisons with other groups, and create negative ethnocentric attitudes. In order to maintain and increase a positive group distinctiveness and identity, the individual will make intergroup comparisons which enhance the qualities of the ingroup and denigrate the characteristics of the outgroup. These types of linkages between self-esteem, ingroup glorification and outgroup derogation can also be traced back to psychoanalytic theory and theories of personality based on the self-concept. Levine and Campbell[42] point out that Freud saw ethnocentrism as a form of narcissim at the group level, wherein ingroup love as a form of self-love facilitated the displacement of aggression from the ingroup onto hated outgroups. Variations of "self-esteem theory" also provide explanations of how groups protect self-esteem through the enhancement of ingroup virtues and the exaggeration of outgroup deficiencies. Through a variety of mechanisms, self-esteem and the need for a positive social identity can result in perceptual distortions, emotional hostility and negative comments directed toward outgroups. Thus the need for identity, which is seen as a positive aspect of the human condition and a requirement for development, may also operate as a negative driver in the causation and escalation of intergroup conflict.

There is at least one possible direction for Needs Theory in seeking a resolution of this potential contradiction – affirming the need for identity as basically a positive force in human affairs, but accepting that it may be met through positive or negative satisfiers. Policies which foster a realistic pride and satisfaction in one's group without invidious comparisons to others are much different from a fanatical jingoism that requires the denigration if not the oppression of others. In other words, the need for identity can be met either through multiculturalism or ethnocentrism, internationalism or nationalism, with the latter options being much less desirable from a humanistic point of view. This approach requires the acknowledgement both by Needs Theory and the field of conflict resolution of the pivotal position of the identity group. Human needs are largely satisfied through the identity group, which in some cases and times is coterminus with the nation-state. Certain needs, such as identity, can be satisfied only through the identity group, while other needs, such as security and freedom and their related rights, can be guaranteed only by the nation-state, sometimes with the assistance of the international system. The challenge for workable policies and structures for multiculturalism and for internationalism, particularly in the area of human rights, is all too apparent.

SYSTEM STATES OF THE MODEL IN RELATION TO NEEDS THEORY

System states are conditions of the system being modeled in which all units take on distinctive values that persist over some period of time. The model may therefore exhibit a number of conditions within its boundaries that are not identical and which assist in capturing the reality of the system in question. The transitions among system states and the recurrence of system states constitute the dynamic flow of the model. The existence of system states allows for the asking of important analytical questions about the conditions and values of variables under which a given system state will persist or change to another one.

In the eclectic model, two system states (low intensity and high intensity conflict) and two forms of transition (escalation and de-escalation) are posited (see Figure 4.2). The pivotal variable is intensity, which is defined both as the psychological investment of the parties and the objective difference between winning and losing. The transitions of escalation and deescalation can be described by a set of propositions which are based on principles primarily at the intergroup level of analysis.

In the system state of low intensity conflict, the indicators of intensity include low to moderate threat, ethnocentrism and mistrust as well as a small number of issues. In relation to Needs Theory, the important point is that in low intensity conflict, the basic differences are over significant interests and values, but the parties do not see their fundamental needs for identity or security threatened, nor do they approach the conflict as a power struggle for their very existence. Representatives or boundary role persons who interact over the conflict adopt a mixed competitive/cooperative stance which looks for an acceptable mix of costs and benefits in the outcomes. Interest conflicts over resource or position scarcity are thus likely to be settled by traditional forms of dispute management including direct negotiation, mediation or arbitration. However, one essential characteristic of low intensity conflict is that it can all too easily be shifted to high intensity conflict through the typical responses which individuals and groups display toward situations of difference. Many of these processes of escalation are covered in the principles of the eclectic model.

In high intensity conflict, the primary sources are the denial and frustration of basic needs and the struggle for power: both groups

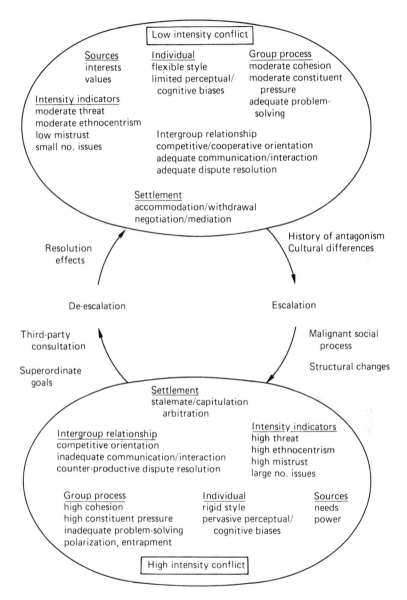

Figure 4.2   System states of the eclectic model

perceive that their inexorable needs for identity, recognition, security and self-determination are being threatened or thwarted by the other. This fundamental threat requires that they mobilize every available form of influence in order to acquire or maintain the satisfaction of needs that are non-negotiable. This situation may occur in one of two ways. First, low intensity conflicts which begin over interest and value differences may escalate to the point where fundamental needs are threatened where they were not threatened before. This is particularly true where threat escalates to a level where each (or one) party is now threatening the other's very right to existence – at least as a social entity if not a physical one – and therefore obviously threatening its security and identity. This is the case, for example, with the conflict between the superpowers wherein value and to a lesser extent resource conflict have escalated to the point where each threatens the other's very identity and existence and wherein peaceful coexistence with such an alien system seems unacceptable to either. Second, some high intensity need conflicts may be created at the outset when groups are placed in positions where the existence of one appears to threaten the existence of the other. This is especially true in cases where identities are fused with overlapping territory. For example, in the process of decolonization, the power vacuum created by the withdrawal of the imperialist nation has often created a situation where groups previously in competition for resources are now threatening each other's identity and/or security. Examples are India and Pakistan or Sri Lanka. Similarly, the creation of Israel produced a situation where the security and identity (and in a sense, sovereignty) of the Palestinians was immediately threatened at the very time that the Israelis were attempting to establish these same conditions for themselves. A conflict thus exists where the recognition of one group by the other seems automatically to deny the legitimacy of the first group. Such situations indicate that the inexorable press for the fulfillment of basic needs will continue to have a significant impact on international relations and the flow of history. In addition, these situations demonstrate why high intensity conflicts are typically protracted and apparently insoluble, and are not amenable to the usual methods of dispute management. Thus, if settlement occurs in some temporary fashion, it will likely be through capitulation of one party or through arbitration by a powerful third party. However, such settlements will deal only with the surface issues relating to interests, and the problem of not addressing fundamental needs will guarantee that destructive interaction will occur in the future. As

Burton[43] has pointed out, only full analysis of the conflict within a problem-solving approach which works toward resolution is likely to be successful in addressing high intensity conflicts. If it is possible to address concerns about needs in this manner, the conflict may be de-escalated to the point where differences related to interests and values can then be addressed through traditional dispute management.

CONCLUSION

Humanistic psychology and applied social psychology yield a number of conceptual and theoretical complements that provide direct and indirect support for Needs Theory as capturing the essence of what it means to be human. In particular, the frustration and satisfaction of the need for identity are seen as central elements in the causation, escalation and potential resolution of intergroup and international conflict. In addition, the social-psychological study of conflict as expressed in the eclectic model supports the validity of Needs Theory as an important avenue for understanding and dealing with intractable social conflict.

The model is eclectic in terms of drawing on a wide range of sources, but it is essential rather than comprehensive in terms of the variables, relationships, and processes that are specified. In that vein, Needs Theory is seen as part of the core explanation of protracted intergroup conflict in communal and international settings.

The analysis has clear implications for the strong support of problem-solving approaches to conflict resolution as a means of establishing viable intergroup and multicultural relations in which the fundamental needs of individuals and groups are effectively addressed. Destructive high intensity conflict may thereby be de-escalated and resolved or in some cases prevented from reaching the point of violence and increased intransigence.

NOTES AND REFERENCES

* Portions of this chapter are taken from R. J. Fisher, *The Social Psychology of Intergroup and International Conflict Resolution*, Springer-Verlaag Publishers, New York, 1990, with permission of the publisher.

1. P. Kurtz, editorial, "A Definition of Humanism," *Humanist* 28 (1) (1968).
2. P. Kurtz, editorial, "The Moral Revolution: Toward a Critical Radicalism," *Humanist* 31 (1971): pp. 4–6.
3. J. F. T. Bugental (ed.), *Challenges of Humanistic Psychology* (New York; McGraw-Hill, 1967).
4. J. F. T. Bugental, "The Humanistic Ethic – The Individual in Psychotherapy as a Societal Change Agent," *Journal of Humanistic Psychology* 10 (1971): 11–26.
5. A. H. Maslow, "A Theory of Human Motivation," *Psychological Review* 50 (1943): 370–96; A. H. Maslow, *Motivation and Personality* (New York: Harper & Row, 1970) 2nd edn.
6. K. Lederer (ed.) with Johan Galtung and David Antal, *Human Needs: A Contribution to the Current Debate* (Cambridge, MA.: Oelgeschlager, Gunn & Hain, 1980).
7. J. Galtung, "The Basic Needs Approach," in Lederer (ed.), *Human Needs*.
8. Galtung, "The Basic Needs Approach."
9. O. Klineberg, "Human Needs: A Social-Psychological Approach," in Lederer (ed.), *Human Needs*.
10. Klineberg, "Human Needs."
11. H. Cantril, "A Fresh Look at the Human Design," in J. F. T. Bugental (ed.), *Challenges of Humanistic Psychology* (New York: McGraw-Hill, 1967): 14–17.
12. Cantril, "A Fresh Look at the Human Design."
13. R. J. Fisher, *Social Psychology: An Applied Approach* (New York: St Martin's Press, 1982).
14. R. J. Fisher, "Third Party Consultation: A Problem-Solving Approach for De-escalating International Conflict," in J. P. Maas and R. A. C. Stewart (eds), *Toward A World of Peace: People Create Alternatives* (Suva, Fiji: The University of the South Pacific, 1986).
15. H. C. Kelman, *A Time to Speak* (San Francisco: Jossey-Bass, 1969).
16. K. D. Benne, "The Moral Orientation of Laboratory Methods of Education and Changing," in K. D. Benne, L. P. Bradford, J. R. Gibb and R. J. Lippitt (eds), *The Laboratory Method of Changing and Learning: Theory and Application* (Palo Alto, CA: Science and Behavior Books, 1975); R. J. Fisher, *The Social Psychology of Intergroup Conflict*, from manuscript to be published (New York: Springer-Verlag, 1990).
17. O. Nudler, "Human Needs: A Sophisticated Holistic Approach," in *Lederer* (ed.), *Human Needs*.
18. Nudler, "Human Needs."
19. Galtung, "The Basic Needs Approach."
20. Klineberg, "Human Needs."
21. Klineberg, "Human Needs."
22. Galtung, "The Basic Needs Approach."
23. M. Sherif, *In Common Predicament: Social Psychology, Intergroup Conflict and Cooperation* (Boston: Houghton M.:.lin, 1966).
24. H. Tajfel, "Experiments in Intergroup Discrimination," *Scientific American*, 223(5) (1970): 96–102; H. Tajfel and J. C. Turner, "The Social

Identity Theory of Intergroup Behavior," in S. Worchel and W. G. Austin (eds), *Psychology of Intergroup Relations* (Chicago: Nelson-Hall, 1986) 2nd edn.

25. M. B. Brewer, "Ingroup Bias in the Minimal Intergroup Situation: A Cognitive Motivational Analysis," *Psychological Bulletin*, 86 (1979): 307–324.

26. D. M. Taylor and F. M. Moghaddam, *Theories of Intergroup Relations: International and Social Psychological Perspectives* (New York: Praeger, 1987).

27. As in T. F. Pettigrew, *Racially Separate or Together?* (New York: McGraw-Hill, 1971).

28. Pettigrew, *Racially Separate*.

29. Y. Amir, "Contact Hypothesis in Ethnic Relations," *Psychological Bulletin*, 71 (1969): 319–42; Y. Amir, "The Role of Intergroup Contact in Change of Prejudice and Ethnic Relations," in P. A. Katz (ed.), *Towards the Elimination of Racism* (New York: Pergamon, 1976); G. W. Allport, *The Nature of Prejudice* (Cambridge, MA: Addison-Wesley, 1954); S. W. Cook, "A Preliminary Study of Attitude Change," in M. Wertheimer (ed.), *Confrontation: Psychology and the Problems of Today* (Glenview, IL: Scott, Foresman, 1970).

30. M. Hewstone and R. Brown (eds), *Contact and Conflict in Intergroup Encounters* (Oxford: Basil Blackwell, 1986).

31. R. J. Fisher and H. McNabb, *A Social Services Planning Approach to Native/nonNative Relations in Saskatoon* (Ottawa: Federation of Canadian Municipalities, 1979).

32. R. J. Fisher, "Conflict and Collaboration in Maori–Pakeha Relations: Ka Taea Anoo e Taatou te Whenua Houkura," *Occasional Paper 20* (Hamilton, New Zealand: Centre for Maori Studies and Research, University of Waikato, 1984).

33. J. W. Berry, "Multicultural Policy in Canada: A Social Psychological Analysis," *Canadian Journal of Behavioral Science*, 16 (1984): 353–70.

34. Berry, "Multicultural Policy": 353.

35. R. J. Fisher, "Approaching the Enigma of Intergroup Conflict: Social Psychological Theory, Research and Practice," invited lecture, Carleton University, Ottawa (May 1987); Fisher, *The Social Psychology of Intergroup Conflict*.

36. D. T. Campbell, "Ethnocentrism and Other Altruistic Motives," in D. LeVine (ed.) *Nebraska Symposium on Motivation*, 13 (Lincoln: University of Nebraska Press, 1965); R. A. LeVine, and D. T. Campbell, *Ethnocentrism: Theories of Conflict, Ethnic Attitudes and Group Behavior* (New York: Wiley, 1972).

37. M. Sherif, O. J. Harvey, B. J. White, W. R. Hood and C. W. Sherif, *Intergroup Conflict and Cooperation: The Robbers' Cave Experiment* (Norman: University of Oklahoma Book Exchange, 1961); Sherif, *In Common Predicament*.

38. M. Deutsch, *The Resolution of Conflict: Constructive and Destructive Processes* (New Haven: Yale University Press, 1973); M. Deutsch, "The Prevention of World War III: A Psychological Perspective," *Political Psychology*, 4 (1983): 3–32.

39. R. Dubin, *Theory Building* (New York: The Free Press, 1969); R. Dubin, "Theory Building in Applied Areas," in M. D. Dunnette (ed.), *Handbook of Industrial and Organizational Psychology* (Chicago: Rand-McNally, 1976).
40. E. E. Azar, "Protracted International Conflict: Ten Propositions," *International Interactions*, 12 (1985): 59–70; E. E. Azar, and J. W. Burton (eds), *International Conflict Resolution: Theory and Practice* (Brighton, England: Wheatsheaf, 1986); J. W. Burton, *Deviance, Terrorism and War: The Process of Solving Unsolved Social and Political Problems* (New York: St. Martin's Press, 1979); J. W. Burton, "The History of International Conflict Resolution," *International Interactions*, 12 (1985): 45–70.
41. D. Katz, "Nationalism and Strategies of International Conflict Resolution," in H. C. Kelman (ed.), *International Behavior: A Social-Psychological Analysis* (New York: Holt, Rinehart & Winston, 1965).
42. LeVine and Campbell, *Ethnocentrism*.
43. Burton, "The History of Conflict Resolution," *Resolving Deep-Rooted Conflict: A Handbook* (Lanham, MD, University Press of America, 1987).

II
Needs and Conflict Resolution

5 Conflict and Needs Research
Katrin Gillwald*

According to Burton, in his opening remarks to our conference, the phenomenon called deep rooted conflict "involves cases of conflict . . . that arise out of demands on individuals to make certain adjustments in behavior that are unacceptable, and probably beyond human tolerance and capabilities." This definition might well be read as a paraphrase to conflicts over needs. It is therefore worthwhile to consider the question of whether needs research can help resolve deep rooted conflicts.

The present chapter deals with theoretical, methodological, and empirical issues of needs research that contribute to the explanation and handling of conflict. The conclusions are quite simple: (1) needs research is capable of guiding clarification and creativity for conflict mitigation in a limited and describable number of cases; and (2) the resolution of deep rooted conflicts goes beyond the capacity of needs theory and methodology. The development of these inferences is more complicated, including a home-made controversy between two schools of needs theory.

AN ADEQUATE NEEDS CONCEPT

Many prominent scholars and social scientists going back as far as Artistotle and Thomas Aquinas have elaborated categorical systems of human needs. The significance that their efforts lend to the concept of needs and the great compatibility and mutual transformability of these systems permit a demanding definition of needs: needs are all the exigencies of human existence and development and are an important driving force thereof.

As a matter of fact, this definition reflects one of the two "schools" in needs research, which have been described in greater detail elsewhere.[1] It suggests a universal character of needs as well as their omnipresence in principle. It is implied that needs are expressed as human sensibilities, degrees of awareness, and patterns of behavior.

This, however, is the case neither for all needs at the same time, nor for individual needs permanently. The overt structure of needs is thus individually and contextually variable.

The universal needs concept cannot be falsified. Needs are non-temporal and non-spatial entities; their methodological status is that of theoretical constructs. The methodological status of categorical systems of needs is that of heuristic models. Needs cannot therefore, be measured directly, they can be measured only on the basis of their manifestations.

Furthermore, the universal needs concepts is axiomatic. It is based on an undisguised, but interpersonally and interculturally indisputable, normative, humanist, and idealist view of human beings and the world. By definition it rules out so-called negative needs, suggesting that needs are only one among other driving forces behind human behavior (others being personality traits and environmental conditions). It also contains methodological devices for identifying (and discrediting) certain counter-productive satisfiers. Contrary to popular belief, not only are they distinct phenomena, their contents are not completely identical.[2]

While the universal needs concept may thus be attractive from a holistic and ethical perspective, it is also theoretically substantive. For example, it has the potential of providing criteria for analytically separating needs from related and neighboring concepts. The most important of these concepts are desires (or wants), defined as the manifestations of needs, and satisfiers, defined as the needs-fulfilling devices.

The situational/subjective concept of needs deals only with what, in universal terminology, is called desires. A situational and subjective character of needs, and thus their propensity to change and adaptation, is postulated. In this concept the latency potential of needs is neglected. Maslow's analyses,[3] however, clearly reveal the situationally and environmentally determined change between the latent and manifest statuses of needs. On the basis of extensive clinical studies, Maslow arrived at the conclusion that humans seek to satisfy their physiological needs above all else. Only then do security needs become relevant, followed in order of urgency by needs for belonging and love, esteem, and self-actualization (the "Hierarchy of Basic Needs").

In general, the universal school of thought on needs may be preferable because of its theoretical provisions. Specifically, it is suited to discriminating between avoidable and plausible conflicts.

The subsequent discussion will therefore be based on the universal needs concept. For the sake of simplifying the argument, however, the focus will be confined to needs and satisfiers. Needs manifestations – i.e., desires – will not be considered, for desires are closely linked to existing or creatable satisfiers.

A LINE OF CONFLICT

About twenty years ago – in connection with the student movement of 1968 – fierce disputes flared up over needs, particularly over their basis in truth and their objectivity. Looking back, it seems as though the focus on the debates that were triggered was inappropriate. From the point of view of the theory of science, conflicts over needs in terms of their evaluation as such are nonsense. Truth and objectivity are not among the virtues required of methodological constructs or heuristic models. All they are expected to be is a conceptual and explanatory aid.

At the level of needs, conflicts should arise only in the establishment of priorities if the appropriate satisfiers involved are limited. The proper subjects of conflict are thus the satisfiers. It would be much easier to separate avoidable conflicts from plausible conflicts, however, if needs and satisfiers could be distinguished.

Such a distinction has heretofore been used only in individual cases, if at all, and the label of needs has been widely used. The ostensibly fluid transition between needs and satisfiers may abet a certain arbitrariness in this practice because there are categories of needs and satisfiers at each of many different levels of abstraction. Mallmann[4] has analyzed and summarized this diversity in terms of needs, drawing on various categorical systems of human needs elaborated by other authors (see Table 5.1) and on his own systems analyses. What elevates Mallmann's typology from the status of a mere collection of needs to a virtual system of needs is its intrarelation through the satisfiers (which are not included in Table 5.1; see the first paragraph in the next section below, which deals with the complexity of needs). Satisfiers have not yet been typologized in the way Mallmann dealt with needs, but they, too, apparently cover a wide range of abstraction levels. The number of overlapping categories alternately labeled as needs or satisfiers is presumably high. The point is to define what, on this continuum, is still a need in the interface categories of needs and satisfiers and what is already a

Table 5.1 **A human needs system**

Classification of needs according to categories of needs / Classification of needs according to categories of satisfiers that mainly satisfy them	Personal	Extrapersonal	
	(A) Psychosomatic or intrahuman	(B) Psychosocial or interhuman	(C) Psychoecological or extrahuman
I. Maintenance	(a) Nutrition, rest, exercise	(b) Earning-work, reproduction, social habitability	(c) Shelter, clothing physical habitability
II. Protection	(a) Prevention, cure, defense	(b) Prevention restitution defense	(c) Prevention, restitution, defense
IV. Love	(a) Belief in one self, self love, identity	(b) Friendship, sexual and family love	(c) Rooting, attachment
VII. Understanding	(a) Psycholization, introspection, study	(b) Socialization, education, information, observation	(c) Habitatization, observation
IX. Autonomous participation	(a) Liberty, independence, autonomy	(b) Autonomous participation in decision	(c) Autonomous participation in management
XII. Recreation	(a) Self recreation	(b) Social recreation	(c) Recreation in the habitat
XIV. Creation	(a) Creation by oneself	(b) Creation of social environments	(c) Creation of habitational environments
XVII. Meaning	(a) Self-realization	(b) Historic, prospective and religious meaning	(c) Weltanschauung
XIX. Synergy	(a) Authenticity equanimity, security humility	(b) Solidarity, justice, altruism, generosity, responsibility	(c) Beauty, ecological equilibrium

Left-hand groupings:

III Subsistence · V Security · VIII Belongingness · X Dignity · XIII Development · XV Renewal · XVIII Transcendence · XX Maturity

VI Existence · XI Coexistence · XVI Growth · XXI Perfection

XXII Living · XXIII Actualizing · XXIV Health

Source: Mallmann.[5]

satisfier, or vice versa.

The lowest level of abstraction in the synopsis by Mallmann is what he calls "Classification of Needs According to Satisfiers that Mainly Satisfy Them." It is next to them that the line is to be drawn; categories of satisfiers begin at a lower level of abstraction to be imagined thereafter. The reason is that the categories listed by Mallman can be considered to represent universal human requirements – i.e., needs – and that the categories at levels of abstraction lower than the one included in Mallmann's table would be a function of geographic, historical, and social variations – i.e., satisfiers.

For example, Mallmann lists "Earning-Work" in category (B)I, not "gainful employment." Most people must work to secure their livelihoods – or, in the Marxist interpretation, to appropriate nature. One form of work typical for societies based on a division of labor is the activity oriented to wages and income – gainful employment. Gainful employment (and its dark side, unemployment) were unknown to closed tribal and barter societies, and dropouts from industrialized societies have recently been seeking alternatives.

Accordingly, gainful employment is a function of place, time, and situation. In other words, it is a historically and societally defined means of satisfying the need for work. Within the category of satisfiers, one can further specify a certain kind of gainful employment having particular characteristics of a substantive, organizational, or other nature. Not only are such specifications historically and socially conditioned, they also relate to needs beyond work, needs like "Creation" (category (A)XIV) or "Recreation" (category (A)(C)XII) in Mallmann's synopsis. One can think of other examples to demonstrate the viability of this distinction between needs and satisfiers, such as different family and partnership models, all created in their space and time in order to meet the friendship, sexual, and family-love needs.

For a tentative classification within the realm of satisfiers, one could say that the more abstract categories of satisfiers primarily comprise historically shaped social institutions and deeply rooted conventions – the very categories upon which the 1968 leftists focused demands for fundamental changes. By contrast, the less abstract categories of satisfiers relate to ways of life specific to individuals or social classes. The general criticism by the 1968 leftists in this context was based on the insight that ways of life are, of course, also historically and socially shaped and that the chances for having a life in which needs are satisfied can be improved by changing the historical and social conditions (as noted above). The specific leftist reproach of manipulation was leveled at the strategy that the market inevitably breeds in the consumer-goods industry: the suggestion that material satisfiers in particular are well suited to meeting needs.

The clear delineation between needs and satisfiers inspires a reinterpretation of the scientific discussion about latent/manifest, objective/subjective, true/false, and material/non-material needs that was taken up approximately a decade ago.[6] The differentiation now made is that "latent" and "manifest" are statuses of needs and that "true" and "objective" are irrelevant criteria with respect to needs (as already discussed).

The attribute "false" is likewise not applicable to needs; at the most, it can refer to satisfiers. The terminological pair "material" (referring to things) and "non-material" (referring to knowledge, meanings and relations) applies to needs as well as to satisfiers: the higher the abstraction level, the more likely it is for needs usually to be non-material. In conflict treatment, however, the more important distinction is that between material and non-material satisfiers. At this level, subjective notions justifiably dominate, and except for the setting of general priorities, the choice and distribution of the satisfiers is the logical place for conflicts.

CONFLICTS OVER SATISFIERS

In the terminology of needs research, the diversity of human life is described as the "Complexity of Needs." Generally, a need can be met by a number of different material or non-material satisfiers, just as individual material or non-material types of satisfaction can serve to meet different needs.[7] Theoretically, then, there would seem to be unlimited possibilities in the choice and combination of apparently suitable satisfiers.

In reality, however, the choice of satisfiers is restricted, the competition for them intense, and the potential for conflict accordingly great. In the confines of spatial and temporal reality, all satisfiers are scarce. Economic political, social, and cultural conditions and conventions limit the freedom of choice. Competition and potential conflict exist in both material terms (as a distributional issue) and in non-material terms (as a matter of attitudes). Burton[8] associates material conflicts with conflicts of interest and non-material conflicts with value conflicts.

The theoretical significance of this association lies in linking the concept of needs with two other key social-science concepts – interests, and values. Unlike needs, they are temporal; like satisfiers, they are historically determined. This connection thereby endows the concept of needs with a dynamic dimension. The practical significance of this association lies in the various numbers of "degrees of freedom" that arise from these links. Some of the material satisfiers are based on resources that are exhaustible in principle, with the focus of interest being correspondingly rigid. Some of the values may be persistent, but non-material satisfiers are based on human resources that are inexhaustible in principle. Burton's train of thought gives rise to an approach to reducing occasions for conflicts by seeking ways to substitute non-material satisfiers for material ones.

EMPIRICAL AND FORECASTING POTENTIALS

When it comes to the contribution that empirical "needs" research can make to conflict treatment, the focus is, logically, on satisfiers. Concerning present situations, the type and scope of the satisfiers used are identified through observations, and secondary analyses. The contribution that satisfiers make to meeting needs is reconstructed primarily from results obtained through surveys on satisfaction with available satisfiers and on satisfiers that are aspired to.

Empirical research can help to increase rationality in conflicts over satisfiers in two extreme cases – unconscious or repressed denials, and counter-productive satisfiers. One example of the first case is an investigation into the social acceptability of environmental impacts.[9] In a blind experiment regarding tolerance for environmental impacts, a ceiling was found beyond which psychosomatic as well as psychosocial needs were frustrated – without the persons in question being necessarily or totally aware of this link. In such cases, scientists can raise awareness and urge corresponding political action. The same is true in the case of counter-productive satisfiers. Schaefer,[10] for example, demonstrated the clear inadequacy of excessive food consumption and drinking with respect to needs.

In most cases, however, a choice of satisfiers is only a question of their higher or lower suitability. Then science has little to say – partly for lack of interpersonally transferable sensibilities, partly for reasons of otherwise undue interventions into subjective matters of the individuals concerned.

Empirical needs research focused on the present enjoys the advantage that the conditions governing needs satisfaction are known and that the subjects under study are physically present. Prospective needs research must rely instead on sound models of future conditions that will shape the future manifestation and satisfaction of needs. Although such research is impaired by several imponderables, it is worthwhile for the sake of reducing foreseeable conflicts over satisfiers.

For the purpose of illustrating future manifestations of needs, prospective needs research can make use of homeostatic theories of regulation, learning and reference-group theories, theories of diversification, and the theorem of diminishing return.[11] Lastly, it is advisable to look at currently experimental ways of living for their satisfaction effect and perspective.

Through prospective needs research functional equivalents of satisfiers that seem to be adequate under present conditions must be designed for altered conditions. It goes beyond customary forecasts of demand in that special attention is given to non-material satisfiers that will be necessary, not only or primarily to material ones. It is particularly important for such future-oriented blueprints to consider simultaneously the whole range of needs categories and a set of related satisfiers. Selective and priority-setting approaches along the lines of Maslow's Hierarchy of Basic Needs (see above) for example, would inevitably lead to misconceptions and scarcities of satisfiers and preprogram conflicts; they are justifiable only in crisis situations.

In terms of conflict regulation, one clear limit to needs research oriented to the present and needs research oriented to the future is that both can deal only with cumulative concerns. Needs theory and methodology offer no instruments with which to regulate competing, conflicting, or mutually exclusive concerns. In other words, needs research offers no tool for conflict resolution. Its utmost contribution could be that of developing and promoting creativity in finding compatible satisfiers.

CONCLUSION

In the needs concept put forward in the present chapter, conflicts over the legitimacy or justification of single needs or categorial systems of needs are regarded as nonsense for reasons originating in the theory of science. Vice versa, needs research has nothing to contribute to a resolution of deep rooted conflicts concerning needs apart from raising an awareness of the universality of needs – or, at most, of the indispensability of mutual tolerance among human beings.

By contrast, conflicts over satisfiers are plausible because they are subject to individual and group interests and values as well as to differences and changes over space and time. Needs research can help to clarify acute conflicts over satisfiers through status analyses and to minimize future conflicts over satisfiers through forecasts of the ways in which needs will be manifested. In both cases, innovative thinking and creativity can be developed and promoted in order to discover inexhaustible and/or compatible satisfiers that make conflict baseless.

NOTES AND REFERENCES

* The author extends her thanks to her colleagues Martin Diewald, Hans-Joachim Fietkau, and Bernhard Glaeser for their discussion of and comments on previous drafts of this contribution.
1. Katrin Lederer, "Needs Methodology: The Environmental Case," in Katrin Lederer (ed.), with Johan Galtung and David Antal, *Human Needs: A Contribution to the Current Debate* (Cambridge MA: Oelgeschlager, Gunn & Hain, 1980): 259–78.
2. As will be demonstrated later under "Empirical and Forecasting Potentials." See also Katrin Gillwald, "Prospektive Bedürfnisforschung," paper presented at the 4th Berliner Bedürfniskolloquium, organized by the Institut für Soziologie und Sozialpoliltik der Akademie der Wissenschaften der DDR, Linowsee (14–18 November 1988).
3. Abraham H. Maslow, "A Theory of Human Motivation," *The Pychological Review*, 50 (1943): 370–96.
4. Carlos A. Mallmann, "Society, Needs, and Rights: A Systemic Approach," in Lederer (ed.), *Human Needs*: 37–54.
5. Mallmann, "Society, Needs": 40–1.
6. Lederer, "Needs Methodology."
7. Konrad K. Waltuch, *Entwicklungsproportionen und Befriedigung der Bedürfnisse* (Berlin: Die Wirtschaft, 1972).
8. John W. Burton, "Analytical Problem-Solving Conflict Resolution," paper presented at a Human Needs conference at Warrenton, Virginia (July 1988).
9. Katrin Gillwald, *Umweltqualität als sozialer Faktor. Zur Sozialpsychologie der natürlichen Umwelt* (Frankfurt am Main; New York: Campus, 1983); Katrin Gillwald, "Environmental Elasticity – Social and Psycho-

logical Effects of Environmental Deterioration," in Allan Schnaiberg, Nicholas Watts and Klaus Zimmerman (eds), *Distributional Conflicts in Environmental Resource Policy* (Aldershot, England: Gower, 1986): 49–58.

10. Hans Schaefer, "Bedürfnisse und Bedarf des Menschen in medizinscher Sicht," in Simon Moser, Gunter Ropohl and Walther C. Zimmerli (eds), *Die "wahren" Bedürfnisse oder Wissen wir, was wir brauchen?* (Basel; Stuttgart: Schwabe, 1978): 19–24.

11. Manfred Murck, "Voraussetzungen und Methoden planungsrelvanter Bedürfnisforschung," in Herbert Stachowiak, Thomas Ellwein, Theo Herrmann and Kurt Stapf (eds), *Bedürfnisse, Werte und Normen im Wandel*, vol. 2 (Munich: Fink/Schöningh 1982): 131–62; Karl Otto Hondrich and Randolph Vollmer, (eds), *Bedürfnisse. Stabilität und Wandel* (Opladen: Westdeutscher Verlag, 1983).

6 Social Conflicts and Needs Theories: Some Observations

Ramashray Roy

I

The goal of a perfect social order, a frictionless society, composed of well developed individuals, is very old. This goal has yielded venerable social theories through the ages, each theory claiming for itself the exclusive wisdom of speaking for the troubled humanity and blueprinting its emancipation. But changing human sensibilities, circumstances and concerns have robbed these theories of their utility. Out of the ruins and scattered debris of these theories has now emerged, Sphinx-like, a new theory claiming to put an end to all theories by indicating how a perfect society of perfect individuals could be realized. This is human needs theory.

Several versions of human needs theory exist. However, common to them all is the assumption of certain universal needs rooted in the biological conditions of man. True, the means of satisfying these needs are culturally conditioned or determined. But needs themselves are innate and form a part of the biologically transmitted framework within which personality develops. If these needs are not fulfilled or fulfilled in an unsatisfactory way, individual development is distorted and mutilated and the personality becomes crippled. If this happens on a large scale, society becomes conflict ridden; conflict marks relationships among individuals, groups, within nations and between nations.

In order, therefore, to purge conflicts from society, needs theories emphasize the absolute necessity of satisfying basic human needs. They do so by marshaling two arguments. First, they insist that it is only on the basis of the fulfillment of basic human needs that the possibility of creative, whole, free, sociable, and multilaterally developed persons can become real. Second, even if the goal is not the individual happiness, needs-satisfaction is a *sine qua non* of a harmonious society.

In John Burton's words:

> The behavioral interest in human needs is not in making the individual happier, though this may be the outcome. It is in determining the conditions necessary for social organisations to survive harmoniously. Problem-solving at the social level – be it the small groups, the nation-state or interactions between states – is possible only by processes that take the needs of the individual as the basis for analysing and planning.[1]

A little further on, Burton makes it more specific:

> The emphasis on human needs as the basis of analysis and problem-solving is oriented towards the stability and progress of societies: the human needs of the individual that enable him to operate as an efficient unit within a social system without which no social organisation can be harmonious.[2]

But the linkage between human needs satisfaction and social harmony and progress has more than functional significance. Contributions to social harmony and progress are made by individuals who, in order to realize their purposes, exploit the opportunities made available by society. In this process, they acquire new needs and develop capacities to satisfy these needs. It is also in this process that individuals change themselves as well as the social conditions in which they have to operate. But this entails a process of continuous change which can either be destructive or constructive. For this process to become constructive, individuals must develop an orientation to society which allows them not only to work for their own wellbeing but also for that of society as a whole. The development of such an orientation, needs theories insist, is possible only when basic human needs are satisfied. It is only against this backdrop that analysis and problem-solving become possible.

Given the linkage between needs satisfaction and social harmony, there are at least three senses in which this linkage can be interpreted. First, it can be argued that if basic human needs are fulfilled, conflicts could be checked at source. Conflicts arise because certain basic individual needs are systematically frustrated or prevented from becoming manifest. Suppression or frustration of needs leads to attitudinal and behavioral distortions which, in turn, create conditions for conflicts. If these needs are satisfied, no conflict will arise. On this view, social institutional arrangements may be such that they either frustrate needs satisfaction, only unsatisfactorily fulfill them, or create alienating needs. As a result, distortions in individual development produce personality imbalances and disturb and disrupt social harmony. It is, therefore, necessary radically to reorganize society so that proper development of the individual as well as harmonious social existence can be assured.

Second, as Burton makes it explicit, it is the frustration of needs that produce disturbing consequences for the harmonious functioning of social institutions. Once needs are made the basis of analysis and planning, conflicts will be easier to identify and handle. They will be easier in the sense that, in a political system which is committed to satisfying certain given basic needs and has devised an appropriate institutional arrangement for this purpose, there will exist a wider acknowledgement of and commitment to satisfying these needs. Conflicts may arise but they will involve mainly two types of question. They may entail the question of whether or not particular needs of the entire population or a particular section of it have been satisfied; or, alternatively, if they have been satisfied, then to what extent, in what manner, and with what results! Needs will thus provide factual, objective and rational criteria for analyzing and evaluating an emergent social situation that may contain in its womb the potential of conflict generation and conflict escalation.

Needless to say that, on this view, conflicts may still occur. However, what this view underlines is either that conflicts will be minimized or that, when conflicts do occur, proper solutions for resolving them could be easily found. This assumption is based on the belief that certain standards, values and norms will be widely shared in society, that conflicting beliefs and ideologies – in short, the ways of looking at the world – will not exist, or if they do, the difference will only be mildly held, and that differences of principle can be reduced to the technical question of facts.[3]

There is, finally, yet another interpretation of the linkage between needs satisfaction and conflict resolution, an interpretation which is a variant of the second. It is argued that every event of conflict incorporates within itself the issue of need satisfaction. Conflict arises because certain needs felt by a particular group have not been recognized – or, if recognized, have been frustrated or not satisfactorily fulfilled. Once the needs in question are identified and recognized as legitimate and requiring satisfaction, the way to the resolution of the conflict opens up. In this search for solution, needs theories can be of great help since these theories are objective, factual and rational. As such, they are instrumental in not only identifying the causes of conflicts but also in apprehending their solution. All these meanings of the linkage between needs satisfaction and conflict resolution may seem, on the surface, to be quite different. However, a closer look will show that they share a common perspective. While they refer formally to three different facets of the linkage between needs satisfaction and conflict resolution, superficially and substantively they are but three facets of one and a single dimension: the belief, usually without any validation, that once basic human needs of the individual are fully satisfied, individuality will merge into and become identical with sociality. In other words, the concern of the individual for protecting and promoting his own interests without taking into account the consequences of his actions for others will, need theories assume, give way to an active concern for others. This will prove instrumental in modifying egoistic motivations and behaviors of the individual. This will, in turn, bring about compatibility between individual wellbeing and social good.

The growing identity between individuality and sociality will, it is assumed, be reflected in the gradual whittling away of what Rousseau calls "*amour propre*" (vanity) and the strengthening of "*amour de soi*" (self-love) which constitutes the firm foundation for concern for others. This growing identity between individuality and sociality releases rationality from its bondage to egoistic self-interest and restores to it (or reorients it to) a wider concern for the good of others, an orientation that submits individual action to the consideration of common interest (or, at least, the recognition that, among individuals participating in human interaction, all of them share similar human capacities and must be treated as equals). In short, it is assumed that if basic human needs are fully satisfied, the individual will not only be fully developed but also will be a fully moral person.

The growing identity between individuality and sociality can be interpreted in at least two senses. First, it may mean nothing more than a compatibility between the individual's striving for worthy purposes and others' striving for similar ends. What is meant here is not that different individuals will pursue different purposes; they might very well do that. And if they did, there might not be any question of incompatibility. What is meant here is that the actions that the individual takes in order to realize his purposes do not in any way get in the way of or adversely impinge on the freedom of others in taking action to pursue their own purposes. It means that the individual refrains from acting in a way that creates difficulty for or curtails the freedom of others in so far as the realization of purposes is concerned. Second, it may also mean going beyond the negative action of simple refraining; it may mean positively, deliberately and consciously adopting an orientation of not only refraining from infringing others' freedom but also of doing good to others.

Are these two means of morality, of the identity of individuality and sociality, rooted in two different perspectives? A moment's reflection will show that they are not. The difference between these two means is only of degree, not of kind. To be able to refrain from action that hinders others' freedom is to be conscious of and concerned with the fact that others have the same right to pursue whatever purpose they as particular individuals find worthy. This necessarily means that one's action must not aim at one's own good alone; it must also incorporate the consideration of the good of others. If the consideration of the good of others guides the choice of action, the action will be moral. It will conduce to social harmony inasmuch as it will not hamper others in doing what they want to do. The compatibility principle, then, already incorporates the idea of the good of others as a standard, a reason, and a guide bearing on individual choices. Stopping at just refraining from such action that may cause harm or injury to others and not taking the further step of actively and consciously pursuing the good of others is an entirely different matter. Whatever may be the case, the identity of individuality and sociality subsumes the development of a moral sense, and the adoption of a conscious and active orientation of rising above narrow self-interest. Without such an orientation, conflict resolution will prove difficult, if not impossible.

Needs theories insist that only by satisfying or creating opportunities for individuals to satisfy their basic needs can there exist the possibility of a fully developed human person, a whole man, and a harmonious, progressive society. If needs are satisfied and individuals grow into "healthy," multilaterally developed, mature persons, the pursuit of individual good will become the vehicle of social or public good. The claim of needs theories is not simply that the satisfaction of basic human needs ensures the healthy and proper development of the individual. It is also that need satisfaction is, in fact, the only way for the individual to become moral. Should this claim turn out to be unfounded and untenable, needs theories lose their validity and, therefore, their viability. This chapter seeks to examine this claim.[4]

II

Basic human needs are not simply only those needs whose satisfaction is *sine qua non* for the well functioning of the individual as a biological organism; it also means those needs that distinguish man from other animals and pertain to him as a social being. These needs are variously described. Apart from the physiological needs, they refer to safety or security, belongingness, self-identity, self-esteem and self-realization needs. These variations apart, the central idea is that when these needs are properly satisfied, the individual realizes his self either in the sense of fully developing his potentialities, attaining psychological health, or becoming a whole, multilaterally developed person. Implicit in this is the idea of self which inheres man's nature as "a pressure toward fuller and fuller Being, more and more perfect actualization and his humanness in exactly the same naturalistic, scientific sense that an acorn may be said to be 'pressing toward' being an oak tree."[5] This pressure manifests itself in the form of various needs.

The modern philosophical articulation of the need for self-realization is of recent origins: a revolt against the debilitating impact of industrialization.[6] In the words of William H. Desmonde:

> The growth of the market had two-fold effect: it destroyed man's feelings of emotional, economic and spiritual security; but at the same time it established him as a rational person capable of free choice. It is the greatest task of the twentieth century to frame institutions which will restore man's feelings of rootedness without sacrificing the integrity of the individual.[7]

The impetus behind industrialization was, of course, the recognition of work as a liberating force. Man interacts with society and nature through work in order to satisfy certain needs. In this process he develops technology which proliferates needs which, in turn, stimulate further development of technology, and so on. In this dialectical relationship, man actualizes his potentialities, constantly raises the level of material wellbeing, and induces civilization's progress. Occupational structure expands and diversifies, choices proliferate, mobility – both physical and social – increases, and the process of rapid change ensues. Through work, man develops himself, restructures society and, through all this, himself changes.

No doubt industrialization has produced certain beneficial results. However, it has also created certain problems. If it has freed man from his subjugation to society and nature, it has also starved him emotionally; it has increased mobility, but it has also made his self-identity uncertain. Man has no doubt free choice, but his increasing dependence on society erodes his freedom. True, work is a liberating force; however, it has also forced alienated labor on him in return for consumer affluence. Ambition is recognized as the central organizing principle of individual life and social relations, but it is hemmed in by numerous mechanisms of control, on the one hand, and unmatched by social infrastructure, on the other. Man is supposed to be a self-creative creature. However, his self emerges simply as a social product.

Given these anomalies, the gap between what the individual has in him to become and what society allows him to become increases. As conditions progressively improve for man to become what he aspires to become, society frustrates his aspirations and uncertainties increase. Since choices are wider, mobility is within the reach of every person, and the opportunity of choosing a life that satisfies is greater, and ambitions grow. But since society changes rapidly, the sense of what is necessary for a satisfactory life becomes less clear. It encourages the aspiration to be highly mobile but difficulties encountered in reaching it create yet another aspiration: to change the structure, create new opportunities and new ways of life. But usually these aspirations are vague or based on a poor knowledge of how society needs to be changed. And a new claim, that of self-realization, emerges. Behind this claim is the notion that the individual must not only assert his identity, but also seek to discover the need for asserting it.

The first ambiguity in the concept of self-realization becomes thus evident because it incorporates the ideas of both asserting self-identity but at the same time discovering it. Two questions arise in this connection: the nature of this self and the way it must be realized. Given the naturalistic bent, the self of needs theories is not the transcendental self representing the spark of the cosmic spirit or a particular manifestation of the absolute. The self is the resident of this phenomenal world and is immersed in the everydayness. It signifies the potentialities inherent in the biological nature of man. When these potentialities are fully developed, the individual is said to attain his true selfhood. The need for self-actualization, then, refers to man's desire for self-fulfillment – namely, to the tendency for him to become actualized in what he is potentially, "the desire to become more and more what one is, to become everything that one is capable of becoming."[8] The specific form that it takes, of course, varies greatly from person to person. In an individual it may take the form of an ideal mother, in another, it may take an aesthetic form, and in still another, the form of an artist.[9]

It is the empirical self that needs theories celebrate. And to actualize this self, what Maslow recommends is to follow the inner law of one's own being. Full health and normal and desirable development consists in actualizing the nature inherent in man's biological condition. But this nature is hidden, covert, and only dimly seen. However, it is not for this reason beyond apprehension and realization. This dimly seen nature presses itself towards fulfillment – i.e., the realization of different potentialities through different needs. This requires growing from within rather than being shaped from outside.[10]

The notion of the self in needs theories symbolizes the return to an intelligible essence which now finds a biological expression. However, biological explanations remain incomplete and therefore misleading because they create a false dichotomy between nature and culture. Culture is not an alternative explanation. It is true that man may have certain biologically coded propensities. However, the individual is shaped by his society in the sense that "he needs it, he cannot grow up without it, and all the particular details of his life are filled in by it; they follow the path that particular society makes possible."[11] The interaction between the biological and the social, makes human nature including human needs, values, motives and wishes, as emergent – "the self-transforming process in which human actions on the world first in evolution then in history, have created conditions that keep bringing new needs, values, motives, and wishes into being."[12]

Needs theories ignore the essential role society plays in the development of the individual. They recognize society only for its instrumental role – i.e., its usefulness for the individual to realize his purpose. A good environment, Maslow emphasizes, "is one that offers all necessary raw-materials and then gets out of the way and stands aside to let the organism itself alter its wishes and demands."[13] On this view, the socio-cultural environment functions only as a support structure. It represents a set of opportunities that individuals may exploit in order to actualize potentialities immanent in them. True, this view celebrates individual freedom. But when society is treated merely as an opportunity structure and is drained of its significance, constraints or obstacles to action are considered to be located not internally, within the individual himself, but externally, embedded in the socio-cultural environment.[14]

The process of self-realization is the process of self-cultivation that may be aborted if the individual is "totally unaware of his potential, if fulfilling it has never arisen as a question for him, or if he is paralyzed by the fear of breaking some norm which he has internalized but which does not authentically reflect him."[15] If this is so, it calls for more than the mere absence of constraints; it calls for individuals to discriminate among motivations, discard those that obstruct the path of true development, and allow those capacities or potentialities to blossom that pave the way of the maturation of humanness. To quote Taylor again:

> the capacities relevant . . . invoice some self-awareness, self-understanding, moral discrimination and self-control, otherwise their exercise could not amount to freedom in the sense of self-direction; and this being so, we can fail to be free because these internal conditions are not realized.[16]

Self-realization may thus be obstructed because of internal blocks. But to acknowledge this is to recognize the possibility of the presence of evil in man. And to admit this and accept that human nature is in conflict with itself is to undermine the normative foundation of needs theories.[17]

Self-realization is the highest stage in man's exploration of his self. The end-results are, among others, desirable civic and social consequences through the wider circle of love-identification.[18] But the self as the end product emerges at the end of the process incorporating the satisfaction of a variety of needs. But man's ideas as to what his self is and what he wants to be are often vague and variable, to begin with. These notions, if they gain in precision and clarity, may change considerably with time. Or, a person may have precise ideas as to what he wants to become but may have illusions about his capacities. Moreover, he may not know from the beginning what he will find; he can know it only when he has found it. What is thus involved in the process of self-realization is a tentativeness, trials and explorations, and the possibility of different pathways to self-realization.

But in this tentative process, the individual lacks a clear understanding of what humanness is. Humanness as an essence is inactive, if not absent, at the beginning of the development. It cannot function as a regulating force guiding an individual's decisions from moment to moment and steering him out of crises that indecision at crucial moments in life produce. But needs theories insist that there is one single dominant pressing line of development in human affairs. Committed to this belief, they look at a series of events in terms of its ultimate outcome, interpreting each of the events with reference to that outcome. They, knowing what did or should in fact eventuate, seek out the lines of connection between it and previous events and are led to consider these events in their roles as contributing to what occurred later. This is what Mandelbaum calls "the retrospective fallacy."[19]

III

Given the tentative nature of the process of self-realization and given also the fact that the essence of humanness does not shine in its effulgence to guide the destiny of the individual in the world of uncertain everydayness, it is quite likely that the path of personal growth may take either constructive or destructive direction. On the path of self-realization are several milestones such as security, self-esteem, belongingness, etc. and numerous cross-roads. It is quite likely that the growing self may take a turn that is pleasing but not beneficial for others. It is also likely that it may stop at a particular point in the journey believing that it has found whatever it sought and that there is nothing more to seek. After all, Maslow himself recognizes that "self-actualization is a relatively achieved 'state of affairs' in a few people. In most people, however, it is rather a hope, a yearning, a drive, a 'something' wished for but not yet achieved."[20]

What do these milestones imply? The need for security, for example, is not totally satisfied in a society which simply preserves law and order. Security involves more than the preservation of life; it also involves preservation of liberty and its possible expansion so that the individual is confident that he can not only choose whatever way of life he prefers, but also maintain it. To this end, he must be able to acquire appropriate resources and rely on keeping the resources he has.[21] To be able to feel secure requires a stable environment.[22] A stable environment does not simply mean stability in expectations with respect to social conditions but also, in a more important sense, it means a feeling that the individual has a recognized place in society. If he is not sure that others recognize his place, he feels the need to make it known to them; and if he does not know their places, he feels the need to find out. The implication of security is thus that the individual feels that he is located in a social space where he knows others' places and others know his own. And the wants and the way of life of the individual are bound up with that place.

Put this way, the concept of security already incorporates the concept of self-identity, because without some notion of one's own identity the individual is unable to define what security means for him. It does not matter whether he has a particular identity for life, or for only a part of it. He must somehow make a connection between his identity, his place in society and the capacities and resources necessary to maintain his identity. For the individual, then, self-identity and security are not two distinct and distinguishable entities: they presuppose each other. However, it is the notion of self-identity that is primary in lending meaning to the sense of security. If this is so, then we expect some rough weather for the concept of self-identity and for sociality as well.

In George Mead's scheme, personal identity is a construction that emerges in the process of social interaction. Through the assumption of roles and the learning and use of language, individuals internalize the attitudes and beliefs of others and develop the faculty of seeing themselves as others see them. Thus, "in the origins of the personal there is the impersonal or, more exactly, the interpersonal."[23] But self-identity as a social emergent is not acceptable to needs theories simply because they visualize a self that is not reducible to the experience of the internalized attitudes of others. They insist on a self-identity which does not depend on a particular group of rigidly upheld attitudes and beliefs.

If the self is the sum total of all that a person can call his and represents his total subjective environment – his inner world – then it not only needs to be separated sharply from the outer world consisting of other peoples and things but also securely held against the encroachments of the outer world. It should be a strong identity but not a closed one. It should be autonomous, secure and open to experience. To be open to experience may signify encounters with diverse and often incompatible situations. But the individual with a strong self-identity treats his identity as the centre of experience that organizes these encounters in terms of the categories inherent in self-identity itself, assimilates and transforms them. In this, he may undergo the processes of differentiation and transcendence.[24] However, what matters is that, in all this, his identity remains neither static nor unstable.

What is indicated here is the fact that out of the list of numerous selves, the seeker of his truest, strongest, deepest self, as William James insists, "pick[s] out the one on which to stake his salvation. All other selves therefore become unreal, but the fortunes of this self are real."[25] All other selves must be suppressed. Apart from this selectivity in what one wants to become, there is also the additional dimension of the belief about one's relative and absolute worth. In building his self-identity, the individual does not only lay claim to the distinctness of what he is or aspires to be; he also claims that others should recognize him for what he is or aspires to be. Self-identity as the bulwark of self-realization has two components: self-esteem and social recognition. If the individual himself is in doubt about the validity of his identity, he may suffer anxiety, tension and conflict. He must therefore respect what he is or aspires to be and assert his identity. But this is not enough. He must also depend on others not only for recognition as a fit aspirant but also for assurance that he has succeeded (or, at least, has failed worthily).

It is thus apparent that the insistence of needs theorists to treat needs as needs of unique individuals is misleading since they ignore the fact that needs are needs of social beings, are socially conditioned and are the means to an individual's needs being socially provided. In Plamentaz's words:

> Society not only produces in the individual the need to assert and realize himself, and provides him with the means of doing so, and is the witness and confirmer of his success; it is also the medium in which he asserts and realizes himself. It is all these things at once: for he becomes self-assertive and self-realizing in acquiring a culture, and uses social resources, and depends on social acceptance and approval for confirmation of his claims, and his acts of self-assertion and self-realization are essentially forms of social intercourse.[26]

If this is true, the individual faces two alternative paths to self-realization. The individual may need powers to develop if he is to become what he aspires to be or to achieve what he thinks worthwhile. Alternatively, he may choose to develop those powers that would make him or his achievements admirable.[27] While these two senses of self-realization are related, the selection of one path forecloses the other. Needs theorists are, however, already committed to the first path since they talk of individuals following the law of their own being, an internal law. And yet they cannot completely reject the idea of social acceptability and belongingness. It is no wonder that Neil McInnes finds the concept of mental health to be full of weasel-words, and contradictions.[28]

Whatever may be the case, needs theorists remind us of Aristotle's conception of human virtue, or excellence, as a life-long process of maturation and exercise of man's characteristic nature. In this process of maturation, only a few can ever hope to reach the destination while numerous others may find it difficult to proceed beyond a short distance. And for these many, the enlightenment produced by self-realization will in all likelihood not be available to guide them in preserving or developing their unique individuality. If they follow the path of social acceptability and admiration, they surrender to society. If they do not, it is very likely that they will want power first to provide for their needs and later to want it for its own sake. The possibility is there and can be obviated only if the individual is endowed with the sense of responsibility for his action. A person is responsible when he owns responsibility for his own actions.[29] In doing so, he also expects from others the same attitude. This means that there is or should be a body of rules which must guide everybody's behaviour. "When he appeals to a rule against another person, he recognizes implicitly that he too would be bound by that rule were he situated as the person is against whom he makes the appeal."[30] This implies an appeal to justice, and to a common interest, an appeal which has significance only among equals. But needs theorists are disturbingly silent about how people caught in the struggle of life and propelled by the need to establish their uniqueness in an uncertain world make a transition from their selves as the suns of the social system to the stars of the social solar system.

Needs theorists, even when they realize that not everyone can cultivate excellence, hope that everybody will. They propose to democratize what is essentially an aristocratic conception. But the pursuit of excellence, even if only by a few people, means a high price for society. It is so not simply because the privileged ones tend to live off the labors of those who lack either the capacity or the opportunity to cultivate and display their own talent but also because the striving for superiority that the cultivation of rare gifts entails is socially divisive and a source of misery. To be ruled by a strong passion is, in many cases, to be willing to sacrifice others and oneself in the attempt to get for that self, by the exercise of special gifts, a recognition setting him apart from and high above others. Since the pursuit of excellence involves inequality, it proves divisive in a society that claims to be based on equality.[31]

But this does not mean that the pursuit of excellence is *ipso facto* undesirable. The cultivation of excellence can also be constructive provided the person engaged in its cultivation does not live *for* himself; he also lives *for* others. But then we have already moved away from the need to follow some internal law to the need for assimilating culture. For living for others is largely "a life of gestures, of acts whose significance depends on ideas common to the actor and his 'witness,' as sharers in a culture."[32] But culture can itself deny or dissipate those standards which promote and sustain living for others. If this is so, how does a person come to have principles that make living for others possible? Equality and freedom without the constraining hand of fraternity can rip society apart.[33]

Broadly speaking, there are four different ways in which this may be possible. First is the Freudian reality principle which suggests that the ego, caught as it is in the struggle between two objective forces – irrepressible desires and overbearing culture – must interpolate between desire and action and check the advisability of satisfying a particular desire against that of leading reality. It may mean suppression of the Id, but it is unavoidable. But this is not acceptable to needs theorists. Second, the individual can attach himself passionately to a principle that is either his own or is shared only by a few. But such an attachment breeds absolutism and ignores the distinctions that must be made in real life.

The third course is to accept only those rules whose observance, in the experience of the individual, is conducive to his own and the good of others. What is involved here is more than the mere internalization of the existing social rules or norms. It also involves a critical examination of these rules on rational grounds and the acceptance of them without reservation as guides to proper conduct. These rules are, then, not maxims of prudence but properly moral laws. The individual feels bound to keep them even to his own harm, even when he could continue, to his own lasting advantage, not to keep them. Here what is important is testing the validity of certain rules on the touchstone of reason and accepting them if they prove to be right. If to act morally is to be bound to a rule which has been accepted on rational grounds, it presumes that there is a prior consensus which make discursive, rational discourse meaningful.[34] Without such a consensus, the rule may turn out to be merely idiosyncratic and may simply reflect rationalization concealing some individual interest. Moreover, acting on this principle may lead to the erosion of a person's moral sensibility by accepting on rational grounds a principle requiring him to do in difficult circumstances what is unjustly required of him.

And, lastly, there is Kant's categorical imperative which asks us to seek a law for ourselves – a law grounded not in motivation of happiness or pleasure which belongs to the realm of a contingency, but a law grounded in will. This law is binding *a priori* and does not depend on the particular nature of objects we desire or the actions we project. It must be purely formal: that is, we must apply a purely formal criterion to prospective actions of rationality – i.e., thinking in universal terms and thinking consistently so that we can universalize the maxim underlying a proposed action without contradiction. No doubt, this is a very attractive idea. However, it is vacuous because the categorical imperative cannot distinguish between situations where it may or may not be appropriate. By avoiding any appeal to the way things are, either to an order of ideas or a constellation of *de facto* desires, the categorical imperative is in danger of degenerating into a maxim that allows any thing as a possible moral action.

If none of the four alternative pathways leads to moral action, where do we go from here? Moral freedom does not lie in making a choice because the choice made may not reflect considerations for others. As such, the argument that the increasing diversity of opportunities and the extension of the range of choices open to the individual make it more likely that people will realize this themselves, and thus be moral, is inadmissable. For morality lies in a sense of discrimination between situations and between action choices proper to each situation without a person's being swayed by the considerations of self-interest.

And here we enter the realm of contingency, not absolute certainty but the realm of *praxis*, not that of *techne*. If situations vary not simply in terms of structure but also in terms of import, then what is essential is to avoid two kinds of error: relativism and absolutism. If the homogenization of contexts leads to the error of absolutism, the attenuation of the universalizing tendency of a principle produces the error of relativism. As Heinrich Zimmer observes:

> Relativism and absolutism equally, when total, are perverse – because convenient. They oversimplify for the purpose of fruitful actions. They are not concerned with truth, but with results . . .
>
> Exclusion, the rejection of anything, is sin and self-deception, is the subjection of the whole to a part, is violence enacted against

the omni-present truth and essence, the finite superordinating itself to the infinite . . .

But, on the other hand, anyone who, in order to be closed to nothing, takes in all without distinction is equally fooled and guilty; for then it is the distinction between things that is being disregarded, and the hierarchy of values.[35]

The relevance of the diversity of situational contexts for moral choice discredits the application of a principle supposed to be universally valid. It also argues against absolutization of values. This is inherent in needs theories which theorists either do not recognize or, if they recognize it, choose to render this absolutization unimportant. As was pointed out earlier, McInnes criticizes needs theorists for projecting contradictory attributes of a self-realized person. But this contradiction is apparent only because needs theorists project not absolute values but postures to be adopted in different situations. Given this, the attainment of moral freedom does not depend so much on the satisfaction of the needs of a social being as on the development of an orientation towards others that is untouched by the corroding effect of vanity. To recognize this is to move away both from the individual and society to somewhere in between wherever lies the ground of morality.[36]

The satisfaction of needs does not necessarily overcome vanity. The attributes that needs theorists identify as the sign-posts of a self-realized person, such as, "creativity," "wholeness," "mental health," etc. may be very catchy, but as indicators of morality they are unsatisfactory because what we need is precisely a measure by which we can judge when a person with these attributes is moral, and when he is not. Freedom too cannot be a criterion of morality because freedom itself is subordinate to an ethical evaluation. What makes a person moral is the incorporation of sociability in individual choices of action.

IV

If there is no direct relationship between the satisfaction of needs and the development of moral sense, how can needs theories be of help either in conflict elimination or conflict resolution? Even if it is conceded that there is such a direct relationship, can we assume that conflicts will be eliminated or resolved? After all, even in a society composed of self-realized persons, there may be conflicts about the validity of needs claims.[37] But why should it be assumed that conflict *per se* is bad? In situations where objective conditions become oppressive and the managers of the system turn a deaf ear to valid or legitimate claims, conflict remains the only alternative to shake the system and force it to find a solution to an emergent problem. The very fact that conflict takes place points to certain anomalies that characterize a particular system.

Be that as it may, when conflict surfaces, it is necessary to find a solution for its pacification. Protagonists of needs theories see in the concept of needs not only a diagnostic possibility of clarifying and putting into a proper context a particular conflict but also a basis for the resolution of conflicts. It is claimed that a particular cluster of needs – i.e., identity needs – not only facilitates a depth analysis of a wide range of types of violent conflicts but also facilitates a final solution by satisfying this needs cluster.

Conflict may be said to exist if two or more groups seek something that each of them wants; seek as large a share of it as each can; seek something that each of them claims is rightfully its own, either as legal or moral right; and seek to get it by getting its claim recognized, either by others or by some authority to which they are subject. These groups, when in conflict, may also seek to get what they want by compelling others to let them have it.[38]

If conflict concerns the effort, peaceful or violent, to have a legal or moral right and its appurtenances recognized, in what way can self-identity of a group be in contention? To talk of the self-identity of a group is, to say the least, very odd. Does it mean the sum total of individual self-identities? If it is so then it loses its significance because there is no way to combine individual self-identities in a way that produces a coherent and durable group self-identity. If individuals have different self-identities the problem, then, is to find a common ground, a common denominator that can form the basis of a strong group identity to emerge. If we cannot find it in individuals, can it be found in the group itself? It is possible only when the group constitutes the major source of identity formulation and the support for identity maintenance for its numbers: that, because of its active role in the social production of culture, it constitutes the focus of its members' affection and allegiance; and that it is the primary entity to which its members meaningfully relate to.

The fact is that such groups are the characteristic of a stable, traditional society where economic opportunities are limited and tied up with the agricultural mode of production; mobility is limited; rights and obligations are definite; and social interactions are intimate. However, the institutional concomitants of technologically induced economic growth has changed all this. In a society undergoing rapid changes, uncertainties grow and the demand for self-realization, for self-identity, becomes very vocal. Lying in the womb of history for long, the idea of self-determination has since the French Revolution, as Dov Ronen notes, "spread throughout the world, unifying peoples into nations, crumbling empires, freeing colonies, and threatening modern states."[39]

Self-determination symbolizes the aspiration of the individual to create, fashion and rule his self and not to be created, fashioned or ruled by others. This is never a group aspiration although it manifests different aggregates through identities associated with different groups "because individual self-determination as an institutioned socio-political entity is inconceivable."[40] However, this does not detract from the fact that this quest, "at its core, is not a national or group aspiration, but the aspiration of the individual human being to the vague notions of 'freedom' and 'the good life'."[41] It is the quest by individuals for freedom and good life in a situation of scarcity that makes it necessary for individuals to identify themselves with particular groups.

As indicated earlier, the uncertainties and the insecurities produced by the rapid pace of social change bring to the fore the question of self-identity. The process of homogenization itself leads to the quest for self-identity. Where inequality in the distribution of and access to societal resources is coupled with the inequality in the distribution of power in a situation where the good things of life are promised but are not accessible to all, political mobilization for preferential access to resources pushes individuals to form groups from which individuals perceive their environment from the same vantage point.

Once the quest for freedom and good life becomes urgent, it needs to be coupled with such quests of others in an institutional arrangement that facilitates the individual quest. The coupling is based on similarity of interests and brings aggregates into being. However, if the vantage point from which to view the environment changes, it brings about a corresponding change in the perception that makes aggregates possible. To quote Ronen again:

But each aggregation is only a temporary "us," because it does not, cannot, provide self-determination for each "I." The aggregation splits into a new "us" and "them" and becomes the stage for a new drive for self-determination, fueled by the hope that after freedom from "them," *my* self-determination will be realized. Because the new "us" often becomes just another framework that appears to limit the freedom of the individual, of the real "self," the perception of a new "them" is promoted, and hence the formation of a new "us" for the further pursuit of the aspired-to "freedom" and "good life." And so a new quest for self-determination evolves, with another new "us," and then another, possibly ad infinitum.[42]

Individuals can thus pick and choose identities depending on particular issues relevant for self-determination. The quest for self-determination takes various forms at different times and places and renders different identities meaningful because they serve as its vehicle. In this sense all aggregations are arbitrary, temporary and instrumental. They represent at any particular moment the constellation of not the whole identity of individuals but just one or a few components of it.

Self-identity as an abstract notion is the end product and can be experienced through the individual's own image of himself expressed through interactions with others, his beliefs and values. The formation of self-identity depends on the individual's access to material and cultural resources that society makes available. As indicated earlier, the sense of security is an integral part of self-identity, and it can be threatened if individuals are denied access to societal resources. This may produce a highly differentiated and fragmented social structure. Differential location of individuals in the factual order may be instrumental in the formation of groups with different and, perhaps, antagonistic interests. These groups may also engage in conflicts for what they consider to be their right. But, then, self-identity as a concept becomes indeterminate because of its tendency to slide into the concepts of "interest" and "right." But can the argument be sustained that the nature of objective reality is the sole and decisive influence on the formation of subjective reality – that is, self-identity?

Behind conflicts, supposedly occurring for the assertion of or the satisfaction of the needs of self-identity, masquerades a concrete material interest which creates and sustains groups. Once this interest is served, other interests will emerge to hasten the formation of newer groups and instigate the eruption of newer conflicts. A never-ending process of conflict and conflict resolution thus ensues because in changing the external world, man also changes his own nature and with it the notion of his self-identity as well as the things required to maintain this identity. In the conflict of interests, morality becomes the first victim. Only power serves as the most appropriate instrument of the pursuit of self-interest. There is no doubt that efficacy (or competence or control) is one of the props of the modern identity of man. But to treat it as the most important one in terms of which society must be analyzed or which is instrumental in meeting individual needs or which brings moral freedom is a distortion. It is forgotten that personal control "is only a slight variant, with different conceptual associations and connotations, of Hobbes' old concept of power as a rational prerequisite for the satisfaction of the whole range of other human appetites."[43]

V

The preceding discussion highlights some of the problems that attend the assumption of compatibility between individuality and sociality via the satisfaction of needs. This assumption now fuels the drive for launching a policy perspective insisting on the radical restructuring of society for fulfilling "basic" human needs. This insistence conceals a subtle change in the vantage point from which the concept of self-realization has historically been viewed. Formerly, self-realizations pertained to autonomous individuals. Now it is grounded in a universalistic principle which emphasizes the prior significance of a harmonious and just social order and then deduces the necessity of satisfying "basic" human needs as a means of establishing such a society. It is in this universalistic garb that needs theories acquire their theoretical and practical relevance.

Needs theorists rely on three assumptions for making good their claim of the compatibility between individuality and sociality via the satisfaction of needs. First, it is assumed that needs are complementary, compatible and harmonious. The second assumption underlines the fact that once needs are properly satisfied, the possibility of a mature and multilaterally developed personality becomes real. And, lastly, it is assumed that needs satisfaction provides a firm basis for forging an identity between individuality and sociality. All these assumptions are problematic.

If the foundation of a strong self-identity is the selection of one self as the source of personal salvation and the suppression of others, it means that certain needs not intrinsic to the preferred self must be shed or suppressed. In that case, it is confusing to talk of either satisfying all needs or working for a multilaterally developed personality. But this is not all. A strong self-identity is the bulwark of autonomy and creativity. It requires the suppression of other competing selves. But while we can try to suppress them, we cannot eradicate them. And if they are not fully controlled, they, like the Freudian Id, are always on their look out for opportunities to break out of the constraints and demand attention. To the extent that this happens, the individual fails to be at peace with himself, and with others.

If it is true of individuals, it is also true of societies. Needs theories are a-historical (it is more appropriate to say that they universalize a particular historical experience), but societies are not. Societies differ in terms not only of the ways of looking at the world and doing things but also in terms of historical experience, production system, etc. As a result of this difference, different societies judge a particular set of needs as desirable and other sets as undesirable. Since socially approved needs do not serve the purpose of certain individuals and groups, one way in which these purposes can get recognition is conflict. Conflict therefore becomes the avenue through which certain needs can be satisfied.

Conflict is a necessary complement of order. But order requires for its maintenance certain principles for claim recognition and adjudication of claim disputes. Some notion of justice has to be accepted for formulating such principles. This calls for uniformity. But uniformity itself then becomes a problem. It tends to rule certain needs claims out of court, or turn a blind eye to them. This again fosters conflict. The emphasis on justice, furthermore, militates against the notion of excellence inasmuch as justice demands equality and excellence calls for inequality.

If conflicts are the necessary complement of order, compatibility between individuality and sociality becomes necessary in order to mitigate the adverse consequences of the tension between the drive towards freedom and the requirements of order. But, as we have already seen, the satisfaction of needs does not automatically produce this compatibility.

NOTES AND REFERENCES

1. John W. Burton, *Deviance, Terrorism and War: The Process of Solving Unsolved Social and Political Problems* (Oxford: Martin Robertson, 1979): 79.
2. Burton, *Deviance*: 81.
3. The aspiration of substituting doctrines for opinions, or reducing opinions to doctrines, is very ancient. However, in its scientific incarnation, this quest goes back to liberals. For a useful discussion on this point, see Thomas H. Spragen, Jr, *The Irony of Liberal Reason* (Chicago: The University of Chicago Press, 1981): 29–90.
4. Obviously, to examine this claim requires the examination of the adequacy of the concept of need itself; but this is beyond the scope of this chapter. However, for a discussion on the inadequacy of biological explanation, see Mary Madgley, *Beast and Man: The Roots of Human Nature* (London: Methuen, 1979) and M. Brewster Smith "Metapsychology, Politics and Human Needs," in Ross Fitzgerald (ed.), *Human Needs and Politics* (Rushcutter Bay, N.S.W., Australia: Pergamon Press, 1977, private limited edn): 124–44, and other papers for ambiguity in the concept of needs. For a discussion of naturalistic fallacy involved in needs theories, see John H. Schaar, *Escape from Authority; The Perspectives of Erich Fromm* (New York: Basic Books, 1961) Chapter 1; for a discussion of needs as insufficient grounds for justice see David Miller, *Social Justice* (Oxford: Clarendon Press, 1979) Chapter 4; and for a discussion of the elusiveness of the concept of self-realization, see John Plamenatz, *Karl Marx's Philosophy of Man* (Oxford: Clarendon Press, 1975) Chapter 12.
5. Abraham Maslow, *Toward a Psychology of Being* (Princeton: D. Van Nostrand Co. Inc., 1962): 151.
6. It was Fichte who voiced this need. See Maurice Mandelbaum, *History, Man and Reason: A Study on Nineteenth Century Thought* (Baltimore: The John Hopkins University Press, 1971) Chapter 11.
7. William Herbert Desmonde, *Magic, Myth and Money: The Origin of Money in Religious Rituals* (New York: The Free Press of Glencoe, 1962): 179.
8. Abraham Maslow, *Motivation and Personality* (New York: Harper & Row 1954): 98.
9. Maslow, *Motivation and Personality*. Maslow also talks of cognition as symptomatic of self-actualization. But it is shrouded in too much of mystical claptrap to be of any use. See his *Toward a Psychology of Being*, Chapter 6.
10. Maslow, *Motivation and Personality*: 340.
11. Mary Madgley, *Beast and Man*: 95.
12. M. Brewster Smith, "Metapsychology, Politics.": p. 141.
13. Maslow, *Motivation and Personality*: 349. It is true that Maslow imposes a condition that the organism must remember that other people also have demands and wishes. However, this is a problem need theories have to contend with rather than assume that this condition prevails.
14. Complete freedom, in this view, becomes situationless and consists of

removing obstacles to untrammeled action. "Full freedom would be situationless. By the same token it would be empty. Complete freedom would be void in which nothing would be worth doing, nothing would count for anything. The self which has arrived at freedom setting aside all external obstacles and impingement is characterless, and hence without defined purpose however much this is hidden by such seemingly positive terms as 'rationality' or 'creativity'." Charles Taylor, *Hegel and Modern Society* (Cambridge: Cambridge University Press, 1979): 157.
15. Charles Taylor, "What's Wrong with Negative Liberty," in Alan Ryan (ed.), *The Idea of Freedom* (Oxford: Oxford University Press, 1979): 117.
16. Taylor, "What's Wrong with Negative Liberty": 179.
17. Leonard Geller, "The Failure of Self-Actualization Theory: A Critique of Carl Rogers and Abraham Maslow," *Journal of Humanistic Psychology*, 22 (2) (Spring 1982): 65.
18. Maslow, *Motivation and Personality*: 149.
19. Mandelbaum, *History, Man and Reason*: 134.
20. Maslow, *Toward a Psychology of Being*: 151.
21. On this point, see Plamenatz, *Karl Marx's Philosophy*: 325.
22. Maslow admits as much although he talks of familiar things. See his *Motivation and Personality*: 88.
23. Oscar Nudler, "Human Needs: A Sophisticated Holistic Approach," in Katrin Lederer (ed.), with Johan Galtung and David Antal, *Human Needs: A Contribution to the Current Debate* (Cambridge, MA: Oelgeschlager, Gunn & Hain, 1980): 144.
24. Nudler, "Human Needs." 144–5.
25. William James, *Principles of Psychology* (New York: Henry Holt, 1890) vol. I: 91.
26. Plamenatz, *Karl Marx's Philosophy of Man*: 334–5.
27. Plamenatz, *Karl Marx's Philosophy of Man*: 349.
28. "The Politics of Needs – Or, Who Needs Politics?," in Fitzgerald (ed.), *Human Needs and Politics*: 232.
29. The Weberian ethics of responsibility, it must be noted, is grossly inadequate since it excludes the critical examination of the basic value premises either in the realm of action or in the realm of science.
30. Plamenatz, *Karl Marx's Philosophy*: 327.
31. The pursuit of excellence inevitably leads the economy to a stage where competition for positional goods becomes acute and intemperate. It creates demands that cannot be met and shatters public morality. See Fred Hirsch, *Social Limits to Growth* (London: Routledge & Kegan Paul, 1977): 67.
32. Hirsch, *Social Limits*: 335.
33. Cf. Martin Buber, "The abstractions freedom and equality were held together there through the more concrete fraternity, for only if men feel themselves to be brothers can they partake of a genuine freedom from one another and a genuine equality with one another. But fraternity has been deprived of its original meaning, the relationship between children of God, and consequently of any real content. As a result, each of the remaining watchwords was able to establish itself against the other and,

by so doing, to wander farther and farther from its truth. Arrogant and presumptious, each sucked into itself ever more thoroughly, elements foreign to it, elements of passion and greed for possession," quoted in Roy Oliver, *The Wanderer and the Way: The Hebrew Tradition in Writings of Martin Buber* (Ithaca: Cornell University Press, 1968): 53.

34. If by rationality we mean prudential, calculative reasoning relating means to ends, rational action becomes problematic not simply because the individual lacks information about how his action is going to influence others but also because he is not sure what principle to apply in which situation. In the lack of complete information, he is forced in his action to take account of his own self-interest. See Kenneth N. Waltz, *Man, the State and War: A Theoretical Analysis* (New York: Columbia University Press, 1959): 110.

35. Joseph Campbell (ed.), *Philosophies of India* (London: Routledge & Kegan Paul, 1953): 175–6.

36. Martin Buber calls this "between." *The Knowledge of Man*, with Introductory Essay by Maurice Friedman (New York; Harper Torch-books, 1965): 11; Tu Wei-Ming, *Humanity and Self-Cultivation: Essays in Confucian Thought* (Berkeley: Asian Humanities Press, 1979): 23.

37. On this point, see David Miller, *Social Justice* (Oxford: Clarendon Press, 1976): 136.

38. Plamenatz, *Karl Marx's Philosophy*: 404–5.

39. D. Ronen, *The Quest for Self-determination* (New Haven: Yale University Press, 1979): 6.

40. Ronen, *The Quest for Self-determination*: 53.

41. Ronen, *The Quest for Self-determination*: 8.

42. Ronen, *The Quest for Self-determination*: 8.

43. Brewster Smith, "Metapsychology, Politics": 140.

7 Necessitous Man and Conflict Resolution:[1] More Basic Questions About Basic Human Needs Theory
Christopher Mitchell

This chapter adopts a fundamentally practical approach to the conception of Basic Human Needs and its attendant theorizing – an approach which arises from my own major interest in the nature of social (mainly international) conflict and its solution. It seeks to throw some light on whether the Basic Human Needs approach can form the core of a general theory of conflict resolution and what clarifications of that approach might be necessary before any systematic development of such a theory can take place.

The chapter will briefly discuss the idea of a "theory of conflict resolution;" review ideas relevant to that theory from contemporary literature on the ending of disputes; attempt to show how the Basic Human Needs approach (hereafter BHN) has become intimately involved with the idea of conflict resolution; and pose some questions about the nature of BHNs that seem relevant to any proposal to use a BHN approach as the basis for achieving a genuine "resolution" of complex, deep rooted conflicts.

TOWARDS A GENERAL THEORY OF CONFLICT RESOLUTION

Ending Social and International Conflicts

Traditionally, international relations scholars have recognized that disputes (whether lethal and violent or not) can have a variety of endings, ranging from a merely temporary (although sometimes quite long) pause in a protracted conflict spanning many decades[2] to the complete destruction of one or other adversary in some kind of "Carthaginian peace" or "final solution" to the dispute. More usually, international conflicts end with some form of compromise solution in which the adversaries compromise by giving up at least some of the goals and interests for which the conflict was originally prosecuted in return for achieving others – plus a cessation of the costs of continuing the conflict through coercion.

In recent years, some scholars have come to distinguish between conflicts which are *settled* and those which are *resolved*, arguing that only in the latter case can a dispute be regarded as having been concluded (or *terminated*) in such a way as to prevent a resurrection of the underlying issues in contention and a recurrence of the conflict behavior between the adversaries.[3]

Such writers emphasize that *settlements* tend to be arranged (or even *imposed*) in situations characterized by successful coercion, either by one of the adversaries or, sometimes, by powerful outsiders. The post-settlement relationship inevitably therefore remains a fragile one, liable to be overturned at the earliest opportunity. The settlement of the 1939–40 "Winter War" between Finland and the USSR provides an example of such a short-term "solution," as does the Anglo–Irish Treaty of 1921 even though, according to one historian, it "conjured the Irish problem out of existence" for Britain.[4]

By contrast, *resolutions* of conflicts (admittedly difficult to achieve and – according to some writers – available only through specialized processes enabling parties to analyze thoroughly and together the underlying causes of their dispute) provide durable, long-term and self-supporting solutions to disputes by removing the underlying causes and establishing new, and satisfactory, relationships between previously antagonistic parties. Writers on the termination of international conflicts have suggested various characteristics by which a true resolution might be recognized,[5] but most would, I think, agree that a genuine resolution of a conflict is characterized by a solution which is:

1. *Complete*, in that the issues in conflict disappear from the political agenda and/or cease to have any salience for the parties to the agreement.
2. *Acceptable*, generally, to all the parties to the dispute, not merely to one side, or to elite factions within the adversaries.
3. *Self-supporting*, in that there is no necessity for third-party sanctions (positive or negative) to maintain the provisions of the

agreement in place.

4. *Satisfactory* to all the parties in the sense of being perceived as "fair" or "just" according to their value systems.
5. *Uncompromising*, in the sense that the terms are not characterized by the sacrifice of goals as part of a compromised, "half a loaf" solution.
6. *Innovative*, in that the solution establishes some new and positive relationship between the parties.
7. *Uncoerced*, in that the adversaries freely arrive at the solution themselves without any imposition by an authoritative (but perhaps non-legitimized) outside agency.

Scholars and practitioners from fields other than international relations will find many of these criteria familiar, particularly when they are compared with some of the criteria for the successful, non-adversarial management of interpersonal, family, industrial, intra-organizational and environmental disputes which have been handled increasingly by non-directive processes under the growing movement for Alternative Dispute Resolution (ADR) in this and other countries.

Moreover, it seems likely that the three basic forms of conflict termination characteristic of international relations may also be familiar to those who study or deal with conflicts at other social levels:

1. *Truces*: arrangements which bring about a cessation of mutually coercive conflict behavior (perhaps for a considerable period) but which do little to deal with the underlying issues giving rise to the conflict and which are acknowledged to be temporary by the parties. (The ending of the four Arab–Israeli Wars since 1949; the ending of the 1982 War over the Falklands/Malvinas.)
2. *Settlements*: arrangements which involve both a compromise and abandonment of goals by the parties who, nonetheless, can genuinely hope that this "best that can be achieved" arrangement will lead to a new, positive relationship based upon compromise and changing circumstances. (The mediated settlement of the Chile–Argentine dispute over the Beagle Channel; the agreement terminating the first Sudanese Civil War in 1972.)
3. *Resolutions*: arrangements which deal with the underlying issues in dispute and establish a new, acceptable relationship between the erstwhile adversaries. (The ending of "Konfrontasi" between Indonesia and Malaysia in 1965; the ending of the dispute over the Aland Islands in 1921.)

Conflict Resolution and Basic Human Needs

In discussing the nature of "conflict resolution," I have emphasized the generally shared view that the label should be applied only to *processes* which result in the production of a complete solution for all the issues in dispute; or to *solutions* that "deal with" the underlying issues in contention (rather than behavioral manifestations arising from those issues).

Expressed in slightly different terms, writers who discuss conflict resolution processes or solutions argue that a "genuine resolution" is one that enables the parties to achieve their "goals and values" without compromise. The conflict is resolved by the basically straight-forward process of removing its underlying causes, defined as the existince of mutually incompatible goals or, alternatively, "opposed interests."

A more recent extension of this view of the nature of a resolved conflict and of conflict resolution processes is one that links the idea of resolving conflict by removing underlying causes to the existence of BHNs in individuals, groups, societies and – thus – parties in conflict, including complex social entities such as "ethnic groups," "communities" and "societies."[6] Fundamental to this view of conflict *resolution* seems to be the idea that only arrangements that fully satisfy BHNs can bring about any final resolution of the conflict – one which "deals fully" with the issues in dispute and establishes a new, self-supporting relationship between the adversaries.

This view is very clearly put in John Burton's latest work on resolving what he terms "deep rooted" conflict which tend to resist conventional efforts at finding a solution and to "protract" over time.[7] Part of this "protraction" is caused by inappropriate conflict management procedures being applied in the search for a settlement of the dispute but the greatest cause of failure arises from an inability (on the part of both protagonists and third parties) to recognize that deep rooted conflicts are caused by the denial of basic, inalienable values or the frustration of BHNs. Conflicts are seen as arising and inflicting costs that are thus attributable to "ignoring, suppressing or failing to promote revealed, non-negotiable needs."[8] BHNs are thus contrasted sharply with "interests that are negotiable" and conflated with "values that are not for trading."[9]

In Burton's view, given that "conflict is likely to be *caused by* the need for identity, recognition, security of the identity group and other such human, societal values" what he terms "facilitated" conflict resolution must aim at determining such human needs and values and then assisting parties "to deduce what alterations in structures, institutions and policies are required to enable the *fulfilment of needs.*"[10] In short, successful and final *resolution* of any conflict must involve satisfying those needs of the parties involved that are being frustrated by existing conditions and relationships. Expressed slightly differently, in contrast to other explanations about the causes of human conflict and war which centre on the concept of "aggressive man," on "power-seeking man," on rationally calculating, "economic man," or on "Hobbesian," "Lockean" or "Freudian" man, Burton proposes "necessitous man" as that starting point. At every social level, man's natural and universal needs are the fundamental, first causes of conflict and disputes, from the simple to the complex.

A similar view is taken by other writers on social conflict. For example, in a recent paper on the Middle East by Alexis Heraclides, the author examines the Arab–Israeli conflict which he characterizes as a prime example of a protracted conflict punctuated by temporary truce arrangements.[11] Having noted how any definition of the issues in conflict in terms of inherently scarce material values (e.g., control of territory, exclusive rights to land) leads to a "quagmire" and a zero-sum *impasse*, Heraclides suggests the possibility of reconceptualizing the disputed issues in terms of higher order values such as "peace" or "security." The major practical difficulty lies in finding some procedures for bringing about such a general reconceptualization among the adversaries. The intellectual difficulty in seeking "win–win" solutions is articulated as "whether other vital, non-material needs such as ethnic identity . . . and the craving for justice, constancy and meaning can be satisfied by moving away from straightforward, tangible values such as territory?" Clearly, Heraclides also feels that any final *resolution* of the Palestinian–Israeli conflict must be sought in the satisfaction of certain basic needs experienced both jointly and separately by Israelis and by Palestinians.

This development of the idea of *resolving* as opposed to merely *settling* a conflict is an interesting and fruitful one, both at the tactical and strategic level of conflict management processes. At the strategic level, it points towards a possible answer to the old question: how can one tell when a conflict is successfully resolved?[12] Using a BHN approach, the basic answer to this query takes the form of stating (presumably with some supporting evidence) that the arrangements reached fulfill relevant BHNs and frustrate none. At the tactical (or process) level, the approach provides procedural guidelines for facilitative exercises which must: (1) seek, together with the parties, to analyze the nature of the BHNs being frustrated on both sides; and then (2) jointly search for acceptable new structures and relationships that permit the fulfillment, rather than the frustration, of those needs.

However, it is at this point that a number of problems begin to arise and these must be addressed and resolved if the conception of BHNs is to be made the centerpiece of any general theory of conflict resolution (whether the latter is to be achieved by facilitated processes, problem-solving workshops or other methods of ADR). Some of the problems, indeed, arise for those originally interested in the nature of human development and from the arguments (1) that the latter consists of the progressively more and more successful satisfaction of Human Needs but (2) that the pursuit of such Needs by individuals and groups may actually *create* major disputes and conflicts. Others, however, are particular to theorists of conflict resolution, who assume that BHNs are either (1) by their nature congruent or compatible, and "benign" in the sense that they do not, by their nature, lead to conflicts or (2) practically capable of satisfaction without the development of logically incompatible tactical goals and/or conflicting behavior in pursuit of need satisfaction.[13]

Given my own interest in the nature of and processes leading to conflict resolution, it is inevitable that the remainder of this chapter will concentrate on problems relevant to that field, but I will begin with two issues of relevance both to development theorists and to conflict resolvers. (1) What justification do we have for assuming that BHNs do not, by their very nature, themselves create conflict (that is, without the intervention of potential satisfiers which may or may not be in limited supply)? (2) What is the basic nature and form of human needs? Secondly, I will discuss the variety of Needs described by different BHN theorists and the problems this variety and heterogeneity poses for systematic conflict resolution. Next, I will consider the issues of the relative salience of different human needs, the question of the way in which BHNs might alter over time and the obstacles and opportunities that differing answers to these two questions might provide for a theory of conflict resolution. Finally, I will take up the matter of "satisfiers" and explore the implications of this conception for conflict resolution.

HUMAN NEEDS AS CONFLICT PROMOTING

At the outset of this discussion, it should be recalled that the conception of BHNs arose in the context of a theory of human development rather than as part of a theory of the causes of social conflict or its resolution. Nonetheless, in much of the development writing it is possible to trace out an underlying assumption about BHNs to the effect that they do not, in themselves, lead to conflict between individuals or groups seeking to fulfill them. Human needs theorists (or some of them) imply that the pursuit of human needs can, indeed, lead to disputes and conflicts in circumstances where there is a scarcity of goods, roles or other rewards to satisfy the sought after needs, and where no alternative "satisfiers" are immediately available. However, the implication is that it is the shortage of satisfiers and not the nature of the needs themselves that leads to conflict. If there are enough appropriate satisfiers, then the pursuit of human needs can take place without "social friction" and avoiding conflicts.

This idea has been taken up by conflict researchers, some of whom argue that conflicts do arise through the frustration of BHNs (often by others' actions in pursuing non-needs-based objectives), while others go further and at least imply that the causes of conflict can never arise from the pursuit of Human Needs but from other, interest- or role-based pursuits. Whatever the nuances of the particular argument, the implications are that conflicts arise only from the strategies used to achieve needs, the nature of the "satisfier-poor" environment in which needs are sought, or the non-needs-based pursuit of other goals.

This tendency to regard BHNs as, in themselves, "benign" or at least "neutral" as regards the creation of conflict is reflected in the way Needs are distinguished and labeled. To some extent, labeling of Needs is merely a semantic exercise, but the kinds of labels attached to particular phenomena often give a clue to the underlying assumptions about those labeled phenomena. In the case of BHNs, it seems clearly to be the case that those who have developed and used the concepts regard them as fundamentally positive and approveable. Needs Theory thus postulates that human development requires the fulfillment of BHNs such as identity, security, recognition, creativity, control, belongingness, love, choice and self-actuation.[14] At the very least, Needs so described appear, *in principle*, fulfillable without strife so long as there are enough satisfiers available, perhaps including a range of appropriate alternatives. Such BHNs could not appear to be conflict promoting in and of themselves.

However, it is perfectly possible to take a less sanguine view of the basic nature of human needs and their own conflict promoting potential. It is not even necessary to return to the traditionally negative view of human nature (to a Hobbes-ian or Morgenthau-ian view of man as essentially grasping, dissatisfied and power-driven or to a Lorenz-ian, genetically aggressive man) to realize that human needs could easily be characterized as basically malign, and conflict promoting by their very nature. The need for "security" could easily become the need for "dominance;" the need for "identity" could become the need for an outgroup and an enemy; the need for "love" could become the need for "admiration" or "status" or "success at the expense of others."

Part of the problem, of course, is that the only clues to the fundamental nature of human needs arise from the observation of human behavior rather than direct observation of the needs themselves (a problem discussed further in the Third Section below). There is a great deal of observable human behavior that is undoubtedly harmful to others, self-serving, aggressive, violent and dominating. It is perfectly reasonable to argue that such behavior might arise from the frustration of needs that are, in themselves, either benign – or, at least, neutral – as regards outcomes from needs pursuit. Unfortunately, it seems equally reasonable to argue that such behavior may merely be the working out of a set of human needs that are fundamentally far more malign than those usually postulated to exist in either the BHN or conflict resolution literature – that are, in other words, conflict promoting, rather than the reverse, in any circumstances.

The implications of this possibility for a theory of conflict resolution need little emphasis. If necessitous man *is* driven by a BHN for domination (only a slight revision of the argument that he is driven by a need for security), or to be dominated as early work on authoritarian personalities might suggest, then any theory of conflict resolution will need to take that need into account in the search for solutions. If, as Vamik Volkan suggests, human beings possess a basic need for enemies as well as allies[15] then theories of conflict resolution will have to take into account the fact that (at least some) BHNs are fundamentally conflict promoting, rather than being neutral or conflict inhibiting. The question then becomes one of which BHNs are benign and which are malign as far as creating conflict is concerned. To answer this question, however, we need to turn to a prior issue, the status of the conception of a Human Need, before examining what range of needs are claimed to underlie human behavior.

THE STRUCTURE OF HUMAN NEEDS

The Nature and Form of Human Needs

A second question, therefore, that arises from any design to make BHNs the centerpiece of a theory of conflict resolution is: what is the essential nature of BHNs, how do they manifest themselves and how are they identified? Only by answering such a question can we return to the issue of whether some BHNs are inherently conflict promoting while others are neutral or conflict inhibiting.

As Lederer has made clear, human needs take the form of *theoretical constructs* if only because "the existence of an individual's needs, or, stronger, the 'truth' of those needs cannot be proven in a direct, physical way."[16] One infers the existence of the phenomenon of "needs" from observable human behavior. To express the idea crudely, one discovers needs "backwards" by observing behavior (including verbal behavior) and then deducing the underlying existence of some reason for the individual undertaking that behavior – this then being labeled a "need." Lederer expresses the process rather more elegantly; "At best, the existence of a need can be concluded indirectly either from the respective satisfiers that the person uses or strives for or from symptoms of frustration caused by any kind of non-satisfaction."[17]

The process of deducing the existence of phenomena from observed behavior is always fraught with problems, which makes it very difficult to say whether observable, conflict promoting *behavior* arises from some basically malign, conflict promoting need (to have an enemy) or some frustrated neutral need (denying people the need to have a sense of security).

It may be, of course, that there are no malign, conflict promoting needs and that malign *behavior* arises from needs being frustrated or from other quite separate causes. The latter argument is often put forward in contemporary writings about conflict resolution.[18] where it is argued that deep rooted conflicts are often caused by the behavior of one party (often those in authority, top dogs, majorities, the powerful) frustrating the BHNs of others in defense of roles, for "institutional values" or in order to maintain "control."[19] The implication of such writing is that this kind of behavior is essentially different from that undertaken (by the other, underdog, minority party) in pursuance of BHNs. The next problem concerning the nature of BHNs, therefore is whether some human behavior does not arise from efforts to fulfill Basic Human Needs and how one can distinguish between behavior of this second type and that which does arise from the pursuit of BHNs.

Approached slightly differently, the question can be posed: how can one clearly tell what (if anything) is *not* a manifestation of a BHN? Obviously, this is a crucial problem for any effort to develop a theory of conflict resolution based upon a human needs approach. If resolutions must fulfill BHNs (perhaps by providing appropriate satisfiers) to be successful and durable, then facilitators and other intermediaries must have some means of distinguishing behavior undertaken to fulfill BHNs from behavior not so directed. (The latter can safely to ignored in helping to construct a resolution.) What criteria might be suggested to assist in the task of differentiation?

Alternatively, it might be argued that all behavior does arise from some (perhaps tactically misguided) efforts to fulfill BHNs (In this case other issues arise about hierarchies of Human Needs which are discussed below.) But this does raise a further question bearing upon the very utility of a BHN approach: if BHNs underlie *all* forms of human behavior in any social conflict, then how do we begin to consider the nature of resolutions as opposed to settlement? In Gilbert Rist's words, "if everything is a need, then need means nothing."[20]

The Variety of Human Needs

A further set of questions that confront anyone trying (1) to develop a Human Needs-based theory of conflict resolution and (2) to discover whether certain needs might be inherently conflict promoting, concern the number and variety of BHNs. Expressed simply, the question is: What are the BHNs, how many of them exist and how can one tell?

In many senses, this is the crucial question. Any theory that says resolution must remove frustration of BHNs (rather than cope with conflict promoting Needs) must also be able to state clearly what such Needs are, as a preliminary to evaluating whether a proposed resolution satisfies them.

Unfortunately, the variety of human needs postulated by different authors seems bewildering in its complexity, particularly when one ventures beyond the basic list of purely material needs that human individuals undoubtedly require for physical survival.[21]

To take only a few examples, some from writers who have tried to use a foundation of *satisfied* Human Needs to discuss the nature of a *resolved conflict*, Banks[22] mention three BHNs that are relevant for conflict resolution: (1) the need for basic resources; (2) the need for self-determination; and (3) the need for association. In a private communication, De Reuck talks of "legitimate" conflict resolution and lists six "supra-biological" Basic Needs that any agreement must fulfill if it is to count as a resolution: Identity,[23] Recognition, Rationality, Respect, Autonomy, and Control. Even in the brief lists of these two close colleagues there only seems to be a limited degree of overlap ("self-determination" and "autonomy," perhaps, or "association" and "respect/recognition"). A similar divergence can be noted if we turn to one of the founders of needs theory, James C. Davies, who implies that Human Needs are not mere theoretical constructs but "organically, genetically programmed predispositions" consisting of (1) physical, (2) social–affectional, (3) self-esteem and (4) self-actualization needs;[24] and Johan Galtung who writes of (1) security, (2) welfare, (3) identity and (4) freedom needs.[25]

The task of determining which is the more accurate list of BHNs appears a difficult one,[26] as does the practical task of shaping a solution to a conflict which satisfies all Needs on any resultant schedule of BHNs. As Galtung suggests, this may be a fruitless task and it may not be reasonable to imagine "that a list of needs can be established, complete with minima and maxima, for everybody at all given social times and social spaces."[27] However, if there is no universal list of BHNs then those involved (either through frustration or being malignantly played out) in one conflict may be very different from those involved in a second, parallel dispute. The implications of this possibility for a sound, general theory of conflict resolution need not be stressed.

Anyone seeking to act in a conflict resolution role must begin by asking Human Needs theorists whether there is any complete list of BHNs and whether such a list will lead (1) to a revelation of the underlying causes of the conflict under review and (2) to a solution that, at least in principle, unambiguously resolves the conflict by removing those causes. If there is no such list, then efforts to develop a theory of conflict resolution based on removing the factors frustrating BHNs seems doomed to failure – or, at least, to a hit and miss strategy that can hardly be said to be based in sound theory. Unfortunately, even if such a list can be produced and contains all fundamental needs that must be satisfied by some solution, a number of subsidiary questions still arise about the nature of the BHNs on that list.

Basic Human Needs: The Problem of Hierarchy

Assuming that it is possible to identify at least those BHNs which are relevant to social and international conflicts, the next issue important to any theory of conflict resolution is whether BHNs have equal value for those holding them. Expressed slightly differently: are all BHNs equally necessary or important, or is there an order of importance (a hierarchy) from most to least, or from essential to peripheral?

The relevance of this question for conflict resolution processes and solutions is easy to see. If a hierarchy of BHNs does exist, then resolutions might become a matter of satisfying the most important needs first, and dealing with the peripheral needs as a secondary consideration. If needs are equally important, then an agreement must deal equally thoroughly with all relevant needs in order to achieve a long term resolution.

On the particular issue of hierarchy versus equal importance, however, many Human Needs writers appear to agree, even if only implicitly, that there is, indeed, some kind of order of importance in the list of BHNs. In this they are, perhaps, following both Maslow's original formulation of the concept as well as Davies's clearly stated view[28] that there is a clear set of priorities for BHNs, running from the physical to the self-actualizing. (Davies does, however, make the point that the order of priorities can sometimes be reversed depending upon circumstances, as when people undergo yet ignore hunger and pain when fulfilling themselves in some salient manner.)

One exception is Rist,[29] who considers the possibility that there might be "non-basic" as well as "basic" needs, the former obviously being less important, but who comes (with Heller) to the conclusion that "All needs felt by humans to be real must be considered as real." However, other writers on Human Needs seem to elevate one or more need as paramount, and make others subordinate to or dependent upon the first. Burton, for example, argues that BHNs such as security and identity will be pursued by individuals "subject only to constraints they impose upon themselves in their need to maintain valued relations,"[30] clearly implying that the last named need is paramount.

In a different context, Oscar Nudler suggests a clearly hierarchical conception of human needs, and begins with the need for *identity*, "the first and most fundamental need of the person system."[31] This is then accompanied by two other *fundamental* needs, the need to grow and the need to transcend, from each of which arises a set of *derived* needs (such as shelter, affection, security, self-esteem or meaningfullness) the exact nature of which depends upon each individual's environment. In Nudler's hierarchy, the *fundamental* needs are invariable, but the *derived* needs differ according to the social system to which an individual belongs.[32]

If, then, it seems generally agreed that there are BHNs which are less important than others, so that needs can be divided (at least) into *essential* and *peripheral*, what are the implications for conflict resolvers? Does a resolution have to deal with both types of BHN or only with the essential ones? If the latter is the case, are we not logically driven to acknowledge that there are differing degrees by which a conflict may be "resolved," that some resolutions are better than others (i.e. they fulfill more peripheral needs, having already fulfilled the essential needs), that there are different levels of "success" in conflict resolution and even that the simple dichotomy between a resolution and a settlement may no longer be sustainable?[33]

This final possibility leads to a further general consideration concerning BHNs, which is the issue of *degree* – in this case, the degree to which they are fulfilled and, hence, the level of success of any resolution. (However, the principle of *degree* is one that might also apply more fundamentally to the nature of BHNs themselves.) To this we might add a further consideration arising out of the apparent consensus regarding the hierarchical nature of BHNs, namely the possibility that the need hierarchy might be a variable one, both *comparatively* (different individuals or groups possessing and attempting to fulfill *different* basic need hierarchies) and *temporally* (the same individual or group possessing differing need hierarchies *at different points in time*). The possibility of a *variable* need hierarchy gives rise to two further fundamental questions:

1. Does the BHN hierarchy vary from person to person or group to group (according to variations in age, gender, education, culture, etc.) or is it fixed and universal?

2. Does the same BHN hierarchy vary within the same individual or group over time, or is it wholly fixed and static irrespective of environmental changes?

Our next section discusses these issues of *divisibility, distribution* and *dynamics* of BHNs, all issues of practical and theoretical importance for conflict research and resolution.

PROBLEMS OF APPROPRIATE NEED FULFILLMENT

Needs and Their Degree of Fulfillment

As already outlined, much recent writing on the resolution of social and international conflict argues that, for a conflict to be genuinely resolved, the underlying issues must be brought to light, analyzed and then dealt with in a mutually satisfactory way that involves the fulfillment of basic needs to achieve a win–win outcome. Human needs are held to be fundamentally non-negotiable so that a resolution must, by definition, fulfill these needs to the satisfaction of the parties involved,[34] otherwise the solution is likely to be merely temporary.

Does such an approach put conflict resolvers in an either/or situation, however? By this, I mean whether it is, indeed, the case that one can fulfil BHNs only completely or not at all. Are BHNs *absolutes*, so that one either has one's needs (or one particular need) fulfilled, or one does not? Is it meaningful to talk about *degrees of fulfillment* of BHNs (and, possibly, "satisfactory levels" or "thresholds of fulfillment") or is this prevented by the very nature of human needs themselves?

Put in slightly different terms: Are BHNs divisible, so that it is possible to talk about varying degrees of fulfillment of a particular need? Is it the case that a person or a party feels secure or does not (or that a settlement provides identity or it does not); or is it the case that a person or party can experience more or less security or identity, depending upon the nature of the situation or of the arrangements proposed for ending a dispute?

If it is the case that BHNs are *divisible* (what Zartman, in another context, calls "inch-able") a number of consequences concerning arrangements for terminating conflicts follow. The first is that it becomes meaningful to talk about a person's or a party's sense of security (experience of having the need for security satisfied) *increas-*

ing over time as a result of some termination arrangements, rather than about that party being insecure at one point in time and secure later. Secondly, it also becomes meaningful to talk about different solutions (termination arrangements) offering *different degrees* of fulfillment of particular BHNs, so that such solutions can be *compared* according to the degree of need fulfillment they offer. Solution *A* might offer a higher degree of security to the parties than Solution *B*, but the latter offers a greater level of identity or of recognition.[35] The point about the *divisibility* of BHNs is that, unless they are absolutes (and not at all inch-able), then one is not inevitably talking about the achievement of a resolution rather than a settlement of any conflict, but about various kinds of solution which differentially fulfill the parties' BHNs. Successful conflict resolution then becomes a matter of the extent to which alternative termination arrangements will fulfill the parties' basic needs. Some resolutions will cover a wider range of BHNs more satisfactorily than others.

A related issue to that of *divisibility* of BHNs – although the connection may not be immediately apparent – is that of *substitutability*. Whether one can or cannot have varying degrees of security or of identity, it is still possible to enquire of needs theorists: are BHNs substitutable one for another and does the possession on one (say, security) make up for the absence of another (say, identity)?

Perhaps the question makes more sense if we combine the principles of divisibility and substitutability, and assume that it is reasonable to talk both about possessing different degrees of fulfillment of BHNs and about exchanging a marginal amount of security for greater opportunities to be creative. Instead of enquiring whether a person has to satisfy all BHNs all the time, one asks whether a person or a party can exchange some security for some identity, or vice versa, without necessarily having to be coerced into such an arrangement at the ending of a dispute.

The implication for arguing that BHNs are *substitutable* – and, hence "swap-able" – one for another, so that (at least above some minimum threshold) parties in conflict might be prepared to exchange a little less identity for a little more security or autonomy, appear to be the same as deciding that BHNs are "inch-able," like traditional "interests" or "bargaining dimensions." Conflict researchers arrive at a position from which there can be some discussion of solutions that, at least in principle, offer varying degrees of BHN satisfaction to adversaries. Different termination arrangements that offer different "packages" of fulfillment of BHNs can be envisaged, even if the actual process of agreeing on one such "package" as a resolution for a particular conflict may remain intractable. However, this is a markedly different position from that which argues that frustrated BHNs *all* have to be fulfilled *completely* if a self-sustaining and durable resolution of a conflict is to be achieved.

Dynamic Aspects of Basic Human Needs

Much of the foregoing discussion of the basic nature of BHNs has an underlying theme of *stability*, assuming – as do many writers on conflict resolution – that the needs to be satisfied through a resolution are not merely fundamental and universal but also *static* rather than *dynamic*. Is it generally felt to be the case that BHNs remain constant and unchanging, and what are the implications of such a view for any theory of conflict resolution?

It may be the case that the accepted view of needs theorists is that *basic, fundamental* human needs are static, and do not alter over time. If so, a fundamental question arises about whether needs are at all useful in trying to explain something as variable as human behavior. This issue seems to be a contemporary version of familiar arguments about human nature as an explanatory factor for human behavior. Whatever one's view about the basic nature of man – whether this be aggressive, power seeking man, rational calculating man or necessitous man – one always has to confront the difficulty that viewing human nature as a constant renders any explanation of a variable (such as human behavior) impossible, unless attention is shifted from the constant (human nature) to other variables. One cannot use a constant to explain variation in a variable. If one adopts a Hobbesian view of the nature of man – as do many international relations scholars – with its emphasis on the struggle for power and dominance, then one can explain war, but one is left with the problem of explaining the occurrence of peace – or, at least, the alternation of periods of war (theoretically attributable to warlike human nature) and peace (not so attributable). If BHNs *are* basic, fundamental and unchanging, then do they genuinely act as an explanation of conflict, rather than explaining the changing social and cultural circumstances that, at times, lead to the frustration of those needs on a massive scale (and thus to massive conflicts) but at other times do not?

There is considerable evidence that some human needs theorists regard at least the hierarchy of human needs as subject to change over time and according to circumstances. James Davies writes of occasions when need priorities are reversed, so that fundamental physical needs remain unfulfilled while others are being pursued, at least for short periods of time. Davies argues that such reversals of the need hierarchy are "very unusual in frequency and brief in duration,"[36] but the fact that they can take place indicates that need hierarchies are dynamic and can alter in response to environmental conditions. Given that Davies's discussion concentrates upon the issue of when very basic physical needs will be downgraded in the hierarchy, he also implies the possibility that, at the level of less basic needs, changes in the salience (and hence order) of individual needs in the hierarchy may be more frequent and durable.

Johan Galtung takes a similar view about the dynamic nature of need hierarchies and, indeed, of needs themselves, and he argues strongly that theorists should not take a rigid view of the nature of the two phenomena, but rather admit the impact of environmental factors so that needs and need hierarchies are not "socialisation- (and hence culture-) independent."[37]

In contrast to Davies, Galtung indicates his belief that, in certain dire circumstances ("utter deprivation"), failure to fulfill the very basic "material" needs would produce wholly similar patterns of behavior from any person or group. On the other hand, when the environment permits the pursuit of "non-material" needs, much flexibility can be exhibited, both among groups and individuals from different cultures and even within the same people at different points of time. In the first case, different individuals and groups "will have their priorities and indeed their own conceptions of needs" so that "basic human needs differ between individuals and groups and vary over time; they are malleable (but not infinitely so)."[38] Even in the second case, needs can also change even though "once they are sufficiently internalised in a human being, that individual is no longer malleable without considerable risk."[39]

While there seems to be no general concensus about the issue of whether needs or need hierarchies are static or dynamic (or about the issue of whether people from different backgrounds can have differing need hierarchies), there is enough evidence to say that some needs theorists clearly take the view both that (1) need and needs hierarchies change over time and according to circumstances; and (2) that different people can have different need hierarchies and even "conceptions of needs." Given that this is so, and conflict researchers can regard BHNs as *dynamic*, then a number of further questions arise concerning the nature of that dynamism.

The first focuses on the nature of the change that BHNs undergo. If a person's or group's needs hierarchy alters, does this not mean that the felt needs themselves change in overall intensity, such that persons' (and parties') experience of the needs can vary over time, with some periods being characterized by weakly felt needs, others by strongly felt ones?[40]

Secondly, are BHNs dynamic only in the sense that the needs hierarchy changes, with the relative salience or order of importance of particular needs altering from one time period to the next? Persons or parties may experience time periods in which security is the most salient need and later periods when identity becomes the most salient and security (or efficacy) much less salient. But are there other forms of change that occur, such as particular needs disappearing completely from the range experienced by particular persons or groups?

Lastly, there is the question of *how* and *why* changes occur in a person's (or a party's) BHNs. It might be that the change occurs quite randomly, which makes the task of any conflict resolution process rather difficult. Alternatively, BHNs might change in some patterned way, over time. It seems a reasonable hypothesis that we might change the salience, ordering and intensity of our BHNs as we get older. Alternatively, it is equally reasonable to argue that BHNs might alter in response to external inputs or environmental circumstances.[41] If needs and need hierarchies are "malleable," in Galtung's terms, what is the nature of that malleability?

The whole issue of static versus dynamic needs can easily be seen to be of great importance for any theory of conflict resolution through the satisfying of frustrated BHNs. If needs are essentially static then particular, limited, strategies become the only ones available to achieve a resolution of a needs-based, deep rooted conflict. If needs change over time, then a range of other strategies become, in principle, feasible for dealing with the adversaries. Different satisfiers can become appropriate in different circumstances and at different times. However, the problem of identifying *relevant* BHN hierarchies then becomes a problem.

SATISFIERS AND THE THEORY OF CONFLICT RESOLUTION

It may be the case, as some conflict researchers have argued, that concentrating on the phenomenon of BHNs as the starting point for a theory of conflict resolution is an error, given the unchanging nature of these sources of human behavior; Instead, it is argued, a theory of conflict resolution should begin with the *satisfiers* available to fulfill those needs and overtly pursued by individuals, groups – and, hence, "parties" – in conflict. In this line of argument it is not the needs themselves but the choice of means for fulfillment (satisfiers) that can create conflict. For example, if everyone possesses or is driven by a need for recognition and the *only* appropriate satisfier for that particular need is a valued, respected and rewarded role, then the relative scarcity of such roles can (and will) become a source of conflict. However, resolution of such "need-for-recognition" based conflicts can be based upon:

1. Expanding the number of such roles (*additional* satisfiers) available within the social system affected by such conflict (provide recognition in new cultures – pop music, sport, scholarship – in addition to existing social hierarchies).
2. Providing *alternative* satisfiers to fulfill needs for recognition among those being frustrated by non-fulfillment of such needs (increase material rewards for individuals and groups in the social system with low status – for example, pay garbage collectors more than lawyers). In this approach, it can be argued that needs theory can outline the conditions necessary for human development and, while it does not *automatically* form a starting point for a theory of conflict resolution, at least it *can* also indicate why conflict arises (inevitable pursuit of BHNs and a scarcity of satisfiers) and how it might be avoided or resolved (provision of more satisfiers).

Conflict researchers adopting this approach to the conception of BHNs as an explanation for the fundamental sources of human conflict can, therefore, argue that it is either competition for scarce satisfiers or the pursuit of particular satisfiers at the expense of other individuals and groups that makes for conflict within and between socio-political systems. Conflict resolution then becomes a matter of:

1. emphasizing the likely resistance and costs inevitably to be met as others find their BHNs unfulfilled in the latter case; and
2. providing additional or alternative satisfiers (the creation or discovery of optional sources of need fulfillment) in the former.

As long as alternative satisfiers that are non-damaging to others are, in principle, available then conflict resolution is possible.

The Issue of Alternative Satisfiers

However, as with human needs themselves, the conception of "satisfiers" as a basis for a theory of conflict resolution requires refinement and the answering of a number of basic questions about a *satisfier's* nature and form, as well as the role that it might play in any such theory. The first query concerns the issue of *substitutability* implied in the conflict researchers' argument that alternative satisfiers for BHNs can always, in principle, be found in order to bring about a resolution of a conflict.

Clearly, the implication of this argument is that specific human needs do not demand specific satisfiers and can be fulfilled by a variety of satisfiers (or, at least, a limited range of satisfiers). The view that one satisfier can successfully be substituted for another (scarce or non-available) satisfier implies at least a *limited* substitutability for satisfiers, and this view also implies that it is not the case – at least for the less fundamental needs in a needs hierarchy – that only one satisfier will "do the job." The rejection of what might be called the "single key satisfier that fits each needs lock" view may take the form of arguing that *all* needs have a variety of potential satisfiers that can be substituted one for another; or the modified view may argue that it becomes progressively more difficult to find alternative satisfiers the further one moves in a needs hierarchy from, say, derived to fundamental needs. (After all, there seem to be few substitutes for food as a satisfier of the most basic material need, although it could be argued that what one culture defines as "acceptable" food can alter under extreme circumstances where survival is at stake – hence the rare cases in extremis of cannibalism.)

However, to argue that satisfiers can be substituted one for another (the need for creativity can be fulfilled by having an interesting job or by playing a musical instrument in one's leisure time) is not necessarily to argue that all satisfiers are equally fulfilling of a particular need or a range of needs. (Satisfiers, presumably, can simultaneously fulfill a number of needs.) It is quite possible that, for each need, there exists a *hierarchy of satisfiers* that are more (or less) effective in fulfilling that need. If there are what some theorists have called "partial satisfiers," then the possibility of conflict resolution through substitution becomes more problematical as alternative satisfiers of frustrated needs may fulfill those needs less well than the satisfiers being sought over the opposition of others. We might here be dealing with a "Methadone model"[42] of alternative satisfiers offered to parties in conflict by a conflict resolution process. Options may, indeed, exist but they may be less fulfilling than those currently being pursued, in which case conflict resolution becomes involved in the question of whether or not the options revealed are fulfilling *enough* to produce a self-sustaining and durable solution.

Deriving the Range of Satisfiers

Inevitably, the issue of more or less effective satisfiers for fulfilling particular needs raises the basic question of the nature and range of satisfiers, which is yet another way in which questions raised by adopting a "conflict resolution through satisfiers" approach parallel those raised by a "conflict resolution through BHNs" approach. We need to know what is the range of potential satisfiers available and which satisfiers fulfill which needs (and with what degree of effectiveness!). It may be that this is an unanswerable question, posed in the abstract. The sheer number and variety of satisfiers mentioned in the existing literature on human needs seems almost infinite. Moreover, it seems clear from some of the human needs writing that both *material* and *non-material* satisfiers suffer from the problem of *volatility*, by which I mean that what may be a satisfier at one point of time and in one set of circumstances may not act to fulfill the same need(s) in a different environment. Galtung, for example, provides an interesting list of satisfiers "*held* to be relevant in *some* societies,"[43] ranging from food and water through jobs, recreation and schooling to elections, labor markets and transportation. In the list he includes "police and military" as satisfiers of the need for security, but he would probably agree that, in other circumstances, those very "satisfiers" might play a major role in frustrating other basic needs including, quite probably, the need for security.

Indeed, a major theme of Galtung's work on human needs and satisfiers concerns the *relativity* of satisfiers to the context in which human needs are being pursued and (particularly) with the theme that one should never assume that Western satisfiers can be used to fulfill basic human needs experienced in non-Western societies. He comments that "satisfiers do not fall from heaven" and argues that "they are produced in and by a social context and are dependent on that context."[44] If this is the case (and it would seem perverse to argue otherwise, particularly given the observable variety of ways in which people satisfy an inferred need, for example, for creativity or for identity), then the argument that conflicts may be resolved by discovering alternative satisfiers is undeniably a powerful one, provided it is modified to include the probabilities:

1. that particular satisfiers are more likely to be acceptable need fulfillers in one context than are others which work perfectly well in other contexts; and
2. that satisfiers which are *highly* effective in meeting needs in one context may be *less* effective in others.

The problem for developing a general theory of conflict resolution becomes that of discovering which satisfiers can work well in which contexts and which are easily transferable from one context to another.

Socially Learned Satisfiers

This line of thought does indicate that an approach to a theory of conflict resolution via need satisfiers raises an issue beyond those encountered in respect of the nature of BHNs. If it is the case that satisfiers of needs are substitutable but vary in their likely effect from context to context, then it seems likely that, while BHNs may be general and universal aspects of the nature of man, satisfiers are culturally derived from – or, at least, affected, influenced or even determined by – cultural variables. To a degree, this argument follows naturally from that concerning the (at least theoretical) availability of alternative satisfiers and the conception of "socially learned satisfiers" used by some needs theorists. If different individuals and groups can learn what are appropriate and acceptable satisfiers for their human needs then, even if they can learn (perhaps to their surprise) that other acceptable satisfiers may be available, there may be cultural barriers to the *ready* acceptance of such substitutes, even if this enables parties to resolve their conflicts. The discovery of conflict resolving options may not, in itself, mean that these options are automatically perceived as attractive to people from a particular culture accustomed to another (admittedly scarce) range of satisfiers. (Even in the case of a physical BHN (for food), the availability of a dietetically quite appropriate alternative satisfier (roast pork) may not appear a realistic option to members of particular cultures (Muslim or Hindu) and it may thus not prove a means of removing the frustration of the need.) The question for conflict resolution then becomes one of discovering:

1. what range of satisfiers have conventionally been regarded as acceptable fulfillers of which needs in society or culture X;
2. what new satisfiers might usefully be added to that range in order to increase the availability of need fulfillers and thus resolve conflicts arising from frustration of needs; and
3. how relatively appropriate might such innovative satisfiers be in fulfilling the un-met needs, and to what extent will the latter then be fulfilled.

At present, it has to be admitted that the literature linking cultures to socially learned satisfiers, and the literature exploring the successful introduction of new forms of satisfier to resolve needs-based conflict is sparse, whether one searches in the field of needs theory or that of conflicts arising from frustration of needs; and
to construct a theory of conflict resolution based on the substitution of alternative satisfiers in situations of "traditional" satisfier scarcity.

CONCLUSION

In the light of the above discussion of the nature of human needs theory and its corollary, and of the nature of satisfiers that must exist to fulfill those needs if full "human development" is to occur, what might be concluded about the use of a BHN approach to develop a theory of conflict resolution?

At first I might suggest determining the extent to which a variety of conceptual and theoretical problems have to be overcome if the BHN approach is to be useful in underpinning such a theory. At the present moment, a number of essential clarifications have to be made in the theory of BHNs and a number of contradictions resolved. For one thing, it is necessary to attain an agreed consensus about the nature and number of BHNs and about whether there is a need hierarchy, ranging from needs which are essential for full human development to those which are desirable but peripheral. Secondly, it is important to clarify the issue of whether or not needs and need hierarchies are, indeed, universal and fundamental in forming part of "human nature", irrespective of whether the human(s) in question come from a hunter–gatherer or subsistence farming culture, or from one of the so-called advanced industrialized cultures of the late twentieth century. Thirdly, there is the issue of whether or not human needs remain the same, fundamental and unchanging, over time and through altering environments and circumstances. It may be that this is the soundest assumption to make – after all, if needs *are* basic they will remain basic irrespective of age, circumstance or upbringing. However, there are distinct indications in some of the early writings on BHNs that at least some scholars consider it likely that human needs (and needs hierarchies) are dynamic, particularly those that are peripheral rather than fundamental.

Next there is an issue that connects the nature of BHNs with that of satisfiers. This issue involves the question of whether it is possible to fulfill BHNs partially, or whether they are either fulfilled completely or not at all. From the view point of satisfiers, the issue becomes one of whether there are satisfiers that partially fulfill felt needs, and whether there are particular satisfiers that fulfill particular needs better than others. A corollary of this issue is whether a satisfier's degree of successful need fulfillment is at all culturally determined, and what might be the implications of this possibility for a *general* theory of conflict resolution are applicable in any culture.

One of the main effects of raising such issues, I would suggest, is that they begin to cast doubt on conflict researchers' stark distinction between conflict *settlement* (incomplete and temporary) and conflict *resolution* (durable, acceptable and permanent because it fulfills all previously frustrated needs completely). If some satisfiers fulfill particular needs completely and other needs partially, then conflict researchers are back in the business of providing better or worse solutions to conflicts (depending upon the degree to which satisfiers are found and the degree to which they succeed in fulfilling the parties' BHNs) rather than in the business of providing wholly satisfactory resolutions that *totally* fulfill all frustrated needs. It may be that there is a continuum of need fulfillment underlying potential solutions to conflicts: one pole represents total satisfaction of all relevant BHNs and is labelled "Resolution." A central area represents less fulfilling solutions labeled something different; and an opposite pole is labeled, "Settlement," at which no improvement in fulfillment has occurred but a temporary compromise of interests has been arranged. However, once one has admitted the possibility of a partial fulfillment of a need through a less successful satisfier, the key question remains one of *the degree* to which a solution successfully fulfills the parties' needs, not whether or not it does fulfill them.

In conclusion, it may be that the BHN approach to human development could provide the possibility of a firm foundation upon which to build a general theory of conflict resolution. One way of concluding the discussion is by pointing out that the conception of frustrated BHNs could provide both a *theory of conflict causes* (even though, it could be argued, such a theory would merely be another one attributing conflict to scarcity – this time, scarcity of appropriate satisfiers); while the conception of alternative or substitute satisfiers (even if limited by cultural variables) could provide a *theory of conflict remedies*. At the moment, however, the key word used in making such a claim is "could." Many issues must be thought through before any real progress can be made on the issue of needs theory as a basis for "genuine" conflict resolution; not least is the matter of the methodological propriety of using a theory devised to explain individual behavior in pursuit of individual development as a way of understanding aspects of complex, collective (as opposed to aggregated) behavior.[45]

Let me end by saying that I hope that this chapter will generate an interesting debate and, at least, some heuristic answers. The study of conflict and its resolution is badly in need of a sound foundation from which both analysis and practical strategies for resolution can proceed. Human Needs Theory appears to offer a fruitful possibility for developing such a foundation.

NOTES AND REFERENCES

1. Several people have protested at the use of the word "man" in this context. I have retained the expression partly to remain in line with a long (admittedly sexist) tradition in political, social and economic writings that uses phrases like "economic" man or "rational man" in place of "human being" or "person;" and partly to follow George Orwell's stylistic advice about breaking any rules of English expression rather than write something downright ugly, such as "necessitous person."
2. What one writer once described as "an entry ticket to the next round."
3. J. W. Burton, *Conflict and Communication* (London: Macmillan, 1969); J. W. Burton, *Deviance, Terrorism and War: The Process of Solving Unsolved Social and Political Problems* (New York: St. Martin's Press, 1979); A. V. S. De Reuck, "Controlled Communication; Rationale and Dynamics," *The Human Context* VI (1) (Spring 1974): 64–80; M. Light, "The Problem Solving Workshop," in M. Banks (ed.), *Conflict in World Society* (Brighton, England: Wheatsheaf, 1984).
4. J. P. Taylor, *Dictionary of World History* (London: Nelson, 1973).
5. For example, Burton, *Conflict and Communication*.
6. I assume that the latter includes what a traditional international relations

scholar might mis-call "nation-states."

7. J. W. Burton, *Resolving Deep-Rooted Conflicts: A Handbook* (Lanham, M. D.: University Press of America, 1987).

8. Burton, *Resolving Deep-Rooted Conflicts*: 23.

9. Burton, *Resolving Deep-Rooted Conflicts*.

10. Burton, *Resolving Deep-Rooted Conflicts*, italics added.

11. A. Heraclides, "The Contours of the Gordian Knot: The Arab Israeli Conflict," *Paradigms* 2 (1) (June 1988).

12. Or, if one takes the position that resolution is not necessarily an absolute but can come in degrees, to what extent has it been successfully resolved?

13. Since writing a first draft of this chapter, I have read Katrin Gillwald's paper on "Contributions of Needs Research to Conflict Prevention," (Chapter 5 in this book) and seen that she approaches basically the same problems from a different but complementary angle. While this present chapter discusses the possible contribution of needs theory to conflict resolution by concentrating on the nature of needs themselves, the Gillwald chapter interestingly deals with the nature and availability of need *satisfiers*, and the impact these might have on the possibility of achieving the resolution of any deep rooted conflict. This is discussed further in my fifth section below.

14. Johan Galtung, "International Development in Human Perspective," in Roger A. Coate and Jerel A. Rosati (eds), *The Power of Human Needs in Society* (Boulder, CO: Lynne Reinner, 1988): 136.

15. Vamik D. Volkan, "The Need to Have Enemies and Allies; A Developmental Approach," *Political Psychology* 6 (12) (June 1985): 219–48.

16. Katrin Lederer (ed.) with Johan Galtung and David Antal, *Human Needs: A Contribution to the Current Debate* (Cambridge, MA: Oelgeschlager, Gunn & Hain, 1980).

17. Lederer (ed.), *Human Needs*.

18. Much writing on conflict resolution argues, or implies, that deep rooted conflict arises from the frustration or deterrence of BHNs by "authorities." The implication of such arguments is that there are two parties involved in the conflict; (a) a minority/set of underdogs who are having their own BHNs frustrated by the actions of (b) some majority/set of top-dogs, whose own behavior is *not*, however, similarly the result of attempting to fulfill their own BHNs, but rather some other set of goals (often negatively described), such as "role defense" or efforts at "social control." On what ground can it convincingly be argued that the latter might not equally be seeking to fulfill *their* BHNs and searching for their "security," "identity," etc.?

19. Are people whose behavior we dislike also trying to fulfill their BHNs? Do the Contras have BHNs?

20. G. Rist, "Basic Questions about Basic Human Needs," in Lederer (ed.), *Human Needs*, Chapter 10: 241.

21. See Galtung, "The Basic Needs Approach," in Lederer (ed.), *Human Needs*: 123, his chapter on BHNs (*Chapter 15 in this Volume*), where he discusses the vast list of 28 (!) needs proposed by E. J. Murray in his work *Motivation and Emotion*, a list including a number of needs that seem likely to promote conflict rather than resolve it. The need to

exercise power, the need to control others, the need to gain possessions and property are examples of needs which contrast very much with the more usual approaches of needs theorists, which present a view of human needs producing harmonious and cooperative behavior (if not frustrated) and a conflict free world.

22. M. H. Banks, *Conflict in World Society* (Brighton, England: Wheatsheaf, 1984).
23. There seems to be some confusion over this particular need. In some work, it is treated as a concept relating to an individual's need to preserve and strengthen a sense of individuality – that is, to be clearly and surely *separate* and apart from others. In other works, the concept is treated as an individual's sure and secure sense of belonging to a group, community or nation, such membership being unhampered and such groups being respected by others. In this second version, the concept deals with *belonging* (or being allowed to belong) rather than being apart.
24. James C. Davies, "The Existence of Human Needs," in Coate and Rosati (eds), *Power of Human Needs*: 26.
25. Other common BHNs in the literature on conflict resolution include (1) some form of efficacy or control and (2) some form of self-determination. Galtung, "International Development": 136.
26. See Rist, "Basic Questions," in Lederer (ed.), *Human Needs*: 236 where he emphasizes that social scientists using a basic needs approach are in a much more problematical position than biologists, who "restrict their investigations to the needs that can be established empirically."
27. Galtung, "International Development": 131.
28. Davies, "Existence of Needs," in Coate and Rosati (eds), *Power of Needs*: 30.
29. Rist, "Basic Questions," in Lederer (ed.), *Human Needs*: 241.
30. Burton, *Deep-Rooted Conflicts*: 15–16.
31. O. Nudler, "Human Needs: A Sophisticated Holistic Approach," in Lederer (ed.), *Human Needs*: 143.
32. Nudler, "Human Needs": 146–7.
33. Is a settlement merely an arrangement that fulfills no BHNs either essential or peripheral, or merely one which fulfills a few, peripheral, BHNs?
34. Some needs theorists make a distinction between *manifest* and *latent* needs, the latter being unconscious and (at least for some of the time) undetectable. I need hardly emphasize the additional difficulties for conflict resolvers created by the possible existence of such phenomena.
35. It might well be argued that, for all BHNs, there are "thresholds" of fulfillment, below which the level of need satisfaction is insufficient to make termination arrangements acceptable to conflicting parties. This seems a sensible argument but does raise a whole host of questions about how one identifies such thresholds, whether they vary from person to person and whether they vary over time.
36. Davies, "Existence of Needs": 30.
37. Galtung, "International Development": 139.
38. Galtung, "International Development".

39. Galtung, "International Development".
40. Note that this is a separate question from that which enquires about the degree to which BHNs are being satisfied (or not) by circumstances in the environment.
41. In connection with this latter possibility, one could envisage a situation in which an environment manages to satisfy a large number (if not all) *fundamental* human needs, together with some peripheral ones. In such circumstances, do other (previously peripheral) needs become more salient, so that persons or parties seek satisfaction of those unfulfilled needs that have risen to the very top of their needs hierarchy by the fact that they remain unfulfilled? *Are needs, or some of them, infinitely expendable* so that one form of change is merely *replacement*? If some BHNs are satisfied to some (reasonable) degree, do individuals start to want more satisfaction of those needs already fulfilled (does the need for identity become a need for fame and adulation once some level of identity has been achieved) or do other unfulfilled needs become salient?
42. Methadone is one of the substitute drugs given to addicts who are trying to withdraw from reliance on hard drugs. It could be regarded as an option and as some kind of a satisfier, but it is obviously less satisfactory than the original drug – perhaps so much less satisfactory as to disqualify it as a satisfier at all.
43. Galtung, "International Development": 136, italics added.
44. Galtung, "International Development": 134.
45. For example:
    (a) Can parties that are not individuals be said to have needs, save on some aggregated basis?
    (b) What are the implications of using the term "societal" needs?
    (c) How might the distribution of BHN satisfaction within a complex party (that is, among the individuals composing that party) affect whether the conflict can be resolved? One can posit any number of plausible scenarios whereby some key individuals – or factions – are all having their BHNs nicely fulfilled by the conflict and their roles within it, whereas others are not; yet alternative solutions or arrangements would have the effect of reducing the former's BHN satisfaction.

8 On Conflicts and Metaphors: Toward an Extended Rationality

Oscar Nudler

This chapter focuses on world and frame conflicts. In the first section, after introducing the problem, it is argued that conflicts of this kind require the use of non-conventional analytic tools. The second section addresses the issue of world and frame conflicts in science as an example, showing their wide scope. In the third section the emergence of these conflicts is explained by relating them to needs theory. In the fourth section the main contribution of this chapter to the conflict resolution field is outlined: metaphor dialogue. The fifth section summarizes the whole argument and concludes with the presentation of a pattern of conflict resolution stages.

WORLDS AND FRAMES

I would like to focus on a special kind of conflict, namely, conflicts between worlds or frames. Let me first say something about the way in which these key terms will be used in what follows.

William James, in his *Principles of Psychology*,[1] introduced "world" in the sense that concerns us here. After asking himself the Copernican question: *under what circumstances do we think things are real?* he answered by stating that it is our selective attention that makes different "worlds," or "subworlds," real for us: "each world, *whilst it is attended to*, is real after its own fashion, only the reality lapses with the attention."[2] We thus, switch from one world to the other: the world of science, the world of myths, the world of games, and so on. However, one of these worlds is stronger, "realer" than the others because it provides the foundation or substratum of them. James called it the world of the senses and in the phenomenological/hermeneutic tradition it has been variously referred to as the life world, the world of everyday life or just the *World* with a capital W; "A World then fulfills the most general set of preunderstandings one has about reality."[3]

English speaking authors, with the exception of the yet comparatively few phenomenologists who write in this language, prefer as a rule to avoid the term "world" in James' sense. They use instead terms like "code," "schema," "paradigm," etc. but, for one reason or another, these terms cannot be regarded as good substitutes. Erving Goffman, after pondering James's use of "world" and some other possible substitutes decided to adopt the term "frame": "I assume that definitions of a situation are built up in accordance with principles of organization which govern events – at least social ones – and our subjective involvement in them; frame is the word I use to refer to such of these basic elements as I am able to identify. That is my definition of frame."[4]

Curiously enough, we find an essentially similar use of "frame" in a rather different context, namely, artificial intelligence research. Marvin Minsky says: "A frame is a data-structure for representing a stereotyped situation, like being in a certain kind of living room, or going to a child's birthday party . . . We can think of a frame as a network of modes and relations. The 'top levels' of a frame are fixed, and represent things that are always true about the supposed situation. The lower levels have many terminals – 'slots' – that must be filled by specific instances or data."[5]

Both "world" and "frame" refer then to a set of assumptions or principles which enable us to structure situations and, by the same token, make them real for us. However, the two terms, though overlapping to some extent, seem nevertheless to have a different scope. While "world" can be properly applied only to the great domains of human experience – science, art dreams, everyday life – "frame" is more suited to more limited, specific fragments of experience like a given social interaction situation, a particular theory or view, and so on. It seems thus advisable to keep both terms in use.

A common characteristic of worlds (and to some extent of frames, too) is the non-reflective, uncritical acceptance of the basic assumptions on which they lie. As soon as we become critical of the assumptions on which a world is based, we somehow step out of it, no matter how strongly we continue to believe in such assumptions. Polanyi says:

When we accept a certain set of presuppositions and use them as our interpretative framework, we may be said to dwell in them as we do in our body. Their uncritical acceptance for the time being consists in a process of assimilation by which we identify ourselves with them. They are not asserted and cannot be asserted, for assertion can be made only *within* a framework with which we have identified ourselves for the time being.[6]

The idea that our most basic presuppositions remain beyond the scope of critical analysis was also stressed by Wittgenstein:

Giving grounds, however, justifying evidence, comes to an end; but the end is not certain propositions striking us immediately as true, i.e., is not a kind of *seeing* on our part; it is our *acting*, which lies at the bottom of the language-game.[7]

Personal worlds are to some extent unique. Sometimes the uniqueness is so deeply built-in that they may remain essentially closed to anyone else. Such is the mark of madness, or genius for that matter. However, language and culture provide a common framework thanks to which most of the people within its range share a great deal of their worlds.

Worlds may run into conflict. Such conflicts arise when people living in different worlds get into a situation which requires social contact or exchange among them. But not every conflict between people living in different personal worlds is an interworlds' conflict. Suppose, for instance, that we observe that two individuals whose worlds differ considerably are quarreling and finally fighting for some available piece of food. In this case hunger and not worlds' diversity may provide a sufficient account for their behavior. Thus conflicts between worlds are conflicts for which worlds' diversity is the *main* reason. In other words, worlds' diversity *per se*, and not any other reason (having to do, for instance, with scarcity of material or non-material goods) is the main cause of such conflicts. Of course, more often than not conflicts are due to an interrelated set of factors which sometimes makes it difficult to discern the world (or frame) basic component. Intergenerations and interethnic conflicts are cases in which such component is more easily visible. To take an example, a description made by M. Maruyama of ethnic conflicts in the United States may be read, substituting our term "world" for his term "epistemology," as a clear illustration of a conflict between worlds:

The basic epistemology of the American culture was essentially derived from the Greek–European epistemology based on deductive logic, assumption of one-way causal flow, and hierarchical social order mixed with the peculiarly American world view of uni-dimensionally rankable universe, competition, conquest, techno-centrism, and unicultural assimilation . . . This epistemology is being challenged by the emergence of other epistemologies. Some of these epistemologies have long existed among the ethnic minority groups in the United States unrecognized by the social majority: for example, the non-hierarchical mutualism of Navajos and Eskimos, the philosophy of balance of nature among most of the Native Americans (American Indians); and the world view of mutual complementarity brought in by Chinese and Japanese immigrants.[8]

Now the question arises: how it is possible that *mere* diversity, not necessarily opposition, between worlds and frames becomes a source of conflict, even of violent conflict? Before addressing this question let me add a few more remarks on the nature of world and frame conflicts.

In principle, these conflicts, though referring to facts, do not involve essentially disagreements that could be settled by appealing to factual evidence. Gestalt ambiguous figures are often used to illustrate this point (see Figure 8.1).[9]

Source: Hanson (1965)

Figure 8.1   The antelope/pelican ambiguous figure

If one party says that this figure represents an antelope and the other says that it represents a pelican, no empirical evidence would be conducive to settling the dispute. Obviously, one can say that the dispute is pointless since each party becomes right or wrong as soon as we adopt or reject its way of framing experience. There is an antelope-world and a pelican-world and both stand within the limits of a given perspective. No party is *just* true but true within a particular frame or world.

However, I am afraid that such a way out of the conflict, if not properly elaborated, may show only the limits of the Gestalt analogy. In real cases of conflicts in which discrepancy between worlds of frames is involved, people may refuse to accept that theirs is *just* one perspective and that there may be other equally respectable alternatives. Needless to say, this is the usual case. However, one can argue that if both parties are consistently rational – that is, if they in practice follow the principles and rules of ordinary logic – then sooner or later they should reach a point in which they will discover, by tracing their conflicting assertions up to their respective fundamental premises or assumptions, the world or frame nature of their dispute and will thus see it as a pelican/antelope case. Such a move would take the discussion to a different (presumably "superior") level in which each party would at least admit the right to exist of the other party's world and consider it as much as possible in its own terms. As a result, each of the opposite worlds may remain unchanged but a true dialogue, not just blind confrontation, would become possible.

Reaching this point is certainly not easy. It requires usually the help of a *third party* endowed not only with good will but also with very particular skills. According to an influential view, these are *analytic* problem-solving skills. In the challenging paper entitled precisely "Analytic Problem-Solving Conflict Resolution"[10] a quite articulated defense of this stance is made. A main key for successful conflict resolution processes is, according to the authors, the *ability* to *analyze*:

> This is the ability to think clearly, to be precise in the use of terms, to question basic assumptions, to be logical, and thus to reach valid conclusions. It is in this way we can arrive at an adequate theory or explanation of any situation or phenomenon. It is this case process which is the core of facilitated conflict resolution.[11]

The confidence shown by the authors in such ability to analyze is really great:

> Analysis of this kind is something within the capabilities of all persons from all cultures and all levels of education, especially when guided by the questioning and help of a third party. It is this analytical component which makes possible conflict resolution procedures which cut through cultures, religions and classes. This facilitated analytical focus also removes military, economic or role power from the interactions of disputants. The analytical approach serves to inform the more "powerful" that an outcome that it is not based on such an analysis is likely to be temporary.[12]

Now, it is my contention that the ability to analyze, to be logical, may eventually lead to conflict resolution in within-frame or within-world conflicts but that this is not the case in conflicts between frames, and even less so between worlds. This is not to imply that analytical conflict resolution procedures are useless in world or frame conflicts. My point is rather that in these cases they must be *complemented* by other procedures, appealing to quite different abilities, in order to make conflicts solvable or, what is sometimes a better outcome, creative and not *just* disruptive.[13] I will turn to this issue in the last section of this chapter. What I intend to do now is to take the case of science in order to show how it has come to be seen, as a result of developments taking place over the last thirty years, as a domain of human experience in which frame and world conflicts play a most significant role. If this view of science is, as I think, correct it immediately implies that analytic problem-solving is not enough to face all types of conflicts in science. The moral is obviously that if this is so in the case of science – the analytic domain *par excellence* – it should be *a fortiori* true in connection with other domains of human life.

CONFLICTS IN SCIENCE

The idea of world or frame conflicts as conflicts for whose resolution neither empirical evidence nor logic are relevant or sufficient, is by no means new. Nineteenth century German historicism had already developed the notion of the *Zeitgeist* (spirit of the age) as a framework which possesses unique and widely disparate standards of intelligibility and reality. Actually, the distance between different *Zeitgeists* was seen by historicists as so large that not even conflict between them seemed conceivable. Conflict requires sharing something – namely, a territory or stage on which it may be acted out. But historicism, by positing radical uncommensurability among *Zeitgeists* removed such common ground. The French philosopher Michel Foucault, whose *Les Mots et les Choses*[14] is possibly one of the best expressions of this view in our century, depicted the "archeological history" of European *epistēmēs* as a history of extreme discontinuity between worlds:

> Within an epistēmē, he proposes quite as much conflict and disagreement between opposing theories as we ordinarily allow for. But between epistēmēs, he proposes something much more

than we ordinarily allow for: a discontinuity so deep and unbridge-able as to be beyond even conflict and disagreement.[15]

This radically pessimistic view about the possibility of interworlds dialogue found only limited support in the Anglo-Saxon milieu despite some influential developments like the Sapir–Whorf thesis on the linguistic determination of thought which might have favored it. As a matter of fact, the realm of scientific knowledge was not significantly touched, at least until the late 1950s, by the historicist–relativist wave, even in its milder forms. Philosophers of science belonging to quite different schools – logical positivists, Popperians and even Marxists like Althusser – shared the view that science is rational in the sense that the acceptance or rejection of scientific hypotheses and theories – though not necessarily their invention or discovery – is not a matter of subjective or cultural preference but is subject to objective, universal criteria based on a combination of empirical, replicable evidence and logical argument. The specific nature of such criteria was a matter of intense disagreement (for instance, between inducti-vists and deductivists) but its objectivity was generally not put in doubt by anybody. Most philosophers of science used to define their task as *rational* or *logical reconstruction* of actual scientific practice at its best (which meant natural sciences, particularly physics). Science was thus seen by logical reconstructionists not only as an essentially rational enterprise but also as *the* paradigmatic case of application of the higher human rational capabilities.

Competition and conflict within science was, of course, admitted by orthodox epistemology, and even seen as one of the motivating forces of scientific progress. However, a notion like world or frame conflict as defined above – conflict for whose resolution neither empirical evidence nor logic is relevant or sufficient – would have been considered as totally alien to the realm of science. No matter how relevant for conflicts of other kinds – religious, political, ideological, cultural, and so on – its application to conflict in science was totally out of the question. In fact, the idea was that far from profiting from procedures developing in other domains, problem-solving in science may provide a model to be applied – *mutatis mutandis* – to almost any problem, particularly social problems. The rationale was simple: if the methods used in science have achieved such a tremendous amount of success, why not try them in other areas too?

As is well known, the orthodox image of science began to be

increasingly challenged by a group of scientists, philosophers and historians of science in the late 1950s and, more particularly, after the publication in 1962 of T. S. Kuhn's *The Structure of Scientific Revolutions*.[16] One by one, all the basic components of such image were brought to the surface and became the subject matter of a fascinating debate which somehow still goes on. I would mention, for example, the attack against the classic view that the empirical basis of science, represented by observational language, is neutral or independent with respect to scientific interpretations of it that use theoretical language. Such independence, traditionally assumed as the guarantee of scientific objectivity, was now strongly challenged.

It is clear that from the orthodox perspective science does not constitute a *world* in the sense introduced above. According to the latter, a perceiver's world cannot be separated from the perceiver's preunderstandings of reality for the very reason that they contribute to his perception as such. As early as 1958, N. Russell Hanson argued at length against the dichotomy between observation and theory. For example, he said that Tycho Brahe and Kepler saw – in one sense of the word seeing that – the same sun but, in another sense – seeing as – they saw quite different suns rising above the horizon: "There is a sense, then, in which seeing is a 'theory-laden' undertaking."[17]

In other words, our accepted theories cannot be exclusively considered as *post hoc* interpretations of a pure, neutral seeing but should be also recognized as incorporated into it.

We might thus summarize this changed view of scientific theory and practice by saying that science started to be seen as giving rise to a *world* – or, more exactly, to as many worlds as scientific revolutions and breakthroughs have brought to life

in a sense that I am unable to explicate further, the proponents of competing paradigms practise their trades in different worlds. One contains constrained bodies that fall slowly, the other pendulums that repeat their motion again and again. One is embedded in a flat, the other in a curved, matrix of space. Practising in different worlds, the two groups of scientists see different things when they look from the same point in the same direction.[18]

M. Polanyi had already introduced the idea of world in his description of the learning process in science:

Think of a medical student attending a course in the X-ray diagnosis of pulmonary diseases. He watches in a darkened room shadowy traces on a fluorescent screen placed against a patient's chest, and hears the radiologist commenting to his assistants, in technical language, on the significant features of these shadows. At first the student is completely puzzled . . . he can see nothing that [the experts] are talking about . . . eventually, if he perseveres intelligently, a rich panorama of significant details will be revealed to him: of physiological variations and pathological changes, of scars, of chronic infections and signs of acute disease. He has entered a new *world* (italics added).[19]

The picture of scientific activity in term of worlds, with all the subjective and cultural "thickness" attached, made oscillate violently the epistemological pendulum to the opposite extreme to orthodox logicism – that is, to the total rejection of transworlds' standards of rationality and progress – and, hence, to extreme relativism. Some statements by Kuhn – like the one quoted above – and by other critics of orthodoxy – particularly Feyerabend's uncommensurability thesis – strongly suggested a necessary link between the critique of logical reconstructionism and relativism. Richard Rorty, in his remarkable *Philosophy and the Mirror of Nature*[20] contributed further to strengthen such a link by rejecting the traditional claim of philosophers to be dealing with the foundations of knowledge beyond any specific conceptual framework. It may be assumed, however, that there is an intermediate space between extreme logicism and extreme relativism. Standards of intelligibility and rationality do not seem to be totally independent from certain scientific theories which reach the status of Kuhnian paradigms, or research programmes in Lakatos' sense, but they do not seem totally theory-dependent either. As Larry Laudan has shown[21] there is in practice an interaction between internal and external standards.

However, what in my view has been established beyond any reasonable doubt by three decades of epistemological debate is that the orthodox belief in universal, unchangeable logical patterns which are supposedly followed – consciously or not – by scientists in dealing with their conflicts is a naive philosopher's myth. Science seems to be more "human" than logical reconstructionists are prepared to admit. Scientists, while doing science, dwell in worlds in essentially the same way as people immersed in other meaningful frameworks do. But worlds are not necessarily uncommensurable, closed to each other, as relativists claim. A basic reason I have to assert a common ground among worlds is the existence of forms of interworlds' dialogue which are beyond the scope of a narrow definition of rationality. Before addressing fully this crucial point, let us see why, after all, human beings are compelled to build worlds. This question can be answered only in the context of needs theory.

THE NEED FOR MEANING

Needs theory is, indeed, a most controversial field. We can find opposite claims in connection with all the basic issues, ranging from the definition of needs – if they differ from wants, where should one draw the dividing line? – to the organization of the "needs system" – is it hierarchical or not? – and its cultural foundation – are there universal needs and, if so, which ones? I cannot enter here into the details of this debate; let me just mention some relevant aspects of an approach to the matter which I have proposed elsewhere.[22]

According to this approach, needs are divided into two categories – fundamental and derived needs. This distinction does not coincide with the usual distinction between biological and non-biological (social and psychological) needs. It is assumed that needs, so to speak, cut across the whole person and achieve a multidimensional – organic, mental, symbolic – inner resonance.

In this approach three fundamental needs were posited: subsistence, growth and transcendence. The need for subsistence is the force which impels the individual to preserve his existence both at the physical and at the psychical levels (where it is usually known as the need for *identity*). The need for growth, in its turn, moves the individual to unfold his potentialities and, by so doing, to change in the direction of an ever-increasing differentiation and integration (complex unity). Lastly, the need for transcendence is the force which prompts the individual to go beyond his individuality and unite – physically, mentally and/or spiritually – with other human beings, with Nature, God, the Party, and so on.

In this model needs are not seen as isolated entities but as making up a *system*. Within this system there are tensions, changes and dynamic interactions. Whereas fundamental needs are universal, the pattern that connects them – the system of needs – is variable according to specific cultural and personal circumstances. The difference between the universality of fundamental needs and the variability of needs systems arises from the fact that fundamental needs undergo a series of transformations which are mediated by culture. For

example, the fundamental need for subsistence transforms itself into a set of *derived* needs, ranging from the needs for food or shelter to the need for reducing uncertainty. In a second stage, derived needs turn out into desires or wants, pointing to specific satisfiers.

One of the advantages which I still attribute to this model is its capacity to integrate the universal and culture-dependent aspects of needs into one explanatory framework. Needs systems, though always made up of the same basic elements, may be in different *states* which are shaped by varying internal and external conditions. Some of these states may imply hierarchical organization, some may be better described as networks, some may be seen as equilibrium systems, some as non-equilibrium systems: no fixed, universal pattern determines the architecture of human needs.

On turning now again to this approach to needs theory I sketched ten years ago, I can see that something very important was left out. Under the influence of Viktor Frankl, I recognize now that at least one more fundamental need should be added to the model, namely, the need for meaning. Maddi[23] described this need as "the push to symbolize, to imagine and to judge." Though I find Maddi's description interesting, particularly in view of his purpose of exploring the pathologies of meaning in industrial society, I would rather characterize the need for meaning as the need which every human being has for building – and living in – a world (in the subjective sense introduced above). As with all living beings, the human being requires an environment but with the help of symbolic devices he transforms such an environment into a world.[24]

Worlds would thus be rooted in a fundamental human need, perhaps the *most* fundamental one since it is a precondition for making room for the push of the others: "As soon as we accept that any activity may or may not have meaning for us, we can no longer avoid the existential question of why we get out of bed in the morning at all and, just beyond that, of why we continue to live."[25]

Now we can see why conflicts between worlds may be so hard to handle: they may imply alternative, competing ways of meeting the need for meaning and, therefore, they may be perceived as putting in danger our own way, a way on which all the rest of what we are depends. Positions in the context of conflicts implying such a threat may be more emotional and less open to rational bargaining and compromise than in conflicts over scarce material goods. Of course, conflicts which combine both components – as, for example, when class and ethnic cleavages coincide – are among the most difficult to face, particularly when they are approached by ignoring or reducing their complexity. Some neo-Marxists' approaches to problems in which there is a world or frame conflict involved are a case in point. They focus on processes of capital accumulation but do not even take into account, as has been rightly pointed out by Anthony Judge,[26] other forms of accumulation, particularly the accumulation of significance or meaning. This last form of accumulation implies depriving people of their worlds and colonizing their minds for the sake of the expansion of one particular world. It represents an extreme form of oppression, probably harder to face than pure economic exploitation.

We have come now to the heart of our matter. If world and frame and conflicts cannot be settled by referring to empirical evidence and logic, shall we then accept the pessimistic conclusion that they are not amenable to any rational approach? In order to deal with this question let us take a step aside and refer once more to some developments in epistemology which in my view shed a new light on the problem.

METAPHOR DIALOGUE

Stephen Pepper,[27] reflecting on the nature of "world hypotheses" in the history of science, reached the conclusion that each of these hypotheses – formism, mechanism, organism, contextualism – is grounded in a "root metaphor": the ideal model or form of natural or man-made objects, respectively the machine, the organism, and the historic event. But Pepper's insight, advanced in the mid-1940s – that is, in the golden days of logical positivism in North America – was premature and had to wait for two decades to find receptive ears. The implied suggestion that even the most advanced branches of science may rest on some all-encompassing metaphors would have sounded preposperous in an intellectual atmosphere dominated by logical positivism. In fact, almost all great Western philosophers of knowledge, whether rationalist or empiricist or whatsoever, would have rejected it. The role traditionally reserved to metaphors and other figures of speech – that is, to tropological language – was, following Aristotle, a purely ornamental one. Its realm comprised poetry, literature, rhetoric; science was certainly excluded. The shared view was that if some terms loaded with non-literal meaning are nevertheless found in scientific discourse, a logical reconstruction of it should allow their complete elimination without any loss of cognitive content.

Such mainstream views started to be challenged in the early 1960s, particularly since waters were stirred by the publication in 1962 of Max Black's now classic little book *Models and Metaphors*.[28] As a result, the cognitive role of metaphors has been recognized and explored by an increasing number of scholars. It has turned out to be a respectable subject for seminars and discussions between "appreciators" and "depreciators" of metaphor.[29] Such on-going debate has certainly had consequences for a great variety of fields, from epistemology to education and politics. This is not in the least surprising since by definition metaphor connects different domains. I shall leave aside here most of these consequences and focus on our specific concern – namely, conflict resolution theory and practice.

I would like to refer first to a nice example of analysis of metaphors underlying conflicting approaches to a concrete social problem. This example, provided by Donald Schön,[30] will allow me to reach a few general points.

Schön tells us two typically American stories (though they may have happened in other places as well):

The first is a story out of the fifties . . . The community, once healthy, has become blighted and diseased. The planner, beholding it in its decayed condition, conceives the image of the community become healthy once again, with "new homes, schools, churches, parks, streets and shopping centers." But this can be achieved only through redesign of the whole area, under a balanced and integrated plan. Otherwise the area will revert again to a . . . slum area, as though possessed of a congenital disease.

According to the second story [but of the sixties] the places called "slums" are not all the same. Some of them are, indeed, decadent and impoverished, the victims of cycles of decay . . . Others, such as the West End and the North End in Boston, or the East Village in New York City, are true low income communities which offer to their residents the formal services and informal supports which evoke feelings of comfort and belonging. The task is not to redesign and rebuild these communities, much less to destroy buildings and dislocate residents, but to reinforce and rehabilitate them, drawing on the forces for "unslumming" that are already inherent in them.[31]

Schön describes then the metaphors underlying the two stories: "the urban-housing situation is seen first as a disease which must be cured and then as the threatened disruption of a natural community which must be protected or restored."[32]

Of course, the two metaphors lead to conflicting interpretations of the same facts and to quite diverse kinds of planning and action courses. In most cases no integration between these conflicting frames is attempted. A decision usually means that one frame is adopted and the other is just discarded without any further consideration of its possible value. Whatever the decision, it is not made – in fact, it cannot be made – on the sole basis of empirical evidence (both stories seem to account for all the known facts) and logic (both stories are in principle consistent). It is rather a matter of choosing a preferred metaphor. Interests, values, prejudices and culturally rooted constraints on social imagination can be surely found as the basis of such decision. If "rational" is considered as equivalent to "analytic problem-solving," any decision made in such a way can hardly be called rational. The dilemma we face here is either to keep the meaning of "rational" unchanged and to accept therefore that decisions as the one implied by the preceding example (that is, decisions in which world or frame conflicts are involved) are non-rational, or to enlarge the scope of "rational" beyond the analytic, Cartesian sense. This latter alternative does not imply, however, the assumption that *all* non-rational elements affecting conflict resolution can (or should) be eventually eliminated. If implies only that rational procedures other than classical problem-solving may be tried. In other words, an extension and not an elimination of the limits of rationality is advocated.

Schön proposes in this connection a procedure which he calls *frame restructuring*: "we respond to frame conflict by constructing a new problem-setting story, one in which we attempt to integrate conflicting frames by including features and relations drawn from earlier stories, yet without sacrificing internal coherence or the degree of simplicity required by action."[33] As a concrete illustration of this work on problem-setting (as opposed to problem-solving), Schön refers to a program which was devised in Lima, Peru, in order to deal with a problem essentially similar to the one mentioned above: "Such a program grows out of a complex coordination of the two perspectives held by municipal officials and by partisans of squatter settlements. The squatter behavior is seen neither as criminality nor as self-sufficiency . . . . Individual settlers are seen neither as passive recipients of government services nor as independent violators of governmental regulations."[34]

Now what is the precise nature of frame restructuring in the context of conflicting frames? If it implies, as Schön seems to suggest, keeping some features of the conflicting frames and excluding others, how should such sorting out of "positive" and "negative" features be performed? And how shall we avoid the danger of eclecticism so as to preserve coherence and meaning? If, on the other hand, frame restructuring is conceived in a more radical way, as implying the building of a *third* frame which "transcends" the conflicting ones, what does such transcendence exactly mean and how can it be reached by the parties? These are basic questions which, most likely, cannot have general answers but only case by case replies. But before dealing with the frame restructuring issue we should consider a previous problem, namely *frame dialogue*. This is indeed a *sine qua non* requirement for frame restructuring and should thus be analyzed first. Actually, it is in my view the main issue. Even if case frame restructuring does not happen at all – and it would be certainly unrealistic to think of it as an outcome which may be expected in more than in a few, exceptional cases – frame dialogue would still be a legitimate target and a helpful tool for frame conflict resolution.

If frames (and worlds) are rooted, as argued above, in metaphors, frame (and world) dialogue imply *metaphor dialogue*. What is the nature of such a dialogue? I should confess that in spite of having been working on the subject for some time now I have been unable to arrive at a general theory. I managed to develop the matter only in connection with some particular cases. I will refer as briefly as possible to one of these cases in the hope that it may provide some cues to the concrete meaning of metaphor dialogue.

The example I have chosen highlights the role of spatial metaphors in the construction of psychological theory. Actually, spatial orientation polarities (like up–down, in–out, left–right, front–back, central–peripheral) are a source of metaphors which structure many of our ordinary concepts. For instance, the up–down polarity provides, as Lakoff and Johnson[35] have shown, the metaphorical basis for an immense variety of conceptual domains ranging from health and life versus sickness and death (Lazarus *rose* from the dead; he *fell* ill) up to virtue versus depravity (she has *high* standards; that would be *beneath* me).[36]

Now, the basic role of at least three orientational metaphors (up–down, left–right, central–peripheral) in psychological theory may be easily shown. Among these three orientations in space, the main basis for metaphors used by Western psychology is up–down. This is not strange since it is perfectly in line with what may be observed in Western culture as a whole, where the up–down or vertical dimension is clearly dominant. The point rightly made in this connection by Lakoff and Johnson is that although all spatial metaphors lie on an experiential, physical ground – orientations of the body in space – and concepts referred to them which are universal, each culture selects and emphasizes only some of these orientations and concepts as the literal support of its preferred metaphors.

Starting thus with the vertical orientation metaphor, we can illustrate it, for instance, with Freud's first purely psychological model, as presented in detail in *The Interpretation of Dreams*.[37] Freud divides the "psychic apparatus" into an upper, conscious and preconscious level, and a lower, unconscious level. As is well known, Freud draws a sharp, qualitative distinction between the two levels: while the upper one is the domain of cognitive functions – from perception to conception – the "deep" one is the land of instinctual drives and repressed desires. Time, logic, causality are, according to Freud, totally absent at this level.[38] This model thus presents a combination of an up–down root metaphor and a discontinuity postulate.

Among those who remain within the up–down metaphor while at the same time challenging Freudian dualism, we may distinguish two subgroups: those who look at the system from *above* and those who look at it from *below*. Most of cognitive psychology and artificial intelligence work falls within the first subgroup. These two interconnected, rather active research programs, share an additional metaphor: the computer model of the mind. This model – naturally suited to abstract thought, problem-solving and "higher" mental skills in general – has been extended to cover first some "lower" cognitive functions like perception or memory and secondly "deeper" mental processes like imagery, dreaming, and so on. From the perspective of this model, Freud's theory is reinterpreted as a computer-like or information-processing approach *avant la lettre*.

Within the subgroup which looks at the system from below we may mention some cognitive psychologists who strongly criticize their colleagues for taking problem-solving and behavior in highly standardized situations as their exclusive data basis. Ulric Neisser[39] (in his second stage), John Bransford[40] or Walter Weimer[41] are examples of this type of cognitive psychologist. Weimer, for instance, advocated using motor skills (and not abstract thought) as the basis for understanding the mind as a whole.

If we now turn to the central–peripheral metaphor, a good example at hand is Milton Rokeach's model of the belief system.[42] According to this model, "connectedness" is the quality which determines the position of beliefs in the belief system: the more connected a belief, the more central it is, and vice versa.

Rokeach's central–peripheral model was devised to explain what happens when new information reaches the belief system. The information is first scrutinized to determine whether it is compatible with the system. If it is, its direct incorporation into the system is allowed, but if it is not compatible a negative reaction takes place whose magnitude is inversely proportionate to the degree of centrality of the belief involved. Cognitive strategies in cases of information incompatible with central beliefs are usually either rejection (the information may be declared false, irrelevant, etc.), reinterpretation (so as to eliminate its incompatible aspects) or non-distorted recording which keeps it isolated, at the periphery of the system. Normally, the cognitive dissonance introduced into the system by beliefs incompatible with the central ones is reduced using one of these strategies. There exists, of course, considerable individual differences in this regard. At the one end we have people whose belief systems are unchangeable beyond the peripheral region ("closed mind" to use Rokeach's term) and at the other end people who lack rigid cognitive defense mechanisms and can therefore change some or most of their central beliefs ("open mind"). Such changes are extremely difficult because they imply major restructurings of the belief system and, consequently, of the personal world in the sense already referred to.

Lastly, let us mention briefly the left–right metaphor which has become so popular after Roger Sperry and Joseph Bogen's work on the functional differences between the two brain hemispheres. The split between the hemispheres has been used to explain differences not only in individual behavior but also in social organization, economic and technological styles, and so on. One-sided preference for one of the hemispheres is often related to unilateral emphases on some aspects of education, some social institutions or even some dominant trends in art and literature. Obviously, the link between brain hemisphere differences and differences observed in all these quite diverse fields cannot be regarded as causal, but (to a great extent at least) as metaphorical.

Having thus outlined three worlds or frames in Western psychology and their respective root metaphors, let me explore what may happen if each of the parties involved, instead of remaining enclosed within their own metaphor, enters a dialogue with the other parties. It is my contention that a learning process of a new kind might then start, leading to a replacement of blind, unproductive conflict by complementary opposition of the yin/yang type. In order to show this I will state briefly what each perspective may learn by internalizing the other two perspectives. Let me do it through the graph in Figure 8.2 and a list of questions and suggested answers.

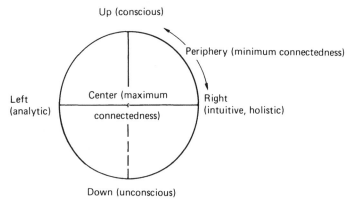

Figure 8.2   Combined three metaphors representation of the person system

1. What can the up–down approach learn from the left–right one? An answer may be that both the upper, conscious level and the lower, unconscious level, have a left and a right side and that these differences are worth exploring. This in its turn may lead, first, to a focus on the psychological differences between types of conscious activities (for instance, science versus art) and their respective languages (digital versus analogical) and, secondly, on types of unconscious activities (for example, oneiric and verbal, as shown by experimental dream research).[43]
2. What can the left–right approach learn from the up–down one? The answer here would be, in the first place, to add to the left–right distinction differences in the degree of consciousness or awareness and, secondly, to set limits to the left–right split. Actually, below the upper, newer (in evolutionary terms) sections of the nervous system there is no such split.
3. What can both the up–down and left–right approaches learn from the central–peripheral one? The answer would be that the up–

down and left–right distinctions are sharp only at the periphery of the system but that they become increasingly blurred as we approach the center.

4. What can the central–peripheral approach learn from the other two approaches? The answer would be that there is not just one periphery but four, each of them related to the center in its own way.

The preceding list of questions may be meaningfully posed with almost no change in a variety of fields other than psychological theory. In fact, it may be applied to all the numerous fields whose orientational metaphors play a guiding role in theory construction. Let us mention, for instance, the field of social and political theory where Marxism,[44] Gandhism and anarchism are respectively clear examples of up–down, central–peripheral and horizontal approaches; or the field of epistemology, where the hierarchical or Euclidean, the network and the holistic approaches are alternative modes of cognitive systematization.[45]

Of course, the brief list given above requires further elaboration. Beyond that, the case of orientational metaphors may look too simple as compared with more complex metaphors which also guide theory building.[46] Whatever the case, the only purpose of the list is to suggest the potential significance of metaphor dialogue as a learning process. It shows how each perspective may become enriched by entering the dialogue process, not necessarily by learning new answers but mainly by incorporating new questions. This process may not mean direct progress in problem-solving but only in problem-setting. However, such progress is necessary in problems involving world or frame conflicts; it is in fact a *sine qua non* condition for their solution or constructive redefinition.

Metaphor dialogue opens the possibility of fully profiting from the heuristic potentiality of metaphors as "condensed" forms of thought, while at the same time helping to overcome the limitation imposed on our vision by our own preferred metaphor. The "logic" of metaphor building and dialogue still requires a lot of work and insight. But what should be in my view clear from the very start is that it is not intended as an "alternative" to classical logic in the sense that non-standard systems of logic have claimed to be.[47] On the contrary, the "logic of metaphor" is truly complementary to analytical, literal logic, particularly useful in the cases of world and frame dialogue and conflict. Kathleen Forsythe[48] has nicely depicted

the two complementary logics as representing the architecture and
the engineering of the mind:

> The fundamental difference in this new view of learning is to see
> *analogical thinking* as the *architecture* and analytical thinking as
> the *engineering* of our mind's view of the world . . . The meta
> design is not built on inference and syllogism but on analogy and
> relation thus allowing form to develop from an underlying logic –
> the morphogenesis of an idea.

SUMMARY AND CONCLUSION

As pointed out at the beginning, this chapter focuses on conflicts
involving different (subjective) worlds or frames. In contrast to
conflicts *within* the same world or frame, any analysis of conflicts of
this kind made solely in terms of opposing interests, discrepancies
over facts and/or the logic of the arguments used by the parties is
bound to be irrelevant or, at least, insufficient. It is argued that by
their very nature, world and frame conflicts require less conventional
analytic tools (like, particularly, searching for the basic metaphors
shaping each party's vision and their modes of operation).

The clearest examples of world and frame conflicts are indeed
provided by intercultural (often interethnic) clashes. People participating in them share the same territory but, as it were, use different
maps of it. On the other hand, there are areas of human activity
traditionally considered free of conflicts of this type. This is especially
the case of science where, according to the orthodox image of it, a
universal language and method transcending idiosyncratic characteristics of scientists always makes possible reaching a common definition
of the problems at stake and a shared judgement about the acceptability of proposed solutions. In other words, science would be a
"within-one-world" business.

After reviewing the challenge posed by Kuhn and others to the
orthodox image of science, it is concluded that, in contrast to such
image as well as to its more radical critics, a better account of the
nature of the scientific enterprise should make room for *both* within-
and between-worlds conflicts. If this is so in the case of science, it
may be asserted that no form of social interaction should be declared
a priori free of conflicts between worlds or frames. And if it is
granted that conflicts of this kind require, as mentioned above, non-

conventional analytic tools, then there is little doubt that the preceding conclusion is highly relevant for conflict analysis and resolution theory.

A remarkable feature of conflicts between worlds and frames is stressed: mere difference, not necessarily opposition, is enough to provoke conflict. In order to explain this feature a proposal in the context of needs theory is presented. In particular, it is claimed that world and frame conflicts involve essentially alternative ways of meeting one of the most fundamental human needs: the need for meaning. Any world differing from our world may be perceived as putting into question our own way of satisfying the need for meaning – and, hence, our identity. So differences of this kind may be threatening and generate deep-rooted conflict.

World and frame conflicts have been regarded as falling outside the scope of rational methods of analysis and resolution. Such a stance is implied, for instance, by Kuhn's or Foucault's claims about the incommensurability between paradigms or *epistēmēs* or by the Sapir–Whorf thesis on the linguistic determination of thought. In contrast to this position, it is claimed that world and frame conflicts are accessible to rational methods, provided that the notion of "rationality" is extended beyond its narrow, Cartesian sense. In particular, it should include the systematic use of metaphor as a cognitive – not just rhetoric or poetic – tool. An example is developed in some detail to show how "metaphor dialogue" may give rise to a learning process and allow the resolution of world or frame conflicts.

It may be useful to close this essay on world and frame conflicts by outlining the ascending path of conflict resolution stages deriving from the perspective presented in the preceding discussion.

Stage no 1: Primitive Conflict

At this stage, each party represents the other in utterly negative terms: mistaken, unjust, immoral, inferior, and so on. True dialogue is impossible since lack of mutual confidence prevails. Depending on the context, different types of occasional or systematic violence are exerted. There may even be a refusal to admit the other's right to exist and keep unchanged his/her own identity.

Stage no 2: Coexistence

At this stage, each party accepts the other's right to exist, though lack of mutual understanding still predominates. Coexistence results more often than not from resignation to the fact that the physical and/or moral strength shown by the opponent makes aggression highly risky and possibly self-defeating. However, in a more advanced phase of this stage, more positive reasons for coexistence may emerge such as an awareness of the potential benefits of dialogue.

Stage no 3: Dialogue

At this stage, each party is prepared to enter a true dialogue with the other, frequently with the help of a third, facilitating party. From a cognitive point of view, "true dialogue" means that each party, though still sticking to his/her own preferred metaphor (or preferred way of building worlds and frames), develops at the same time a capacity adequately to represent the other party's metaphor, and eventually learn from it. Mutual deterrence and mistrust are gradually replaced by dialogue based on an understanding of the other's needs and ways of representing them.

Stage no 4: Restructuring

This is the highest phase in conflict resolution. Both parties now cooperate in building a new frame transcending their original frames and the conflict between them. This does not imply the end of all possible conflicts but only of the old, primitive form of the conflict. New forms of conflict may emerge and new cycles of conflict resolution may then occur.

World and frame conflicts are indeed the most difficult kind of conflicts. They can too easily degenerate into deep seated hatred and violence. However, they are also potentially powerful sources of learning.

An understanding of this nature and dynamics should help to channel the considerable amount of energy invested in them into positive, creative forms. Joint work between theoreticians and practitioners in the field may contribute decisively to such a purpose.

NOTES AND REFERENCES

1. W. James, *Principles of Psychology* (New York: Dover, 1950).
2. James, *Principles* vol. 2, Chapter 21, "The Perception of Reality": 293.
3. P. A. Heelan, *Space Perception and the Philosophy of Sciences* (Berkeley: University of California Press, 1983): 10.
4. E. Goffman, *Frame Analysis*, (New York: Harper & Row, 1974): 10–11.
5. M. Minsky, "A Framework for Representing Knowledge," in P. H. Winston (ed.), *The Psychology of Computer Vision* (New York: McGraw-Hill): 211–77.
6. M. Polanyi, *Personal Knowledge* (Chicago: University of Chicago Press, 1958): 60.
7. L. Wittgenstein, *On Certainty*, G. E. Anscombe and G. H. von Wright (eds), (London: Harper & Row): 204.
8. M. Maruyama, "Toward Cultural Symbiosis," in E. Jantsch and C. E. Waddington (eds), *Evolution and Consciousness* (London: Addison-Wesley, 1976); C. E. Waddington, *Evolution and Consciousness* (London: Addison-Wesley, 1976).
9. This is one of the most commonly used illustrations of Gestalt ambiguous figures. I took it from N. R. Hanson, *Patterns of Discovery* (Cambridge: Cambridge University Press, 1965): 13.
10. "Analytical Problem-Solving Conflict Resolution. An Exploratory Paper," The George Mason University Center for Conflict Analysis and Resolution (March 1988).
11. "Analytical Problem-Solving": 49.
12. "Analytical Problem-Solving": 49–50.
13. The difference between "creative" and "disruptive" in this context is not simple. For example, Mushakoji argues that the process of transcending conflicting paradigmatic approaches includes the creation of a "chaotic pole." See K. Mushakoji, "Scientific Revolution and Inter-Paradigmatic Dialogues" (Geneva: UNU, 1978).
14. M. Foucault, *Les Mots et les Choses*, tran. as *The Order of Things* (London: Tavistock, 1970).
15. R. Harland, *Superstructuralism: The Philosophy of Structuralism and Post-Structuralism* (London: Methuen, 1987): 105–6.
16. T. S. Kuhn, *The Structure of Scientific Revolutions* (Chicago: University of Chicago Press, 1962) 2nd enlarged edn (1970).
17. Hanson, *Patterns of Discovery*: 19.
18. Kuhn, *Scientific Revolutions*: 116.
19. Polanyi, *Personal Knowledge*: 101.
20. R. Rorty, *Philosophy and the Mirror of Nature* (Princeton: Princeton University Press, 1979).
21. L. Laudan, *Progress and Its Problems* (Los Angeles: University of California Press, 1977).
22. O. Nudler, "Human Needs: A Sophisticated Holistic Approach," in K. Lederer (ed.) with Johan Galtung and David Antal, *Human Needs: A Contribution to the Current Debate* (Cambridge, MA: Oelgeschlager, Gunn & Hain, 1980). A new version of this paper is included in O.

Nudler, "On Types of Civilizations: A Comparison through Three Dimensions," in E. Masini (ed.), *Visions of Desirable Societies* (Oxford: Pergamon Press, 1983).

23. S. R. Maddi, "The Search for Meaning," in W. J. Arnold and M. M. Page (eds.), *Nebraska Symposium on Motivation* (Lincoln: University of Nebraska Press, 1970).

24. For the difference between "environment" and "world" see O. Nudler, "The Development–Adaptation Dialectic" in C. A. Mallmann and O. Nudler (eds), *Human Development in Its Social Context* (London: Hodder & Stoughton, 1986).

25. Maddi, "The Search for Meaning": 137.

26. A. J. N. Judge, *Development Through Alternation?* (Brussels: Union of International Associations, 1983).

27. S. C. Pepper, *World Hypotheses* (Berkeley: University of California Press, 1942).

28. M. Black, *Models and Metaphors* (Ithaca: Cornell University Press, 1962).

29. See M. Black, "More About Metaphor," in A. Ortony (ed.), *Metaphor and Thought* (Cambridge: Cambridge University Press, 1979).

30. D. A. Schön, "Generative Metaphor: A Perspective on Problem-Setting in Social Policy," in Ortory (ed.), *Metaphor*.

31. Schön, "Generative Metaphor": 262, 363.

32. Schön, "Generative Metaphor": 264.

33. Schön, "Generative Metaphor: 270.

34. Schön, "Generative Metaphor": 273.

35. G. Lakoff and J. Johnson, *Metaphors We Live By* (Chicago: The University Press, 1980).

36. Lanoff and Johnson, *Metaphors*: 15.

37. S. Freud, "The Interpretation of Dreams," in J. Strachey (ed.), *Complete Works of Sigmund Freud*, vol. 3 (London: The Hogarth Press).

38. Freud, "The Unconscious," *Complete Works*, vol. 2.

39. U. Neisser, *Knowledge and Reality* (San Francisco: W. H. Freeman & Co., 1976).

40. J. Bransford and N. S. McCarrell, "A Sketch of a Cognitive Approach to Comprehension: Some Thoughts about Understanding What It Means to Comprehend," in W. B. Weimer and D. S. Palermo (eds.), *Cognition and the Symbolic Processes* (New York: John Wiley 1974).

41. W. B. Weimer, "A Conceptual Framework for Cognitive Psychology: Motor Theories of the Mind," in R. Shaw and J. Bransford (eds), *Perceiving, Acting and Knowing: Toward an Ecological Psychology* (New York: John Wiley, 1977).

42. M. Rokeach, *The Open and Closed Mind* (New York: Basic Books, 1960); *Beliefs, Attitudes and Values* (San Francisco: Josey–Bass, 1968).

43. See, on this point, R. M. Jones, *The New Psychology of Dreaming* (New York: The Viking Press, 1970).

44. Marxism developed, of course, well in advance of Freudism, an approach also based on an up–down metaphor (infrastructure, structure, superstructure) together with a discontinuity postulate. A significant part of both Marxist and Freudian theories deal with the nature of the links

between the levels of strata previously separated.
45. See in this connection N. Rescher, *Cognitive Systematization* (Oxford: Blackwell, 1979). Actually Rescher considers only the first two modes mentioned above. I added the holistic mode because it cannot in my view be reduced to any of the other two.
46. However, complex metaphors like the computer, the hologram, etc. might be analyzed as combinations or extensions of simpler ones.
47. S. Haack, *Deviant Logic* (Cambridge: Cambridge University Press, 1974).
48. K. Forsythe, "The Cathedrals of the Mind: The Architecture of Metaphor in Understanding Learning." It is interesting to know that this paper won the 1987 award of the American Cybernetic Society for the best paper of the year. I am grateful to A. J. N. Judge for this reference.

III

Needs Theory and Behaviors

9 Self-reflexivity and Freedom: Toward a Prescriptive Theory of Conflict Resolution

Joseph A. Scimecca

Conflict resolution deals with the conflictual behavioral relations of human beings and how these are best resolved. As such, it is classified as a social science. I would hope, however, that those of us who consider ourselves to be working within this field do not consider it a typical social science, one subject to the arguments, problems and controversies that characterize traditional social science. In particular, I would caution against the acceptance of the dichotomy between fact and value which defines contemporary mainstream social science, and which has led to an overemphasis upon quantitative methods in the name of an objectivity which is at best suspect. Conflict resolution should be a normative discipline; it should be prescriptive.

Galtung[1] has succinctly stated the major criticism concerning traditional, mainstream social science in his reference to what he calls the "old science":

> The old science also had its values, implicitly held: the values of the "realist," the man to whom the empirical world is the best of all possible worlds. It also had its criticism: non-criticism, or acceptance, called value-neutrality. It also made its proposals: for the implementation of a values defined by others, by the politicians in power, who also paid the scientists, and to whom they sometimes owed their loyalty. Value-neutrality was interpreted as a non-questioning attitude to these values. And the old science had its action: non-action.

In what follows, then, I will argue that the field of conflict resolution is best served via an emphasis upon a parsimonious modification of *basic human needs* (BHN) theory ("those human requirements calling for a response that makes human survival and development possible in a given society"[2]) which I see as the best available starting point for a prescriptive theory of conflict resolution.

Although a human needs approach to theory has been a part of social science for quite some time, indeed has provided the foundation for the "Goals, Processes, and Indicators of Development" (GPID) project of the United Nations University, which resulted in a major edited publication, *Human Needs*,[3] it is the name of John Burton who is most often associated with human needs theory when one speaks of conflict resolution.

Burton's human needs theory, what he has more recently called "collaborative problem-solving conflict resolution,"[4] draws on the humanistic psychology of Abraham H. Maslow,[5] the sociology of Paul Sites[6] and Stephen Box,[7] and the sociobiology of Edwin O. Wilson,[8] to formulate a theory of conflict and conflict resolution based on the premise that individuals seek to fulfill a set of universal needs which, when thwarted, resulted in deep-rooted and protracted conflicts.

In *Deviance, Terrorism and War*,[9] his clearest statement to date of his theoretical framework, Burton discusses nine distinct universal human needs. They are:

1. *A need for consistency in response*: Only through consistent responses can there be learning and consistency in behavior.
2. *A need for stimulation*: This is the other side of the coin to consistency in response. The individual must be stimulated in order to learn.
3. *A need for security*: Without security there is a withdrawal from response and stimulation.
4. *A need for recognition*: Through recognition the individual receives confirmation that his or her reactions to stimulation are approved. Recognition also provides the encouragement factor in learning.
5. *A need for distributive justice*: Distributive justice provides an appropriate response or reward in terms of experience and expectations.
6. *A need to appear rational and develop rationality*: This follows from the need for consistency of response. Rationality is a function of the behavior of others. Inconsistent responses invoke irrationality.
7. *A need for meaningful responses*: Unless responses are meaningful to the individual they will be interpreted as inconsistent.
8. *A need for a sense of control*: Control is a defense mechanism; if the other needs are met there is no need to control. Since the

other needs are never fully met, the ability to control rather than react to the social environment is consequently a need.

9. *A need to defend one's role*: The individual has a need to secure a role and to preserve a role by which he or she acquires and maintains recognition, security and stimulation.

The first eight are taken from Sites[10] and the last, *role defense*, Burton himself adds to the list.

Burton's human needs theory of conflict resolution has been criticized for its emphasis upon genetic determinism and its subsequent failure to take into consideration culture and social institutions. Avruch and Black[11] for example ask: "Where do these human needs come from? And why these particular needs and not others?" Although Burton originally saw these needs as genetically based, in a response to Avruch and Black,[12] he modifies his position somewhat by accepting the thesis of Boyd and Richerson[13] that humans have a "dual inheritance system," one cultural and the other genetic. According to Burton[14] what is important "is that universal patterns of behavior exist." And in a more recent paper Burton[15] calls for a "theory which is generic and relates ontologically, *perhaps* genetically, to the human person" (italics mine). Although this represents movement from a pure genetically determined position, it still places Burton in the sociobiologists camp and does not answer the question of where the needs come from; nor does it resolve the dilemma of ascertaining just how much culture influences human needs, dual inheritance system or not. It also remains to be shown how human needs can be ontological without being genetic, something which Burton does not even begin to confront. Nevertheless to dismiss Burton because of his failure to overcome genetic determinism and his acultural approach would, to slightly alter a cliché, "be like throwing the almost fully grown adolescent out with the bath water." Thus, even though I question the foundations of Burton's assumptions – i.e., how the needs are derived – nevertheless, I still believe that this human needs theory represents the most sophisticated and fully developed theory of conflict resolution available today. What follows is therefore done in the spirit of supporting and extending Burton's framework for analyzing and resolving deep rooted conflicts by showing that ontological human needs can be derived from a non-genetically determined base.

BEYOND THE GENETIC VERSUS CULTURAL ARGUMENT

The literature criticizing the sociobiological approach to human behavior is almost as extensive as the original formulations of the sociobiological position on human action. To summarize it here is not only beyond the scope of this chapter but most likely beyond that of any non-book-length manuscript. Instead, my position is, quite simply, that at present, there is no empirical evidence for genetically determined needs beyond those for physical survival.[16] In short, unless we can locate a gene for aggressiveness, or for timidity, or whatever, I am in complete agreement with Roy[17] who writes that; "the concept of needs has no relevance apart from organized social existence."

As a way of moving beyond the genetic/cultural argument, I offer, instead, the view that there are two fundamental basic human needs which are universal and thereby transcend culture, but at the same time are not genetically determined. My position is that these basic human needs are (1) *self-consciousness*, which can only be derived from self-reflexivity (the ability to think back and reflect upon one's actions); and (2) the concomitant need for freedom, which is the only condition which enables self-reflexivity fully to develop. By defining freedom as a human need and not a satisfier, I place myself in opposition to Galtung,[18] Mallmann,[19] and Masini,[20] who see freedom differing "according to space, time, and culture."[21]

Human consciousness is what makes us human and therefore transcends culture and genetics. Furthermore, as I will argue later, Burton's basic needs can be subsumed under the needs for self-reflexivity and freedom, thereby providing the ontological base his view lacks.

Consciousness and mind are not reducible to biological characteristics, to a materialistic base. The materialist argument that mental states are either solely dependent upon the physiological brain or are at best epiphenomena cannot be proven empirically. Indeed, just the opposite is the case – the purely materialistic position can be refuted on "natural" or scientific grounds. In order to justify this statement, I rely primarily on the work of the Nobel Laureate in Physiology and Medicine, Sir John Eccles.[22]

Eccles's and Robinson's[23] critique of the materialist position concerning the mind – brain problem is as follows:

First, nowhere in the laws of physics or in the laws of the derivative sciences, chemistry and biology, is there any reference to consciousness or mind. Regardless of the complexity of electrical, chemical, or biological machinery, there is no statement in the "natural laws" that there is an emergence of this strange nonmaterial entity, consciousness or mind. . . . This is not to affirm that consciousness does not emerge in the evolutionary process, but merely to state that its emergence is not reconcilable with the natural laws as presently understood. For example such laws do not allow any statement that consciousness emerges at a specified level of complexity of systems . . .

Second, all materialist theories of the mind are in conflict with biological evolution. Since they . . . all assert the causal ineffectiveness of consciousness *per se*, they fail completely to account for the evolutionary expansion of consciousness, which is an undeniable fact. There is first its emergence and then its progressive development with the growing complexity of the brain. Evolutionary theory holds that only those structures and processes that significantly aid in survival are developed in natural selection. If consciousness is causally important, its development cannot be accounted for by evolutionary theory. According to biological evolution, mental states and consciousness could have evolved and developed only if they were causally effective in bringing about changes in neural happenings in the brain with consequent changes in behavior. This can occur only if the neural machinery of the brain is open to influences . . .

Finally, the most telling criticism of all materialist theories of the mind is against its key postulate that the happenings in the neural machinery of the brain provide *a necessary and sufficient explanation of the totality both of the performance and of the conscious experience of a human being.*

The materialists simply cannot explain the uniqueness of the person. Human consciousness cannot be reduced to inorganic matter or even to animal consciousness. Human beings are like nothing else in nature; it is our unique consciousness that raises us above everything else.

This leads to the relationship of Eccles's notion of a mind–brain interaction, rather than a brain-determined mind. According to Eccles and Robinson,[24] the evidence clearly shows that a non-material mind acts on a material brain.

The history of humanity establishes that there are human attributes – moral, intellectual, and aesthetic attributes – that cannot be explained *solely* in terms of the materialist composition and organization of the brain. Note that we choose the word *cannot*. We *have shown* that all reductionistic attempts fail *in principle* in part through self-refutation and in part through incoherence . . . The environment of our genes can be determinative only through the mechanisms and processes of the nervous system. Thus if personhood is not reducible to these mechanisms and processes, neither the behavioristic nor the hereditarian accounts can be sufficient.

Eccles's conclusions lead him to a religious perspective concerning the notion of consciousness. He believes in the existence of a soul. Whether or not Human Needs theorists will accept Eccles's religious conception of self is less important than the fact that he and his colleagues have shown through a grounding in brain research that human consciousness is unique. Armed, then, with a critique of materialistic and deterministic consciousness, we can assume that the individual is capable of self-reflexivity, and is not simply responding to external stimuli or genetic patterning.

I need now to show how this capacity for self-reflexivity develops. In order to do this, I turn to the theoretical framework of the American social philosopher and Pragmatist, George Herbert Mead.

GEORGE HERBERT MEAD AND THE SOCIAL DEVELOPMENT OF MIND

The basic premises of George Herbert Mead's thought is that the mind cannot develop without some form of social process or interaction between individuals. The mind is not a physical substance with a specific location in the brain, but rather something that functions in relation to what Mead called *significant symbols*. Significant symbols can be words, gestures, even grunts and groans. What makes something significant is consensus of meaning. It must mean the same thing to those who are interacting.

Significant symbols arise only in some kind of social process. Individuals try to guess the intentions of others and then respond according to their suppositions about what the other will do. Cooperative behavior among people is possible only if they understand each other's actions and then guide their own behavior accordingly. Human society rests upon a consensus which is possible only because of significant symbols.

For Mead, human beings acquire a mind in the process of developing the capacity to create significant symbols. Individuals modify and control their own behavior by role playing. Thinking occurs as individuals engage in conversations with themselves and imagine how others would respond to them. The actions of others are completed in our heads. Language is of primary importance because it alone stimulates speaker and hearer in the same manner and speeds the process of developing significant symbols. This mechanism, according to Mead, is found only in human society. Vocal gestures provide the method by which social organization in society becomes possible.

Language and the mechanisms of communication, together with role playing results in the social formation of mind. Mead formulated a theory which produced a shift in the then basic assumptions underlying the nature and function of language. With his friend and colleague, John Dewey, he pioneered a new approach in which the nature of language is not described as the expression of earlier thought, but as communication – the establishment of cooperation in social activity – in which the self and the other are modified and regulated by common action.

For Mead[25] consciousness and will arise from problems. Individuals ascertain the intentions of others and then respond on the basis of their interpretations. If there were no interaction with others, no problematic behavior on the part of others, there would be no development of the mind. Individuals possess the ability to modify their own behavior; they are subjects who construct their acts rather than simply responding in predetermined ways. Human beings are capable of reflexive behavior. The individual, according to Mead, is not a passive agent who merely responds to external constraints, but someone who chooses among alternatives. This is a universal part of the development of consciousness. We predict the actions of others by previsioning the future, and through self-reflexion we modify our actions based on the experience of whether our predictions are accurate. Self-reflexivity enables us to develop a mind. Self-reflexivity, in the form of an active, inquiring, rather than a passive, receptive mind, is the universal we have been searching for. Self-awareness in the form of self-reflexivity is at once a distinctive and necessary component of human life. No functioning society is conceivable without self-awareness.

Although few would argue that self-reflexivity is not an ontological need, the need for freedom is more problematic. And my position is highly controversial in that I assert that freedom is not a satisfier, not a value which may be altered by cultural conditions, but is a *basic human need*. Obviously, some justification is needed for this assertion on my part. And given the importance of the concept of freedom, a fuller description of how I am using the term is also definitely in order.

FREEDOM: A DEFINITION

There are two major categories of freedom: *positive* and *negative* freedom, and under positive freedom there are also two categories, which I shall call "freedom from restraint," and "freedom to develop." Negative freedom can also be referred to as "freedom as a burden."

Freedom from restraint, which can be traced back to the Enlightenment, holds that freedom in and of itself is absolutely desired; it is what separates human beings from animals. In essence, any defects of societies and cultures is reducible to instances of human repression. Liberation, therefore, is *the* answer to all political questions. Society should impose only the minimum of restraints required to safeguard other people. From a mental health position, without freedom, people are unhealthy, and conditions which thwart freedom are to be avoided.[26] There is a problem, though, with this view of freedom – the problem of the individual who may be restrained by external forces but is still free internally, in his or her psyche. The monk who takes a vow of strict obedience and silence serves as a prime example of this, for it would be difficult to argue that the monk in his relationship to God is not free.

It is the second conception of freedom, *freedom to develop*, that I am defining as a basic human need. Freedom to develop is an extension of what can be called "the monk's dilemma." It is related to "freedom from restraint" but is also different in that it primarily involves the development of the individual's capabilities. This type of freedom can be illustrated by the very old joke, which goes as follows:

> After removing a cast from the hand of a patient, the doctor says: "Your hand is as good as new." The patient says: "Doctor, does

that mean I can play the violin?" "Of course," the doctor replies. To which the patient says, "That's great, since I could never play the violin before."

The point is, that although we may have the freedom to play the violin, without the prior lessons, or some capacity to learn how to play, we can have all the freedom we want, but we can not use it.

Fromm[27] here, too, offers insights into the freedom to develop. For Fromm, there are two distinctive constellations of drives within human nature – one oriented toward the satisfaction of human needs in a healthy, progressive fashion, and the other oriented toward the satisfaction of human needs in an unhealthy regressive fashion, what Fromm[28] labels as a "life-furthering syndrome," and a "life-thwarting syndrome." The actual possibilities for the satisfaction of human needs are provided by existing conditions of social reality. These possibilities can allow for the satisfaction in the life-furthering mode, the life-thwarting mode, or both. If these drives generate satisfaction, then the person can progress to a fully human level. Satisfaction in the life-thwarting mode results in neurosis, and the failure of social conditions to provide for any type of need satisfaction results in insanity. In short, for Fromm, the satisfaction of human needs in the life-furthering mode produces and sustains mental health.

Freedom to develop is in my view more important than freedom from restraint, and from now on when I refer to freedom as a human need or to positive freedom, this is what I mean. And if, as I hold, the mind develops only in interaction with others, it must be pointed out that absolute freedom is a contradiction in terms. Only optimal freedom is possible – the freedom to develop in consort with others, to learn skills, to accumulate knowledge, to develop self-reflexivity. This interpretation differs from the Freudian view that society is repressive, and is more in line with contemporary sociologists who stress the interaction of the individual and society for the fullest possible human development.[29]

Positive freedom can be contrasted to *negative freedom*, or "freedom as a burden." Negative freedom is the basis of Erich Fromm's classic analysis of Nazi German, *Escape From Freedom*,[30] where he analyzed why the German people embraced totalitarianism. Is it this fear of freedom that allows a people to yield up their freedom and to submit to dictatorial rule?

Now that we have had a fuller look at the concept of freedom, certain things are apparent. Foremost among these is that freedom is never absolute, and one does not need to be liberated from all restraints in order to be free. Human consciousness and self-reflexivity are predicated on choice, but no choice is ever totally free in the common, ordinary meaning of the word. All choices are made in the presence of some pressures and some risks, some lack of information or skills – nothing is ever decided in a vacuum.[31] So, too, with negative freedom. Although we usually picture Fascism as a system of absolute control, a total order, from which no individual could possibly escape, this does not mirror reality. There are always options available. Not everyone is an Eichmann.

Freedom, then, is both ontological and social as is self-reflexivity. Neither are genetically based.

To reiterate: the basis of my argument for an acceptance of the premise that self-reflexivity and freedom are ontological and social is that the individual is engaged in an active confrontation with the world; mind and self-consciousness develop in a social process. Mead provides an ontological justification for the need for freedom. The mind develops in a social context as it comes into being. Any restriction on the freedom of the mind to inquire and know implies a restriction on the mind fully to develop. Self-reflexivity and freedom are inseparable, both are ontological needs. Freedom is a universal wherever self-reflexive minds develop. Without freedom to develop, the mind is restricted and we become less than human beings.

Not only does the social development of mind and reflexivity offer a counter to the genetic argument, it also counters the position of cultural relativity, which assumes that there are no cultural universals.

CULTURAL RELATIVITY AND HUMAN NEEDS

Cultural relatively holds that any cultural pattern is vindicated by its cultural status – that is, a given pattern cannot be judged outside of the culture in which it is found. The basis of cultural relativity is located in the cross-cultural variations in human customs and institutions, which provide evidence for the plasticity of human behavior. Societies can fulfill human needs by the most disparate kinds of behavior. This leads the cultural relativist to the conclusion that because human needs (with the exception of basic bodily needs) can be met in such a variety of ways, there can be no universal standard by which to determine what is a basic human need.

Let us take a closer look at the cultural relativistic argument in relation to self-awareness and freedom. If the mind develops coterminously with society or a culture, and the mind cannot develop without being self-reflexive, every society or culture must provide positive freedom for the mind fully to develop if the society itself is fully to develop. Contrary to other aspects of human behavior, self-reflexivity cannot be provided for in a variety of ways, but only through freedom in thought and action. If, as anthropologists hold, the only non-relative cultural phenomena is the fact that humans create a culture then I would add that other non-relative facts which transcend culture are self-reflexivity and the freedom to develop. Self-reflexivity and freedom, because they are not culturally relative, can be used for judging whether societies fulfill basic human needs for its members. Societies with less freedom are thwarting human potential and can be rated as more destructive than societies which encourage freedom and human development.

Both totalitarian regimes or authoritarian regimes – which I do not differentiate between (with apologies to Jean Kirkpatrick) – which suppress freedom are destructive for human beings, indeed are evil, because they are not fulfilling basic universal human needs. The more authoritarian a culture, the more likely it will perpetuate deep rooted conflict because it thwarts basic human needs. Authoritarian and totalitarian cultures hinder self-reflexivity and freedom. Given these restrictions, I hypothesize the basis for an empirical test. Societies and cultures, or segments and groups within them, which restrict self-reflexivity are more likely to experience deep rooted conflicts. I stress, here that this is an hypothesis and in order to be supported would need cross-cultural verification.

CONCLUSION

I have postulated the existence of two basic human needs: (1) the need for self-reflexivity, and (2) the need for freedom. At this point I will also argue that Burton's nine human needs, with a critique of which I began this chapter, can be subsumed under the two human needs, thereby answering the fundamental questions concerning basic human needs raised by Mitchell[32] (Chapter 7): just what are basic human needs, how many are there and how can we tell?

Self-reflexivity and freedom are manifestations of the social development of self-consciousness and they are the foundation of all basic human needs. Not only are they compatible with Burton's human needs, his nine needs can be seen as derivatives of them. *Consistency* is an integral part of the social development of self-awareness. Significant symbols arise only as individuals guess the intentions of others. Without consistency in response the formation of significant symbols would be problematic at best. So, too, with *stimulation* which Burton sees as the other side of the coin to *consistency*. *Stimulation* is necessary for learning what others think, as well as for our own responses when we have ascertained what we believe to be the other's position. Without *security*, there would be a withdrawal from social interaction, from response and stimulation. Again, the creation of significant symbols would be rendered problematic. *Distributive justice* provides a reward structure for continuing interaction. Without fairness, there would not be the same willingness to engage in social interaction and significant symbol creation. Without *rationality* and *meaningful responses*, which are based on consistency of responses, the creation of significant symbols would again be problematic. Without *control*, the individual would not be proactive, would not be a creator of social reality, and therefore would not possess an integral part of self-reflexivity. We come finally to Burton's last need, that for role defense. In his response to Avruch and Black's[33] criticism that *role-defense*, unlike the other needs, is subject to zero-sum constraints, Burton[34] maintains that his critics fail to consider "costing" in the conflict resolution process, and that this ninth need is part of a conflict resolution process derived from his theoretical framework. For my purposes, then, role defense, because it is derived from a technique of conflict resolution ("costing"), loses its importance as an ontological need and is better viewed as an empirical question to be looked at when analyzing sucessful (or non-successful, for that matter) attempts at conflict resolution. In short, my concern is whether or not self-reflexivity and freedom provide an ontological basis for the specific human needs postulated by Burton, and of course, I believe they do.

To conclude, self-reflexivity and freedom are the two basic ontological human needs from which a prescriptive theory of conflict resolution can be deduced. If such a theory is to be validated it must be shown that these two needs when thwarted produce deep rooted conflict. This is, of course, an empirical question, one that can be answered only through the accumulation of cross-cultural and trans-temporal evidence. Only then will we be able to resolve deep rooted conflicts. To say that those who will follow this theory-building and research agenda have their work cut out for them is an understatement to say the least. Yet, given the state of the world today, can we afford to do less?

NOTES AND REFERENCES

1. Johan Galtung, *Methodology and Ideology: Theory and Methods of Social Research*, vol. 1 (Copenhagen: Christian Ejlers, 1977): 65.
2. Eleonora Masini, "Needs and Dynamics," in Katrin Lederer (ed.) with Johan Galtung and David Antal, *Human Needs: A Contribution to the Current Debate* (Cambridge MA: Oelgeschlager, Gunn & Hain, 1980): 227–31 at 227.
3. Lederer (ed.), *Human Needs*.
4. John W. Burton, "Conflict Resolution as a Political System," George Mason University Center for Conflict Analysis and Resolution Working Paper Series (1988).
5. Abraham H. Maslow, *Motivation and Personality* (New York: Harper & Row, 1954).
6. Paul Sites, *Control, the Basis of Social Order* (New York: Dunellen Press, 1973).
7. Stephen Box, *Deviance, Reality and Society* (New York: Holt, Rinehart & Winston, 1971).
8. Edwin O. Wilson, *Sociobiology: The New Synthesis* (Cambridge, MA: Harvard University Press, 1975).
9. John W. Burton, *Deviance, Terrorism and War: The Process of Solving Unsolved Social and Political Problems* (New York: St. Martin's Press, 1979): 72–3.
10. Sites, *Control*.
11. Kevin Avruch and Peter Black, "A Generic Theory of Conflict Resolution: A Critique," *Negotiation Journal* 3 (1987): 87–96 at 91.
12. John Burton and Dennis J. D. Sandole, "Expanding the Debate on Generic Theory and Conflict Resolution: A Response to a Critique," *Negotiation Journal* 3 (1987): 97–9 at 97.
13. Robert Boyd and Peter J. Richerson, *Culture and the Evolutionary Process* (Chicago: University of Chicago Press, 1986).
14. Burton and Sandole, "Expanding the Debate": 97.
15. John W. Burton, "The Need for Needs Theory," paper presented at the Conference on Human Needs and Conflict Resolution, Warrenton, VA (July 1988).
16. See especially R. C. Lewontin, Steven Rose, and Leon Kamin, *Not in Our Genes* (New York: Pantheon Books, 1984).
17. Ramashray Roy, "Human Needs and Freedom: Liberal, Marxist, and Gandhian Perspectives," in Lederer (ed.), *Human Needs*: 191–212 at 192.
18. Galtung, *Methodology and Ideology*.
19. Carlos A. Mallmann, "Society, Needs, and Rights: A Systemic

Approach," in Lederer (ed.), *Human Needs*.

20. Masini, "Needs and Dynamics."
21. Lederer (ed.), *Human Needs*: 5.
22. John Eccles, *The Human Psyche* (New York: Springer Verlag International, 1980); John C. Eccles and Daniel N. Robinson, *The Wonder of Being Human* (New York: The Free Press, 1984); Karl Popper and John Eccles, *The Brain and Its Self* (London: Routledge & Kegan Paul, 1977).
23. Eccles and Robinson, *The Wonder of Being Human*: 119.
24. Eccles and Robinson, *The Wonder of Being Human*: 169.
25. George Herbert Mead, *Mind, Self and Society* (Chicago: University of Chicago Press, 1934) 1974 edn.
26. Erich Fromm, *The Sane Society* (Greenwich Conn: Fawcett Publiations, Inc., 1955); Fromm, *The Heart of Man: Its Genius for Good and Evil* (New York: Simon & Schuster, 1964); Rollo May, *Man's Search for Himself* (New York: W. W. Norton and Co., 1967); May, *Power and Innocence: A Search for the Sources of Violence* (New York: W. W. Norton and Co. Inc, 1972).
27. Erich Fromm, *The Anatomy of Human Destructiveness* (New York: Holt, Rinehart & Winston, 1973).
28. Fromm, *The Anatomy*: 254.
29. Joseph A. Scimecca, *Society and Freedom* (New York: St. Martin's Press, 1981).
30. Erich Fromm, *Escape From Freedom* (New York: Rinehart, 1941).
31. Frithjof Bergmann, *On Being Free* (Notre Dame: Notre Dame University Press, 1977).
32. C. R. Mitchell, "Necessitous Man and Conflict Resolution," paper presented at the Conference on Human Needs and Conflict Resolution, Warrenton, VA (July 1988).
33. Avruch and Black, "A Generic Theory": 92–3.
34. Burton and Sandole, "Expanding the Debate": 98.

10 Human Needs and the Modernization of Poverty

Victoria Rader

My research experience in the last six years has been with the very poor in two different settings. One is with homeless Americans on the streets and in the shelters of Washington D.C. The other is with peasant and Indian communities in rural Mexico.[1] The combination of those two experiences has changed my views dramatically in regard to human needs. In this chapter I want to relate the human needs approach to development issues, drawing on this experience with poor people in both the US and Mexico. In a discussion of human needs and development there are interesting comparisons to make between these two groups, because they are located at opposite poles in the modernization process. Homeless Americans are struggling to survive within a highly advanced industrial economy while Mexican Indians continue to resist entry into the Mexican modernization process. Although these two groups face different stages of industrialization, in their struggles to remain human in the face of psychological and physical extinction homeless Americans and Mexican Indians have much to teach us about irreducible human needs and the conditions necessary for their satisfaction.

Poor people have shown me, for example, that well meaning campaigns for affordable housing in the US or debt relief for Mexico are not long-term solutions to their problems. They are only our most recent attempts to solve deep structural conflicts through minor shifts in the balance of power, the distribution of resources, and more efficient bureaucratic management. The housing crisis in the US and the debt crisis in Mexico are only manifestations of the development process itself.

The crises of massive debt and deficit, of government crime and corruption, and the astounding increases in homelessness, hunger, and alienation in both Mexico and the US offer us the shock of entire social systems breaking down. One-fifth of all American children survive below even the official poverty line while four out of five

Mexican children suffer either physical or mental handicaps from malnutrition. Approximately two people are murdered each day in the capital city of the US while the children and elderly in Mexico's capital are warned not to leave their homes in the mornings because of toxic levels of pollution. These crises reflect obsolete, authoritarian political structures and economic systems which are totally blind to human needs. Clearly, all of us have failed to create the necessary changes in our ideals and in our social structures so that ordinary people can create satisfying lives. At the same time, the crises offer us a profound moment of hope: they offer the opportunity to stop tinkering with the status quo and take an honest look at what is going wrong. It is time to challenge our most fundamental assumptions. What does it mean to be a human being? A whole new way of thinking is required.

The human needs approach is a promising way of rethinking development issues, and it resonates with much that I have learned at the grassroots level in the US and Mexico. I also have some reservations. What I find most useful about the argument is that it begins with the individual and embraces the whole human being. What we are studying, in essence, is the humanization process, the ways people struggle for their liberation from dehumanizing forces. My major reservation is with the concept of needs, which is intricately submerged within the thinking of modern industrial society. Let us begin by reviewing the positive aspects of the argument.

The essence of the human needs approach is that there exist certain irreducible needs which individuals *will* pursue. When they cannot meet those needs by conforming to society's norms, people will deviate from the norms, eventually leading to deep seated conflicts and social disorder. From this point of view, the satisfaction of individual needs is the essential requirement for a harmonious society rather than the other way around. The focus here becomes the individual rather than society as a whole.

CRITERIA FOR EVALUATION

This approach is quite the opposite of the conventional model of industrial modernization which takes the needs of the system as the primary concern of development: if national markets are expanding, for example, or production increases, benefits will eventually trickle down. From the perspective of the poor, of course, the ideology of modernization seems bizarre. For them, economic growth never has meant development: poor people in both the US and Mexico today watch their lives deteriorate while their societies continue to modernize. Certainly Mexican Indians, but also most Mexican peasants know that it is modernization itself which has directly led to an increasing incapacity to meet their own needs. Even before the debt crisis, with "miraculous" growth rates in Mexico in the 1960s and 1970s, development occurred on the backs of peasant and urban workers, the huge majority of whom lived at subsistence level and below. The absolute number of those marginalized, those who do not participate in the economic or political life of the country has grown steadily since the 1940s. Meanwhile in the most industrially advanced country on earth, thousands of poor families in the US are evicted every day, their homes torn down, boarded up or converted into condominiums in the name of economic development.

If a human needs approach were applied to these issues, modernization could no longer be confused with development. Thirty years have passed in Mexico with only the unmanageable debt, the stagnant trade, the permanent slump in commodity prices and hunger and oppression trickling down to 65 per cent of the Mexican people. Still, the high ground remains occupied by the modernization experts with their overriding concerns for the "needs of capital." Since there seem to be no solid criteria for evaluating development policy, the old guard continues spending vast sums of development aid and protecting the interests of the powerful. Yet validation criteria for "development" models do exist; they are tragically obvious at the grassroots level. In Mexico, for instance, peasants continue to lose their land, having to leave their villages and families, watching their children waste away, working fourteen hour days for next to nothing, drinking polluted water and being harrassed, imprisoned or murdered if they dare to try changing their conditions.[2]

If development means the development of human beings, any development policy would be evaluated on the basis of what it means for the individuals involved. A human needs approach to development gives us a clear set of validation criteria from the grassroots perspective by which to judge the benefits and costs of modernization in real people's lives. This is very important.

RECONCEPTUALIZING DEVELOPMENT

The human needs approach actually offers us more than criteria of evaluation. With its focus on meeting individual needs as the basis of social order, it radically redefines development goals. If a society is to maintain order while it changes, the identity and autonomy, as well as the physical security needs, of ordinary people must be taken into consideration. What is new in this formulation is the inclusion of social needs – freedom, recognition, security – aside from the usual goal of economic growth.

I think the human needs approach may also imply a very different source – or "engine" – of development. Instead of a top-down model in which powerful external economic structures drive a western style of industrial development, people might find more identity and autonomy as well as physical security if they were given the space to develop within their own environments. How can experts expect to develop a society if the knowledge, the concerns, the resources and the skills of the huge majority of its people are excluded? From the grassroots perspective, development is the unfolding potential of a people applying their own culture in daily projects for shared goals. What has been attempted in Mexico, mestizo and Indian farmers tell me, has not been the genuine development of Mesoamerican society, but the attempt to substitute one civilization for another.[3]

It is thus not just a matter of evaluating development policies on the basis of the impact of structural forces on individuals. We need to remember that it is individual actors who create, maintain, and change the structures themselves. Even macro- economic and political forces, while crucial to understand, are not generated by an invisible hand, but by individual actors. Development experts in the World Bank and IMF, executives of transnational corporations, and housing officials and real estate developers are individuals who, because of the extraordinary centralization of power, have a lot more impact than others.

But even with this concentration of power, authorities cannot forever impose a development approach that denies the essential humanity of large numbers of people without experiencing the consequences. In Mexico, the debt crisis only makes the deeper conflicts more visible. From the viewpoint of actors on the top, for example, the Mexican peasant – and most particularly the Indian farmer – has remained passive, stubborn, and uninterested in improving himself. It does not occur to officials that people are continuing their historical struggle to protect the knowledge, resources, beliefs and practices coming out of a civilization several thousand years old. Poor communities historically have resisted their subjugation in a variety of ways, from the wars and armed rebellions throughout the nineteenth century to passive resistance, land grabs, and other acts of protest in the twentieth. The recent explosion of popular movements among Indian, peasant, and urban marginal communities is forcing the Mexican state and the world to re-examine their version of Mexico as a model of political stability. As the human needs approach predicts, if participation in the system does not allow people their humanity, they will not cooperate, causing conflict and disorder.

Currently there are 3–4 million homeless in the United States. Can there be authentic human development in a society where entire groups of people are permanently marginalized, rendered unable to participate or create meaningful roles in human communities? How else can we explain the thriving drug trade and the war in our inner cities?

A HUMAN NEEDS APPROACH DISTORTED BY AUTHORITIES

Under conditions of social unrest, dire human misery begins to be a concern for authorities. Ironically, one frequent response is a human needs approach. For example, a "basic needs" approach was adopted by the major international aid institutions in the 1970s and it is interesting to examine the timing. This "revolution" in development thinking had a variety of origins; undoubtedly, the most important source was the very success of the aid regime in the 1950s and 1960s in promoting market based outward-oriented growth throughout the Third World. The United Nations had set a growth target of 5 per cent per annum for the "development decade" of the 1960s and overall this target was exceeded. It certainly was by Mexico. By the 1970s, however, those within the aid community increasingly admitted a more basic failure within the success. The most famous indictment came from Robert McNamara, the relatively new president of the World Bank before the Board of Governors in 1973: "The basic problem of poverty and growth in the developing world can be stated very simply. The growth is not equitably reaching the poor."[4]

Other factors led to such a realization, namely the Vietnam War, especially given McNamara's move from US Secretary of Defense to president of the World Bank. South Vietnam was touted in US aid literature as a major success story in the 1950s, but by 1967 only the presence of 535,000 US troops could keep the South Vietnamese regime in power. The war as a whole was estimated to have cost the US $168 billion – more than all the economic aid from all sources to all developing countries between 1962 and 1975.[5] In South Vietnam the trickle down assumption of capitalist growth theory had not worked and the spector of "two, three, many Vietnams" was on the horizon. The movement to a basic needs approach to development aid was a commitment to a new focus on "defensive modernization," as one World Bank observer put it: "The strategy rests on the assumption that reform can forestall or pre-empt the accumulation of social and political pressures if people are given a stake in the system. Reform thus prevents the occurrence of full-fledged revolution."[6] It is worth noting that international elites have at least partially adopted the logic of the human needs approach in their understanding of rebellion and revolution. But it is also crucial to understand how authorities with a vested interest in maintaining the current political and economic order define "human needs."

When the World Bank began to discuss strategies of redistribution, economic and political reservations immediately surfaced. Redistribution would inhibit economic growth and encourage resistance from governmental and business elites. In the end, basic needs was thus seen as an approach different from and preferable to both traditional trickle down and to direct redistribution. The Bank's *Poverty and Human Development Report* emphasizes how investment in "human capital" will promote growth through raising the productivity of the poor.[7]

Most observers agree that the basic human needs approach had a very limited effect in terms of the AID regime's goals. Aid allocation changed little. (There was some shift of the more concessional types of aid toward the poorest countries and some shift in sectoral priorities, particularly toward agriculture. But these changes might not have resulted from the needs approach.) The Bank itself concluded that its rural and urban development projects had generally failed to benefit the poorest sectors of the population.[8] Certainly with the more recent structural adjustment requirements, the Bank has given up its concern for the poor and reverted back to its high growth priorities.

While AID goals floundered, the effect of basic needs strategies on poor people brought a new round of debilitating dependence. In Mexico, one of the expressions of this new approach was in the Mexican Food System, an innovative strategy which, for the first time in the post-war era, discarded the notion of "effective demand" to quantify food needs in Mexico. After adopting international standards which identified these needs in terms of calories and proteins, the Mexican government officially recognized in 1980 that half of all Mexicans did not have access to minimum food requirements. Society was compelled by this new strategy to produce and distribute enough food to satisfy those needs. During the three years of its short life the strategy was a brilliant economic success; Gustavo Esteva reports that production and productivity increased, food supply, as well as food distribution improved.[9] But as Gustavo Esteva explains, because this strategy reinforced economic linkages in the food chain, dependency and scarcity were created. It contributed to the dissolution of the peasants' traditional routines of subsistence. Because "improved" seeds and fertilizers were made available at very tempting prices, the stock of peasant seeds were lost and traditional practices of organic fertilization or natural regeneration of the soil were abandoned. Peasants thus became addicted to industrial inputs. When the supply of improved seeds and fertilization fell short of the demand created by this strategy, the peasants confronted a two-pronged scarcity: scarcity of improved and native seeds, and scarcity of chemical inputs and natural cycles.[10] Given their experience, Mexican peasants are understandably skeptical of human needs models.

Another example of the adoption by authorities of a "needs" approach is the US War on Poverty. Once again, the source of unrest originated in the modernization process; when automated agriculture was adopted in the southern United States, it forced millions of people from their rural communities into the cities looking for work. Four million blacks alone migrated from Southern rural areas to cities in less than four decades. This massive migration occurred just at a time when industry began needing a more skilled labor force; racism among white employers plus automation resulted in large scale unemployment and underemployment among black migrants. This unemployment and the loss of traditional community supports led to the erosion of the family system as well. Men who were chronically unemployed were not as likely to marry or retain stable relationships with women and children who they could not support. The community support systems which northern black urban neighborhoods were able to generate, were largely demolished by the massive urban renewal efforts of the 1950s and 1960s, which removed hundreds of thousands of blacks from inner cities in the guise of slum clearance. Being locked out of the labor force along with the breakdown in community supports led to the inevitable. With riots flaring up in the northern inner cities and the civil rights movement shifting its focus to economic rights, the Kennedy Administration generated a new focus on "poverty," largely as a way to evade civil rights demands without losing black support. Johnson's State of the Union announcement of an unconditional "War on Poverty" greatly expanded the array of service programs which Kennedy started. Given the momentous forces of mass civil rights protest and the urban disorder arising out of modernization, migration, urban unemployment and the destruction of black community, the government moved to moderate unrest by naming poverty as a national issue and offering massive new grants to the "needy."

The War on Poverty operated within the context of an advanced industrial economy, however, and served not so much to integrate the poor into the post-industrial workforce as to create vehicles through which black ghettoes mobilized to demand government services. Most significantly, hundreds of thousands of families were added to the welfare rolls. For example, relocation services that were part of the "urban renewal" process discovered thousands of families who were elegible for benefits but had never applied. Anti-poverty lawyers began litigation in courts reducing punitive welfare eligibility restrictions and whole new categories of people were granted assistance.[11]

The liberalization of relief practices designed to meet the "needs of the poor" should be seen as a concession to the victims of modernization. What it did, however, was extend dependency on a welfare system that dehumanized people in every aspect of their lives. Once on welfare, for example, there was the continual threat of one's termination, sometimes for participation in political protest, more often for the infraction of welfare rules. Many of the anti-poverty programs further weakened traditional sources of identity, recognition and support. Welfare mothers, for example were kept on the rolls only as long as they did not work and in half of the states, so long as there was no man in the house. Whole communities were "relocated" out of existence: church congregations, community leaders, and long time neighbors scattered in all directions. Then when the relief programs were drastically cut in the 1980s, the poor found themselves without either the traditional community or state support system.

Homeless residents at the Federal City Shelter have inherited this history and they face a very concrete dilemma. There is no work available to them that pays a living wage, and there is little community left to which they might turn. (Many do have family members who care about them, but the lives of the relatives themselves are too close to the edge, with lay offs increasing, rents going up, and living space severely overcrowded.) While we do not yet have the massive social unrest of the 1960s, the current level of deviance in the inner cities is serious enough for authorities to express mounting concern. And while drug dealing, theft, and murder among poor young blacks, or the panhandling and idleness among some homeless is not political in intent, it does challenge the legitimacy of the system by repudiating the obligation to enter a labor market where blacks are denied any but the most menial of jobs.

THE MODERNIZATION OF POVERTY

The human needs approach adopted by authorities will necessarily be distorted by their desire to control human beings as interchangeable units in the political economy. Fortunately, this view of people as passive producers and consumers is too small for whole human beings, and while needs such as identity and autonomy are denied in domestic welfare and international aid ideologies, they are not as easily extinguished in real human beings.

What I want to emphasize here is that the basic needs approach adopted by authorities in times of social unrest assumes not only the oppressive political order but the oppressive economic order, which is the source of powerful dehumanizing forces: the obsession with material standards of living, the creation of artificial and chronic scarcity, the separation of needs from their means of satisfaction, and the weakening of family and community supports. The dehumanization which I am most sensitive about in my relations with poor people is this modernization of poverty, where people are not only locked out of the labor market but systematically denied any alternative process for meeting their own needs.[12]

Industrial capitalism is organized to encourage economic growth by turning people's activities into commodities, specialized goods and services which people buy and sell. The extraordinary productivity of this system and its expansion into nearly all areas of life results in a growing emphasis on the accumulation of commodities; people learn to think in terms of material rather than spiritual or social values. Both poor Americans in the D.C. shelters and poor Indians in rural Mexico have shown me, however, that the tremendous emphasis on material consumption is the need of an industrial capitalist economy rather than an accurate reflection of ontological human needs. Our physical needs are really quite finite and few.

People on the streets and in the shelters of D.C. have developed their own understandings of irreducible human needs: people need food and shelter for biological survival, but they need dignity and love to remain human beings. Physical needs can be very cheaply provided; the shelter does it every day. Yet, in a society driven by material success, men and women who have lost everything material must struggle fiercely to retain their pride. That is why so many homeless people refuse to go to shelters where they must publicly undress and shower, be searched like criminals, or be required to "prove" their destitution. It is my experience that when individuals are forced to choose their dignity over shelter or food, they will often choose the former even at some risk to their lives. What makes life fully human is social recognition, some semblance of autonomy, some grounds for demanding membership in the human race. There is an exasperating impotence forced upon the poor in modern societies where not only are physical needs frustrated, but identity withdrawn and autonomy undermined.

Mexican Indian peoples who continue to live outside the industrial economy, on the other hand, are more materially impoverished than the US homeless; yet their subsistence communities continue to provide some forms of physical security and a strong sense of group identity and autonomy. Indians say that they learn from their elders how to make do with very little without feeling "poor." Communal harmony, economic self-sufficiency, a focus on the spiritual, and local control are values that traditional Mexican communities have not willingly surrendered, even for the promise of advanced levels of material consumption. As Gustavo Esteva, a grassroots activist writes, "Society does not have to be subjected to the rules of the economy at all costs. This way of organizing society had a concrete beginning in the emergence of industrial capitalism in Europe. And it can have an end. It is possible to put limits on the economy, to resist its dominance . . . Mexico can learn from an apt tradition – the Indian village – which has been capable of avoiding economic forms of interaction which would give up political and economic control to forces outside the community itself."[13]

Conventional wisdom associates the predicament of the poor with the intensification of scarcity, but poor people know very well that the scarcity they experience is artificially produced. The Mexican *campesino* grows sorghum for cattle while his own children go hungry, and homeless Americans freeze to death on city streets lined with boarded up houses and empty office buildings. Material resources are far from scarce; they are simply confiscated from the control of ordinary people.

In Mexican communities, the sense of scarcity comes from colonial and modernizing experiences and is still resisted in areas of their culture where it has not yet penetrated. It is in resistance to the Western creation of scarcity that Gustavo Esteva takes a strong stand against the human needs approach itself, as way of thinking about social problems: "Our wants and hopes, in our way of living, do not correspond to what others call 'needs,' nor to what you designate with the couplet 'needs and satisfiers.' These are nouns denoting lack and scarcity. We have verbs which identify our activities, and these in turn embody our wants and skills."[14] The Mexican peasants have seen from experience that their capacities and skills became inadequate for satisfying their wants once they have been turned into needs for industrial services. They are changed from capable human beings into the "needy." Says Esteva, "In the name of development, our abilities have been transformed into lacks. To produce the need for education and thus the scarcity of schools, our ways of learning and our social recognition of knowledge and wisdom were first depreciated and then prohibited. Our autonomous ability to cope with the environment – as René Dubois defined health – was maimed so as to generate the need for medical services and hence, their scarcity. The autonomous mobility provided by our feet was inhibited so as to create the need for scarce means of locomotion: transportation. The ability to learn and to heal as well as the ability to walk, abilities that embody our wants as well as express our opportunity to lead satisfactory lives, are mortally threatened by their mutation into needs."[15] I agree with Esteva that "needs" is a loaded concept emanating from modernization, which connotes deficit-motivation rather than the inherent drive and capability of ordinary people to create satisfying lives. Human needs theorists should explore this problem carefully.

A crucial aspect of the generation of artificial scarcity is the dissociation of needs from the means of satisfaction. After a certain point in the industrial process, this separation destroys peoples' experience of being active agents in their own lives. As Ivan Illich has explained for years, the peculiar modern inability to use personal endowments, communal life, and environmental resources in an autonomous way infects every aspect of life where a professionally engineered commodity has succeeded in replacing a culturally shaped use-value.[16] In fact, most poor people know that they possess the abilities to meet their own needs: they are capable of working, of producing food and building shelter, of generating community. These human capabilities are not scarce, although Mexican Indians have more experience in initiating such activities than poor people in advanced industrial societies since the environmental resources and community support systems in Mexico are still in place. The Indians are the most oppressed group in Mexico and most of their land has been confiscated. Still they retain enough independence from the market economy to use their resources and capabilities to build their own shelter, heal their own sick, teach their own children and grow some of their own food. This is not true for homeless Americans in an advanced industrial society, who might be capable of building shelter, for example, but lack the property deeds, the building permits, the bank credit, the standardized building materials, or the occupational certification legally to do the job. Homeless people in the US are not allowed to construct their own refuge: makeshift or temporary shelters, even in freezing weather, are quickly torn down and if the builder resists, he or she is arrested. Similarly, shelter residents are severly restricted in their natural efforts to generate a sense of community within the shelters by 30 and 60 day residential limits.

This separation of means and ends is a product of modernization and results in a serious loss of personal and group autonomy. In the Mexican peasant communities, it is fiercely resisted. Much of Mesoamerican culture involves teaching people to live within their means, and to adjust to considerable material constraints. They have found through harsh experience that their communities cannot survive once they surrender to the modern condition of having means on the one side and ends on the other, needs or lacks here and satisfiers there.

Not only are resources taken out of poor peoples' control, and non-commercial initiatives suppressed, but traditional family and community support systems which formerly were a major source of identity, recognition, and even physical security are gradually weakened and destroyed in the modernization process. Life for black Americans, for example, has always been difficult, with hardships of poverty intermingled with those of race.[17] Ironically – and contrary to conventional wisdom – it was this very precariousness which created the necessity of an exceptional degree of organization in black communities. Peoples' survival depended on the development of cooperative institutions.

The urban black community has always found ways to pool resources, spread survival information, confer recognition, and provide support in times of trouble. The popular practice of taking in boarders, for example, was in many ways a system of informal adoption, where younger and older children, the elderly and single people were brought into family activities and newcomers integrated into the neighborhood. More formal mutual aid societies have always existed. And in a society that traditionally excluded blacks from respectable positions, the Afro-American church provided a crucial forum where community status could be conferred, leadership developed, and social action organized.

We have discussed earlier how the traditional black community was weakened through modernization of agriculture, migration, urban unemployment, and urban renewal. What these processes weakened, the War on Poverty and, more recently, gentrification has almost completely demolished. The destruction of black neighborhoods as stable communities and the substitution of dependence on the larger economy for one's physical security, social recognition, and sense of autonomy puts this group in dire jeopardy. There is no economic, political, or social space for them in modern society, their traditional alternatives have been destroyed, and their very existence is threatened.

SUMMARY AND CONCLUSIONS

The human needs approach calls on us to ask the following theoretical questions: What does it mean to be a human being? Are there irreducible qualities which all peoples predictably require in their lives? In the real world we can explore these questions by studying the humanization process, the struggles of peoples for liberation against dehumanizing forces. In the area of development and human needs, we have argued in this chapter that elites cannot impose a development process that denies the essential humanity of large numbers of people without experiencing the consequences: widespread deviance in US inner cities, for example, or the increase in popular opposition exploding in Mexican communities today. When poor and oppressed communities do rise up, we have suggested that authorities often respond with their own version of a human needs approach. The usual attempt is to define the dehumanized group as "needy" and provide some temporary material relief. I have argued that the major consequence of such aid is increased dependence on an industrial system which not only is unreliable in terms of meeting poor peoples' requirements for physical security, but which further destroys their personal and group autonomy and weakens alternative sources of identity and support. As industrialization progresses, this modernization of poverty becomes an increasing threat to peoples' very survival.

As well as seeing very positive aspects to the human needs approach, I have two reservations about the concept of "needs." In modern industrial society, at least among the poor, I have found that physical security, autonomy, and identity are not separate needs but inherently inter-related aspects of being a full human being. I think it is a mystification to separate them even for analytical purposes. The idea of a needs hierarchy, for example, that begins with material requirements, may be accurate at a purely biological level but it does not reflect the way real people behave. Such an analysis also plays into the hands of authorities who approach popular unrest by offering material aid in ways which deflect attention from the economic, political and cultural oppression which poor people suffer. One very valuable aspect of the human needs approach of such scholars as Burton and Galtung is precisely the inclusion of social *and* physical requirements for a human life. We need to explore further the ways in which these needs are interrelated.

A second problem with the concept of "needs" is its derivation from an industrial mode of thinking, with its focus on scarcity, which seems inadequate in describing the response of people against oppression. The concept of "needs" too easily leads to a view of individuals as having certain deficits, transforming poor people, in particular, into the "needy" suffering a condition to be alleviated rather than an oppression to be challenged and redressed. Such a conceptualization, no matter how sympathetic, ultimately blames the victim and distracts us from the structural origins of the injustice poor people face.

In sum, while there seems to be some ontological human needs, the social organization of the means to their satisfaction is always historically grounded. While Burton emphasizes political oppression in contemporary society in his writing, I have focused in this chapter on the oppression which the modernization process imposes. The loss of control over any productive resources seems inherently connected with the denial of the essential human right to live in community and take initiatives. The modernization process greatly reduces the opportunity of poor people to create satisfying lives. One of the wider implications of such a critique of modernization is to re-examine our preference for industrial growth over the option of encouraging human development within self-reliant communities.

NOTES AND REFERENCES

1. My research experience with homeless Americans began in 1983 and continues to the present. It includes working in women's shelters and the Federal City Shelter Clinic in Washington, D.C., meeting homeless people on the streets and transporting them to shelters, dumpstering for food and preparing it for soup kitchens and living with the D.C. homeless advocacy group, the Community for Creative Non-Violence. My experience with poor people in Mexico is far more limited, with two summer visits in 1987 and 1988 to meet with grassroots social change groups. These included visits with members of several indigenous communities, peasant-*ejidos*, human rights and alternative development groups.
2. Susan George, *A Fate Worse than Debt* (New York: Grove Press, 1988).
3. See Guillermo Batalla Bonfil, *Mexico Profundo* (Secretaria de Educaçion Publica, 1987) for a serious anthropological reformulation of Mexico's development problems in terms of the conflict between Western and Mesoamerican civilizations.
4. Peter Henriot, "Development Alternatives: Problems, Strategies, Values," in Charles Wilber (ed.), *The Political Economy of Development and Underdevelopment* (New York: Random House, 1979).
5. There needs to be further documentation of the "lessons" learned by elites from the Vietnam War. Robert Woods makes a good start in this direction in his book *From Marshall Plan to Debt Crisis* (Berkeley: University of California Press, 1986).
6. Robert Ayers, "Breaking the Bank," *Foreign Policy*, 43 (1981): 82.
7. World Bank, *Poverty and Human Development* (Oxford: Oxford University Press, 1980): 206.
8. *From Marshall Plan to Debt Crisis*: 255.
9. Gustavo Esteva, newspaper interview in *El Gallo* (10 August 1988).
10. Gustavo Esteva, personal interview in *Cindad Oaxaca*, Mexico (12 August 1988).
11. See P. Piven and Richard A. Cloward's book on *Regulating the Poor*

for the classic sociological treatment of the shifts in relief policy resulting from relief in relation to civil disorder in the US. Their historical analysis remains very useful today.

12. We are not referring here to the radical inequality of distribution systems in industrial capitalist society. This aspect of poverty can best be understood and changed through a Marxist analysis.

13. Esteva, *El Gallo*: 1.

14. Gustavo Esteva, "Alternatives to Economics," *Alternatives* (Spring 1988): 3.

15. Esteva, "Alternatives": 2.

16. See Ivan Illich's provocative writings over the last two decades on this subject. His analysis has been profoundly felt in Latin America, in particular, and carried further by activist intellectuals each as Gustavo Esteva, director of Anadegas, a radical grassroots social change organization.

17. Lois Horton and James Horton, "Pluralism and Fragmentation: Race, Ethnicity, Class and Gender," in Marcus Cunleffe (ed.), *The Post-Vietnam Decade* (Mary Knoll, N.Y.: Orbis, 1986).

11 Taking the Universality of Human Needs Seriously
Christian Bay

INTRODUCTION

As a political theorist concerned with human emancipation I consider myself a specialist in how things ought to be, in this country, and in this world. As a social scientist, however, I am interested only in conceptions of the future that in principle appear realistically attainable, by and by, by way of reasonably non-violent strategies. This chapter will try to convince you that the idea of an evolving struggle toward a human rights world order can be seen as an essential supplement to the stagnating, stability-serving agenda of liberal democracies and as an alternative to the dangerous vision of a Marxist world revolution.

Human Rights will be understood to refer to all entitlements and immunities that, as a matter of moral urgency, must belong to every human being *qua* human being. That human rights in this sense must be protected, to the fullest possible extent, is for me the pre-eminent normative premise in the political legitimation of power; it transforms the power of force into (legitimate) authority, according to the rational-humanist, maximalist perspective to be articulated and defended in this paper.

But the good sense of this key premise hinges on the issue of *what* are (the legitimate and legitimating) human rights; and what are the priorities among them, and why? The pre-eminent legitimation principle must itself, for its own legitimation, be grounded in compelling assumptions.

I want to make an argument in four parts:

First I want to link human rights to basic priorities of human need, to come up with a broad range of categories of human rights; not a flat range but one with mountains and valleys: some categories of rights are more urgent than others and should, generally speaking, prevail over others. I shall distinguish my rational-humanist perspec-

tive from the prevailing liberal construction of human rights.
Secondly I shall argue for a highest-priority commitment to human
rights, in the maximalist sense that makes loyalty to and legitimation
of the state contingent on whether, or the extent to which, the state
protects and champions human rights. This part of my argument will
take up the issue of authentic and inauthentic *language* of human
rights as well: since the powers that be tend to have priorities other
than human rights, and yet will want to claim to stand for freedom,
human rights, and other good words, they will tend to use these
words perversely, inauthentically. Their critics who are genuinely
committed to human rights must therefore push harder for authenticity in the use of the language of human rights and we must
endeavour to expose inauthenticity more promptly and effectively.
    Thirdly I shall distinguish two broad categories of human rights
issues (as distinct from democratic issues): the task of giving prompt
aid to victims of human rights abuses and other calamities; and the
task of prevention of such calamities in the future. Rescue-mission
priorities must be guided by a strictly negative-utilitarian scheme of
priorities; as in a good hospital, the most endangered or suffering
victims must have the prior claim on relief resources. Still within the
parameters of negative utilitarianism, with respect to policies of
prevention, I shall argue for the first priority to be our green ecological
rights, which are collective as well as individual human rights; for a
second priority to be the red rights of socialism; and for a third
priority to be the blue rights of liberalism.
    Fourthly I shall argue that the universality of basic human needs
and of need-based rights should be taken more seriously – seriously
enough to make all other legal and political priorities secondary, in
our own country and also worldwide. Human beings are social as
well as individual beings, which is why we must insist that the need-
based collective rights are individual rights as well. Provided we take
the universality of basic human needs and of need-based rights
seriously enough, we may envisage an expanding worldwide human
rights movement as a viable third way toward a more humane and
sustainable world, post-liberal and post-Marxist. As we shall see, this
new movement is already well on its way. It consists of countless
organizations and agencies – non-governmental, national, regional
and international – all seeking to make governments and other
powerful agencies more accountable for abusive or contemptuous
treatment of human rights in disregard of human needs and rights,
including the needs and rights of future generations.

To be sure, there are many powerful vested interests that oppose the on-going efforts to build a human rights world order. Yet the movement has been gaining strength in the last half century, as we shall see, helped along by new qualities of citizenship, inspired by a new awareness of what is at stake.

HUMAN RIGHTS AND HUMAN NEEDS

Every human being has *needs*, as distinct from wants, demands, and preferences. Unlike needs, the latter phenomena can be observed and measured, surveyed and demonstrated. Needs, too, are in principle empirical phenomena but, like human nature, cannot be directly observed. Needs are inferred objective requirements (including psychological requirements: emotional, cognitive, motivational) for individual safety, wellbeing, and growth.

The fact that human beings have individual needs that may differ from their wants will hardly be disputed by any thoughtful parent, social worker, or health professional; one has almost to be an academic to doubt it. But in the prevailing traditions of liberal philosophy, and of liberal-democratic political institutions, attention to needs issues is low. Utilitarians have sought to base political institutions on wants and demands, and so have contract theorists, Rousseau excepted. Our time's liberal-democratic or Tory-democratic governments tend to claim to be righteous when they "give the people what they want."

Democrats, as believers in voting, must emphasize responsiveness to popular wants as a primary legitimation principle. A primary commitment to human rights, on the other hand, requires a different kind of legitimation, for a human right cannot in principle be validated or invalidated by popular votes. *Vox populi, vox Dei* will not do for a human rights-ist.

How to ground human rights philosophically? There are many *ad hoc* assumptions in the literature. Orwin and Pangle speak of "every human being" possessing "certain desires that are uniquely human and cannot be chosen or rejected but are simply given."[1] Henry Shue makes it his first principle that "degrading inequalities ought to be avoided."[2] Matthews and Pratt assert, on both logical and empirical grounds, that the following four human rights are "more fundamentally basic" than other important rights: "the rights to freedom from detention without trial, to freedom from torture, to freedom from extra-judicial execution and to subsistence." These rights are given a logically based priority, to the effect that "no other rights are meaningful" unless these are protected, and the empirical point is made that these four points "are now receiving near-universal acknowledgement."[3] Jack Donnelly, in a paper in which he wisely rejects a grounding of human rights in a Rawls-type theory of justice, settles for the general idea of grounding the concept in some kind of natural rights theory, and concludes rather openendedly that what rights one is assumed to be entitled to "simply as a person is a function of a theory of human nature, a philosophical anthropology, which presents an account of what it is to be a human being or moral person."[4]

I think these and other writers head in the same direction, without quite getting there: toward a grounding of human rights in human needs. At the risk of sounding dogmatic I shall adopt this grounding explicitly; not only that, I shall state what I think are the most basic categories of human needs, in their natural or "rational" order: Survival needs, first of all; then safety or health needs; the dignity of social identity needs; and then liberty or freedom needs.

You are free, of course, to proclaim that freedom is our highest, noblest human need, and to prepare to sacrifice your life to the ideals of freedom of your choice. But you should not feel free to sacrifice other people's lives for *your* ideals of liberty, or for Mr Bush's or Mr Mulroney's. Chances are that the less privileged among us, especially those who live in the Third World, if given a real choice would value guarantees of nutrition for their children above freedom of the press, assuming they could not have both.[5]

Before I return to the issue of the philosophical grounding of rights in human needs, allow me a digression about how I think this issue applies to the Cold War between the so-called democratic and the so-called socialist super-power. The US government, like other liberal regimes, focuses on wants and demands as all-important for its political legitimacy; even outrageously brutal, need-destructive domestic and foreign policies are assumed to be justified if based on the apparent will of the people. The USSR and its allied regimes, on the other hand, claim legitimation on the ground that they meet their peoples basic needs. In principle, this is a better kind of legitimacy claim, from a humanist perspective, except that these regimes tend to undervalue the importance of individual freedom needs; and, what is worse, their Politiburos tend to be so sure that *they* know what the people's needs and not-needs are that they often close off debate about need limits and priorities, and stagnation may set in, under the lengthening shadows of a bureaucratic administration of ideas along with other commodities. One system is more like a jungle, with limitless liberties for the jetsets and abysmal poverty elsewhere; the other is more like a zoo, with well cared for but over-regulated human lives. Let us hope that this contest between liberties and basic rights will not bring about the end of the world, when a much better resolution would be to push for a little more zoo into the jungle, and a little more jungle into the zoo! I believe that Mr Gorbachev would agree; perhaps Mr Bush as well?

The Philosophy of Rights

Now back to the question of the philosophical grounding of human rights. The historical linkage of human rights with liberalism is clear enough, but it is philosophically indefensible, assuming that we think of these rights as universal rather than social class-restricted.

Liberalism originated in the social contract theories of Hobbes and Locke, in the utilitarianism of Hume and Bentham, and in the political economics of Adam Smith and Ricardo. The simultaneous rise of demands for civil or human rights gave useful slogans to the struggle of the rising bourgeoisie against monarchs and feudal lords, but they fitted badly into the subsequent struggles of the working class for a new, more humane, socialist order. Indeed, it could be termed a giant, bad joke of history that the cause of (allegedly universal) human rights became associated with the rise of capitalism, an economic system based on exploitation and on the reduction of workers to commodities in a merciless labour market, or to outright redundancy and starvation within the growing industrial reserve army. Another unsuitable feature of mainstream liberalism was its pessimistic ontological assumption that man is by his nature, and always will be, a narrowly selfish utility maximizer, unfit for any better kind of life in any more humane future kind of social order.[6]

We must look to Rousseau for a more viable philosophical basis for a theory of human rights based on need priorities. Let me for brevity's sake refer to his outlook, as I interpret and adopt it, as rational humanism: *humanism* here will refer to the orientation that is committed to a human rights order based on basic need priorities, and *rational* means being ready to question all related assumptions, possibly excepting the commitment to the supreme inherent value of every human.

Rousseau envisioned a social contract that was to serve, not some individuals or classes at the expense of others, but the General Will – that is, the best interests of all, without exceptions. He was a pessimist about societies and governments but an optimist about man. Societies and regimes tend to corrupt us by stimulating within us all kinds of false needs that make us avaricious, spiteful, envious, and above all dependent on fashions and on the powers that be; yet we are in principle, he believed, capable of striving for the best life, even for *moral liberty*, which we achieve when we come to see the common good as our own good, and to act accordingly.[7]

Rousseau was a humanist, not a liberal, also in the political sense that he made it a condition for a regime's legitimacy that it made the General Will prevail over particular wills, and insisted that the Law made no exceptions to the detriment, or to the advantage, of any individual: "Is the welfare of any single citizen any less the common cause than that of the whole State? . . . So little is it the case that any one person ought to perish for all, that all have pledged their lives and properties for the defence of each, in order that the weakness of individuals may always be protected by the strength of the public, and each member by the whole State."[8]

Kant made it his project to develop his own elaboration of Rousseau's ethic in the *a priori* realm of thought, rational rather than empirical, that he called Practical Reason. Rousseau's moral liberty in Kant becomes the "autonomy of the will" – that is, the will being a law to itself, guided by "only a single categorical imperative"; "'Act only on that maxim through which you can at the same time will that it should become a universal law'."[9]

According to Kant, man must be seen to exist as an end in himself "*not merely as a means* for arbitrary use by this or that will . . . In the kingdom of ends everything has either a *price* or a *dignity*. If it has a price, something else can be put in its place as an *equivalent*; if it is exalted above all price and so admits of no equivalent, than it has dignity."[10] For Kant, every human being has dignity, equally.

If Rousseau and Kant had sought to replace liberalism's calculating man with a conception of moral man, it was left to Marx and Engels to develop a viable model of a socialist man. They saw man as social by nature, as a species being, before and beneath alienation. They were confident that men will reaffirm their natural social solidarity, as associated producers and as fellow human beings, after the revolution, when capitalist exploitation and alienation have been brought to an end. "In place of the old bourgeois society, with its classes and class antagonisms, we shall have an association, in which the free development of each is the condition for the free development of all." ". . . only then can the narrow horizon of bourgeois right be crossed in its entirety and society inscribe on its banner: From each according to his ability, to each according to his needs!" "The society that will organize production on the basis of a free and equal association of the producers will put the whole machinery of state where it will then belong: into the Museum of Antiquities, by the side of the spinning wheel and the bronze axe."[11]

Marx derided "Rights of Man" as a symbol of selfish bourgeois individualism. But he was a rational humanist; like Rousseau and Kant, he was out to safeguard the basic needs of every human being without exception, even though he shunned the language of human rights.

After this, let me propose the following reformulation of my rational-humanist definition of "human right": any moral claim to an individual entitlement or immunity validated by the fact that the claimant or the claimee is a human being, whose basic need(s) will be in jeopardy unless the claim is protected.

HUMAN RIGHTS AND POLITICAL LEGITIMACY: AUTHENTIC AND INAUTHENTIC ADVOCACY

We live in an age of the democratic make-believe. We ascribe legitimacy to our political institutions because they are perceived to be democratic. Paradoxically, it was the authoritarian but innovative philosopher Thomas Hobbes who founded this tradition, with his new idea that only real service to the people's most urgent needs could justify the state. The most pressing need that he saw was for civil peace, and the only viable alternative he saw to civil war was the Leviathan state.

John Locke saw the options as less grim and came up with a more liberal social contract. Like Locke, the utilitarians and the Manchester liberals were mainly concerned with popular interests, wants and demands rather than needs. Bentham would assign legitimacy to a regime if it served "the greatest happiness of the greatest number."

Our own time's most influential students of political behaviour have, paradoxically, accepted the liberal-democratic legitimation theory, while at the same time reporting voluminous research findings to the effect that, in fact, small minorities are running our political shows. Behavioral political scientists, of all people, should have resisted the democratic make-believe. This research tradition was inaugurated by Robert Michels with his 1915 book, *Political Parties*, which made a strong empirical case for expecting all organizations to be run by oligarchies, even trade unions and parties ostensibly struggling for democracy and equality.[12] We must assume the same to be true, only more so, of so-called democratic states (and, of course, of so-called socialist states, no less).

Not surprisingly, some contemporary theorists, most conspicuously Habermas, have announced a *legitimation crisis*,[13] in view of the loss of credibility of the liberal legitimation theories of the Lockian contract or of utilitarianism, in the present-day context of the rapid and massive accumulation of society's economic resources in private-corporate hands. On the other hand, other empirical findings, discussed by Robert E. Lane, strongly suggest that, especially in the US, there remains a broad, implicit support for the system, at least in the sense that relatively few Americans as yet can see any viable alternative on the horizon.[14]

I accept Lane's facts and his empirical interpretations of them, but I strenuously try to resist the democratic make-believe.[15] Consequently, I see a mammoth challenge to political education in our time. Essentially, this is still Rousseau's rational-humanist challenge to his own time: how to resist a powerful regime's false legitimation claims, and thus try to nurture the hope for a more humane future political order?

The US and Freedoms

The fraudulence of such democratic legitimation claims in behalf of a regime that serves privileged interests has rarely been more starkly visible, it seems to me, than in the present Reagan–Bush era in the United States (in Canada there is, in any event, much more decorum). Most baffling of all the many challenges to our credulity are perhaps the recurring statements from Washington officials that attribute democratic virtues to terror regimes like those of Guatemala and Salvador but not to the populist Sandinista regime of Nicaragua.

How to characterize Washington's current official position on international issues of human rights? Like "democracy" and "freedom" (cf. "the Free World"), "human rights" is a powerful symbol, and it serves the interests of power and privilege to use the term *inauthentically* – i.e., for the extraneous purpose of gaining propaganda points in a confrontational world. As the opposite, *authentic* human rights language is language serving a dialogue on how to promote human emancipation: discourse seeking universal criteria for assessing relative burdens of oppression, for purposes of fair comparisons and evaluations of human rights achievements, and as a guide to strategies in the struggles for further advances, in any part of the world.

Governments and their advocates, least of all superpower representatives cannot be expected to speak authentically about democracy or human rights. Also our Canadian government must to some extent speak with "forked tongue" on human rights issues, as on other issues that may affect concerns of power and diplomacy. That makes it all the more necessary, however, that those of us who are not obligated by such concerns should be as forthright and as forceful as possible in our own examinations of human rights theory and issues, in order to try to limit as much as we can the persuasive impact of the many inauthentic, more or less deceptive official and semi-official communications.

For an extreme case of inauthentic human rights discourse, which no doubt has been widely persuasive, consult ex-Ambassador Jeane Kirkpatrick's famous and infamous essay, "Dictatorships and Double Standards," first published in 1979, after years of mass-murderous rightwing regimes in Chile, Argentina, and Central American countries. Kirkpatrick there asserted flatly that "traditional authoritarian governments are less repressive than revolutionary autocracies . . . and . . . more compatible with U.S. interests."[16] In effect she tacitly encouraged the continuing use of torture and death squads in "friendly" dictator-ruled Latin American countries, in the righteous cause of anti-communism; and these signals became more significant when she republished the essay during her time as US Ambassador to the United Nations.[17]

I don't have to remind you that her boss at the time has extravagantly exceeded even *her* inauthentic rhetoric on related human rights issues, on many occasions; speaking, for example, of today's Nicaragua as "a totalitarian dungeon;" and of Somozist-led, CIA-salaried "Contras" as "freedom fighters" of the same moral stature as his own country's Founding Fathers.[18]

It was discouraging that even a President of the US could be taken seriously after indulging in such extremes of fanciful rhetoric. One must hope that in the longer run he will have helped to strengthen the case, *malgré lui*, for the two propositions with which I conclude this part of my discussion:

1. A government should be considered legitimate, or deserving of respect and loyalty, only to the extent that it endeavors to protect human rights, according to rational humanist priorities, at home and, when possible in terms of influence and legality, also abroad.
2. The task of advancing human rights requires strategies of action but also of words: a continuing struggle to push for a more authentic, critical discourse on human rights-related issues, and to expose inauthentic apologies for oppressive policies and institutions.

A NEGATIVE-UTILITARIAN PERSPECTIVE ON PRIORITIES AMONG HUMAN RIGHTS ISSUES

"Nature has placed mankind under the governance of two sovereign masters, *pain* and *pleasure*. It is for them alone to point out what we ought to do, as well as to determine what we shall do," according to the famous opening statement in Bentham's *Introduction to the Principles of Morals and Legislation*. Neither he nor his utilitarian followers have perceived the deepgoing moral asymmetry between the pursuit of pleasure and attempting to escape from pain. The pursuit of pleasure is largely a subjective matter which requires individual freedom of choice, while escaping from pain is largely an objective matter which requires solidarity and assistance, especially when the pain is severe. Bentham called the principle of imprescriptible natural rights "nonsense upon stilts," and yet I shall argue that the negative half of Bentham's utilitarianism, if properly conceptualized, will provide a useful perspective for judgements on priorities among categories of human rights.

The one amendment that is necessary even to the negative half of Bentham's utilitarianism is the stipulation that the worst kinds of pain and danger afflicting only one or a few persons must have first claim on relief or remedy, prior to lesser pains afflicting larger numbers; as will be taken for granted in any hospital emergency ward.

In a pluralist society there can be no human right to happiness or pleasure, only a right to define and choose one's own conceptions of pleasure or happiness. These goals raise democratic issues that should be settled by way of voted upon public policies – unlike, in principle, human rights issues, where the victims of the worst kinds of violence or oppression should have a prior claim on relief, compared to those who are in a less precarious or suffering state. It is inappropriate to *vote* on whether to permit torture in our jails, or the death penalty, from this point of view, unless we can be virtually certain that the Nays will prevail. On human rights issues we need enlightened Courts who can push our civilization step by step away from remnants of barbarism which may still be tolerated by public opinion, parties, and/or legislatures.

As in the field of medicine, so is there in the field of human rights a difference between priorities in treatment and in prevention. Claims of actual victims of violence (physical, social or economic) should have to yield only to claims of persons or groups that are suffering even worse or are in even more immediately life-threatening situations. There should be no discrimination on any grounds other than urgency of need, and the feasibility of assistance reaching the victims before it is too late; ideally speaking, since human rights are universal, physical proximity should not by itself make a difference, outside the immediate family, groups of friends, or community.

Priority issues in prevention raise more complex problems and there is less of a clearcut distinction between democratic and human rights issues, chiefly because elements of uncertainty in predictions are unavoidable. Legislatures and courts must both take part in law-making efforts to prevent future human rights abuses (as well as in efforts, of course, to curb ongoing abuses, first of all), in support of future as well as now living people. Priorities in prevention might well begin with the green ecological health and safety rights (such as the right to breathe uncontaminated air); these are collective as well as individual rights, of persons and groups now living as well as of people yet to be born. Almost equally momentous in scope and weight are the red safety and dignity rights of socialism (like the rights of equal access to adequate nutrition, or to quality health care). Last but also of great weight are the blue dignity and freedom rights of liberalism, an area in which the economically advanced Western countries have made great advances in the last two centuries (such as the right to free speech, or the freedom of association); however, the record of colonial and neo-colonial policies has not evidenced consistent concern, to put it mildly, for the human rights of citizens of politically or economically dependent countries.

WHAT DOES "WE TAKE THE UNIVERSALITY OF HUMAN RIGHTS SERIOUSLY" MEAN?

In his important work, *Taking Rights Seriously*, Ronald Dworkin states that the US constitutional system "rests on a particular moral theory, namely, that men have moral rights against the state." So rests, according to my argument, the legal and political order of *any* legitimate state; to this extent the present argument goes beyond Dworkin's; but so it does in a different way as well: Dworkin says that not only do people have rights, and incidentally expresses his indebtedness to John Rawls's theory of justice, but one right among all others is for him "fundamental and even axiomatic. This most fundamental of rights is a distinct conception of the right to equality, which I call the right to equal concern and respect."[19]

In my own scheme of human rights priorities this is one fundamental dignity right, to be sure with implications for personal security rights and freedom rights as well. But the most basic security rights must, in principle, be prior: the rights to collective and to individual security of survival and to protection against serious injury and disease. From a practical legal or public policy perspective I grant that the right to equal concern and respect is a much neater first premise, but I contend that Dworkin's normative position fails to take the most basic needs seriously enough.

Along with Rousseau and Kant, as I have pointed out above, I take human lives and each human life as the ultimate value, each life being equally an end in itself and therefore priceless. For actuarial and insurance purposes and to resolve various public policy dilemmas pricetags may, to be sure, be attached to human lives (e.g., how much to invest in accident-prevention?);[20] but as a matter of moral principle the primary task of politics and government must be to serve all human beings according to priorities of need.

Now, people and governments may go about meeting basic needs in different ways, depending on historical and cultural experience; but since humans all are of the same species we may reasonably assume that we share our most basic need categories. However, ethnocentric patriotism or nationalism often tends to create illusions to the contrary. These illusions, usually welcomed and nurtured by the ruling powers, must be exposed, as a first step toward becoming serious about the universality of need-based human rights.

Next I shall argue, along with John Burton, that basic needs carry a heavy weight as facts, which political leaders may ignore, and often do ignore, only at heavy costs, for unmet basic needs don't go away in peace.

The remainder of the chapter will argue for an extension of our concern with (need-based) human rights so as to make it the core of a political program rather than just a list of discrete claims; first in the American context and then in the context of the global public interest and I shall conclude with an assessment of the prospects for a longterm struggle toward a world order of human rights.

The Issue of Standards

In our age of government reinforced nationalism we tend to apply different terms and different standards of judgement regarding human rights observance, depending on whether we have our own or foreign countries in mind, or depending on whether a given country is perceived as similar to, or as friendly to, our own. Correspondingly, epithets like "terrorist" are applied liberally to those who kidnap and detain US or allied nations' citizens, but not to Israeli military incursions or to punitive airstrikes in Shiite Moslem areas in Lebanon.

The double standards applied by the most powerful state today, in extracting from other countries an inordinate respect for the dignity of *its* citizens, even after their deaths, is nowhere better illustrated than in post-war Vietnam, where the American government is still pressing for a more complete accounting for the earthly remains of every last US Air Force or Army combatant, in contrast to the same government's apparent indifference to the countless and unaccounted-for remains of the Vietnamese victims of the war.

As Bertrand Russell pointed out many years ago, patriotic rhetoric thrives on the idea of the presumably sacred duty to be prepared, when called upon, to "die for our country;" while there is little explicit attention paid to the presumably corollary obligation, of being prepared to "kill for our country."[21] Much of the conventional patriotism amounts to collective self-aggrandizement, circuitously phrased to look idealistic and virtuous. It tends to be taken for granted, for example, that international negotiations involving one's own country must always be conducted as bargaining sessions, to seek outcomes reflecting realities of power, not considerations of justice. National governments, just like liberal individuals or capitalist firms, are invariably supposed to look out for their own countries only, not for the safety or wellbeing of other nations. A once familiar American roadside warning comes to mind: "The life you save may be your own!" As if to kill someone else by careless driving would have to be a lesser calamity.

I write this not to build up to the obvious and facile statement that we would all be better off if we were more concerned about the safety and wellbeing of others. True enough, but the point I want to reach is at once more limited and more compelling as an *empirical* argument for a new perspective on needs and human rights.

The Political Reality of Needs

This point, most ably argued by John Burton, is that basic human needs are powerful *facts*, which decision makers in international politics may keep on disregarding only at their own peril. "Protest behaviour – legal, antisocial and all forms – emerges as the symptom of a significant gap between human needs and expectations, on the one hand, and opportunities within the international structure for satisfying these, on the other."[22] Take the view that terrorism can be effectively deterred, even in the Middle East, by American sponsored counter-terrorism, a view supported by syndicated columnist James J. Kilpatrick, Henry Kissinger, and others;[23] this view, which would not be concerned to examine the depth of frustration on the other side, is effectively laid to rest, I think, in Burton's analysis. And he has followed up his theorizing, and in turn contributed to it, by way of extensive practical experience with facilitating processes of international conflict resolution. He relies on the principle of a third-party facilitator, when this is acceptable to the two parties at conflict. The third party's principle task is to look for innovative ways of analyzing the basic need structure on both sides, to try to come up with multiple ideas for partial outcomes that can benefit both sides, or alternatively benefit one side without hurting the other; in any event, to try to bring alternative ideas forward which could leave both sides better off in terms of total need satisfaction.[24]

If basic needs are to be seen as hard facts for purposes of international negotiations, they are just as hard facts for purposes of domestic legislation and public policies as well. A society or government that keeps on violating basic needs of large numbers will encourage violent crime in the streets – and more so when the wealth of the affluent glaringly contrasts with dire poverty and other indignities for the less privileged classes. Calling American society "a civilization without a conscience," the eminent social psychologist Kenneth B. Clark comments as follows on the Bernhard Goetz case in New York City (the subway passenger who shot three teenagers who, he claimed, were about to attack and rob him). "In Cities, Who Is the Real Mugger?" Clark asks, and he replies as follows: "The educationally rejected and despised 'muggers' – the pool of unemployed and unemployable from which they come – will increase in numbers, defiance and venom. Not able to express their frustrations in words, their indignation takes the form of more crime."

Is it a basic security right to be able to walk the city streets unmolested? Clark does not dispute this right, but argues that New York's "rejected, dehumanized 'muggers' are the products of the silent 'respectables' who make a hero of one [namely Goetz, who was praised in many letters to the press] who fights the fire of urban deterioration and crime by firing a gun . . . They seek to protect themselves from increasing violent crime while they remain silent about the crimes of deteriorating neighbourhoods, job discrimination and criminally inferior education."[25]

What has prompted the writing of this chapter is my sense that human rights issues have not yet become as central to political thought and action as they might be, especially for those of us who place ourselves on the left side of the traditional political spectrum, and/or on the Green side of the modern political colour spectrum. To be sure, specific human rights issues deeply concern many constituencies of activities; and many of them, as well as many jurists and academics, are keenly committed on fairly broad ranges of human rights issues. But few see the problem of human rights as the core issues, as I do, in future strategies for national and transnational political emancipation. To come to this view requires, as I have argued, taking the universality of need-based human rights seriously, and incorporating a concern with the whole range of basic needs as the end of politics and the only source of political legitimacy.

Ronald Dworkin, as we have seen, took an important step in this direction with his call to take rights seriously; he issued one of the first persuasive arguments for making the legitimacy of the state contingent on its respect for and protection of the basic human rights. However, Dworkin's argument is about some, not all, basic rights; and it is about the American constitution, not about world politics.

Another jurist, Arthur S. Miller, has probed beyond Dworkin's perspective in a paper entitled "Taking Needs Seriously: Observations on the Necessity for Constitutional Change," in which he argues cogently in favour of activating an orderly process of accelerating constitutional change, to achieve for the United States something akin to a "constitution of human needs."[26] Other legal scholars have argued effectively for the continuing development of new and improved international human rights law; so effectively, in fact, that one of them felt bound to urge a slower pace, and to advocate a procedural "quality control" over new United Nations-sponsored "enactments".[27]

But there is more that needs to be done on the political scene, especially in the countries of the First World: internationally powerful, politically "open" (i.e., pluralist), but as yet less serious, compared to the Second and Third Worlds, about the most basic human needs. In this relatively privileged part of the world, neither the Greens nor the Greys (if we may call opponents of the Greens by the colour of cement), and neither the left, the center, nor the right, have as yet articulated their central political concerns in needs and rights language. The exception, it might perhaps seem, could be the political right's fondness for the language of individual liberties and property rights, but in their case there is little attention to human needs. Robert Nozick, to refer to one of the most articulate philosophers of the near-Libertarian right, seem to make respect for property rights, regardless of human needs, the ultimate political value.[28]

My hope is not only to impress on much of the left and on the Greens that they are really human rights-humanists at heart (although Green animal rights people will dissociate themselves from the *term* humanist), *provided* the human rights cause is seen to be associated, not with liberal individualism but with the whole range of the most basic human needs. I also think inroads will be made among people now in the political center and further right, and among people who are not yet Green. Very few people of any political colour are really opposed to, or even *not* in favour of, the meeting of basic needs according to just priorities. There are quite a few people around who are prepared to commit gruesome crimes, with the easy conscience of fanaticism; yet there is hardly any large constituency available, for example in the United States, for an openly "pro-victimization league," or for an "anti-basic needs association." In brief, I believe that a need-based, universalistic human rights coalition could become the basis of a political movement with clout.

Political Practice

Now let us look at some of the actual developments in the last fifty years which appear to point toward a world order of human rights as a future possibility; I shall argue that the steps that have been taken are valuable accomplishments in their own right and not only as possibly being waystations on the road toward a new world order.

The United Nations was founded as an alliance of the nations allied in the war against Hitler's Germany, Italy, and Japan, but after the end of the war it has gradually expanded its membership, until by now nearly every state has become a member of the world organization. Only sovereign states can be members of the UN, and they remain sovereign states as members; and yet their sovereignty is no longer as unimpaired as it was when the UN was founded. A new concept entered the world stage of the UN: the idea of international human rights, as protection against the state. The near-universal revulsion against the Holocaust made most of the world's public opinion ready for the idea that there should be some limits to what any government could do to silence or punish even "its own" citizens, even though this new idea took time to articulate, let alone to be thought of as a concept incorporated in the evolving international law. When in 1946 the UN established the Commission on Human Rights, the original idea was that it should consist of independent experts, but this plan was voted down, in favour of government appointees as Commission members.[29] When the Commission went to work on drafting the Universal Declaration of Human Rights, it was just as well that the government had had a hand in it from the outset; it undoubtedly added to the political weight of the Document, which was adopted by the UN General Assembly in December, 1948.

Early in 1976 followed the International Covenant on Economic, Social and Cultural Rights, which by then had been ratified by the requisite number of States, and the International Covenant on Civil and Political Rights, the latter followed by an Optional Protocol, by now acceded to by some 30-odd states which were prepared to be in principle accountable to the international community for their compliance with the Covenant on Civil and Political Rights.

There are no sanctions as yet, even under the Optional Protocol, let alone under the two Covenants, but the process of establishing the principle of legal force for global human rights has been established, and awaits the political will to build some procedural muscle. Some regional Coventions, notably the European one, go further;

there is now the opportunity for West European citizens to take their own governments to court (The European Court of Human Rights) and obtain binding judgements in their own favour.

There are innumerable non-governmental agencies in many countries; individually and collectively they yield an enormous and growing influence in the United Nations agencies, on member governments and on world opinion. *The Human Rights Internet Reporter*, published quarterly at the Harvard Law School, documents a wide range of human rights agencies and on-going activities; there is indeed a fast-growing international human rights movement ready to speak up and seek ways to act against abuses – even if, to be sure, their working conditions in many countries remain both difficult and hazardous.

To these organizations must be added other categories, if you accept the broad conception of human rights – the green and the red as well as the blue rights. The ecology movements, the peace movements, and the feminist movements all work to protect human rights that bear on essential human needs. So do community-based health-promotion agencies, anti-poverty agencies, and parts of the union movements. In pluralist societies there is increasing potential for new experiments with coalition building and a new concern with the national interest, but also with aspects of the global public interest.

The Future

Coalitions toward what kinds of goal? What kinds of conceptions of the global public interest? Let me now cite Article 28 in the Universal Declaration of Human Rights: "Everyone is entitled to a social and international order in which the rights and freedoms set forth in this Declaration can be fully realized."

This statement expresses a political aspiration, not yet an achievement; and it could be called a utopian aspiration since such a state of affairs in the world cannot be approximated even in the foreseeable future. And yet the Article poses a challenge to us: the challenge to take the universality of human rights seriously. In practical terms this challenge can and should have consequences for our self-awareness as citizens, and for our political conduct.

First of all, we are reminded that any individual's human rights become morally unacceptable privileges if they are enjoyed by some at the price of excluding others. In Sweden, for example, some socio-economic writers have asked whether the material standards of life have not become too high in their country, since the Swedish affluence that has made the welfare state entitlements affordable derives in part from the unjust terms of international trade that have kept most of the Third World mired in poverty.

Secondly, Article 28 should remind us that humans are social as well as individual beings, when not too corrupt, oppressed, or alienated; it pains many of us to know that Africans starve, or that many Canadians are homeless; if given a choice, many of us would gladly sacrifice if thereby the world's poor could be helped. More than that, many of us would, if this kind of human rights language were available to us, demand as our human right that a Canadian government should help to make a better world for all people.

Thirdly, when Article 28 demands a world order in which (all) the "rights and freedoms set forth in this Declaration can be fully realized," we are reminded that the socio-economic as well as political rights are to be protected; and whenever Washington lectures Havana about human rights shortfalls we should remind the media that in Cuba the right to health and to education is far better protected today than it is under any one of Washington's client regimes in all of Latin America.

The very profusion of rights listed in the Declaration and in the two Covenants should also underscore the need for discussion and for rational decisions about priorities; for example, Article 24's stipulation of a right to "periodic holidays with pay," while by no means unimportant, hardly is of the same urgency as Article 5's ban on torture.

While liberal writers often make a distinction between (individual) human rights and collective rights, the Declaration and the Covenants include both kinds of rights as human rights, with the Declaration's Article 28 as good an example as any of a reference to both collective and individual human rights. Since human beings are social animals, it is to be assumed that rights of collectivities, if based on needs, are individual human rights as well.

In conclusion: The two best-known secular agendas in the struggle for human emancipation, away from the barbarism of our distant and recent past (including the Holocaust), are liberal-democracy and Marxism–Leninism. The former kind of states, the liberal democracies, have tended to produce rather passive citizenries with a high tolerance for socio-economic injustice; the latter, the so-called socialist states, have produced more equal access to health services, education, and to other social amenities as well, but at the price of stiffening bureaucracies and setting tight limits on public access to critical political knowledge. And the tension between the two kinds of system has led to fears of war and to massive armaments on both sides. Clearly, in our nuclear tinderbox world the time for ideas of a bloody world revolution is over; that strategy is much too dangerous for all of humanity.

The third kind of agenda envisaged here, as a struggle for worldwide human rights, with priorities based on needs, seeks a gradual strengthening of citizens and their independent organizations against the states and their power elites, with potential allies among the latter on specific human rights issues. A negative-utilitarian perspective of relief and remedies always for the least privileged or the most endangered will lead to many coalitions, often with United Nations agencies seeking to assist, and with articulate professionals from many countries, and many church and union leaders, helping to push forward in the general direction suggested by Article 28: toward a strengthening of the vision and the demand for an eventual world order of human rights.

NOTES AND REFERENCES

1. Clifford Orwin and Thomas Pangle, "The Philosophical Foundation of Human Rights," in Marc F. Plattner (ed.), *Human Rights in Our Time* (Boulder, CO: Westview Press, 1984): 1–22 at 3.
2. Henry Shue, *Basic Rights: Subsistence, Affluence and US Foreign Policy* (Princeton University Press, 1980): 119–23 at 119.
3. Robert Matthews and Cranford Pratt, "Human Rights and Foreign Policy: Principles and Canadian Practice," *Human Rights Quarterly*, 7 (2) (May 1985): 159–88 at 160.
4. Jack Donnelly, "Human Rights as Natural Rights," *Human Rights Quarterly* 4 (3) (1982): 391–405 at 392 and 398.
5. A proclaimed and perceived necessity of making such a choice (between freedom rights and welfare rights) may itself reflect elite strategies of oppression. "Scientific comparisons [of human rights implications of strategies of development] may be used as explanations, but should never be used as excuses, for human rights abuses. The Nigerian writer Wole Soyinka speaks of 'power morality.' Power morality is undoubtedly the most enduring enemy of human rights, in Africa as elsewhere." Rhoda Howard, "Evaluating Human Rights in Africa: Some Problems of Implicit Comparisons," *Human Rights Quarterly*, 6 (2) (May 1984): 160–79 at 179.

6. "We can see now that men are not by nature infinitely desirous creatures, but were only made so by the market society, which compelled men to seek ever greater power in order to maintain even modest levels of satisfactions." C. B. Macpherson, *The Real World of Democracy* (Toronto: CBC Publications, 1965): 62. Also see his *Democratic Theory: Essays in Retrieval* (Oxford: Clarendon Press, 1973): 3–23.

7. Jean-Jacques Rousseau, "The Social Contract," in *The Social Contract and Discourses*, Book 1 (London: Dent, 1973), Chapter 8: 178.

8. Rousseau, "A Discourse on Political Economy," in *The Social Contract*, Book 1: 114–53 at 132.

9. Immanuel Kant, *Groundwork of the Metaphysic of Morals* (New York: Harper & Row, 1964): 108 and 188, italics deleted.

10. Kant, *Groundwork*: 95 and 102, Kant's italics.

11. Robert C. Tucker (ed.), *The Marx–Engels Reader* (New York: Norton, 1972, 1978): 491, 531 and 755, 2nd edn. The first statement is taken from Marx and Engels, "The Manifesto of the Community Party;" the second from Marx, "Critique of the Gotha Program;" the third from Engels, "The Origin of the Family, Private Property, and the State."

12. Robert Michels, *Political Parties* (Glencoe, IL: Free Press, 1915, 1949).

13. Jurgen Habermas, *Legitimation Crisis* (Boston: Beacon Press, 1975).

14. Robert E. Lane, "The Legitimacy Bias: Conservative Man in Market and State," in Bogdan Denitch (ed.), *Legitimation of Regimes* (London: Sage, 1979): 55–79.

15. Cf. C. Bay, "Foundations of the Liberal Make-Believe," *Inquiry*, 14 (1971): 213–37.

16. Jeane J. Kirkpatrick's "Dictatorships and Double Standards" was initially published in *Commentary* in November 1979. See her *Dictatorship and Double Standards: Rationalism and Reason in Politics* (New York: Simon & Schuster, 1982): 23–52 at 49.

17. She served in this position during President Reagan's first administration, 1980–4 and for a couple of months into the second; she stepped down in March 1985.

18. Like Ambassador Kirkpatrick, President Reagan appeared oblivious to well-established facts about atrocities in Latin America; he, too, constructed his own sense of reality by way of reasoning deductively from the evil of alleged communism as his first premise. In a 1985 address the then President Reagan dismissed the many authenticated reports of "Contra" atrocities in Nicaragua by stating that atrocities in that country are largely "the work of the institutionalized cruelty of the Sandinista Government . . . a cruelty that flows naturally from the heart of totalitarianism. The truth is Somoza was bad, but so many of the people of Nicaragua know the Sandinistas are infinitely worse," *New York Times*, 16 April 1985: 4.

19. Ronald Dworkin, *Taking Rights Seriously* (Cambridge, MA: Harvard University Press, 1978).

20. See William R. Greer, "Value of One Life? From $8.37 to $10 Million," *New York Times*, 26 June 1985: 1 and 9.

21. Bertrand Russell, *Which Way to Peace?* (London: Michael Joseph, 1936).

22. John W. Burton, *Deviance, Terrorism and War: The Process of Solving Unsolved Social and Political Problems* (Oxford: Martin Robertson, 1979): 206.

23. Kilpatrick recommended the following message to the Shiites holding American hostages in Beiruit after a hijacking and murder in late June 1985: after shooting a Shiite, held in Israel and picked at random, in retaliation for the American who had been killed by the hijackers we, "For every American passenger you kill thereafter . . . will kill 10 of your brothers." James J. Kilpatrick, "Eye for Eye . . . Stripe for Stripe," in *Washington Post*, 20 June 1985, section A: 21. Henry Kissinger, who was interviewed in the same week on the major television networks, was less specific but nonetheless fierce in his pleas for retaliation, and for taking strong measures to deter future hostage taking, though he stopped short of recommending that the Israelis be urged to stop taking Lebanese Shittes forcibly to internment in Israel.

24. See Burton's statement "Procedures for Facilitated International Conflict Resolution," from the Center for International Development, the University of Maryland (April 1985).

25. Kenneth B. Clark, "In Cities Who Is the Real Mugger?," *New York Times*, 14 January 1985: 17. Also see C. Bay, "The Triple Insult of Poverty: Notes Toward a Study of Liberal Society," *Sociological Inquiry*, 46 (1976): 223–34.

26. Arthur S. Miller, "Taking Needs Seriously: Observations on the Necessity for Constitutional Change," *Washington and Lee Law Review*, 41 (Fall 1984): 1243–1306 at 1305.

27. Philip Alston, "Conjuring Up New Human Rights: A Proposal for Quality Control," *The American Journal of International Law*, 78 (1984): 607–21.

28. Robert Nozick, *Anarchy, State and Utopia* (New York: Basic Books, 1974).

29. Cf. Asbjurn Eide, "The Human Rights Movement and the Transformation of the International Order," *Alternatives*, 11 (3) (July 1986): 367–402 at 386. I am indebted to Eide's paper in this section of the present discussion.

12 The Role of Knowledge in Conflict Resolution
Yona Friedman

WHAT IS "NEEDS THEORY?"

It is widely questioned if a "needs theory" can be useful for conflict resolution. This is an important question and leads to the necessity for clarifying the definition of "needs theory." Like many other "theories," this one has a name without having substance. I shall try here to sketch the structure of what could be labeled a "unified needs-conflict theory."

Let us start with a few fundamental statements which could become the axioms of such a theory:

- A need is a conscious or unconscious recognition of a lack of something "indispensable" for a state of personal equilibrium, physically or emotionally.
- The indispensable something, the obtaining of which relieves that feeling, is a "satisfier." A need can be defined only as it is relieved by the specific satisfier. Therefore we will consider a need and its satisfier as an inseparable pair.
- Need–satisfier pairs cannot be considered as isolated entities. A satisfier that eliminates a particular need can create other needs related to other satisfiers.
- In order to clarify a complex system of need–satisfier couples, drawing a "needs diagram" can be helpful. In such a diagram each satisfier is represented by a "node" (as in graph theory) and each need represented by a "link." The central node (the "root") is the representative of the particular individual whose needs are to be mapped. Such a diagram shows the needs directly linking that individual to the particular satisfiers and to the direct needs, which are created through the process of engaging those satisfiers. The simplest needs diagram is based on a particular individual and connected to the primary satisfiers, which, in their turn, are linked with the secondary needs. A needs diagram thus shows the different "needs levels."
- A needs diagram mapping the needs of a group of people is the

result of interrelating the needs–satisfiers of the individuals making up that group.
– A community needs diagram indicates the eventual conflict zones where intra-community conflicts might arise. It indicates as well at which particular level a conflict deflating intervention could be achieved.

LEVELS OF CONFLICT AND CONFLICT RESOLUTION

If we assume these statements are fundamental, we can proceed to deduce some observations. These observations might be of practical use when studying possibilities for resolving conflicts. The grassroots level is the level where it is the most difficult to intervene as opposed to the highest level (Level III: the political level) which is relatively the least complex. Level II (the economy level) is somewhat complex, and when we get to Level I (individual needs level) the system becomes practically inextricable.

We can also assume that the true conflict level is often undetected: the visible part is only a small part of the conflict (generally of Level III). The important task for conflict resolution may be to find both the level where conflict is acute and to find the level where intervention can be made. These two levels are not necessarily the same. Communicating the right information to be grassroots level might be the most efficient method of conflict resolution. The fact that a "need to know" is always present at this level might facilitate the procedure.

The "need to know," which is the second part of the topic of this chapter and is a principal part of the unified needs–conflict theory we sketch here, is a very particular need–satisfier pair. Indeed, knowledge is not a characteristic satisfier as it does not relieve its correlate need; I would consider knowledge as an "enabler" for satisfying other needs. The "need to know" is thus really a need to have access to a tool which helps to satisfy other needs. This characteristic of the need to know assures it a very important place in a needs theory, and a no less important place in any conflict theory. But the need to know has other characteristics as well. If we observe an animal society, we can surely recognize in it all need categories but one that need theorists identify in human society. This unique need–satisfier pair is the "need to know." It is not an exaggeration to state that the need to know is the most human need of all. We can guess that it is exclusively human.

KNOWLEDGE AS NEED AND SATISFIER

I would start this chapter by citing from an earlier article I wrote on needs theory entitled "Implicit Limitations Upon Satisfiers." That paper stated that satisfiers of needs are unavoidably of limited access, these limitations becoming "heavier when growing social organization can cope with certain specific needs." This statement is particularly true about knowledge. A solitary being knows the world more profoundly (comprehensively) than does a group having interrelations in matters of knowledge; in many cases the effect of other people's knowledge on that knowledge that one learns alone is simply perturbing.

Knowledge, as already stated, is an enabler to satisfy both material and other needs. In a certain sense knowledge is an instrument for reducing material scarcity: it can lead to making the universe more habitable to more humans and to increasing its "carrying capacity." Knowledge can also be considered a power source on which domination over other people can be based. On the other hand, knowledge can be a satisfer of individual wellbeing (without involving the material universe) by leading to a feeling of equilibrium with the universe, a feeling called "wisdom" in current language.

I have always been intrigued by the enigma of knowledge and have tried to examine aspects of it in other papers ("The Right to Understand;" "The New Physiocratia: Information, Communication, Knowledge"). In these papers, I stated a few simple facts.

First, about the nature of knowledge: knowledge is not stored information; information is the raw material of knowledge. Knowledge is realized through a process called "insight." This insight is a particular ability within individuals similar to a creative instinct: everybody has it, but with many people it stays latent and unproductive. Training might develop it but cannot evoke it *ex nihilo*. Insight thus cannot be a merchandise as is knowledge. Information, in spite of existing in unlimited quantity, can also be merchandise when it is withheld. However, the amount of information necessary to develop knowledge (provided one possesses insight) is generally available.

Knowledge thus is a curious satisfier of a particular need, a satisfier which provides a particular element of wellbeing for an individual. It cannot be manipulated from the outside; it cannot be imposed upon or withheld from the one who looks for it (unlike information). As insight is the key to knowledge and as insight is strictly personal, people try to develop it through training and through persuasion.

The effect of that development is to form a process. All religions, political ideologies, scientific and educational processes try to create a method to reach insight, to keep insight from automatically following a predetermined path.

ANTAGONISM, A BASIC CONCEPT

The concept of conflict seems to be a basic image we refer to when trying to represent the universe for ourselves. In natural sciences, even physics, we represent reality as being a result of antagonistic forces fighting one another: if there are no antagonists, there are no events. A state of no-event (an equilibrium) can be understood as the apparent cancellation of such basic conflict; this state corresponds, in the view of present sciences, to the image of the universe ceasing to exist.

I have to note here that I am not considering whether this image of the world-made-through-conflicts can be accepted as true; what serves my analysis is that such an image of the world is produced by our insight and that we fit all observed phenomena into the frame of that image. But – and this is my personal conviction – this image comes from transplanting our social experience into a model that we build up to represent the world in which we live.

With regard to social events, we revolt against the idea that conflicts should be resolved purely by an equilibrium of antagonistic forces. We need a justification of that resolution: it has to be fair. We need to feel that it corresponds to our logic as well: we refuse (emotionally) all randomness (even in games). We want transparency: we look for a hidden mechanism, and we can accept more easily a secret one than we can accept the idea that it does not exist. We look for these characteristics in our image of the universe – justice, logic, transparency – which are not implicit in the information we get from things as they are. These characteristics are our poetic emotional invention, and they are tightly linked with the process of insight. It is through insight that these justifications of the information received as fundamental facts become our knowledge.

Religion, ideologies, science, all human institutions endeavor to insert into our processes of insight the need of justice, the need to understand and the need of the certitude that our explanations about events are comprehensive and without gaps. This need (let us call it Faustian) can be satisfied only in a very obvious way: we adapt ourselves to the imaginary world model we invented, and correct this model by additional information in all areas where contradiction between experience and the model might be too harsh.

To state simply that our knowledge is based on illusions would be too banal. But if we recognize that many conflicts result from the unsatisfiable need for knowledge, the statement loses its banality.

THE DIFFICULTY OF COMMUNICATION: A SAFEGUARD

One might conclude from these reflections that human insight in itself is intolerant and aggressive. Indeed, as the process of insight is the most important link between information from the external world and our consciousness, is the major link between ourselves and the universe that forms our holistic image of the universe, we instinctively consider it an aggression against ourselves if somebody tries to demolish that image (and thus "our" universe) by affirming one different from our own. As insight basically different from ours is thus unacceptable.

Ideological (religious, scientific or other) conflict is thus the only kind we cannot resolve, and the need of recognition of our insight is a need without any known or acceptable satisfier (as I consider brainwashing or "ideacide" unacceptable). Ideological struggle does not benefit those who participate in it, but they feel that they cannot avoid it: it is part of their very existence. The image of the universe one builds up for oneself (an ideology or a cosmology) is thus a source of intolerance and conflict. The only fact that softens this situation comes from the largely incommunicable character of one's very personal image of the universe.

To be more exact, it is not the image itself which is incommunicable. What is nearly impossible to communicate is the personal interpretation that led one to that image and that determines this intellectual adventure: the process of insight. An image of the universe can be conventional but is felt and visualized by each person in his/her own unique way which, luckily, cannot be kept secret. We thus arrive intuitively at what we assumed at the start: it is not the insight but the "need to know" that is the direct conflict source.

THE AMBIGUOUS NATURE OF INSIGHT

We now arrive at another statement. Referring to the paper already mentioned about Implicit Limitations Upon Satisfiers, and referring to the classification there described, we first have to distinguish between the two factors of which the "need to know" is composed: the need to "be informed" and the need for insight. Indeed, the need to be informed does not necessarily involve a material satisfier: the satisfier cannot be created by the subject of the need; it comes from the outside, and the simple fact that the subject has the information makes some contextual transformation within the information itself (i.e., it loses its quality of secrecy). Finally, such information contains what it contains and will never contain more (this does not concern its validity or truth).

Insight has the same characteristics as knowledge without being "symbiotic" – i.e., it cannot be changed from the outside, and it does not provoke any change in a person other than the one whose insight is in question. But beyond this first characteristic, insight is a very special need satisfier.

First of all, quite obviously, no normal human being exists without any capability of insight; to exist without insight would mean to exist without a mind. But the processes of insight of different human beings can be qualitatively very different. I would even risk the statement that it is precisely the particular quality of insight that makes up the "personality" of a human being. And, perhaps, personality is one of the most important conflict sources both for individuals and collectivities.

On the other hand if we consider the need to know as an important conflict source, we arrive at some unexpected ideas. We stated that information is translated into knowledge through insight, and the differences between particular personal processes of insight trigger intolerance and aggression leading to conflict. We stated further that the explosion of such conflict is diminished through the difficulty of communicating the differences in the personal processes of insight. As a thought experiment, imagine a "telepathic society": either it would possess a banalized process of insight (thus the lack of individual personalities), or it would mean a struggle of everybody against everybody else (one would have to accept the others' different images about the world).

Thus, it seems to me, the need for knowledge could be satisfied without leading to serious conflicts particular to that kind of need by making it easier to acquire information and by making it even more difficult to communicate that which insight produces from such information. Insight is thus, in its very nature, a conflict-triggering factor, and though it is essential in avoiding conflict we might presume that the latter characteristic is the more decisive. A practical problem thus arises: could the ability to gain insights be increased and if so, how?

PRACTICAL CONCLUSIONS

Many currents of thought try to achieve the goal of increasing insights and most of them do so in order to establish a "conflict dampener." Religions, political ideologies, art and science all consider themselves catalysts to a higher level of insight – practically all that we consider as making up a "culture" (in the largest sense). Knowledge, insight and information are elements of culture. The error of our time seems to be the trend to increase the information factor without caring about the insight factor. This one-dimensional development incites conflicts. Perhaps we should endeavor to pay more attention to how information becomes knowledge.

Certain conflicts originating from the need to know can thus be defused by an appropriate information policy. First of all the mass media can be dangerous. An appropriate policy seems to me one that pays attention to the following points:

– What are the kinds of information that are "knowledge generating?"
– What are the subconscious goals of knowledge generated through such information: understanding the world or manipulating it? To what extent is such knowledge communicable?
– How can knowledge be kept from being the exclusive property of an elite?

But such a policy leads to other, important questions which we have referred to in the second section of this chapter. We mentioned there that the only real way to deflate a conflict was through appropriate information at the grassroots level. The purpose of such information for conflict deflation is to trigger individuals' personal insights. It is only insight that can produce what we could call "mentality" (i.e., a routine way of thinking), and it is mentality which leads to rejection of a given conflict source (only by esteeming it non-important). Appropriate information is not "brainwash": indeed, brainwashing does not apply to insight. On the contrary, brainwashing makes a thought automatic without appealing to understanding.

To act at a grassroots level is very difficult. It is easier to act at other levels, easier and easier as we go "higher" in the needs diagram from biological satisfiers to socio-economic organization and to government (the most abstract of all levels). Action might be easier there, but will be surely less efficient. Only grassroots' acceptance is really efficient. Action at other levels is generally a form of wishful thinking.

As a practical conclusion, we could state that knowledge at the grassroots level is the best way to resolve conflict. The need to know is thus the best ally of the "conflict hunter."

13 Processes of Governance: Can Governments Truly Respond to Human Needs?
William R. Potapchuk

CONFLICT RESOLUTION AND HUMAN NEEDS THEORIES

Several scholars in the field of conflict resolution have been searching for a generic or foundational theory to unify the disparate disciplinary strands traditionally brought to bear on conflict and conflict resolution theory.[1] A recent effort by John Burton and Dennis Sandole attempts to use human needs theory as a generic adisciplinary theory of conflict and conflict resolution that encompasses the arenas of practice of interpersonal to international.[2]

If a mature human needs theory is developed, Burton suggests, then conflict resolution practitioners could understand which aspirations of a party are truly driven by basic needs and which are merely "wants." Needs cannot be compromised. Means must be found in a conflict resolution process to satisfy human needs in order to resolve (as opposed temporarily to settle) a conflict while wants, the theory holds, can be compromised.[3]

Each human needs theorist has offered their list of human needs. The lengths of the lists range from over a dozen to the one superordinate need – control – defined by Sites,[4] from which he derives eight additional fundamental needs. Each list of human needs[5] has in common one or more needs that can be met only through a process of interacting with others. Davies dubs these needs "instrumental" needs which can be contrasted with "substantive" needs.[6] Instrumental needs cited by needs scholars include control,[7] identity,[8] recognition,[9] power,[10] and security.[11] Substantive needs can be met in the absence of another human: for example, they would include physical sustenance and security from predators.

Substantive needs and instrumental needs can be further differentiated by looking at how they are satisfied. The satisfiers of substantive
needs can be looked at in a static state: a person's need for physical
sustenance can be satisfied by a certain number of calories per day.
Instrumental need satisfiers are the net result of social interaction
over time. For example, it is often said that "respect is earned." One
can feel recognized when the pattern of interaction with another is
systematic and based on mutually held criteria. If, however, the
interaction is irregular or based on criteria held by only one person,
the other may believe that they are no longer recognized. Rarely will
one isolated interaction fully determine whether an instrumental need
has been met.

These needs theorists, expressing their intent through comprehensive definitions or longer lists of needs, all assert that individuals seek
recognition, predictability and security in social interactions. While
the theorists differ in nuance, all believe that persons everywhere
have a need (a) to be treated as well as others are treated no matter
how they are linked to a particular identity group, (b) to have some
level of surety in forecasting the result of interactions with others,
and (c) to be safe or protected from others as each pursues his/her
individual goals.

International relations theorists have often defined this triplet of
needs as self-determination. The United Nations charter suggests
that self-determination is met when "all people have the right freely
to determine, without external interference, their political status and
to pursue their political status and to pursue their economic, social,
and cultural development, and every State has the duty to respect
this right in accordance with the provisions of the Charter."[12]

This explanation of self-determination uses the word "rights"
instead of "needs," but in any case neither word captures the various
methods persons use to satisfy these needs. In fact, few of the needs
theorists explore what has been called "the dark side of needs
theory."[13]

The starkest examples of the dark side are what Johann Galtung
calls the "chosen people phenomenon."[14] He suggests that currently
the Islamic majority in Iran, the Afrikaners, the Israelis, and at times
leadership in the United States talk and behave as if they were God's
chosen people. In order to satisfy their recognition and identity
needs, these groups pursue strategies that they believe will cause
others to recognize them as superior to all others. If, indeed, these
actions reflect an honest search by these peoples to satisfy their

basic human needs, are these satisfiers just? Can there be unjust, illegitimate, or dysfunctional satisfiers of legitimate needs? Needs theory currently has little to say about this question.

I believe that not only are there illegitimate and unjust satisfiers of human needs, there are false satisfiers as well. While continued exploration of universal human needs may provide a wellspring of information to conflict resolution practitioners seeking to understand the motivations of parties in conflict. The notion of satisfiers is bound by fuller, cultural and developmental issues that may minimize the potential contributions of human needs theory to the conflict resolution process.

This chapter will examine how the various processes used in the "democratic" governance of politics may satisfy instrumental human needs and what implications this has for the field of conflict resolution. In the next section I will explore the process of satisfier formation. The subsequent two sections view instrumental needs satisfaction from the view of the powerful and powerless. Two principles are offered to guide the development of the processes of governance, and some ramifications for the field of conflict resolution are then explored.

INSTRUMENTAL HUMAN NEEDS AND THE NATURE OF THEIR SATISFIERS

If we were focusing on substantive needs, it would be relatively easy to establish that if all people sought to satisfy their need for adequate nourishment as Americans do there would not be enough food to go around. Americans, as the highest *per capita* red meat consumers in the world, eat food at higher levels in the food chain where the amount of output in calories and usable protein is less efficient than at points lower in the food chain. Indeed, it might be argued that Americans eat more than their share of the world's food supply and, in fact, seek to satisfy their need for nourishment at an unjustly high level. Needs theory correctly identifies the need for physical sustenance, but fails to suggest how scarce satisfiers should be allocated among competing parties.

Within the realm of instrumental needs, there are satisfiers that are scarce as well: for example, power, status, and authority are often the satisfiers in systems of governance. Is there any scenario under which power and status can be distributed disproportionately among groups where the result is perceived as equal satisfaction of their instrumental needs?

Richard Rubenstein, an observer of revolutionary and other "out" groups, has analyzed the goals of these groups and the various responses of the "in" groups or governors.[15] In US history, he states, many groups have sought not true independence, but quasi-independence. Quasi-independence he defines as "the maximum degree of local autonomy consistent with membership in a legally unified nation."[16] Examples of situations that support this characterization include the goals of white Southerners prior to the Civil War and the goals of blacks in the civil rights movement a century later. In each movement, however, there were radicals who demanded secession from the larger government as the *only* method of self-determination. The radicals could not envision a society where they could freely pursue the satisfaction of their needs if their polity included a former oppressor class. Is the search for quasi-independence a search for false satisfiers? Have blacks in America, for example, truly satisfied their basic human needs? If blacks in South Africa completely managed their black townships, would their human needs be satisfied in this quasi-independent state?

Before we can understand the notion of false satisfiers, it is important to look at how satisfiers are formed.

How Are Satisfiers Formed?

Galtung states clearly that "human beings develop their need consciousness in a social context and that most of them have their needs satisfied in a social context."[17] Renshon hypothesizes that an individual develops a need for personal control through socialization that begins at birth.[18]

The human child, he states, comes into the world totally unprepared to take care of itself. The child comes into the world with hunger and thirst needs, but with no knowledge of how to satisfy them. Eventually these needs cause physiological discomfort but the child has no way of expressing those needs. The child starts crying. The mother at some point interprets those cries and feeds the baby. After repeating this routine many times a day, the child starts to learn that crying is linked to the appearance of food. It is the child's first experience in being the initiator of action that allows the child to successfully meet biological needs.

When the child is born, the child does not recognize the connection between his or her crying and the arrival of food. The child is experiencing two unpleasant experiences – the discomfort of unmet needs and the anxiety or fear that these needs might not be met in the future. Renshon posits that out of these twin discomforts, the need for personal control is born.[19]

Renshon carried this hypothesis further by surveying over 300 students to ascertain if their sense of personal control originated in the family situation. By a wide margin, the most important single influence was the extent to which the parents themselves had achieved a sense of personal control.[20]

Christian Bay links Renshon's findings with Melvin Kohn's in a study of the relationship between social class child-raising in Italy and the United States. Kohn found that lower class parents make clear to their children that they will have little control over the circumstances affecting their life. Parents of a higher class or socio-economic status tend to make their children expect a good measure of personal control over their lives.[21]

Bay further reports on a study conducted by Herbert Kelman and Lee Lawrence of American reactions to the trial of Lt William Calley, convicted in 1971 for the My Lai massacre. In a large national sample they discovered that hawks and doves were fairly evenly split in their reaction to Calley's conviction. The only factors found significantly related to these reactions were the subjects' level of education and socio-economic status. Those who considered themselves pawns in the social order, empathized with Calley as the perceived "fall guy" or scapegoat. Respondents of higher socio-economic status (and presumably those who achieved greater control in their lives) apparently felt Calley could have and should have refused to conduct the massacre.[22]

Galtung,[23] in much the same way that Bay suggests that social class affects satisfier formation, asserts that Western and non-Western societies have significantly different world views which alter the process of satisfier formation (see his contribution to this collection, Chapter 15).

Galtung stresses how significantly non-Western cultures differ from this cosmology and the effect of this difference on the formation of satisfiers.

Davies takes a third approach to this question. He believes, in keeping with the original hierarchy of needs hypothesized by Abraham Maslow, that individuals do not become acutely aware of their self-actualization needs until their physical needs are met. Implicit in this analysis is a belief that satisfiers also are hierarchically ordered. Using

United Nations statistics from 1957, he points out that countries with inadequate diets also have low levels of political activity on a national level. Citizens of countries with adequate diets have much higher levels of national political activity. He believes that a national consciousness forms only when physiological needs are met and persons start looking beyond their immediate community.[24]

The innovative power theorist, Steven Lukes, takes a fourth approach. He suggests that in systems where severe power disparities exist, the powerful may exercise power over the powerless "by getting him to do what he does not want to do, but *he also exercises power over him by influencing, shaping, or determining his very wants.*"[25] Lukes characterizes this as the third dimension of power. If one of the manifestations of power is the use of the system to manage expectations, needs theorists might need to determine how to satisfy the needs of those who are unable to express those desires themselves. This danger – that needs can be satisfied and conflict suppressed by the (ab)use of power – troubles Lukes. He details this fear by stating:

> is it not the supreme and most insidious exercise of power to prevent people, to whatever degree, from having grievances by shaping their perceptions, cognitions, and preferences in such a way that they accept their role in the existing order of things, either because they see it as natural and unchangeable, or because they value it as divinely ordained and beneficial? To assume the absence of grievance equals genuine consensus is simply to rule out the possibility of false or manipulated consensus by definitional fiat.[26]

Without suggesting that any of these analyses is perfect, it seems clear to conclude that (a) one's consciousness of one's needs, (b) one's ability to satisfy one's needs, and (c) what one seeks in satisfying one's needs will vary from person to person and from group to group; perhaps most importantly (d) one's sources of power will determine how ambitiously one will set the desired level of satisfier. Class, culture, and contextual power issues, among other factors, are likely to have substantial impact on satisfier formation.

Do Desired Satisfiers Change Over Time?

Of all the needs theorists, Davies remains the most wedded to the Maslovian hierarchy of needs and therefore believes that a person must move sequentially through the four stages of needs – physical, social–affectional, self-esteem or dignity, self-actualization.[27] Davies asserts that an individual can choose to fast, for example, in seeking self-actualization, but an individual who has never satisfied his/her physical needs will seek to satisfy those first before seeking to satisfy higher level needs.[28]

While none of the extant needs theorists speculate in this area, I believe the so-called information revolution and western cultural imperialism have over time had a global impact on the formation of satisfiers to instrumental and substantive needs. Even in the countries where the most restrictive controls possible are placed on the spread of information, violations regularly occur. Whether it be Solidarnosc in Poland, the United Democratic Front in South Africa, the *refuseniks* in the Soviet Union, Eritreans in Ethiopia, the Chinese students in Tiananmen Square or the Palestinian Liberation Organization in the Middle East, each has direct ties to Western social change movements and sources of information. This link, I think, only heightens the expectations of what lower class or "out"-groups believe is possible.

The satisfiers to instrumental needs in Western culture leads the world toward Western-style representative democracies while the satisfiers to substantive needs lead to increased materialism that surpasses the ability of the earth to meet the demand. The global links between all types of change movements tend to bring more similarity to these movements than the culture or class difference between groups might have us infer. The difficulty the linkage creates, albeit one that can be overcome, is that the positions of social change groups around the world tend to sound very Western and similar when the appropriate satisfying responses may not be Western, but culture and situation specific.

Indeed, if the focus of a generic conflict resolution theory is that individuals need to express their needs and find how they can be satisfied, then we have encountered some potentially fatal obstacles. First, some groups may pursue satisfiers that will expressly prevent other groups from satisfying their needs. Second, some groups may pursue false satisfiers – changes in the political, social, or economic order that do not truly satisfy the need. Third, and perhaps most damaging, the desire for some satisfiers may never be expressed because the powerful have manipulated the powerless into accepting the status quo.

Satisfiers may vary from group to group and from time to time, but are there clear criteria used to judge satisfaction? In particular, now that we have explored the changing nature of satisfiers to instrumental needs, can we determine how satisfiers manifest themselves in the processes of governance?

HOW ARE PROCESSES OF GOVERNANCE ANALYZED FROM A NEEDS PERSPECTIVE?

First, the question of whether the systems of governance are a class of satisfiers to basic human needs needs to be examined. Renshon posits in his "Needs Theory of Political Efficacy and Political Participation," in which personal control is the dominant need, that an individual seeks "sufficient personal control over political processes to satisfy the need for control in relevant life areas." He then suggests that it is only when political systems are perceived to be salient (i.e., "having an impact on the individual's social or physical life-space"), that the individual will seek to satisfy his/her needs through the political system.[29] The NIMBY[30] phenomenon clearly reflects this analysis.

In the first sentence of *Control: The Basis of Social Order*, Sites states:

> We intend to show that the most fundamental component in individual and social life is that of control; that the individual, either on his own or in coalition with others, attempts to control the situational context by controlling the behavior of others as well as his own, thus making control the most important dynamic of social as well as individual life.[31]

If not personal control, certainly recognition and identity needs are affected by the role of government. Governments have declared that:

- a slave is 3/5 of a person;
- a person of color cannot vote;
- a Jewish person must be confined to a concentration camp;
- a Japanese–American person must be confined to a concentration camp; and
- a Palestinian has no right to a homeland.

If the processes of governance are occasionally salient and their nature determines whether individuals and groups perceive their needs are being met, how can they be evaluated from a human needs perspective? Processes of governance are judged on both process terms – how the decision was made – and outcome terms – what the decision was. This creates a supra-significant role for political process because the process helps determine whether instrumental needs are being met while the outcome often establishes whether substantive needs are being met.

How is the *Process* of Governance Evaluated From a Needs Perspective?

First, it may be helpful to review the list of instrumental needs created by needs theorists. Instrumental needs cited included control, identity, recognition, power, and security. These were summarized as the need (a) to be treated as well as others are treated no matter how they are linked to a particular identity group, (b) to have some level of surety in forecasting the result of interactions with others, and (c) to be safe or protected from others as each pursues his/her individual goals.

These needs are often expressed as the right to self-determination. Article 21 of the 1948 Universal Declaration of the UN attempts to define how this need should be satisfied:

1. Everyone has the right to take part in the government of his country, directly or through freely chosen representatives.
2. Everyone has the right of equal access to public service in his country.
3. The will of the people shall be the basis of the authority of the government; this will shall be expressed in periodic and genuine elections which shall be by universal and equal suffrage and shall be held by secret vote or by equivalent free voting procedures.[32]

Lung-chu Chen, a scholar of movements for self-determination, suggests that it is not only freedom to participate in political processes but "in different value processes (e.g., power, wealth, wellbeing, respect, enlightenment) which is fundamentally at stake." He adds, "the sharing of power is of paramount importance."[33]

Now that several potential criteria have been discussed, it may be helpful to explore contrasting case studies. The social change movement in South Africa is one of the clearest current examples where the whole system of governance is being challenged. Simply put, the change forces in South Africa are seeking to institute the one-man, one-vote principle into all levels of governance. Blacks and other people of color believe their identity and recognition is challenged while the system of apartheid denies their participation in the normal affairs of government because of their race and that the maintenance of apartheid by the oppressive regime threatens the security of all who oppose the system. Blacks earn less, live shorter lives, and are prohibited from participation in any systems of governance except for the cooptive township governments or the relatively powerless so-called "colored" and "Indian" legislatures.

Women in the United States, on the other hand, received the right to vote in 1917, can own property, and have sensitized Americans to the severe problem of violence against women. Yet women's rights activists continue to fight for changes in the political culture and to remove perceived impediments to full participation in the political process. Women hold only two of 100 US Senate seats and 25 of 435 seats in the House of Representatives. Many women still feel alienated from the political process because the informal network of fundraisers, party organizations, and consultants usually make it more difficult for a woman than for a man to run for office.

While these examples are not representative of the vast range of efforts by individuals to change the systems of governance, examination of these two case studies suggests that each group is seeking some greater level of personal control on issues important to them. What is illustrative is that in both situations it appears the change forces believe they will not achieve their need for sufficient personal control because the opportunity for significant personal participation in the decision making process is being denied.

Of further significance is the women's movement in the United States. On the face of it, the US system meets the minimum needs criteria set forth. Women have achieved the right to vote and run for any political office in the country. What seems to be important to the women is that, despite changes in the laws and the opening of the political system, the resulting participation by women in governmental bodies is significantly less than if their representation were determined by the proportion of women in the population. The ultimate test of a new or modified process, "does it work?" has been employed here, and many women have determined that the system does not work for them.

Renshon suggests that another method for determining if the need for personal control in systems of governance exists is whether the system allows the development of two important abilities: the political skills necessary to influence the process, and the ability to engage in successful reality testing. The necessity for political skills is obvious. Reality testing is defined as the ability to formulate a problem-based analysis of one's needs and of the current status of the political system.[34]

The development of political skills, as Renshon suggests, is essential to being able to affect decision making in a forum in a way that advances one's own needs. Evans and Boyte coined the term "free spaces" to describe "settings between private lives and large-scale institutions where ordinary citizens can act with dignity, independence, and vision . . . where people gain new skills, a new sense of possibility, and a broadened understanding of whom 'the people' include."[35]

Based on the analyses of Freud and McClelland, Renshon posits that "needs are not directly translated into human motives, but rather acquire motive status through social learning."[36] Davies goes further and argues that the social and political development of individuals is necessary for politics and political systems to mature.[37] Mature political systems, he suggests, are those that better meet the human needs of all individuals.

Pateman, in her analysis of participatory democracy theorists suggest that the "'social training' for democracy . . . takes place through the process of participation itself."[38] In addition, she suggests that "participation has an integrative effect and that it aids the acceptance of collective decisions." The participatory model, in her eyes, is "one where maximum input (participation) is required and where output includes not just policies (decisions) but also the development of the social and political capacities of each individual."[39]

Instrumental human needs, then, cannot be satisfied without the potential for participation in the process of governance on issues that are perceived to impinge upon a person's individual, social or physical life-space. If this potential is present, individuals believe that the threshold or personal control they need is met.

If individuals are motivated to participate in the processes of governance, the processes must allow room for persons to develop their social and political capacities so that they can participate in an efficacious manner. Through participation, or the belief that fair participation has occurred, individual instrumental needs will have been satisfied. Processes which satisfy instrumental needs may still reflect a strong majoritarian or totalitarian influence, and may produce outcomes that frustrate the search to satisfy substantive needs of certain groups and prompt further action by those groups.

How are the Outcomes of the Processes of Governance Evaluated From a Needs Perspective?

A full discussion of this issue is beyond the scope of this chapter but I would suggest that one often overlooked area requires consideration. Processes of governance are often used to initiate thousands of additional processes for decision making, for receiving citizen input, and for adjudication. The role a federal government has in creating and implementing state and local processes, judicial and administrative processes and international processes is enormous. One of the types of outcomes of systems of governance is thus the creation of systems for citizen participation.

IF THE POWERFUL GET WHAT THEY NEED, ARE THE POWERLESS PREVENTED FROM SATISFYING THEIR NEEDS?

The issues of who has power, how power is used, and the potential effects of significant disparities in power between groups pervades – as it should – the discussions of needs theorists. In the discussion of how satisfiers are formed, it is clear that those of Western culture and upper class background will surely have their physical needs met, wield significant power, and will probably develop desires that can be fulfilled only through oppression and exploitation. This section explores the issue of satisfiers in the processes of governance from the point of view of the powerful. The following section considers the problem from the perspective of the powerless.

Since different societies improve and change at different speeds and start at dramatically different places, powerful groups most advanced in meeting their human needs will develop satisfiers that are not mitigated by equally developed satisfiers of other less powerful groups. In the worst case, more advanced and powerful societies may establish their domain over other societies and nations in order to achieve economic, military, and ego goals. Only when less powerful groups attain power and expand their view of how their needs should be satisfied will powerful groups and societies be challenged to satisfy their needs in ways that do not oppress, coerce, or cause structural violence to less powerful groups.

If we assume that in our current world order power disparities do exist, can needs theory be used to identify satisfiers that are legitimate (i.e., those that meet basic human needs) and those that are just (i.e., where attaining the satisfier will not prevent other societies from meeting that level of satisfaction)? I believe the answer is a definitive NO.

Secondly, many satisfiers are often in scarce supply. Positions of status within a polity, decision making positions in a bureaucracy, and sources of power are all items that may be scarce when there are competing claims. Does needs theory have the capacity to determine how these scarce resources should be allocated in these situations? Once again, the answer is NO. The allocation of these scarce resources should be made by the parties who are making the competing claims. In this way, there is at least a chance that the process of making a decision on these difficult issues can meet the parties' instrumental needs. Even if broad identity and recognition needs have been met by all parties in a particular situation, the consistent adjustment and readjustment to the political system necessary to reflect the will of the people will make the reallocation of these scarce satisfiers a regular task.

Even if there were a global consensus to act with force and vigor to meet the basic human needs of every person, it would not be possible to create a plausible scenario without invoking theories of justice, culture, and governance that focus on satisfier allocation and using decision making mechanisms that allow for the satisfaction of instrumental needs.

ARE YOU GETTING WHAT YOU NEED, OR JUST WHAT SOMEONE THINKS YOU NEED?

The process of satisfier development would suggest that unempowered persons and groups tend to be socialized to seek less than the powerful. As groups move toward more ambitious satisfiers of their human needs, they may seek satisfiers or be offered satisfiers that may be of questionable value. Recall the discussion of quasi-independence above. Can needs theory determine if a satisfier will truly meet the need? In other words, can needs theory identify false satisfiers or Trojan horses?

Again, I believe the answer is NO. The Model Cities program in the United States that commenced under the Great Society program of President Lyndon Johnson called for the maximum feasible participation of residents in the affected area. Unprecedented openness in the White House allowed a range of civil rights groups, neighborhood interests groups and others to help develop the legislation. Michael Harrington, author of *The Other America*[40] and a socialist also had a major hand in shaping the legislation. The legislation provided for greater recognition of long-unempowered groups, dramatically increased the likelihood of personal control, and through service programs attempted to respond to substantive needs as well. Did it work? With minor exceptions, the program was a failure. The reasons for failure are not well understood, but the reasons adduced usually include:

- Leadership in the neighborhoods was coopted when they agreed to serve in leadership capacities with the Model Cities program.
- Model Cities did not address systematic discrimination by corporate America, and large-scale private investment never occurred.
- The program did not have enough money.
- The type of development program was much better suited to persons who were less desperate.
- The program implementation was subverted in city halls across America.

The detailed specification of these reasons is not important here. What is important is to note that the body of knowledge and theory necessary to build a similar program is not encapsulated in needs theory. Rather, at best, by drawing upon the latest and best practice from a range of fields parties can develop programs that both meet their needs and actually work and, at worst, only through the process of social experimentation guided by past mistakes will we be able to respond to these types of tasks.

In addition to the need to draw upon a wide range of theories and bases of knowledge, it is important to remember that many persons are often transfixed by the *symbols* of governance and are not familiar with the actual workings of governance. Edelman, in his groundbreaking book *The Symbolic Uses of Politics*, states that "mass publics respond to conspicuous political symbols: not to 'facts,' and not to moral codes embedded in the character or soul, but to the gestures and speeches that make up the drama of the state."[41]

The manipulation of symbols and the general lack of information on governance in the general public creates "false" satisfiers that can mislead the public. Many are well-intentioned if inappropriate, and needs theory cannot always spot them.

HOW ARE SATISFIERS REFLECTED IN THE POLITICAL SYSTEM?

In an earlier draft of this chapter, I attempted to create a typology of decision making processes and assess their worth from the perspective of needs theory. In the redrafting process, I came to realize the richness of needs theory despite the limitations that I believe accompany it. This richness makes it all but impossible to conduct this type of speculation without the specificity of context, culture, polity, size of geographic area, and other factors that would guide the application of needs theory.

Instead of that exercise, which were it feasible could possibly be illuminating, I propose to draw out several principles from the preceeding discussion. I suggest the principles with the caveat that they must be developed and adapted by those involved in a polity and should not be externally enforced.

> *Principle 1* Processes of governance should, to the maximum extent possible, provide for interaction between disparate groups to allow (a) each group to learn about the needs and proposed satisfiers of the other group, (b) the development of joint understanding of the problem(s), and (c) the maximum opportunity for the development of consensual approaches.
>
> *Principle 2* In order for these processes to work at the higher system levels (federal, international) there should be maximum opportunity through the neighborhood, the workplace, and other smaller units for persons to develop the skills necessary to be effective in these forums. Without these skills, it is unlikely that any group or individual will feel that their needs have been met.

To go beyond these basic principles would I believe move them toward a more Westernized, linear mode of decision making. In a specific situation, needs theory could be applied more systematically to ensure that a particular process was as responsive as possible to the needs of the participants.

RAMIFICATIONS FOR THE FIELD OF CONFLICT RESOLUTION

Beyond the principles stated above I believe the most urgent need for the field of conflict resolution posed by the preceding discussion is the need for a theory of representation. Since most conflict resolution processes are *ad hoc*, representation is often determined by the practitioner in consultation with the parties.

How should a practitioner determine how the various cultures and subcultures, the diverse perspectives on the issue, the different functional and role orientations toward the issue, and the links to the formal structures of governance be represented? In other words, which advocates for which satisfiers should be brought to the table? Should the criteria be power or skill at problem-solving or racially-, class-, or geographically-based systems of representation, or some combination of the above?

And, perhaps more importantly, how should the conflict resolution process be linked to the members of a policy not at the table? In order for their instrumental needs to be met, they may need acute awareness of the nature of the conflict resolution process and have a vehicle for participation other than the observer role.

It was helpful for me, as a practitioner, to realize that conflict resolution processes provide for the interaction set forth in Principle 1 through the face-to-face interaction that occurs at the negotiation table. The growth of the field of conflict resolution is along the lines suggested in Principle 2. The opportunity to participate in face-to-face systems of conflict resolution to resolve interpersonal disputes may help people develop the skills necessary for effective participation at higher system levels.

Needs theory, I believe, can make great contributions toward helping practitioners understand the motivations of the parties. Needs theory can also help practitioners understand the parameters for constructing a process that meets instrumental human needs. Practitioners will need to move beyond needs theory in order to gain a full appreciation for the diverse and culturally sensitive potential satisfiers present in a given situation. Conflict resolution should be about the business of helping parties achieve true satisfaction of their needs. In order to achieve that goal, similar exploration of other fundamental social theories and their relevance for conflict resolution should be conducted to lead us to the point where a truly comprehensive explanatory and predictive conflict resolution theory can be developed.

NOTES AND REFERENCES

1. See John W. Burton and Dennis J. D. Sandole, "Generic Theory: The Basis of Conflict Resolution," *Negotiation Journal*, 2 (4) (October 1986): 333:44; Lawrence Susskind and Larry Weinstein, "Toward a Theory of Environmental Dispute Resolution" (Cambridge, MA: Harvard Program on Negotiation, 1979).

2. See Burton and Sandole, "Generic Theory"; Burton and Sandole, "Expanding the Debate on Generic Theory of Conflict Resolution: A Response to a Critique," *Negotiation Journal* 3 (1) (January 1987): 97–100.

3. Burton and Sandole, "Generic Theory": 340–1.

4. Paul Sites, *Control: The Basis of Social Order* (New York: Dunellen Publishing, 1973): 31–52.

5. For the purpose of this article Davies, Sites, Burton, Galtung, Renshon and Park are included.

6. James C. Davies, "Human Needs and the Stages of Political Development," in J. Roland Pennock and John W. Chapman (eds), *Human Nature in Politics* (New York: New York University Press, 1977): 168; Johan Galtung, "The Basic Needs Approach," in Katrin Lederer (ed.) with Johan Galtung and David Antal, *Human Needs: A Contribution to the Current Debate* (Cambridge, MA: Oelgeschlager, Gunn and Hain, 1980): 101. Galtung differentiates between "actor–dependent" and "structure–dependent" needs. There is a large overlap between instrumental and actor–dependent needs.

7. Sites, *Control*: 1; Stanley Allen Renshon, *Psychological Needs and Political Behavior: A Theory of Personality and Political Efficacy* (New York: Free Press, 1974): 43–4; and Han S. Park, *Human Needs and Political Development: A Dissent to Utopian Solutions* (Cambridge, MA: Schenkman Publishing, 1984): 61.

8. John W. Burton, *Deviance, Terrorism, and War: The Process of Solving Unsolved Social and Political Problems* (New York: St. Martin's Press, 1979): 165; Galtung, "The Basic Needs Approach": 59.

9. Galtung, "The Basic Needs Approach": 72; Davies, "Human Needs": 170.

10. Davies, "Human Needs": 170.

11. Burton, *Deviance, Terrorism*: 72; Galtung, "The Basic Needs Approach": 59; Davies, "Human Needs": 170.

12. Jordan J. Paust, "Self-Determination: A Definitional Focus," in Yonah Alexander and Robert A. Friedlander (eds), *Self Determination: National Regional and Global Dimensions* (Boulder, CO.: Westview Press, 1980): 4.

13. The Human Needs and Conflict Resolution Conference was sponsored by the Center for Conflict Analysis and Resolution of George Mason University and held on 6–9 July at Airlie in Warrenton, Virginia. Hereinafter it will be referred to as the Human Needs Conference.

14. Human Needs Conference conversation.

15. Richard Rubenstein, *Rebels in Eden: Mass Political Violence in the United States* (Boston: Little, Brown & Co., 1970).

16. Rubenstein, *Rebels in Eden*: 71.
17. Galtung, "The Basic Needs Approach": 60.
18. Renshon, *Psychological Needs and Political Behavior*: 59–74.
19. Renshon, *Psychological Needs and Political Behavior*: 60.
20. Renshon, *Psychological Needs and Political Behavior*: 123–152.
21. As reported in Christian Bay, "Human Needs and Political Education," in Ross Fitzgerald (ed.), *Human Needs and Politics* (Rushcutters Bay, N.S.W., Australia: Pergamon Press, 1977): 17.
22. Bay, "Human Needs": 18.
23. Galtung, "The Basic Needs Approach": 72.
24. James C. Davies, *Human Nature in Politics: The Dynamics of Political Behavior* (New York: John Wiley, 1963): 26–30.
25. Steven Lukes, *Power: A Radical View* (London: Macmillan, 1974): 23.
26. Lukes, *Power*: 24.
27. Galtung, "The Basic Needs Approach": 67–71 objects to the notion of a hierarchy of needs, for he believes it gives permission to First World governments to respond only to the physiological needs of people residing in the Third World, and to ignore their needs for identity, recognition, and security.
28. James C. Davies, "The Development of Individuals and the Development of Politics," in Ross Fitzgerald (ed.), *Human Needs and Politics* (Rushcutters Bay, N.S.W., Australia: Pergamon Press, 1977): 76.
29. Renshon, *Psychological Needs and Political Behavior*: 75.
30. NIMBY is the acronym given to traditionally complacent citizens who rise up in anger at the prospect of an unwanted change in their communities and say "*not in my backyard!*"
31. Sites, *Control*: 1.
32. Paust, "Self-Determination": 8–9.
33. Lung-chu Chen, "Self-Determination as a Human Right," in M. Reisman and B. Weston (eds), *Towards World Order and Human Dignity* (New York: Free Press, 1976): p. 244.
34. Renshon, *Psychological Needs and Political Behavior*: 43–4.
35. Sara M. Evans and Harry C. Boyte, *Free Spaces: The Sources of Democratic Change in America* (New York: Harper & Row, 1986): 17, 21.
36. Stanley Allen Renshon, "Human Needs and Political Analysis: An Examination of a Framework," in Ross Fitzgerald (ed.), *Human Needs and Politics* (Rushcutters Bay, N.S.W., Australia: Pergamon Press, 1977): 60.
37. See Davies, "Human Needs;" and Davies, "The Development of Individuals and the Development of Politics" for a more complete exposition.
38. Carole Pateman, *Participation and Democratic Theory* (London: Cambridge University Press, 1970): 42.
39. Pateman, *Participation*: 43.
40. Michael Harrington, *The Other America: Poverty in the United States* (Baltimore: Penguin Books, 1963).
41. Murray Edelman, *The Symbolic Uses of Politics* (Urbana: University of Illinois Press, 1967): 172.

14 Applying a Human Needs Perspective to the Practice of Conflict Resolution: The Israeli–Palestinian Case[1]

Herbert C. Kelman

How can a human needs perspective inform the *practice* of conflict resolution? This chapter attempts to answer this question on the basis of my own experience with "interactive problem-solving," an approach to the resolution of international conflicts that finds its fullest expression in the problem-solving workshop.[2] This approach derives from the work of John Burton[3] and follows the general principles that he has laid out. My own work has concentrated heavily (though not exclusively) on the Israeli–Palestinian conflict and I will draw most of my illustrations from that arena.

THE CONCEPT OF HUMAN NEEDS

My use of the concept of human needs is very broad and is not anchored in any particular needs theory. For my purposes, I find it best not to circumscribe the concept with too many specific assumptions. Thus, I do not assume that needs are necessarily organized in hierarchies, such that lower-ranked needs must be satisfied before higher-ranked needs can assert themselves. I do not assume that all needs will somehow be satisfied – in deviant fashion, if legitimate avenues for need satisfaction are closed off – although I view the large-scale frustration of basic human needs as a threat to peace and social order. I do not assume that the lists of human needs identified by various needs theories are necessarily universal, although I do believe that certain basic needs are widely shared across cultures and societies.

My view of human needs in relation to social order is, very simply, that the satisfaction of basic needs is central to the functioning of social and political institutions. Normatively, the satisfaction of human needs is the ultimate criterion by which the quality of institutions and their policies must be evaluated. Empirically, the degree to which institutions satisfy basic needs is an important determinant of their perceived legitimacy and thus, at least in the long run, of their stability and effectiveness.

When applied to international conflict and conflict resolution, a needs perspective focuses our attention on a set of collective psychological needs, including needs for identity, security, recognition, participation, dignity, and justice. Failure to fulfill these needs or threats to them contribute significantly to the causes of conflict, and perhaps even more so the escalation and perpetuation of conflicts. The profound resistance to change – despite changing realities and interests – that characterizes intense, protracted conflicts is typically rooted in the impact of such needs and associated fears on the perceptions and beliefs of the parties. Thus, in the Israeli–Palestinian conflict, the major obstacle to change is each side's perception that the very existence of the other as a national entity constitutes a fundamental threat to its own identity and security.[4] In order to break through such resistances in change, conflict resolution efforts must address the parties' needs and fears.

A needs perspective contributes not only to overcoming the barriers to a negotiated solution, but also to improving the quality of the solution achieved. Solutions that address the basic needs of both parties are likely to be more satisfactory and more durable. Furthermore, such solutions are likely to be more just and morally superior if we take the satisfaction of human needs – articulated through people's core identity groups – as the ultimate criterion for evaluating policies and practices within the international system.

INTERACTIVE PROBLEM-SOLVING

Before describing more specifically how a human needs perspective enters into my particular practice of conflict resolution, I must summarize the main features of interactive problem-solving and of the problem-solving workshops in which this approach is utilized.

Interactive problem-solving is an unofficial third-party approach to the resolution of international conflict. The third party typically consists of a panel of social scientists with expertise in group process and international conflict and at least some familiarity with the conflict region. The role of the third party in our model differs from that of the traditional mediator; it can be best described as a facilitative role. We do not propose (and certaintly we do not impose) solutions. Rather, we try to encourage a process whereby solutions will emerge out of the interaction between the parties themselves. The task of the third party is to provide the setting, create the atmosphere establish the norms, and offer occasional interventions that make it possible for such a process to evolve.

In the work of my colleagues and myself, our academic base serves as the major venue of our activities and source of our authority and credibility. The academic context has several advantages for our enterprise. It allows the parties to interact with each other in a relatively non-committal way, since the setting is not only unofficial, but also known as one in which people engage in free exchange of views, in playful consideration of new ideas, and in "purely academic" discussions. Thus, an academic setting is a good place to set into motion a process of successive approximations, in which parties that do not trust each other begin to communicate in a non-committal framework, but gradually move to increasing levels of commitment as their level of working trust increases.[5] Another advantage of the academic context is that it allows us to call upon an alternative set of norms to counteract the norms that typically govern interactions between conflicting parties. Academic norms favor open discussion, attentive listening to opposing views, and an analytical approach, in contrast to the polemical, accusatory, and legalistic approach that conflict norms tend to promote.

The setting, norms, ground rules, agenda, procedures, and third-party interventions in problem-solving workshops are all designed to facilitate a kind of interaction that differs from the way parties in conflict usually interact – if they interact at all. Within the workshop setting, participants are encouraged to talk to each other, rather than to their constituencies or to third parties, and to listen to each other – not in order to discover the weaknesses in the other's argument, but in order to penetrate the other's perspective. Workshop discussion are analytical in the sense that participants try to gain a better understanding of the other's – and indeed of their own concerns, needs, fears, priorities, and constraints, and of the way in which the divergent perspectives of the parties help to feed and escalate their conflict. Analytical discussions proceed on the basis of a "no fault" principle. While there is no presumption that both sides are equally at fault, the discussions are not oriented toward assigning blame, but toward exploring the causes of the conflict and the obstacles to its resolution. This analytical approach is designed to lead to a problem-solving mode of interaction, based on the proposition that the conflict represents a joint problem for the two parties that require joint efforts at solution.

Workshops have a dual purpose, which can be described as educational and political. They are designed to produce both *changes* in attitudes, perceptions, and ideas for resolving the conflict among the individual participants in the workshop, and *transfer* of these changes to the political arena – i.e., to the political debate and the decision making process within each community. The political purpose is an integral part of the workshop approach, whatever the level of the participants involved. Workshops provide opportunities for the parties to interact, to become acquainted with each other, and to humanize their mutual images, not as ends in themselves, but as means to producing new learnings that can then be fed into the political process.

Because of their dual purpose, problem-solving workshops are marked by a dialectical character.[6] Some of the conditions favorable to change in the workshop setting may be antagonistic to the transfer of changes to the political arena, and vice versa. There is often a need, therefore, to find the proper balance between contradictory requirements if a workshop is to be effective in fulfilling both its educational and its political purpose. The selection of participants provides a good example of a central workshop feature for which the dialectics of the process have important implications. The closer the participants are to the centers of power in their own communities, the greater the likelihood that what they learn in the course of their workshop experience will be fed directly into the decision making process. By the same token, however, the closer participants are to the centers of power, the more constrained they are likely to feel, and the greater their difficulty in entering into communication that is open, non-committal, exploratory, and analytical. Thus, on the whole, as participants move closer to the level of top decision makers, they become less likely to show change as a result of their workshop experience, but whatever changes do occur are more likely to be transferred to the policy process. These contradictory effects have to be taken into account in selecting participants for a given occasion, or in defining the goals and agenda for a workshop with a given set of participants. In general, the best way to balance the requirements for change and for transfer is to select participants who are politically influential but not directly involved in the execution of foreign policy. The workshops and related encounters that I have organized over the years have included participants at three different levels of relationship to the decision making process: *political actors*, such as parliamentarians, party activists, or advisers to political leaders; *political influentials*, such as senior academics (who are leading analysts of the conflict in their own communities and occasional advisers to decision makers), community leaders, writers, or editors; and *pre-influentials*, such as younger academics and professionals or advanced graduate students, who are slated to move into influential positions in their respective fields. The lines between these three categories are not very precise; moreover, many participants who may have been "pre-influentials" at the time of their workshop have since become influential, and some of our "influentials" have since become political actors. Whatever the level of the participants, a central criterion for selection is that they be politically involved – at least as active participants in the political debate and perhaps in political movements. From our point of view, even this degree of involvement is of direct political relevance since it contributes to the shaping of the political environment for any peace effort. Another criterion for selection is that participants be part of the mainstream of their community and that they enjoy credibility within broad segments of that community. We look for participants who are as close as possible to the center of the political spectrum, while at the same time being interested in negotiations and open to the workshop process. As a result, workshop participants so far have tended to be on the doveish ("moderate" or pro-negotiation) side of the center.

Although workshops proceed on the principle that useful ideas for conflict resolution must emerge out of the interaction between the parties themselves, the third party plays an essential role (at certain stages of a conflict) in making that interaction possible and fruitful. The third party provides the context in which representatives of parties engaged in an intense conflict are able to come together. It selects, briefs, and convenes the participants. It serves as a repository of trust for both parties, enabling them to proceed with the assurance that their interests will be protected even though – by definition – they cannot trust each other. It establishes and enforces the norms and ground rules that facilitate analytic discussion and a problem-solving orientation. It proposes a broad agenda that encourages the parties to move from exploration of each other's concerns and constraints to the generation of ideas for win/win solutions and for implementing such solutions. It tries to keep the discussion moving in constructive directions. And, finally, it makes occasional substantive interventions in the form of observations about the content of what has been said, observations (at the intergroup level) about the ongoing process, and theoretical inputs.

Problem-solving workshops may vary in their substantive focus, depending on the particular point in a conflict relationship and a larger conflict resolution effort at which they are introduced. They are not intended to substitute for official negotiations, but to help prepare the way for negotiations, to supplement them, and to feed into them. Our work on the Israeli–Palestinian conflict is primarily a contribution to the pre-negotiation process: Workshops in this context are designed to identify conditions required for negotiation and to help create a political environment conducive to movement toward the negotiating table. Workshops may also be useful at a point at which negotiations are already in progress: For example, they may provide a non-committal forum to explore ways of breaking a stalemate that has been reached in the negotiations; or they may allow the parties to work out solutions to specific technical, political, or even emotional issues that require an analytical, problem-solving approach; these solutions can then be fed into the formal negotiating process. Finally, workshops may be useful in the post-negotiation phase, when they can help the parties explore patterns of coexistence and cooperative efforts and thus contribute to a transformation of their relationship.

Our own experience has pointed to some of the ways in which problem-solving workshops and related activities can contribute to a pre-negotiation process, helping the parties to overcome the fears and suspicions that inhibit negotiations and to create the conditions that enable them to enter into negotiations. Workshops can help produce a more differentiated image of the enemy and help the participants discover potential negotiating partners on the other side. They can contribute to the development of cadres of individuals who have acquired experience in communicating with the other side and the conviction that such communication can be fruitful. They enable the parties to penetrate each other's perspective. They contribute to creating and maintaining a sense of possibility – a belief among the relevant parties that a peaceful solution is attainable and that negotiations toward such a solution are feasible. They contribute to the development of a deescalatory language, based on sensitivity to words that frighten and words that reassure the other party. They help in the identification of mutually reassuring actions and symbolic gestures, often in the form of acknowledgements – of the other's humanity, national identity, ties to the land, history of victimization, sense of injustice, genuine fears, and conciliatory moves. They contribute to the development of shared visions of a desirable future, which help reduce the parties' fears of negotiations as a step into an unknown, dangerous realm. They may generate ideas about the shape of a positive-sum solution that meets the basic needs of both parties. They may also generate ideas about how to get from here to there – about a framework and set of principles for getting negotiations started. Ultimately, problem-solving workshops contribute to a process of transformation of the relationship between enemies.

THE ARTICULATION OF A HUMAN NEEDS PERSPECTIVE IN PROBLEM-SOLVING WORKSHOPS

The approach to conflict resolution that I have briefly described is significantly shaped by a human needs perspective. Indeed, it would be fair to describe the approach as an application of a human needs perspective to the practice of international conflict resolution. I propose that human needs enter into three aspects of the workshop approach that are themselves highly interrelated: the *definition* of the entire enterprise, the *structure* of workshops, and the workshops *process*. The enterprise is defined as an effort to find – through joint, creative problem solving – *solutions to the conflict that would satisfy the needs of both parties.* Workshops are structured so that the *focus of conflict analysis and resolution is on the parties whose needs are at the core of the conflict.* The process is specifically geared to *enabling the parties to identify and understand each other's needs and to take the two sets of needs simultaneously into account* as they work on the shape of an overall solution. I shall address each of these aspects of the approach in turn and draw out some of the implications of a needs analysis.

Definition of the Enterprise

A key element of the definition of the entire enterprise is our interest in contributing to the search for solutions that would satisfy the basic needs of both parties. The main task of workshops is to redefine or restructure the conflict so that it can move from a zero-sum to a positive-sum definition.

The Israeli–Palestinian conflict, like other intense conflicts, tends to be defined by the parties in zero-sum terms. Its origin is a conflict over territory, which is clearly zero-sum in nature, at least as long as the focus remains on the possession of territory: Any gain by one party represents a loss to the other. But the zero-sum definition of the conflict goes beyond the territorial issue. The conflict can be described as an existential conflict, perceived by the parties as zero-sum not only with respect to territory and other material interests, but also and primarily with respect to national identity and national existence. Both parties have tended to the view that only one can be a nation – that acknowledgement of the nationhood and the national rights of the other is tantamount to denial of their own national status.[7]

Paradoxically, focusing on the needs for identity and security and the existential fears associated with them may actually enhance the possibility of achieving conflict resolution. The territorial issue is indeed zero-sum in nature. An agreement at that level can be achieved only by a compromise – by some formula for sharing the territory that both parties claim, such as partition. But any suggestion of territorial compromise immediately arouses profound existential concerns among the parties, which have greatly inhibited movement toward negotiation in the Israeli–Palestinian conflict. Each party has been concerned that conceding the other's right to any part of the land would jeopardize its own claims and set into motion an inexorable process in which it loses everything. When we move from issues of territory to such issues as identity and security, however, it becomes at least possible to explore positive-sum solutions. As Burton has pointed out,[8] ontological needs – in contrast to material interests – are not inherently zero-sum in nature. Establishment of the other's identity or enhancement of the other's security does not diminish one's own identity or security. In fact – contrary to the zero-sum thinking engendered by the dynamics of conflict – the opposite is often true. Thus, at the level of ontological needs, integrative, positive-sum solutions become more readily attainable in intense, interethnic conflicts with existential overtones.

By focusing on such needs as identity and security, interactive problem-solving can help redefine the conflict in a way that makes it susceptible to a solution that satisfies the basic needs of both parties. Once the parties' existential concerns have been addressed and the parties have been reassured at that level, they can turn, as necessary, to serious distributive bargaining over issues of territory and resources. Thus, if Israelis can be reassured that Palestinian self-determination can be achieved without threatening Israeli security, and if Palestinians can be reassured that Israeli security concerns can be accommodated without denying political expression to Palestinian national identity, the two parties can move toward a historic compromise over the issues of territory and sovereignty.

An important qualification is in order here: I do not assume that a win/win solution is always achievable. It is quite possible that some conflicts may be entirely refractory to a mutually satisfactory solution, no matter how much effort and skill third parties may bring to bear on them. Any given conflict's susceptibility to a win/win solution certainly varies with time, depending on historical developments, on the constellation of interests, necessities, and opportunities at the moment, on the available alternatives, and on the regional and international environment. I do believe, however, that creative, mutually satisfactory solutions are more often available than conventional wisdom realizes. When parties probe beyond their stated positions and presumed interests into their underlying needs, they may find that these needs are in fact not incompatible (or no longer incompatible in the light of changing circumstances) and that an apparently intractable conflict can in fact be resolved. It is incumbent on third parties to encourage such probing, while recognizing that the search for a positive-sum solution does not inevitably meet with success.

Furthermore, I do not assume that all needs can be – or, indeed, ought to be – satisfied. When we speak of solutions that satisfy the needs of *both* parties, we are by definition excluding needs of one party that can be satisfied only at the expense of the other (or, to be more precise: needs so defined by a party that their satisfaction depends on negating the needs of the other). As a third party, I am not prepared to facilitate satisfaction of a party's need, for example, for domination or control over the other. While all perceived needs must be taken seriously by the third party, it is necessary to make a distinction between legitimate and illegitimate *satisfiers* of needs. When such needs as domination or control over the other emerge in the course of a workshop, it is important to explore their meaning to the party expressing them. The third party might encourage participants to push more deeply in order to see what lies behind these statements of needs. Such probing may perhaps reveal that the need to dominate the other reflects a deeper need for identity, or that the need to control the other reflects a need for security. It may then be possible to redefine these needs and to identify different satisfiers that would provide the party the identity or security it seeks without negating the other's needs in the process. Such a search may not always meet with success, but it is consistent with the overall task of workshops to help the parties define and satisfy their respective needs in ways compatible with one another.

Structure of workshops

Defining the enterprise in terms of human needs – rather than, for example, in terms of power politics – has some definite implications for the structure of workshops. In essence, problem-solving workshops are structured so that the focus of conflict analysis and resolution is on the parties whose needs are at the core of the conflict. Specifically, a needs perspective has three major implications for the structure of workshops.

1. Individuals invited to participate in workshops are usually representatives of the parties that are most directly and immediately involved in the conflict under consideration – individuals for whom the conflict raises existential concerns. Thus, participants in workshops on the Israeli–Palestinian conflict are Israelis and Palestinians, not Egyptians or American Jews, participants in workshops on the Cyprus conflict are Greek and Turkish Cypriots, not mainland Greeks and Turks.

   There is no implication here that the immediate adversaries are the only relevant parties, just as there is no implication that problem-solving workshops are the only relevant settings for the conflict resolution process. Resolution of international conflicts generally requires a larger, multilateral, and ultimately official process. In the Israeli-Palestinian case, the larger process must include the Arab states, whose interests are significantly affected by the outcome of Israeli–Palestinian negotiations and who have the capacity to facilitate the process or to block solutions that ignore their interests. It must include other states, particularly the superpowers, who play an essential role in providing incentives and guarantees. The larger process must represent a mix of bilateral and multilateral fora, and of unofficial and official contexts for communication. An essential part of this process, however –

and one that is too often neglected in traditional diplomacy – is active, direct interaction between the parties most immediately involved, whose basic, existential needs are at stake. That part of the work can generally be carried out most effectively at the unofficial, bilateral level, as exemplified in problem-solving workshops, and then fed into the official process. Agreements must ultimately be reached at the official level (and usually within a multilateral framework), because only such agreements are binding. But problem-solving workshops can contribute significantly to such agreements precisely because of the *non-binding* character of their proceedings, which allows them to generate ideas for resolving the conflict that are responsive to both parties' needs.

2. In focusing on the parties most immediately involved in the conflict, we make the assumption that enduring, high-quality solutions, that are responsive to the parties' needs, cannot be imposed. They must emerge out of the direct interaction between the parties. The setting, norms, procedures, and third-party role for problem-solving workshops are all geared to facilitating such direct interaction. Workshops, in short, are so structured that the kind of interaction capable of generating ideas for conflict resolution that satisfy the basic needs of both parties becomes necessary and possible: interaction in which the parties focus on each other, rather than on extraneous audiences, with the goal of understanding other's concerns and constraints and penetrating each other's perspective.

3. Workshops must be structured on a basis of equality, if they are to provide both parties the opportunity to satisfy their basic needs without violating the needs of the other and in a manner consistent with the principle of reciprocity. Unless equality between the parties is built into the structure of the workshop, it is unlikely that the discussions will yield ideas for resolution that are responsive to the needs of both parties and that do not systematically deny one party the benefits and assurances garnered by the other.

Establishing a structure of equality is a major challenge to workshop organizers in conflicts that involve asymmetries in the power relationship between the parties (or, as if often the case in protracted intercommunal conflicts, double asymmetries, such that one party enjoys a power advantage on some dimensions and the other party on others). Participants from the stronger party must be *willing* to deal with the other on a basis of equality, which generally means that they have come to accept the illegitimacy of past patterns of discrimination and domination; participants from the weaker must be *able* to deal with the other on a basis of equality, which generally means that they have reached a stage of confrontation in the conflict.

The third party can help ensure a structure of equality by selecting participants who meet the above criteria and by communicating and reiterating the values and purposes of the workshop at the time of recruitment of participants and over the course of the workshop itself. Without favoring one side or the other, the third party must make it clear that, if workshops are to fulfill their goal of generating ideas for solution that meet the needs of both parties, the basis of workshop interaction must be equality, even if there is asymmetry in their power relationship. Clear presentation of the workshop in these terms tends to encourage self-selection of participants, so that those who agree to come to a workshop are usually willing and able to accept a structure of equality. Selection and self-selection of participants, of course, do not fully ensure that the principle of equality will govern all of the proceedings; continued attention to this issue is part of the task of the third party.

In Israeli–Palestinian workshops my policy has been to select Palestinian participants who support and identify with the Palestine Liberation Organization (PLO), although most have not been formally affiliated with the organization. The primary reason for this selection criterion is the same as the reason for inviting only Israelis who are within the Zionist camp: As already stated, we are looking for participants who are within the mainstream of their political communities. At the same time, this selection criterion reinforces the structure of equality required for workshops. Palestinians who support the PLO are able (and in recent years have also been willing) to interact with Israelis on a basis of equality, because they are clearly asserting their entitlement to an independent, sovereign state, on a par with Israel. Israelis who agree to meet with such Palestinians are demonstrating by their action that they are willing to interact with Palestinians on a basis of equality.

Workshop Process

The workshop process is specifically designed to enable the parties to identify and understand each other's needs and to take the two sets of needs simultaneously into account as they work on the shape of an overall solution. The typical workshop agenda begins with an exploration of each party's concerns: the needs that a solution will have to satisfy and the fears that it will have to allay if it is to be acceptable. From there, the agenda moves to a discussion of the overall shape of a solution that would be responsive to both sets of concerns; of the political and psychological constraints that stand in the way of such a solution; and of ways of overcoming these constraints, including efforts that require direct or indirect cooperation between the parties.

Workshops focus on concerns rather than positions. By encouraging the parties to go behind their stated, incompatible positions and explore the needs and fears that underlie them, it often becomes possible to redefine the conflict in terms that are susceptible to a win/win solution. For example, in a conflict over territory, such as the Israeli–Palestinian conflict in its current phase (with its focus on the West Bank and Gaza), the parties would be urged to talk about why each wants the contested territory. At the risk of oversimplifying the issues for the sake of illustration, let us propose that the Palestinians want it primarily to establish and express their national identity, while the Israelis want it primarily to safeguard their national security. Once the conflict is redefined in terms of these underlying needs, the parties may be able to invent solutions that would satisfy Palestinian identity needs and Israeli security needs without threatening the other's existence.

It is important to our workshop model that the proceedings begin with exploration of the parties' concerns and needs, rather than – as participants are sometimes inclined to do – with discussion of formulas for solution. We ask participants to describe their needs to the other side and reflect on them. We try to make sure that these needs have been understood by the other. We encourage the parties to explore where the two sets of needs that have been presented are similar; where they differ, either in content or in the priority assigned to them; where they suggest mutually incompatible satisfiers; and where perhaps they could actually be satisfied by the same set of arrangements. Only after both sets of concerns have been placed on the table and each party seems to have understood the other's needs and fears and the perspective from which these arise, does the agenda move on to a search for solutions that take both sets of concerns simultaneously into account. Workshops encourage the parties to think actively and creatively about solutions that would meet not only their own needs, but also the needs of the other. The exploration of both sides' needs and fears also informs the discussion of the two remaining items on the typical agenda: the constraints that inhibit the discovery and implementation of mutually satisfactory solutions, and ways of overcoming these constraints.

When probing for needs in the course of a workshop, our focus is entirely on *collective* needs, in keeping with the group and intergroup level at which workshops operate. The terms we use to describe collective needs are identical to those used to describe individual needs: identity, security, recognition, autonomy, dignity, justice, development. And, indeed, what a human needs perspective ultimately refers to is the needs of individuals. It is the satisfaction of the needs of human individuals that constitutes the fundamental criterion for evaluating public policies and institutional arrangements, including those that bear on the resolution of international and intercommunal conflicts. To justify policies in terms of the needs and interests of institutions is to commit what Floyd Allport has called "the institutional fallacy."[9] Institutions do not have needs and interests; only people do. Individuals do, of course, have an interest in maintaining the integrity of institutions, but only insofar as they serve human needs, not at the expense of these needs.

The focus on collective needs in problem-solving workshops is consistent with the fact that people pursue satisfaction of their needs through collective entities – particularly through "identity groups" at the national, subnational, and transnational level. The identity, security, dignity and recognition *of these groups* (which is what we focus on in workshops) are relevant to the fulfillment of individual needs for two reasons. First, these groups serve as the *vehicles* for satisfaction of some of the basic needs of their members, such as security, self-development, self-expression, self-transcendence, and ultimately personal identity. Second, in view of the members' identification with these groups, the status of the groups is itself a *source* of the members' personal identity, self-esteem, and sense of dignity and meaning. In short, by searching for solutions that satisfy the basic collective needs of both communities, problem-solving workshops put a human needs perspective on conflict into practice.

NOTES AND REFERENCES

1. This chapter is a product of an action research program funded by grants from the US Institute of Peace and the Ford Foundation to the Harvard University Center for International Affairs. I am grateful to the two funding agencies and to the Center for their generous support of my work. The chapter was completed while I was a Distinguished Fellow at the US Institute of Peace. The views expressed in this chapter are those of the author alone; they do not necessarily reflect views of the Institute.
2. Herbert C. Kelman, "The Problem-Solving Workshop in Conflict Resolution," in Richard L. Merritt (ed.), *Communication in International Politics* (Urbana: University of Illinois Press, 1972); 168–204; Kelman, "An Interactional Approach to Conflict Resolution and its Application to Israeli–Palestinian Relations," *International Interactions* 16 (1979): 99–122; Kelman, "Interactive Problem Solving: A Social-Psychological Approach to Conflict Resolution," in William Klassen (ed.), *Dialogue Toward Inter-Faith Understanding* (Jerusalem: Tantur Ecumenical Institute for Theological Research, 1986): 293–314; Kelman, "Interactive Problem Solving: The Uses and Limits of a Therapeutic Model for the Resolution of International Conflicts," in Vamik Volkan, Demetrios Julius, and Joseph Montville (eds), *The Psychology of World Politics, Volume 2: The Tools of Unofficial Diplomacies* (Lexington, MA: Lexington Books, 1990); Kelman and Stephen P. Cohen, "Resolution of International Conflict: An Interactional Approach," in S. Worchel and W. G. Austin (eds.), *Psychology of Intergroup Relations* (Chicago: Nelson-Hall, 1986): 323–42.
3. John W. Burton, *Conflict and Communication: The Use of Controlled Communication in International Relations* (London: Macmillan, 1969); Burton, *Deviance, Terrorism and War: The Process of Solving Unsolved Social and Political Problems* (New York: St. Martin's Press, 1979); Burton, *Global Conflict* (Brighton, Sussex: Wheatsheaf, 1984).
4. Kelman, "Israelis and Palestinians: Psychological Prerequisites for Mutual Acceptance," *International Security* 13 (1978): 162–86; Kelman. "The Political Psychology of the Israel–Palestinian Conflict: How can we Overcome the Barriers to a Negotiated Solution?" *Political Psychology* 18 (1987): 347–63.
5. Kelman, "Creating the Conditions for Israel–Palestinian negotiations," *Journal of Conflict Resolution* 26 (1982): 67.
6. Kelman "An Interactional Approach" and Kelman and Cohen, "Resolution of International Conflict."
7. Kelman, "The Political Psychology of the Israeli–Palestinian Conflict."
8. See, for example, John W. Burton, "Conflict Resolution as a Function of Human Needs," in Roger A. Coate and Jerel A. Rosati (eds), *The Power of Human Needs in World Society* (Boulder, CO; London: Lynne Rienner, 1988): 196.
9. Floyd H. Allport, *Institutional Behavior* (Chapel Hill: University of North Carolina Press, 1933).

IV
Assessments

15 International Development in Human Perspective

Johan Galtung*

WHY A BASIC NEEDS APPROACH?

From the very beginning let it be stated unambiguously: a basic need approach (BNA) is not *the* approach to social science in general or development studies in particular, but only one approach. There are others. They may focus on structures (particularly of production–consumption patterns of any type of goods and services), on processes (e.g., of how the structures change over time), and on how structure and process are constrained and steered by culture and nature, to mention just some examples, In more classical approaches there is also heavy emphasis on actors, their strategic games in cooperation and conflict and their motivations and capabilities. Nor is it assumed that one can pick any one of these approaches at will; they are probably all (and more could be added) indispensable for a rich picture of the human condition. The only thing that is assumed in the following is that a BNA, although not sufficient, is at least necessary; that a basic needs approach – or its equivalent in other terminologies – is an indispensable ingredient of development studies.

To justify this position we shall make use of two arguments, one negative and one positive. The negative argument would be based on the futility of other approaches as the single or dominant approach, because they fail to make development human. In the name of a human theory, considerable anti-human crime can be committed.

Pitted against this there is the single and clear idea that development is development of human beings, because "human beings are the measure of all things." This does not mean that one cannot talk about development of things other than human beings, but that changes in these "things" can be shown only in relation to the development of human beings. If this is not the case, reification will set in – that is, what should be seen as means after some time attain goal character. Instead of difficult, complex, ever-changing, very often

301

dissatisfied, contradictory human beings, infinitely diverse, manifold, and volatile, "development" escapes into production and distribution patterns, institution building and structural transformation, cultural "aspects," and natural balances.

The negative argument is thus based on the futility of other approaches, not because they are not feasible, but because they are not valid – either theoretically or practically. Indeed, pragmatically they often lead to anti-human practices because there is no built-in guarantee that such development really aims at improving the condition of human beings. We may be free to have the intuition that democracy is better than dictatorship, that socialism is better than capitalism, and that democratic socialism (not the same as social democracy) may be the best of them all, but how do we know? These terms all refer to social formation, not to human beings. To assume that human beings *develop* inside them is like assuming that inside a beautiful house there must by necessity be beautiful people. We know well enough today that a rich country may have many very poor people, that a democratic country may very often evidence authoritarian relationships, that a socialist country may have very capitalist ways of doing things, and so on. In short, these other approaches are futile not only because they make development studies too easy by dodging the real issues; they may also lead to most dangerous development practices that ultimately serve only the interest of those managing the "things" singled out as the objects undergoing development – the production managers, distribution bureaucrats, revolutionary leaders, institution builders, nature con-servers, and culture preservers.

The basic needs approaches (BNAs) constitute one answer to this type of dilemma, and this is where the positive argument starts. The expression "a fully developed human being" may have no precise meaning; and that may be just as well, for if such a being existed, he or she would in all likelihood either be rather arrogant or be lifted by admirers on to a pedestal from which the arrogance of power, as well as the power of arrogance, might be exercised . . . However, we may still know something about what it is to be underdeveloped as a human being, and one approach here would be to say, "when basic human needs are not satisfied."

Development would then be seen as a process progressively satisfying basic human needs, where the word "progressively" would stand for both "more and more need dimensions" and "at higher and higher levels . . ."

In the pages to follow some of the perplexing and difficult, but also highly interesting and fruitful, problems connected with BNAs will be discussed. At this point let it be said only that other approaches for conceiving of human development should be explored.[1] What is needed are very rich, many-dimensional and many-faceted, views of human beings, ranging from the most material to the most non-material aspects. As far as we know, the BNAs are the only ones that bring that entire range of aspects under the same conceptual umbrella.[2]

WHAT IS A BASIC HUMAN NEED?

A need should be distinguished from a want, a wish, a desire, a demand. The latter are subjectively felt and articulated: they may express needs, but they also may not; and there may be needs that are not thus expressed. There is thus no assumption that people are conscious of their needs. Correspondingly, it is well known that we may want, wish, desire, or demand something that is not really needed in the sense of being necessary. Necessary for what? For the person to be a human person – and this is, of course, where the difficulties start.

One aspect of "need" is thus tied to the concept of necessity, which means that we have an image of what is necessary to be human – or, at least, of what it is to be non-human. Moreover, we shall claim that there is something universal to this image. This does not mean that a list of needs can be established, complete with minima and maxima, for everybody at all given social times and social spaces as *the* universal list of basic human needs. The claim is much more modest – namely, that it does make sense to talk about certain classes of needs, such as "security needs," welfare needs," "identity needs," and "freedom needs," to take the classification that will be used here, and to postulate that in one way or the other human beings everywhere and at all times have tried and will try to come to grips with something of that kind, in very different ways. It may even be fruitful to look for needs in the least common denominator of what human beings are striving for: if one were capable of making lists of what everybody at any time had wanted, as inferred from words and deeds, from conscious and unconscious wishes – and they would be many lists indeed – then there would be a certain overlap. That overlap would be a guide to (basic) needs.

When we say "something universal," this applies to the needs, not to the satisfiers; they may vary even more than the needs. Moreover, there is no assumption that needs can universally be satisfied. There are, as is rather well known, needs that cannot be met because of some empirical scarcity – even needs held by the same person. And there are needs, like a possible "need to dominate," "need to be dominated," "need to be more educated and/or healthy than my neighbor," "positional needs," that cannot be met by everybody for logical reasons.

Let us then proceed to "human," the second term in the expression "basic human needs." Our concern is with human needs, and by that is meant needs that are located, if not necessarily perceived, in individual human beings. The need subject is an individual, but that does not mean that the satisfiers, the "things" necessary in order to meet or satisfy the needs, are in the individual or can be met by the individual alone, without a social context. The problem is that the term "need" is also used for non-subjects; there is talk about "national needs" (for prestige of a country), "social needs" (e.g., for a good urban sewage disposal system), and "group needs" (e.g., for a place to meet, to be together). The argument here would certainly not be that there are no necessary conditions for these social entities or actors to function, but that the term "need" will be used only with reference to need subjects – and the only subjects we know of in human affairs are individual human beings. It is only in them that the "click of correspondence" between need satisfier can be experienced. That these individual human beings develop their need consciousness in a social context, and that most of them have most of their needs satisfied in a social context, does not change the circumstance that groups, cities, and countries do not have minds in which needs can be reflected or even articulated. On the contrary, the usual experience is – and this brings in the negative argument from the preceding section – that such "collective needs" usually express wishes and wants, the desires and demands of the ruling elites in these collectivities, more or less poorly disguised.

The term "basic" serves to further qualify the notion of a need as a necessary condition, as something that has to be satisfied at least to some extent in order for the need subject to function as a human being. When a basic human need is not satisfied, some kind of fundamental disintegration will take place.[3] This is not an *obscurum per obscurius* definition, for we know at least something about fundamental forms of disintegration. At the individual level they show up in the form of mortality and morbidity, the latter divided into the two interrelated categories of somatic and mental diseases. However, even if needs are seen as individual, the disintegration resulting from deficient need satisfaction may not necessarily show up in the individual or be classified as such. It may also show up elsewhere, for instance as *social disintegration*.

Two relatively clear types of social disintegration can now be identified, using the metaphors of freezing and boiling: on the one hand, the society that suffers from lack of participation, from apathy, withdrawal; on the other hand, the society that suffers from overactivity, mutiny, revolt. Just as with individual biological death, social disintegration may not necessarily be bad; it may put an end to something that is no longer viable. But both are signs of disintegration. Whether societies disintegrate because individual human needs are not sufficiently satisfied or the societies are incapable of satisfying them because they are disintegrating is less interesting. The two would probably be part of the same process, and from our point of view social disintegration is an indicator (as opposed to a cause or an effect) of insufficient satisfaction of basic human needs in concrete historical situations.

All that has been said in this section now amounts to one thing: although we do not want to be rigid in the conception of needs, one should not be totally free in the use of this term either. No doubt all of this raises the important problem of who are to judge what constitutes basic human needs if the person himself or herself is not considered sufficiently capable of judging – and we shall have something to say about that later. In conclusion, as we have defined it here, needs equal basic human needs, for "needs" are (1) "human and (2) "basic." For other concepts, other terms should be used.

TOWARD A TYPOLOGY OF BASIC HUMAN NEEDS

So far we have touched upon a distinction between material and non-material human needs, preferring "non-material" to the term "immaterial" because of the connotation of "unimportant" also carried by the latter expression. There are at least two ways of trying to clarify this distinction, one relating to the need subjects, one to the satisfiers.

There is a tradition, and it is not Western in general nor Cartesian in particular, to distinguish between the bodies and minds of persons and, correspondingly, between somatic and mental (spiritual) needs. One of the difficulties with this, of course, is that mind and body are related. Is the satisfaction that derives from eating food, even unappetizing food and in an environment devoid of good company and esthetic pleasures, really merely somatic? Of course, there are digestive processes that perhaps may be referred to as merely somatic, but there is also a feeling of hunger abatement, of increasing satisfaction that, if not spiritual, at least is mental. In short, it does not appear that the body–mind distinction serves as a good guide here.

A distinction based on satisfiers is not unproblematic either. It is relatively clear what are held to be material satisfiers: military or police hardware, food, clothes, shelter, medical hardware, schooling hardware, communication–transportation hardware. All these objects are scarce, ultimately due to the finiteness of nature, so that they obey the principle, "if you have more, I have less, and vice versa."

Then there are clearly non-material satisfiers, the major example being social structures or arrangements. But it is not quite as simple as that. To enjoy togetherness, proximity is needed if one's needs are not met by telecommunication; to enjoy loneliness, geographical distance may not be absolutely necessary, but it is helpful, and certainly sufficient (provided one avoids telecommunication). Both can be referred to as "human settlement patterns" and put in the category of "structural arrangements." But whereas the former does not require much geographical territory, the latter does, and geographical territory is scarce, given the finiteness of our globe. There seems always to be material constraints somewhere, and hence some opportunity costs.

How would one classify human beings? It may be argued that it is not my wife who is a "satisfier," but her love – her capacity both to love and to be loved – and that that has to do with some expression in her eyes, the tone of her voice, the feeling when we look at a full Easter moon together. It is hard to refer to all of this as material, but it certainly does obey the principle that "if I have more of it, somebody else has less." It may be objected that if I have more capacity to love or to be loved, that does not mean that somebody else has to have less of either, and this may be very true and very important; yet I may be less interested in love in general than in love in particular. Most human beings who live and have lived and much of human literature can testify that there is a scarcity principle involved here. In short, there is some scarcity in the non-material sphere, too.

Like the needs, the satisfiers do not fall from heaven, and they do not exist from eternity to eternity: they are produced in and by a social context and are dependent on that context. Since any social context can be looked at in at least two ways — as a set of actors and as a structure – it may make sense to distinguish between actor-dependent and structure-dependent needs.[4] An actor-dependent need would be one where the satisfaction depends on the motivation and capacity of some actor to meet or impede the satisfaction; a structure-dependent need would have the level of satisfaction more built into the social structure itself, as an automatic consequence, not dependent on the motivations and capabilities of particular actors. To this could be added a third category – nature-dependent. For social analysis, however, we shall take that for granted and be more interested in how actors and structures – in other words the social context – impede or meet needs over and above what nature yields.

Table 15.1　A typology of basic human needs

	Dependent on Actors	*Dependent on structures*
Material	Security (violence)	Welfare (misery)
Non-material	Freedom (repression)	Identity (alienation)

The above very tentative typology (Table 15.1), giving four classes of needs, is based on the two distinctions made above.[5] It is readily seen that the distinction actor-dependent versus structure-dependent is also highly problematic. In the case of security, the fact that military and police hardware relate to security is one reason for classifying it as a material need. No doubt insecurity may also stem from the evil motivation of capable actors. But then security may also be highly structure-dependent, something provided for by a structure that makes the members more able to resist any attack, violently and non-violently.[6] And insecurity may also stem from structure – for example, from exploitative relations between groups in general and societies in particular. And then both factors may be operating together, as they usually are: the structures produce the "evil" actors, and those actors make use of bad structures.

Nevertheless, the typology may serve as a rule of thumb, as some kind of guide, at least sensitizing us to some problems in connection with satisfiers and need satisfaction. When people starve, for instance, it is usually not traceable to strong actors with a motivation to kill through starvation (except during a siege), but to structures that are distributing the fruits of nature and human production unevenly. The same applies to alienation: it is generally a non-intended rather than an intended effect of the workings of the social context. But repression is different: at least the forms reflected in human rights are highly actor-dependent (although also structure conditioned).

As mentioned, the four types in Table 15.1 stand for classes of needs. One effort to spell them out in a way that may be particularly relevant for rich, industrialized countries is given in Table 15.2. The list in Table 15.2 no doubt has a Western bias – and may be of some use as a check-list to discuss problems of Western societies. There is certainly no assumption that the satisfiers to the right really meet the needs; they may do so up to a certain point. The hypothesis is that they are held to meet the needs. It should also be pointed out that these needs are posited; there is no systematic empirical research behind them. They are included here as an example of a need set to facilitate discussions.

IS THERE A HIERARCHY OF NEEDS?

In most literature about needs there is an explicit or implicit assumption of a general hierarchy of needs. Usually, there is a distinction, putting some of the "physiological" or "animal" – in general very somatic or material – needs at the bottom of the hierarchy and mental or spiritual needs – in our terms identity needs and freedom needs – higher.[7] The thesis may be seen as an axiological thesis (the higher needs are higher in the sense that they are less shared with animals, for instance), as an empirical thesis (the lower needs are pursued, in fact), or as a normative thesis (the lower needs should be satisfied first before attention is given to the higher needs).

Any such thesis is dangerous because it limits the range of possibilities that should be opened by any good theory of needs. As such, these theses constitute threats not only to cultural diversity but also to human diversity within cultures and throughout any individual human being's life cycle. The idea that non-material needs are "higher" than material needs can be seen as a way of legitimizing the

Table 15.2   A list of basic human needs: a working hypothesis

	Satisfiers held to be relevant in some societies
Security needs (survival needs) – to avoid violence	
– against individual violence (assault, torture)	Police
– against collective violence (wars, internal, external)	Military
Welfare needs (sufficiency needs) – to avoid misery	
– for nutrition, water, air, sleep	Food, water, air
– for movement, excretion	Physical freedom
– for protection against climate, environment	Clothes, shelter
– for protection against diseases	Medical treatment
– for protection against excessive strain	Labour-saving devices
– for self-expression, dialogue, education	Schooling
Identity needs (needs for closeness) – to avoid alienation	
– for self-expression, creativity, praxis, work	Jobs
– for self-actuation, for realizing potentials	Jobs and leisure
– for wellbeing, happiness, joy	Recreation, family
– for being active and subject; not being passive, client, object	Recreation, family
– for challenge and new experiences	Recreation
– for affection, love, sex; friends, spouse, offspring	Primary groups
– for roots, belongingness, support, esteem: association with similar humans	Secondary groups
– for understanding social forces; for social transparence	Political activity
– for partnership with nature	Natural parks
– for a sense of purpose, of meaning with life; closeness to the transcendental, transpersonal	Religion, ideology
Freedom needs (freedom to; choice, option) – to avoid repression	
– choice in receiving and expressing information and opinion	Communication
– choice of people and places to visit and be visited	Transportation
– choice in consciousness formation	Meetings, media
– choice in mobilization	Organizations, parties
– choice in confrontations	Elections
– choice of occupation	Labor market
– choice of place to live	?
– choice of spouse	Marriage market
– choice of goods and services	(Super-) market
– choice of way of life	?

position given to intellectuals in many societies and to ascetics as sacred or holy in some societies (presumably specialists specializing in the non-material). As their lives seem to be built around higher needs, should that not also give rise to a higher position? As theories about needs are more likely to be formulated by intellectuals than by non-intellectuals, the point is worth considering – as reflected in utopias, for example.

This does not apply so much to the hierarchy thesis as to an empirical thesis: if it can be ascertained empirically that people in fact do pursue material needs first and then non-material ones, even under conditions where they cannot be said to be forced to do so, then this is an important consideration. However, the basic point would be that as an empirical thesis this is certainly not a generally valid rule about human behavior. People are willing to suffer both violence and misery – including the sacrifice of their own lives – in struggling for identity and freedom. What is a general rule might be the possibility that the thesis is valid at an extremely low level of material satisfaction – that in utter deprivation (hunger to the point of starving, thirst, exposure to pain inflicted by nature or by human beings, denial of excretion or basic sanitation, denial of the possibility of moving, suffocation, "starving" for sex) priorities are clear. These are the cases where the ephithet "animal behavior" is often applied – and reference is made to extreme behavior under, for instance, concentration camp situations.

There is no denial that a rock bottom basic physiology of human beings exists that – under what we are used to seeing as extreme situations – would seem completely to control human behavior. But this is not the same as saying:

1. That all human beings under all circumstances first pursue the satisfaction of these needs to a maximum or at least quite completely before any attention is given to other needs.
2. That other needs, "non-material needs," cannot be given immediate attention at least after extreme material deprivation has been overcome or that they are not there all the time, merely overshadowed by the activity to overcome material deprivation.
3. That all human beings have the same minimum borders, the same limits where deprivation is concerned. It is assumed that some cultures and some individuals can stand physiological deprivation much better than others – that some threshold are much lower, in

other words – whether or not this is the result of conscious training and practice.

It is the normative thesis that is the most dangerous one as seen from the perspective of diversity. A presumed empirical regularity is elevated to the status of a norm, with considerable political implications. What the thesis says in fact, is that concrete policies and strategies, on both the individual and the collective levels, should be ordered sequentially in time so as to give first priority to the satisfaction of material needs, and then to non-material needs. The normative thesis may thus serve as a pretext for deliberate inattention to non-material needs, claiming that the "time is not yet ripe." Both individually and collectively, this may serve as a basis for indefinite postponement.

In practice this will serve as a *carte blanche* for the type of policies that might guarantee security and economic welfare, but at the expense of considerable amounts of alienation and repression. And the problem here is not only that non-material needs are put lower down on the priority list, it is also that the structures that have been used in order to satisfy only material needs may later stand in the way of satisfaction of non-material needs.

If need theory is to have any purpose or positive political function in contemporary society, it should be to serve as a basis for revealing such social malconstructions or cases of maldevelopment and to indicate other possibilities. A society that is incapable of giving attention to non-material needs, or a society that is incapable of giving attention to material needs for the masses of the population may be acceptable or compatible with theories of historical processes that define them as inescapable, necessary stages of development.[8] In the name of such theories, any kind of crime can be defended, and any kind of alleged privilege can be legitimized as "historical necessity" or as "the only historical possibility at this stage of development."

A theory of needs should serve as a basis for a rich image of human beings and should demand of social constructions that they respect this richness. The argument is not against having priorities in concrete situations – all of us have – but against any theory of needs that tries to universalize the priorities, freezing them into a general law, and thereby decreasing the diversity. Moreover, the theory of needs should also serve as a checklist, and a warning of possible basic problems that may ensue if priorities are organized in such a way that important classes of basic needs are pushed into the background for large sections of the society and for considerable periods of time. The hierarchy thesis may thus serve status quo purposes, particularly in a structural sense. On the other hand, it should not be denied that the hierarchy thesis may also serve to give much more attention to the material deprivation so prevalent in the world at large and that it has served to build a certain consensus among people and groups that otherwise might have remained inactive because of disagreement about non-material needs and how to meet them.[9]

The position taken here would be one of avoiding any built-in hierarchization of needs. Individuals and groups will have their priorities, and indeed their own conceptions of needs. The purpose of need theory would be to inspire them into awareness, not to steer and direct them into well-structured need sets. A major purpose of development theory and practice would have to be to expand the range of the possible, and this is better served by non-hierarchical than by hierarchical need sets where the priorities are universally given in advance. People should work out their own priorities, and the self-reliant ones will always have the courage to do so in dialogue with others.

NEEDS AND WESTERNIZATION: TEN PROBLEM AREAS

After this preliminary exploration, an effort will now be made to go into greater depth. The basic assumption will be that human beings do have needs, that there is such a thing as basic disintegration or pathology that shows up at individual–personal or societal levels, or both, if and when needs are not met. The expression "human beings" is used; the assumption is thus seen as universal. On the other hand it does not say very much: needs are not specified, nothing is said in precise terms about the breaking points where the pathologies will start developing. Nevertheless there is a position taken: human beings are not infinitely malleable. We do have goals, some of which take the form of basic human needs of which the individual may be more or less aware. Those basic human needs differ between individuals and groups and vary over time; they are malleable (although not infinitely so), but once they are sufficiently internalized in a human being, that individual is no longer malleable without considerable risk. Inside him or her, more or less consciously, some sort of reckoning takes place; satisfaction–dissatisfaction is the term used for that. The theory of socialization will thus have to play a fundamental role for any theory of needs unless that concept is reduced to a physiological level held to be socialization independent (and hence culture independent). And it raises the problem that people may be socialized into trying to satisfy some needs that will stand in the way of their own satisfaction of some other needs or in the way of others trying to satisfy theirs – these others being present or future generations. The theory of conflict is consequently also around the corner of any theory of needs, particularly if one is searching those patterns of development (meaning meeting basic human needs) that are not at the expense of others.

We shall now try to develop some ideas about the relation between this very broad concept of needs on the one hand and something referred to as "Westernization" on the other. Westernization is seen as a process that shapes anything in a Western direction. It is seen as a social code that leaves its imprint on whatever comes its way, transforming it so that the result is compatible with the code. The problem is what happens, or can be expected to happen, to the notion of needs when exposed to Westernization. It is assumed that the code is expressed partly as some general assumptions about how the world in general and human relations in particular are organized and how they evolve – referred to as the social cosmology – and some more specific ideas about social structure. To describe the code, two short lists with five points on each will be used:

The Western social cosmology is characterized by:

1. A Western-centered, universalist, conception of space.
2. A unilinear, present-centered, conception of time.
3. An analytic rather than holistic conception of epistemology.
4. A man-over-man conception of human relations.
5. A man-over-nature conception of relations to nature.

The Western social structure is characterized by:

6. A vertical division of labor favoring the center.
7. A conditioning of the periphery by the center.
8. Marginalization, a division between a social inside and outside.
9. Fragmentation, separation of individuals from each other.
10. Segmentation, separation inside individuals.

Let it be stated again that this is an effort to separate a general theory of needs from Western "perversions" that tend to slant the concept, including the criticism of the concept, in specific directions that are compatible with the Western code.[10] The position taken is thus that much of what has been done, both in theory and in practice, in the field of needs so far bears an unmistakable Western imprint; the following is an effort to help identify that imprint. But the position is not that the concept of need itself is Western – as pointed out above. We shall consider each item on the above list and try to draw some kind of demarcation line between the Western and the general. It is not important that the line is sharp nor that it is generally agreed upon; what matters is the effort and the consciousness of the problem. We will consider each point on our two lists in turn.

1 A Western-centered, Universalist, Conception of Space

Given the tendency in the West to see itself as a universally valid model to be imitated and in addition to promote and institutionalize processes emanating from Western centers, penetrating all over the world (at least to the level of the elites), implanting the Western code, it is obvious how the West will make use of a basic human needs approach. The first step will be to establish a list of needs so that it can serve as a basis for a universal conception of man. Leaving aside whether such lists are meaningful at all, the lists emanating from the West will have a Western slant, meaning that if people attempt to meet these needs all over the world, fewer changes will be needed or expected in the West, thereby being built into other countries as a model. Given the power of the West to institutionalize and implement its conceptions, not the least through intergovernmental (and other international) organizations, this is not an abstract exercise; it becomes political reality. The West may thus make use of such lists, with universal pretensions legitimized through UN and UN-related resolutions, to exercise pressure on other countries to conform and become more compatible with models from the West.[11]

The first answer to this point is simple enough: instead of universal lists of needs, stimulate the search for particular lists. The ultimate in particularity would be one individual, here and now. However, it is generally assumed that there is sufficient overlap between individuals over some intervals in time and some distance in space not to have to disaggregate to that extent. But what, then, is the unit of aggregation sufficiently homogeneous to posit its goals in the form of its list of what for it are basic human needs – or at least to posit some of their goals in such terms? The honest answer would probably have to be we simply do not know; much empirical research would be needed. But if we assume that there are two roots of human needs, one physiological and one cultural, transmitted through the socialization process, no doubt in interaction with each other, then a fruitful point of departure might be to think in terms of groups that, *grosso modo*, are physiologically in the same situation (as to underconsumption, adequacy, or overconsumption) and groups that belong to the same culture.

2 A Unilinear, Present-centered, Conception of Time

There are two problems here, and the first one is similar to the problem just treated – some kind of Western time imperialism in addition to the space imperialism just discussed. The basic logic is the same: a need list reflecting Western society today is postulated as valid for all times – in other words, is seen as timeless. History is seen as the gradual realization of this list, which is then constructed in such a way that approximation toward the West can also be seen as progress, so that the West as model and the idea of progress are both reflected.[12]

There is however, another problem here, hidden in the term "unilinear." More precisely, it is the non- or even anti-dialectic view of processes reflected in this term that has some important implications for how needs are conceived of. Looking at the terms used in most lists of needs, one is struck by their onesidedness, one hears much about the need for security, very little about any need for insecurity. There is much about the need for food, but where is any need for hunger? If there is a need for togetherness, where is the need for separateness, even for isolation? Where is the need for hatred if there is a need for love – perhaps even a need to be hated or at least disliked if there is such a thing as a need to be loved or at least liked?

The answer to this should not be seen in terms of adding the opposites to the lists; that would also be too mechanical. Rather, what is missing is a more dialectical approach to needs and need satisfaction. For the hungry there is a need for food, but for the well sated, the satisfied, there may be a need to be hungry again so as to have the need for food and (if it is available) the satisfier of that need and with it the enjoyment of need satisfaction.

The need for food is thus seen as a process, with no beginning and no end, of satisfaction and dissatisfaction, undulating through time with sometimes slow, sometimes quick rhythms, with no resting point, full of contradictions at any point. The "need for food" should be seen as a shorthand expression for this more complex need. In all needs for something there is also an element of the need for its negation – that is the thesis.

3 An Analytic Rather Than Holistic Conception of Epistemology

Western epistemology, it is often said, is analytic, following the Cartesian dictum of subdividing a problem into components that can then be attacked one at a time, starting with the simplest. The problem is whether a problem can be subdivided or whether anything for that matter can be subdivided and still remain the same. Elephants cannot be subdivided and remain the same; there is something irreducible, the elephant as *holisis* that is (considerably) more than the sum of the trunk, legs, tail, and so on. A list of needs looks like a list of components. The question is, What is the whole that has been subdivided to deliver that list, and what, if anything, has been lost in the process?

In a sense it is the human person that has been subdivided into components. There is hence a double problem here – the wholeness of human beings and the wholeness of our images of human beings. Both problems are difficult; they can be approached but not solved in what follows, written by an admittedly analytically minded Western researcher, probably the worst possible point of departure for this type of exercise.[13]

First, it should be mentioned that people in general, unless they have been trained through need analysis, do not see their own situation in terms of need lists and need satisfiers. If a verbal expression is asked for, the expression "state of well being," used in the WHO definition of health, is probably as good as any. The problem is what happens when powerful analysts subdivide a holistic experience of well and ill being into components called need dimensions, use them to construct images of human beings as need sets, and then propagate these images to the people they are images of asking, or even demanding, that they accept these images as their own.

Second, however, the analytic versus holistic image is not a dichotomy of alternatives; it is or can be seen as a both-and rather than an either-or (using both halves of the brain). The problem is not how to suppress analytical thinking in this field, but how to facilitate and promote holistic thinking. (Some of the dangers of analytical thinking will pointed out under the heading of Segmentation, below.)

Third, how is that done? How can the researcher develop images that are not onesidedly analytical? Probably best by learning from the people, by understanding, through dialogues, how they understand their own situations.

4 A Man-Over-Man Conception of Human Relations

One way of expressing this part of Western cosmology would be in terms of verticality and individualism. Society is seen as some kind of a jungle where conflicts are resolved through processes defining winners and losers rather than through consensus and solidarity-building processes. If such processes are enacted often enough, the net result is a society of vertically organized, mutually detached individuals; as the process is built into the social code, this type of structure will be not only produced but also reproduced. The problem of how a code of that type would affect the theory of needs may be answered, in general terms, by emphasizing those aspects of needs that would give prominence to the three themes just mentioned: conflict, verticality, and individualism.

Conflict
One would expect Western theories of needs to emphasize the need, or the theories of needs that, when translated into political practice, would generate conflict rather than cooperation. One way of doing this would be by giving priority to material needs, remembering that one perspective on such needs is that the satisfiers are high on material components, that such components by definition have some element of scarcity (at least when pursued *ad lib*, because of the finiteness of the world), and consequently, that if I have more, somebody else will have less. This may be one factor behind the Western tendency to give priority to material needs: by doing so conflict is guaranteed, conflict that can serve to arrange human beings vertically and individually.

More emphasis on non-material needs would, in general, produce fewer zero-sum games in society. As will be seen below, there are exceptions to this: there may also be non-material scarcity. The important point, however, is not whether the fine line between competitive and non-competitive needs passes exactly between material and non-material (thus there are also material needs – e.g., for air – that at least so far can be seen as largely non-competitive, but decreasingly so with increasing pollution). The point is only that other codes might steer people and societies in less competitive directions by emphasizing other needs more and the competitive one less – but not, of course, by pretending there are no such things as human needs.

Verticality

There is the point already referred to of promoting images of human beings and their needs so as to foster competition and conflict, ultimately leading to vertical ordering. However, it should be noted that this can also be obtained in other ways. Need dimensions may be used for vertical ordering even when the satisfiers are not competitive.

Behind this is not only the possibility of ranking people, but a cultural norm pressing people to do so. Earlier generations might have talked about competitive instincts.[14] Does this mean that we should talk about a basic human need, at least in the Western context, not only to have and to be, but to have more and to be more?

One possible approach would be to stipulate that what cannot even for logical reasons be met for everybody should not be referred to as a "need" – or at most as a "false" need – for if I shall have or be more than anybody else, others cannot be in the same position; that would constitute a logical contradiction. To rule it out, by definition, however, sounds a little bit like removing sin by outlawing it. The problem still remains that this value persists, and certainly not only in the Western code.

However we choose to look at this, neither conflict nor verticality can be said to be built into the need concept as such. But what about individualism?

Individualism

No doubt there is something individualistic in a need concept stipulating that the only need subjects are individual beings. The position taken is that the need for togetherness is felt inside human beings, nowhere else, and that it is inside human beings that a feeling of wellbeing – because that need is met – is generated, nowhere else, other positions being seen as obscurantist and lacking empirical referents and as politically very dangerous. The need to belong to a society of which one can be proud is also located in members of that society; a country outdoing others in wars or economic competition is a satisfier of such needs, but both the need and the need satisfaction (into the satisfier!) are individual. This trivial point, however, is not enough to label need theory in general as individualist.

A clearly individualist need theory would go further and demand that the satisfaction not only take place inside the individual, but inside the individual in isolation – in other words, that a social context is not needed. No doubt need theory can be slanted in that direction, and this will be discussed in some detail below (under Fragmentation). But nothing in that direction is built into the concept as such. What is built into it as here presented is an effort to rule out concepts of "social needs" because they seem so often to be felt only by ruling elites and to confuse satisfiers with needs.

5 A Man-Over-Nature Conception of Relations to Nature

The assumption that only individual human beings are need subjects draws a line not only against human collectivities of various kinds as legitimate need subjects; there is another borderline with nature on the other side. Nature – animals, plants, and other forms of nature – is not seen as being a subject possessing needs. No doubt this is in line with the Western tradition of de-souling nature and be-souling man and only man – and, as such, an item of Westernness built into the theory, subject to challenge and possible modifications.[15]

In the meantime let it be noted that to deprive nature of the status as need subject does not mean that there is no recognition of necessary conditions for the survival of, say, an ecosystem – just as there are necessary conditions for the survival of, say, the capitalist system (only that we would not identify these conditions with satisfiers of human needs, at least not without having more evidence).

6 A Vertical Division of Labor Favoring the Center

How this vertical division of labor works is obvious: by a group in the center telling the rest of the population what their needs are. Under point 1 above the tendency toward a Western view is discussed in geopolitical terms. The point here is how the same structure is also found inside societies. There are those who work out lists of needs and satisfiers, thereby contributing to the programing of others, and there are those who have their needs defined for them. The system is found in capitalist and socialist countries alike: in the former the corporations play more of a role; in the latter, the state bureaucracies (and the Party).

As pointed out above, there will for several reasons be a tendency to focus on material needs; in the capitalist countries denying the reality of some of the identity needs, in the socialist countries adding to the denial list many of the freedom needs (they are all for "later").[16] The examples are chosen so as to make very clear how profoundly political is the problem of needs and their satisfaction which means that the struggle for the right to define one's own needs is a highly political struggle. In a sense the situation is very similar to the situation that has reigned in the field of "development:" the idea has been coopted by powerful elites, a combination of bureaucrats, capitalists, and intellectuals at national and international levels. That the idea can be abused by those in power is, of course, what power is about. The needs of human beings do not disappear because the idea of needs can be abused, nor does reality change if one should decide to use some other term. The same applies to "development:" it can be used for political, even military, manipulation and for economic exploitation; the problems are still there, particularly if development is seen as a process aiming at meeting human needs.[17]

The problem consequently relates not to the concept of needs, however it is defined, but to the power of defining needs, particularly for others. If anything should relate to a need for identity then it must be the need to define one's own situation – including in this, indeed, the definition of one's own needs. Again, what the unit is defining needs – the individual, the group, the country, the region – can be discussed, but regardless of what level is chosen, participation in the need definition would have to be the general norm. In such dialogues, bureaucrats, capitalists, and intellectuals, national as well as international, should also participate; they are also people. But in the present structure they count too much.

7 A Conditioning of the Periphery by the Center

This conditioning is not merely a question of potential and actual culturocide and depersonfication to be expected when Western need structures (point 1) elaborated by elites (point 6) are beamed in all directions as universal norms to be pursued, but also a question of making people dependent on the satisfiers that will follow in the wake of the propagation of need structures. It is difficult at present to see fully the possibilities of conditioning the periphery by means of basic needs (BN) strategies; on another occasion[18] we have listed six:

1. BN approaches as an effort to sidetrack the new international economic order (NEIO) issue.
2. BN approaches as a new way of legitimizing intervention.
3. BN approaches as an instrument to increase the market.
4. BN approaches as a way of slowing down Third World growth.
5. BN approaches as an effort to decrease technical assistance.
6. BN approaches as a weapon of defense against the poor.

Whether such consequences are intended is of less significance; the problem is that a basic needs-oriented strategy may work this way when operated from the center, including Third World centers.[19]

In a sense, this is to be expected. When fed into a certain structure, steered by a certain code, needs will be structured so as to be compatible. It is possible to do this, however, only with a very truncated need set, singling out from more complete sets the needs that fit, including others (such as the need for self-actuation, for self-expression, for being active and a subject, for challenge, for creativity, etc.). As it is now, satisfiers tend to define the needs rather than vice versa. Needless to say, this leads to an overemphasis on material needs.[20]

8 Marginalization, a Division Between a Social Inside and Outside

What could be better for reproduction of the marginalization of the masses of our societies than a hierarchy of needs, having at the bottom people whose major concern it should be to have material needs (physiological and safety needs in Maslow's parlance) well taken care of before they can or ought to (the ease with which one slides from descriptive to normative statements here is part of the mechanism) proceed to non-material needs? The isomorphism between needs hierarchies and social hierarchies will reinforce either of them, giving a sense of confirmation to either. Elites will be the first in propagating the idea of "material needs first" under the guise of humanitarianism, thereby preserving the marginalization for generations still to come, given the magnitude of the job of "meeting the basic needs of those most in need" when it is done the way these elites suggest – managerially. To meet those needs may even be a low price to pay to retain a monopoly on social management – as is done in the social democratic welfare state.

This becomes even more significant given what is probably a reasonable map of the real situation where need satisfaction is concerned (see Table 15.3). The elites in countries, poor and rich, in the world today certainly have basic material needs satisfied and in addition a lot of material satisfiers (often called "gadgets") beyond that. The masses have less of the latter; this is, in fact, how some of the borderlines between elites and masses are drawn. As to non-material needs the conjecture is simply that in a modern, corporate society based on the typical bureaucrat-capitalist-intellectual top management (with somewhat more power to bureaucrats in the state capitalist and to the capitalist in the private capitalist countries), satisfaction of a broad range of non-material needs is impossible and the consequence of this is probably found, among other places in the rates of mental disorder. For the masses in the poor countries, this is all different: the material situation is deplorable in most regards; the non-material not necessarily so. If one of the keys to identity is closeness, this is where it may still be found; as many authors, often naively startled by this obvious circumstance, report: "in the slums I found the solidarity, the generosity, the warmth so often missing where I come from."

Table 15.3   The level of need satisfaction: a conjecture

		Material needs		*Non-material needs*
		Basic	Non-basic	Basic and Non-basic
Elites		Yes	Yes	No
Masses	Rich countries	Yes	Yes/No	No
	Poor countries	No	No	No/Yes

No doubt a theory of needs draws a line between those whose basic human needs are not satisfied and those whose are, given the specificities of the society. So does, incidentally, the whole tradition of caring for the ill: there is marginalization involved with the institutionalization of the ill, (temporary) non-membership in society, separation from healthy people in family and work, and so on. A good theory of needs, however, should serve as a corrective by constantly reminding us that even if a person is deficient relative to one need dimension, need satisfaction cannot possibly consist in a trade-off that sacrifices other need dimensions in order to make up for the deficit. If a theory of needs is to be of any value at all it would be to serve as a reminder of the needs of the total human being in such a situation.

Our present society makes deficits in material needs visible: poverty can be seen; so can illness. Deficits in non-material needs are less visible: alienation, lack of ability to love and be loved, are more easily tolerated than is poverty, both in the need subjects and in others. Why? Because of the material bias of our societies, implying that material problems are the problems held to be resolvable within these societies, other problems are either defined away or given up – and that consensus for action is built around material "facts" not non-material "values." But in a different culture, with greater emphasis on non-material dimensions, this may all turn out very differently.

The Maslow hierarchy can thus be seen as a very precise sophisticated translation of Western culture into a theory of needs. But did we not argue against that? Yes, and on two levels: First, it is often offered with the pretension of being a universal hierarchy, of being something beyond merely a reflection of Western cultural biases. Second, it reinforces Western-type social stratification, even class formation, further. The critique of that kind of hierarchy is found partly in the contradiction between the West and important parts of the non-West, partly in contradictions inside the West. Our personal bias would be that a society is best served with a theory and politics of needs satisfaction that place the material and the non-material on a more equal footing, as argued several times above. In that case, a hierarchy drawing lines between the material and the non-material would be impossible; no marginalization could be built on that basis. But this is the type of struggle that has to be fought inside each culture and society.

9 Fragmentation, Separation of Individuals from Each Other

If the individuals are the only need subjects there are, why should not this individualization be carried further? The problem has been mentioned above (point 4): "that the satisfaction not only takes place inside the individual, but inside the individual in isolation; in other words that a social context is not needed. No doubt need theory can be slanted in that direction." Actually, "that direction" splits into two, both of them meaningful within a Western tradition of individualism and fragmentation, but very different in their consequences: that the need subject alone provides for the need objects, the satisfiers; and that need satisfaction takes place in social isolation. The hypothesis would be that the Western tradition would pick up both possibilities and slant a theory of needs in these directions.

The basic point is that there is and should be nothing in needs theory as such that would make this type of social formation a logical consequence of needs theory. On the contrary, under the need class of "identity" it would be strange if most need lists did not one way or the other include some reference to "togetherness." A society that systematically counteracts this need will be punished sooner or later, regardless of efforts that it might make to make a virtue of its vices by proclaiming that this is a "natural" tendency.

10 Segmentation, Separation Inside Individuals

We have discussed above – under marginalization – how hierarchies of needs may serve to reinforce social hierarchies, and – under fragmentation – how the individualization of the need subject may spread to the production of need objects, or at least to their consumption. Here an effort will be made to discuss how lists of needs may serve to reinforce tendencies toward segmentation – or, rather, toward a segmented as opposed to an integrated mode of need satisfaction. One way of exploring this may be as follows.

So far we have looked at why need objects/satisfiers are consumed/enjoyed (to meet needs), but not at how. As time progresses – for example, from morning to afternoon to evening to night – a person's action line passes through new points in space and social space, perhaps with family in the morning, workmates in that afternoon, friends in the evening, and back to the family at night. This is the segmented mode; in the integrated mode time also progresses, but all these activities are carried out with the same people, more or less at the same place. The continuity in space and people provides for a carryover, a social continuity, from one activity to the next. The segmented mode is often referred to as "compartmentalized" because transition from one activity to the next implies a change of place and social partners – a new "compartment" in space.

One may now be for and against either pattern. The segmented mode is disruptive, but it also provides for new experience; the integrated mode provides stability, but there may be too much of that. This is not the point, however. The point is that needs theory may be used to reinforce the segmented mode, by assigning to each point in the space one type of need satisfaction, one need dimension, or at least one need class. Without that separation, the place and the people, all the things around that do not change, will provide continuity from one satisfier to the other and from one need to the other. The integration on the satisfier and the social context side may thus constitute one approach to the problem of lack of holism in the basic needs approaches.

Concluding this survey of possible perversion of a general theory of needs, presenting what in reality is adaptation to Western social cosmology and social structure as if it were universal theory, let us now summarize. "Westernization" is like a machinery; something emerges that is recognizable, but twisted in particular directions. Our assumption is thus that Western theories of needs will tend to claim universal validity; that the approach to time will be non-contradictory and mechanistic; that the epistemology of needs will be analytical, non-holistic, that needs whose satisfaction generates conflicts of scarcity will be overemphasized; that nature will be seen as without needs; that there will be a strong division of labor between those who define the needs and those for whom needs are defined and that the former will plan the lives of the latter; that the center will propagate not only need images but also satisfiers and thereby create or awaken needs; that needs will be ordered into hierarchies, thereby reinforcing current stratification into higher and lower classes, engaging in satisfaction of higher and lower needs; that need satisfaction will be individualized; and that need satisfaction will be increasingly segmented, one need at a time and context. If this were needs theory, the present author would be against it; a theoretical tree should be known by its theoretical and empirical fruits.[21]

But it is not. It is not even Western needs theory, although there are strong inclinations in these directions. In this case the distinction made is between a general needs theory and a specification adapted to Western conditions along the ten lines indicated above. From this one should not drawn the conclusion that the general theory is good and the Western specification bad. What is wanted are many more specifications, none of them pretending to be the universal truth. What is needed is a general theory broad enough to help us generate such specifications – in short, let 100 specifications of need theory grow.

BASIC NEEDS APPROACHES: SOME STRENGTHS AND WEAKNESSES

BNAs are certainly not new. Just to mention two traditions, the Western–Christian and Indian–Hindu. "Give us today our daily bread" is an invocation for minimum satisfaction of basic material needs (it certainly does not stand for bread alone); John Ruskin's *Unto This Last* is filled with this idea (but the source of satisfaction is now more secularized); Marx's entire theory is actually based on thinking about needs; and in the history of the United Nations, Lord Boyd Orr's famous Quebec speech when the FAO was founded in 1954 is along the same line.[22] Gandhi, deeply inspired by Christianity and John Ruskin on top of his Hindu roots always had those most in need as top priority, in theory and in practice.[23] The twin ideas, which focus on what is fundamental and on those who lack precisely this, run through history, but not as a mainstream: had it been a mainstream, then there might still have been inequality, even exploitation, but not so much abject misery. And that leads us straight to the major strength of and the major weakness of BNA.

The major strength is that BNAs serve to set priorities. BNA is an effort to cut through rhetoric, focusing on what is essential and basic, and to provide individuals and societies with a measuring rod that lowers the focus of social attention downwards, "unto this last," saying this: "tell me how much material and spiritual misery there is at the bottom of society and I will tell you what kind of society you have." Human suffering, deprivation shall count more and serve to set our priorities straight.[24]

The major weakness is that BNAs say nothing about how misery is produced; they do not comprise a social theory. Thus they say nothing about inequity, for these are relations, even abstract ones, and it would be hard to assume that there is a need not to be exploited or not to live in a society with too much inequality. Equity and equality are social values, and so is social justice. As such they may be so deeply internalized that they attain need character, but one would assume such cases to be exceptional. What is felt inside a person would be concrete deprivation, leading to concrete tension, even suffering; and that is what needs theory is about, not about social analysis. Thus, by raising the floor above a certain minimum agreed to by people themselves so that misery is abolished, basic needs will be satisfied,[25] even when inequity and inequality are constant or even increasing. There is no automatic extension of BNAs to cover all good social values; that would be to stretch the need concept too far. And in this a major danger exists: it is quite possible, even when material and non-material needs are put on a more equal footing, to combine BNAs with many kinds of exploitative processes, channeling most resources toward the rich as long as the poor are above the minimum. One may impose a social maximum, a ceiling, but between ceiling and floor there may still be inequality and inequity; there may be need satisfaction at the expense of somebody else's need satisfaction. Needs theory does not automatically guard against that, except in the (postulated) need to be a subject.

The answer to this should not be to pretend that BNAs can offer what is not within their paradigm, but to call for additional perspectives, theories, paradigms, approaches. Most important would be theories about how misery is produced and reproduced, and such theories exist – they are indispensable to get at the roots of the phenomenon. Further, a theory of conflict is an indispensable additional perspective: satisfiers are often scarce; there may be trade-offs and choices to be made.

A second strong point in BNAs is the rich image they can give of the human being when they are not too narrowly interpreted. A list of needs like the one given in Table 15.2 can so easily be subdivided among the social sciences; and it is rather obvious what the psychologist, the social psychologist, the sociologist, politologist, and economist would focus on, deriving their *homo psychologicus* and so on till we reach *homo economicus*. BNAs transcend such efforts at compartmentalization, aiming at rich biosocial, physiological–cultural images.

But another major weakness is that the empirical procedures for developing these rich images are far from clear. Survey research may get at values, depth interviews may probe more deeply into motivations. But for needs it is more complicated: what the subject says, in spite of being a subject, is not necessarily to be taken at its face value. To use the two distinctions used in this chapter, conscious versus unconscious (also called manifest versus latent) and true versus false needs: the subject is not necessarily conscious of her or his needs, and what are held to be needs may turn out to be false needs – they may not be that important.

The answer would be that empirical methods do exist, but they certainly have to go beyond simply asking the person what her or his needs are. The dialogue should be a much more promising approach, around the theme, "what is so important that we cannot do without it?" A process of mutual probing in depth may reveal to what extent non-satisfaction of the need can really be held to be that crucial, and how much effort or sacrifice one would be willing to make for that need. This would still be verbal, only intense, so that it may explore the deeper recesses of the mind.

The second major approach would be through practice, again with the same subdivision. Empirical situations of deprivation might occur where satisfiers usually present disappear wholly or partly: does disintegration take place or not? And in the concrete situation, what do people in fact sacrifice in order to meet a certain need? More particularly, are they willing to sacrifice along other need dimensions, for if they do, that serves as an indication of relative priority. People are known to be willing to give up their lives for freedom and/or identity, so physical survival is not unconditionally the most basic need. But they are also willing to give up freedom and/or identity in order to obtain security and/or welfare – indicating the futility in trying to establish any universal linear hierarchy. From considerations such as these one arrives at a flatter need landscape in general. For particular situations and groups clear peaks may be visible; we do not deny hierarchies in concrete situations.

Thus we have essentially four empirical approaches, as shown in Table 15.4. Table 15.4 can now be seen as an exercise in methodology, and one may discuss which method is more valid and which method is more reliable. The conclusion is probably that the non-verbal methods are more valid but less reliable, among other reasons because replication is less feasible; and the verbal method is more reliable, but also less valid. The verbal approach is certainly the easier to use.[26]

Table 15.4   Empirical approaches to exploring needs

	Is it possible to do without?	How much sacrifice to have it satisfied?
Verbal approaches (through dialogue)	(A)	(B)
Non-verbal approaches (observation of behavior)	(C)	(D)

But the four approaches can also be seen as a form of social practice. Through dialogue people help each other, raising the general awareness and consciousness of their own true needs – manifest-conscious or latent–unconscious – meaning by that what they really cannot do without.

A third point in BNAs is that they indicate a future agenda for development, and a very rich and open one. BNAs do more than set a list of priorities, of things that must be done. Correctly understood they go beyond discussion of a minimum level of satisfaction in at least three ways. First, they open for the whole exploration of true versus false needs, thereby potentially becoming a tool for enriching human existence. A condition for this, however, is not only to strip one's need set of false needs, but also to enrich it with latent, but true, needs. This is where there is so much to learn from others – a reason why the union approach to universalism in the field of needs is so important. Second, they open for the whole exploration of true versus false satisfiers, questioning all the relationship in Table 15.2 with pretend satisfiers, precisely by being a theoretical construct, something non-observable that can serve to define a class of satisfiers from which the best – the most adequate in terms of a range of needs and resources available – may be picked. Third, they open up the whole exploration of richer relations between needs and satisfiers, particularly how new satisfier contexts can be imagined relating to whole need complexes. The point is to reason from the needs, combining them mentally, asking for rich satisfier contexts that may speak to new, more integrated combinations and not to be steered by existing satisfiers simply because they are there.

The major weakness corresponding to this strength remains: there is a difference between tension relief and human development; and the image is not holistic enough. The preliminary answer would be that needs theory never assumes that needs remain at the same level, a sort of basement level in a building where values constitute the upper floors. Needs can be developed precisely because they are biosocial in character. We have tried to point to the process: through internalization of values, to want so much to do what is good and right that it becomes a need to do so. But this will never exhaust any image of human beings because of our capacity of transcending whatever image somebody has constructed, in good directions, in bad, in both.

In conclusion, BNAs are indispensable in any theory of development that sees development as development of human beings – in other theories BNAs become unnecessary, even disturbing.[27] In one way or the other, BNAs will be present, even under other names.

Thus, instead of letting the needs creep up that building from the basement, one may let the values creep down, into the basement, insisting that it is all culturally conditioned. But one does not escape from the idea of a *conditio sine qua non*. No development theory worth its name can do without an anthropology of human beings, and however vast the variations, the concept of necessary conditions remains. That the approaches are beset with problems is obvious, and constitutes important challenges for future research. But the major problems are those people, adherents or critics, who see them as the only approaches and either pretend that BNAs have answers when not even the question can be formulated within a BNA paradigm or attack it for the answers that BNAs cannot and should not give.

So what we need are a rich range of perspectives, among which BNAs are one, and a rich theory of basic needs, all of which will be very complex. And yet it will never be as complex as human life and social reality themselves, in their infinite variety. And that may turn into a virtue what to many seems like a vice built into basic needs approaches: they are not only complex, but also chaotic. But why not? Maybe they should be chaotic, to guard against the type of clarity that will only too easily serve as a basis for bureaucratic/corporate/intellectual manipulation! There is much wisdom in the tale related by Mushakoji[28] in defense of the alternative of chaos: King Chaos died when the Kings of the Northern and of the Southern Seas "structured" him by giving him eyes and ears, a mouth. For that reason we referred to the subject of this chapter as "approach," not as "model" and not as "strategy" – knowing well that there are strong forces trying to pull basic needs in that direction. Some clarification is needed, but not too much; whether the present effort is adequate is for others to decide.

NOTES AND REFERENCES

* *Editor's note*: Johan Galtung wishes it to be recorded that the inclusion of a contribution by him in no way indicates his support of the sponsorship of this Conflict Series.
1. Thus, there is something negative about the needs approach very well expressed by Dorothy Lee in "Are Basic Needs Ultimate," in D. Lee

(ed.), *Freedom and Culture* (Englewood Cliffs, N.J.: Spectrum, 1959): 72.

The premise that man acts so as to satisfy needs presupposes a negative conception of the good as amelioration or correction of an undesirable state. According to this view, man acts to relieve tension; good is the removal of evil and welfare and the correction of ills; satisfaction is the meeting of a need; good functioning comes from adjustment; survival from adaptation; peace is the resolution of conflict; fear, of the supernatural or of adverse public opinion, is the incentive to good conduct; the happy individual is the well-adjusted individual.

No doubt, there is in the need concept the idea of tension relief. But these tensions are real whatever the mix of the physiological–cultural basis. When Lee argues that "it is value, not a series of needs, which is at the basis of human behavior," she is obliterating the important distinction between values in general and values so basic that the tension resulting from non-fulfilment becomes destructive. Needs are in this latter category, and it is not a fixed category. We can turn values into needs; the question is – Which values should become needs?.

2. World philosophies tend to be relatively silent on material needs, with the important exception of some of the basic Western philosophies in antiquity, which become important to the general materialistic bias of Western thought. (But they may also have been misinterpreted, and at any rate the Middle Ages were less materially bent.) What is generally associated with Oriental thought (for a good survey, see J. K. Fiebleman, *Understanding Oriental Philosophy* (New York: Horizon Press, 1976) has a very non-material bias.

3. Sicinski ("Concepts of 'Need' and 'Value' in the Light of the Systems Approach," *Social Sciences Information* (1978): 73 ff.) speaks of a logical hierarchy of needs:

   (1) needs whose non-satisfaction results in the annihilation system (these could be termed, as in traditional terminology, *fundamental needs*);
   (2) needs whose non-satisfaction results in the system's *inability* to perform *some of its functions*;
   (3) needs whose non-satisfaction results in disturbances in the system's performance of *some of its functions*;
   (4) needs resulting in disturbances in the *development* (emphasis in the original) of the system. (This applies to self-organizing systems in particular.)

4. For more on this distinction see Johan Galtung, *The True Worlds: A Transnational Perspective* (New York: The Free Press, 1979) Chapter 2.

5. I am indebted to my colleagues in the World Order Models Project for stimulating discussions on this subject, especially during the meeting in New Brunswick (August 1976).

6. Thus, both Gandhi and guerilla-type resistance are based on very decentralized, numerous, and autonomous units so that the society cannot be hit at any central point and dominated from that point.

7. The best known author, most worthy of being discussed, is, of course, Abraham H. Maslow. His famous hierarchy was put forward in "A Theory of Human Motivation," *Psychological Review*, 50 (1943): 370–96; also see his books *New Knowledge in Human Values* (New York: Harper & Row, 1959); *Toward a Psychology of Being* (Princeton: Van Nostrand, Reinhold, 1962); *Motivation and Personality* (New York: Harper & Row, 1970) rev. edn; *The Farther Reaches of Human Nature* (New York: Viking Press, 1979). His hierarchy (from 1943) has five levels: at the bottom are physiological needs (hunger, thirst, oxygen, recovery from fatigue) and safety needs (freedom from pain, protection of physiological goals); in the middle, belongingness and love needs (friendship, love, and tender affection); at the top are esteem needs (prestige, achievement, status, and dominance) and need for self-actualization (expression of capacities and talents). We have grouped them in these three levels because that seems to correspond not too badly with what one may associate with lower, middle, and upper classes in our vertical societies, with the middle classes taking physiological and safety needs for granted but not able to actuate the highest group of needs; and with the upper classes deeply engaged in exactly that while taking the others for granted and maybe discovering that in the struggle for esteem and self-actualization belongingness and love needs somehow get neglected. Any vertical ordering of needs is likely to be reflected in social stratification one way or the other, and a theory of needs hierarchy may therefore easily become a justification of social hierarchy.

8. Neither liberalism nor Marxism can be said to be strong on emphasizing the possibility of non-material growth before or together with material growth.

9. Thus, a consensus in the UN around material needs would probably break down very quickly if the intricate "philosophical" problems pertaining to identity and freedom should be entered into with the First World accusing the Second World of repression and the Second World accusing the First World of alienation (and the First World retorting with a *tu quoque*) and the Third World obtaining nothing for lack of consensus. The spiritual poverty of liberalism and Marxism (compared, for instance to Oriental thought) may have been necessary for this consensus to be worked out for good or for bad.

10. In so doing it is also a response to the critique of the needs concept by my colleague Gilbert Rist. At least in earlier versions I perceived his critique as being directed not against needs theory but against the Western perversions of needs theory, or against some of them. For a more effective critique of that kind of needs theory, a map of Western social cosmology and social structure is needed to generate hypotheses about what kind of biases would be likely.

11. One might even say that this is the function of the UN system from a Western angle: what is profoundly Western may look more universal clothed in a UN resolution at least until one starts asking questions about the degree of Westernization in the UN.

12. World history is seen then as some kind of rolling agenda with first welfare, then . . . , and so on – always assuming that the West is tackling the more advanced points on the agenda.

13. Hence, a major topic of research in this field is precisely how to develop more holistic images. In what language can it be expressed without becoming some type of bla-bla?

14. A difference between instinct theory and needs theory, and an important one at that, would be that whereas needs vary greatly and are not only biophysiologically but also socio-culturally determined, instincts would be seen as biophysiological, species-typical, and hence, universal. The transition from one theory to the other thus also permits much more flexibility and variation in general.

15. The efforts to try to draw a line between humans and animals are countless. My own favorite formula is something like this: "Both animals and humans are programmed, but it is given to humans to some extent to reflect on this program and to change it, again to some extent. It is this self-transcending character that renders distinctness to man." According to a view of this kind, animals do not have needs; they have instincts because needs can be the objects of reflection. This certainly does not mean that there are not necessary conditions that have to be fulfilled for any form of life to continue and unfold.

16. "When time is ripe" – the "principle of unripe time" that may serve to legitimize almost any repression.

17. But not at meeting them in any way possible; in a human way (as emphasized by Anders Wirak, 'Human Needs as a Basis for Indicator Formation," *Papers*, CCPR (Oslo: University of Oslo). One way of formulating this might be as follows: development is not only to satisfy the needs of the needs subjects, but to do so in such a way that the needs subjects can control the needs objects, can decide over them. This is also one way of defining self-reliance, like the Chinese *tzu li keng sheng* (regeneration through own efforts). For a very interesting example, see *The Basic Human Needs and Their Satisfaction*, Sarvodaya Development Education Institute, Moratuwa, Sri Lanka, with a preface by the president of the Sri Lanka Sarvodaya Shramadana Movement, A. T. Ariyaratne. The needs are classified in ten classes: environment, water, clothing, food, housing, health care, communication, fuel, education, and spiritual–cultural needs. Thus the focus is on material needs, and the 167 satisfiers listed – based on dialogues with Sarvodaya villagers – are mainly material (cf. 33: to have a raised raft built to keep pots and pans). But they are all within the reach of the villagers with modest means themselves and hence are a basis on which autonomous development can start. Surely it will not necessarily stop at that level, either materially or non-materially. Needs are dynamic!

18. See Johan Galtung, "The New International Economic Order and the Basic Need Approaches," paper presented at the Society for International Development North–South Round Table, Rome (18–20 May 1978).

19. For a good analysis from one Third World point of view see Firouz Vakil, "Basic Human Needs and the Growth Process: The Dimension of Conflict," paper prepared for Aspen-Gajareh Workshop, Iran (June 1977).

20. This is where the obvious linkage with market and sales promotion under capitalist economic structures enters: satisfiers can be promoted (a whole structure exists for that purpose), but they can be sold and consumed

only if some kind of need is created for them. That need has to be implanted in people (see Goulet). In some cases this may bring to the surface latent, but true, needs; in other cases artificial, false needs are created. The experience of children with toys can satisfy – but what kind of toys? Children are fascinated with glittering, expensive-looking toys, but they get tired of them after one day – because they are too well-made, too programmed, too full of already explored possibilities. The moment the toys are discarded, the child may turn to a heap of pebbles, some old brick, or the like. But the market does not press these upon her or him which may mean that the child still has the capacity to be honest, to be faithful to true needs rather than to give in to the forces of the market. Socialization into adult consumer behavior is then, in part, socialization into dishonesty toward oneself.

21. There is thus agreement, by and large, with the points made by Gilbert Rist if they are seen as directed against a special interpretation of BNAs and not BNAs in general.

22. "The hungry people of the world wanted bread and they were given statistics – No research was needed to find out that half the people in the world lacked sufficient food for health," the words of Article 25 (1) of the Universal Declaration of Human Rights of 10 December 1948 are very clearly basic needs oriented:

> Everyone has the right to a standard of living adequate for the health and well-being of himself and of his family, including food, clothing, housing and medical care and necessary social services, and the right to security in the event of unemployment, sickness, disability, widowhood, old age or other lacks of livelihood in circumstances beyond his control.

And then there is the important report on "International Definition and Measurement of Standards and Levels of Living" (United Nations, 1954) that lists categories of material needs and adds at the end "human freedom." The idea has been with the UN from the very beginning, but in different terminology. The debate within the UN about the proper position of basic needs in development strategy, not to mention the selection of development strategies to meet basic needs, is terribly important; and the steps forward should be appreciated not belittled. At the same time, many watchful eyes are needed – there are strong forces at work.

23. The whole idea of "constructive work" and "positive action," so essential as part of a dialectic where "non-cooperation" and "civil disobedience" constituted the other part, was aiming exactly at basic needs for the most needy.

24. That means lower priorities for elite non-basic needs – not so strange that they are skeptical or outright hostile towards BNAs. But a view of basic needs as leading to a zero-sum game between elites and masses overlooks the possibility of generating new satisfiers through self-reliance. Thus, it is hard to believe that the Sarvodaya villages in Sri Lanka, after much volunteerism and hard work, are competitive with elite interests. To many, this would be an argument against them.

25. The history of the last generation or two of the rich, developed countries under controlled, welfare state capitalism is about this. It is possible for the whole world? My own view is YES. What capitalism presupposes is not misery or poverty at the bottom, but inequality which internationally, intra-nationally rewards the entrepreneurs, has vast differentials to play upon for motivation, and above all can find new markets for old products when they have to cater to old markets with new products.

26. There is thus the usual trade-off known from the general methodology of data collection in the social sciences: what one gains in validity one usually loses in reliability, and vice versa.

27. And that is, of course, a major reason why it is rejected by those who have vested academic, intellectual or political interests in some other theory; it becomes disturbing when development as defined by these theories turns out to be not only a-human but anti-human.

28. Kinhide Mushakoji, "Scientific Revolution and Inter-Paradigmatic Dialogues," paper prepared from the GPID project meeting (Geneva, 2–8 October 1978).

16 Basic Human Needs Theory: Beyond Natural Law

Richard E. Rubenstein

Individual psychology discovers the existence of basic human needs in connection with the search for an explanation of individual pathology.[1] Social thought discovers basic needs in the quest for the causes and cures of social disintegrration. "When a basic need is not satisfied," Johan Galtung has written, "some kind of fundamental disintegration will take place."[2] Galtung identifies two broad categories of social disintegration: "freezing" (lack of participation, apathy, withdrawal) and "boiling" (overactivity, mutiny, revolt).[3] Other classifications and metaphors might be more apt, but the essential point remains: what leads us to think about basic needs are the unpleasant consequences of their non-satisfaction.

What Galtung does not say in so many words, but what he understands, is that we do not move directly from the perception of social pathology[4] to the hypothesis of basic human needs. We are driven to embrace the hypothesis, in a sense, by a process of elimination. John Burton has described the process well.[5] It involves, first, the elimination of "malevolent will" theories of individual and collective pathology (for example, the theories of innate sinfulness, the "will to power," and the aggressive drive), and, second, the elimination of mechanistic theories that reduce individuals and identity groups to epiphenomena (for example, the notion of the infinitely malleable "sociological man"). In a broad but definable sense, the basic human needs approach is political: it springs from an unwillingness to blame violent or withdrawn social actors for the pathologies in which they participate, and also from a refusal to see individuals and social groups as mere manifestations of uncontrollable external forces or structures. But these rejections do not constitute a political philosophy; they clear an area in which political philosophy may be constructed.

The purpose of this chapter is to make explicit certain political questions raised by needs theory, and to inquire, in particular, into the relevance to needs theory of natural law thinking. A touchstone will be the adequacy of the philosophy to explain political violence, and hence to serve as a theoretical basis for conflict resolution. I assume that we will want to impose upon ourselves the same sort of discipline Freud demanded of psychoanalytic theorists, when he insisted that they test a theory of normal mental structure originally inspired by interest in abnormal mental states by evaluating its usefulness in the treatment of mental pathology.[6] In Freud's case, referring psychoanalytic theory back to its generative motives demonstrated where its strengths lay (in understanding and treating the common neuroses), where it was less effective (in dealing with schizophrenia and other severe psychoses), and where important new work remained to be done. The analogy of psychoanalysis is useful because we, too, desire not only to understand the world but to change it. To the extent that human needs theory enables us to understand the sources of deep rooted political conflict, it also illuminates the parameters and possibilities of conflict resolution.

HUMAN NEEDS THEORY AND NATURAL LAW

Human needs theory is an attempt to account for the causes of violence and disorder in a manner that is consistent with the ultimate construction of an orderly but non-coercive world society. It is therefore responsive to the same motives that, over the course of the past 2500 years, have produced recurrent waves of Natural Law thinking. Comparing the emergence of various versions of natural law theory among the Greek Stoics, Roman jurisconsuls, late-medieval European churchmen, early bourgeois political philosophers, and modern constitutionalists, A. P. d'Entrèves suggested that this mode of thought has great appeal and utility in certain situations – for example, when authorities lacking effective means of coercion wish to extend their sway over peoples outside the *civis* proper, or when subjects wish to disobey existing authorities in a manner consistent with the preservation of their view of social order.[7]

Natural Law was ever a way of affirming cross-cultural (and, after the sixteenth century, cross-individual) commonalities upon which could be based a regime of "natural" (therefore, minimally coerced) order. The Roman *praetor* used it to create a rough sort of legal order in which Romans and Barbarians could trade and interact on a common footing. ("Natural Law," said the Roman maxim, "is the law of nations.") Medieval jurists used it to create a basis for universal moral order (and Church supremacy) in the rapidly changing European society of the twelfth and thirteenth centuries. And bourgeois theorists used it both to justify the revolt against feudalist authority and to establish the principles of a less coercive political order in the age of the capitalist revolutions. In each of its reincarnations, the theory exhibits certain common elements.

Connection With Human Nature

Natural Law refers to a body of rules prescribing rights and duties that are considered "natural" in the sense that they pertain to human nature rather than to the rules of any particular culture, social system, or historical era. Most theorists of this school conceive of natural law as a body of rules addressed to or emanating from human *reason*, and as derivable from a relatively small number of basic rules that are self-evident.[8] A corollary holds that, since human beings *are* reasonable, they will recognize and observe these rules without intense or massive coercion. (The purpose of the law, says St. Thomas Aquinas, is to assist men to be good.)[9]

Universality

It follows from their intimate relationship with human nature that the rules of Natural Law are universally applicable. Fusing the normative with the descriptive, which theorists of this school are ever wont to do, this means that they are universally obligatory and more or less universally obeyed. This "more or less" obviously poses problems for the theory, particularly when obedience turns out to be quite a bit less than universal.[10] Nevertheless, Natural Law theorists have traditionally maintained that while some disobedience can be attributed to the fact that certain individuals or groups are not reasonable, much apparent disobedience is merely the result of the relativity of custom and the vagaries of local interpretation. Differences in the legal definition of "self-defense" do not abrogate the natural right of self-preservation. Although Natural Law in civil society is not applied as it would be in a state of nature, a right of self-defense is universally recognized.

Permanence

Most theorists hold that Natural Law is unchanging. Again, changes over time can be explained, in many cases (to use St Thomas's terminology) as "additions to" rather than as "subtractions from" the natural law – i.e., as institutional innovations that, while changing the application of basic principles, do not alter the principles themselves. The medieval philosophers believed that slavery and private property represented beneficial additions to a Natural Law prescribing equality and communism.[11] In a similar vein, to cite just one example, modern Constitutional Law theorists have held that legal recognition of a right of privacy adds to the Natural Law without changing it in any essential respect.[12]

Supremacy

In case of conflict between the principles of Natural Law and those of any other law, Natural Law is generally held to be supreme. The principle of supremacy is maintained both by conservative Natural Law thinkers (i.e., those who believe that rule by existing authorities is justified by Natural Law) and by radicals (i.e., those who see existing legal or moral rules as inconsistent with Natural Law). Overall, it is probably fair to say that the effect of this doctrine has been profoundly conservative, since natural rules are held to prescribe both the methods and the limits of civil disobedience. In polities like the United States, where natural rights are believed to be embodied in the Constitution, the right of revolution is thus effectively reduced to a right to amend the Constitution.

Primacy of Interpretation

A final common principle, often unacknowledged, is the primary role implicitly accorded by Natural Law to its interpreters. Positive Law consists of all statements of legal obligation deemed authorized, most of which are quite specific. The first principle of positive legal interpretation is therefore, "Effectuate the plain meaning of the rule."[13] Natural Law, on the other hand, consists of a relatively small number of statements of legal and moral obligation expressed in highly general fashion. It is impossible to apply them in any concrete situation without extensive interpretation, a circumstance that has long placed great authority in the hands of their interpreters. An important difference between conservative and radical applications of Natural Law has thus been that, in the former case, interpretation is limited to an authorized group (or caste), while in the latter, interpretation is held to be a more commonly distributed function. Over time, one notes an apparently inexorable tendency for radical Natural Law to become conservative Natural Law – that is, for the "priesthood of all believers" to be transformed into the priesthood of the authorized priests.

The purpose of this summary of Natural Law should by now be obvious: the theory of basic human needs, as commonly adumbrated, seems to be the latest version of the Natural Law approach to social relations, but with quasi-psychological categories substituted for the quasi-legal categories employed by the earlier theory. Indeed, there are works in the human needs genre which can be translated into the Natural Law medium merely by substituting the phrase "natural rights" for "basic human needs." This suggests, of course, that it is the more radical version of the theory which is being revived: a theory of rights not yet vindicated rather than of duties rightly imposed. But to the extent that human needs theory accepts the assumptions of natural law – in particular, the assumption that human nature is fully revealed in existing relations of production and extant social relationships – its conservative tendancy is inexorable.

Like Natural Law, basic human needs are believed (at least by some commentators) to be universal, permanent, imperative, and an essential part of the definition of what it means to be human. The theoretical difficulties generated by this approach are also familiar: the specific content of basic human needs seems as problematical as the content of specific natural duties and rights. Nor is it an easy matter to explain why "universal" needs are not universally expressed, and how it is that "permanent" needs appear to change. Most important, like Natural Law, human needs theory is vulnerable to the charge that it embodies in absolutistic form the transient ethical norms, political assumptions, or mere prejudices of its interpreters. In general, Natural Law thinking exemplifies those qualities of a-historical "flatness," reified abstraction, and tendency toward tautology that Marxist critics have long identified as the outstanding limitations of bourgeois social thought.[14] If human needs theory is to escape the impact of this critique, reconstruction will be necessary.

IS THERE A BASIC NEED FOR SECURITY?

Let me illustrate the problem more concretely with reference to the alleged human need for security. Immediately, the problem of definition obtrudes. Defined most simply and "externally," security means safety of the individual from violent attack. Defined in a more complex and internal manner, it suggests what R. D. Laing termed "ontological security," that is, the psyche's safety from a host of dangers including engulfment, petrifaction, depersonalization, splitting, and other threats to the independence and coherence of the personality.[15] But security in the ontological sense merges with identity, which is said to be an independent human need, and which is linked in turn with autonomy, freedom to develop, and other desiderata. Laing's subject is really *the security of identity* – an important concept, as we shall see, but a far cry from what most needs theorists mean by the need for security.

The tendency to treat physical needs (e.g., hunger) as archetypical, and to model other needs after them, is a mark of human needs theory's descent from Natural Law philosophy. Security, in the sense of safety from violent physical attack, is a notion drawn directly from the Natural Law thinking of the early modern period. Thomas Hobbes asserted that the sovereign state was created to vindicate humans' natural right to security, which he considered the master right on which all other rights depended. John Locke, more demanding of the state, insisted on specifying the right to include the components of life, liberty and property. It is by no means clear, however, that security in either Hobbes's or Locke's sense of the word is a basic human need. Precisely the same objections that could be registered against considering it a natural right compel us to question the utility of substituting "need" for "right" without altering the natural lawyers' definition.

For example, if the need for physical security is fundamental, universal and imperative, we must explain why some people willingly expose themselves and their loved ones to violence. One explanation suggests that there is a hierarchy of needs, with security ranking lower on the scale than, say, identity or freedom. But Galtung maintains, I think correctly, that no such hierarchy exists; depending upon the circumstances, any need may temporarily be subordinated to any other need.[16] This seems demonstrable – but it also means that the fundamental, universal character of the security need can be proved only in the way that natural rights are proved: i.e., by assuming that it is self-evident. We must assume, in other words, that although the need is always and everywhere present, like the sun at night, in practice, it is frequently nullified or counter-balanced by other unsatisfied needs. This tendency to explain the operation of needs in history as the product of case-by-case prioritization or "balancing" betrays the legalistic origins and limitations of the doctrine, at least as expressed in this form.

By the same token, if we assert that the need for security is a permanent aspect of human personality, we must account for the fact that its expression seems to change greatly over time. It is generally understood that, in an earlier age, security needs were not considered to be as basic or imperative as they later became under the influence of bourgeois ideas of civilization and safety. The natural lawyers had a standard answer to objections based on relativity of time or place: the law was always and ever the same, they said, although its applications differed from time to time and place to place. Today, others may argue in a similar vein that although the security need was always present, the possibilities of satisfying it were not; therefore, the need remained unconscious, etc. But I do not think that this sort of (literal) casuistry advances our inquiry.

Similarly, when we say that satisfaction of the security need is necessary to permit us to live in a truly "human" fashion, we imitate the natural lawyer's propensity to blend the descriptive with the normative. Natural Law consists of those rules which humans *do* obey and which they *ought to* obey, since this is the law addressed by the Eternal to human reason. Human needs are those needs that humans *do* have and that they *ought to* be enabled to satisfy, since without their satisfaction, "development" will not occur. In both cases, the optimistic theorist assumes that, because creation is good, that which exists ought to exist, and that which ought not to exist is in some sense illusory. St Thomas asks "whether there is a law in the *fomes* of sin," and concludes that while the tendency to sin is inherent in post-lapsarian humanity, it is not part of the natural law.[17] Galtung asks whether there is a basic human need to dominate others, and comes to the conclusion that while "needs language should be open" to such "morally unapplauded" needs, they "cannot be met by everybody for logical reasons."[18] This sounds very much like saying that they are not basic.

Can there be "bad" (i.e., anti-social or anti-developmental) basic needs? One taking an essentially Augustinian view of humanity might argue that in a fallen world needs are inherently insatiable; hence that, if uncontrolled by authority or unbalanced by other needs, the security need becomes indistinguishable from a need to dominate others. The conventional response to this challenge is precisely that of St Thomas to St Augustine, or of the natural lawyer to the advocate of *Realpolitik*: insatiable needs are unnatural. Or, needs incapable of universal satisfaction (like the alleged need to dominate others) are not basic human needs. Both Natural Law and human needs theory, expressed in this form, assert that humans are fundamentally reasonable, sociable creatures whose basic requirements do not – can not – conflict internally or with the general welfare.[19]

What is deficient in this approach is not the concept of basic needs itself, but rather an approach to the subject that partakes of the abstraction, moralism, and a-historicity of Natural Law thinking. These defects are inevitable, in my view, the moment that needs theory accepts the natural lawyers' definition of the individual as a body motivated by interests – i.e., as bourgeois man. If we do not define security ontologically (in effect, as the security of identity), there is no way or reason to distinguish between a security "need" and a security "right" or "interest." And if this is the case, nothing has been gained by rephrasing Natural Law theory in the (pseudo-) psychological language of need. We do not need human needs theory to tell us that human beings are calculating machines that "balance" their interest in security against other interests in order to maximize marginal utilities!

To the extent that needs theorists accept the assumptions of Natural Law philosophy, their thought takes on that philosophy's characteristic tautological tendency. Why do men rebel? Some scholars assert that political violence is the result of humans' attempts to close the gap between their "value expectations" and the socio-political system's "value capabilities."[20] But to say that people experience a gap between value expectations and value capabilities is not very different from saying that they are unable to get what they want – i.e., that they are unhappy. And this is not very different from asserting, as John Locke's North American disciples did, that there is a natural right to happiness whose denial activates a right of revolution. If human needs theory is to demonstrate its usefulness in the context of conflict resolution, it will have to advance beyond the level of truism.

One might say of almost any violent political conflict that it is motivated, at least in part, by unfulfilled security needs. As it stands, this statement is not significant; the disputing parties generally believe that their security is threatened, and they resort to violence in a conscious effort to eliminate that threat. The statement becomes interesting only if we can differentiate between true and false security needs – i.e., if we can describe how the parties' perceptions of their needs and of those needs' potential satisfiers differs from reality. Many of us might argue, for example, that true security can be found in the creation of affective bonds rather than in arming the state; but characterizing this as an argument about need satisfiers does not alter the fact that it is an argument that has long been made without reference to needs theory at all.

Needs theory (like Natural Law theory) frequently seems to have this "additive" character – one uses it to restate or to confirm conclusions already arrived at by some other method. Unless it can be used to generate *new* insights, however, the utility of the approach for conflict analysis and resolution will be severely limited. In the next part of this chapter we therefore ask whether the basic human needs approach can, in fact, generate new insights into the causes, nature, and means of resolving violent political conflicts. We want to discover whether it is possible to build the theory in a manner that avoids the pitfalls and limitations of a Natural Law Perspective: that is, that restores the qualities of historicity, concreteness, and theoretical utility to a doctrine that often seems vague, abstract, and conclusory.

NEEDS THEORY AND IDENTITY-GROUP VIOLENCE

Human needs theory offers to provide theorists and practitioners of conflict resolution with both a context and a method. First, it envisions the conflict ridden world as one in which authoritative elites unable to satisfy their subjects' basic needs are bleeding legitimacy, as it were, from every pore. In such an environment, authorities tend to rely increasingly on coercion (armies, police, courts, and power-based negotiations) to defend their roles and visions of social order, while the unsatisfied basic needs of their people provide the tinder for various sorts of violent rebellion, from violence against the self and common crime to terrorism, revolution, and war.[21] This perspective, it seems to me, is both defensible and useful to analysts of political violence, although it does not answer the question why those with unsatisfied needs so often resign themselves to suffering or engage in purely "expressive" rebellion.

Second, the theory defines a substratum of behavior that may serve a function in conflict resolution similar to that served by the unconscious in psychoanalysis. In other words, it indicates specific needs whose non-satisfaction, under certain conditions, will generate particular and predictable types of conflict, as well as characteristic perceptions of "right" and "interest" on the part of the disputing parties. A basic human needs approach in this sense offers analysts of deep rooted conflict a place to stand – a vantage point which permits them to translate the language of right and power generally spoken by conflicting parties into a tongue permitting the identification and solution of conflict generating problems: the language of individual human needs and socially structured satisfiers. This heuristic function of human needs theory is more ambitious and potentially more significant than the contextual function described above. Let us examine the extent to which its promise can be fulfilled.

Recent work on the causes and nature of political violence suggests that one cluster of basic needs in particular facilitates the depth analysis of a wide range of types of violent conflict.[22] I refer to the needs associated with "identity": self-identification, group-identification, recognition, belongingness, and so on. The usefulness of this concept can be demonstrated in three ways.

First, it indicates underlying similarities between certain apparently disparate forms of conflict. The need to defend or create "group identity" (i.e., the identity of the-individual-in-the-group) is an essential component of the mix of factors generating certain types of riots and other forms of "primitive rebellion,"[23] police violence,[24] vigilantism,[25] and terrorism,[26] as well as communal violence, state terror, and war.[27] Indeed, in an earlier work on the subject of mass political violence in the United States, I concluded that the principal actors in a wide spectrum of violent confrontations in that country, ranging from farmer revolts to anti-immigrant riots, racial uprisings, gang warfare, and even some forms of labor–management violence, were "out-groups" defending a threatened identity against the effects of "internal colonialism," and "in-groups" wielding state power in defense of their members' own identity needs.[28] Much work remains to be done, of course, in exploring the dynamics of culture group identity needs and the forms of social organization that might satisfy them.

Second, the notion of "basic" and irrepressible" identity needs helps to explain the power and durability of these needs (as opposed not only to "interests," but to other needs) in generating intense political conflict. One may agree with Galtung that, in general, the assertion of human needs in history is incompatible with a fixed needs hierarchy, and still note that in many cases of ethnic, religious, and national violence, needs for security, welfare, and freedom are systematically subordinated to the imperatives of identity, recognition, and belongingness. The peculiar power of this needs cluster in modern world society enables one to predict that, under certain conditions (for example, an attempt by the state to integrate an incompletely developed identity group into the general population), violent conflict will erupt. Analysts understanding the importance of identity needs have therefore been able to anticipate such phenomena as the Palestinian *intifahda*, the resurgence of the "nationalities problem" in the USSR, and the (as yet almost unnoticed) revival of Black Nationalism in the United States.[29]

Third, the concept of an identity needs cluster has the particular utility of suggesting (and, to an extent, defining) an intimate connection between individual psychology and group behavior. Unlike, say, freedom and welfare needs, identity is the subject of a well developed body of psychological theory with patent political interests and implications. It is hardly coincidental that Erik Erikson, the father (as it were) of "psychohistory," is also the leading psychoanalytic exponent of the importance of the "identity crisis" in the transition from adolescence to adulthood.[30] Erikson's analysis of the roles played by identity, fidelity, and betrayal in the development of post-adolescents provides a bridge between individual and group psychology that enables us to move from one domain to the other without "reducing" or "psychologizing." This sort of theoretical work gives the identity needs cluster an analytical weight that other needs do not have, either because the necessary psychological groundwork has not yet been laid or because the non-satisfaction of other needs does not generate violent conflict so directly.

Finally, the relevance of identity needs to the analysis of conflict becomes apparent when one attempts to fashion solutions to the problems that generate political violence. In many cases (but certainly not all), practitioners of conflict resolution find themselves drawn to options that redefine relationships between groups in dispute – for example, by proposing one form or another of a new "constitution" that promises to satisfy identity needs.[31] Those who recognize the power of this needs cluster are not easily persuaded that such needs will wither away once a new majority group is in power, or once some sort of token autonomy is conceded to a rebellious minority group. On the contrary, the satisfaction of narrow (let us say, without intending any offense, "tribal") identity needs, which may be a prerequisite to the development of species-identity, depends upon structural changes that permit every member of the tribe to satisfy his or her needs for security, welfare, love, autonomy, and meaning. In other words, it appears that identity needs, while central to the understanding of many types of political violence, are derivative in the sense that the satisfaction of all other needs also satisfies them.

THE NEED FOR IDENTITY: BEYOND NATURAL LAW

The assertion that there is a basic human need for identity suggests a departure from natural rights philosophy. For unlike life, liberty, security and other needs commonly referred to as basic, the identity need is not a restatement of any natural right. Or, rather, it has but one analog in the universe of natural rights, and that drawn from a later revival of Natural Law: the right of national self-determination. Some analysts would say that just as there is a basic need for security which can be satisfied by collective arrangements that guarantee domestic order and international peace, there is a need for identity that can be satisfied by arrangements recognizing the political auton-omy of nations and other cultural identity groups. What seems clear, however, is that to the extent national (or group) self-determination is deemed an *adequate* satisfier of the need for identity, we remain stranded in the abstract, reified universe of Natural Law. And, conversely, to the extent that nations and other limited communities are recognized as *partial* satisfiers of the identity need, we begin to move beyond Natural Law, and on to the terrain of an autonomous needs theory.

The chief failing of Natural Law philosophy is that it assumes the permanence and universality of the present, including a known human nature and social institutions responding to the requirements of that nature. Human needs theory commits the same error when it fails to recognize that human nature can be more fully comprehended and expressed only when men and women are in a position to make their own history. When Karl Marx discusses "the production of new needs," he is not referring to material needs alone (and certainly not to apparent needs based on "false consciousness"), but to the fact that people discover what their basic needs are – and hence, what it means to be human – by associating themselves together in ways that permit conscious transformation of the environment.[32] It follows from this that social arrangements that obstruct conscious transformation also obstruct the discovery or development of human nature. Insofar as humans are imposed upon (for example, by elite domination, or by being compelled to sell their labor power at the price set by an apparently "objective" market), they are compelled to accept false satisfiers for true needs, a process that has been described subjectively as producing "false needs." Galtung is absolutely right to oppose the bureaucratic concept of "minimum needs,"[33] although I am not sure that he sees clearly enough that, so far as any need is considered to be fully "satisfied" in an elite dominated, scarcity ridden society, it is to that extent falsified.

The need for identity illustrates this point. Clearly, we would not consider someone identifying himself or herself literally as Jesus Christ, or someone seeking recognition as a member of the Aryan Master Race, to be satisfying an identity need. Personal or social delusions of this sort, rather, represent the acceptance of false satisfiers: false in the double sense that they do not satisfy the identity need, and that they pretend to satisfy it. (False satisfiers are satanic in the Miltonian sense; they not only negate reality, they also mimic it.) The proof of this is the persistence of disintegration: the deluded reincarnation of Christ remains tortured by his incomplete or shattered identity; the Aryan Superhuman must try endlessly to prove the unprovable by eliminating or enslaving dreaded rivals and sources of "pollution." Kurt Vonnegut put the matter nicely: "Bad ideas make you sick."[34]

The problem is how to recognize a true satisfier when we see one. Suppose that a Lebanese woman identifies herself and is recognized as a Shiite Muslim. If Shia is her chosen or inherited religion, and if recognizing that fact causes no personal or social disintegration, the needs theorist might say that she has discovered a true or efficient satisfier. But if this identification were such as to *negate* her identity as a Lebanese, a woman, a worker, or a human being, we would have to characterize it as a false satisfier whose partiality is bound, in time, to cause disintegration. This implies that the only true satisfiers are those that make the identity whole: that is, that satisfy the need for a series of fact-based identities ranging from the most local to the most universal. Any local identity that serves as a stopping point, an obstacle to the achievement of a mere universal human identity, is to that extent false (or falsely satisfied). And any purportedly universal identity that can be secured only by annihilating (as opposed to redefining) fact-based local identities is to that extent false.

The "need for identity," in other words, is really a need for integrated multiple identities, and for the opportunity to realize them.[35] In a world which considers membership in a nation-state or a community of believers the final stage of identity development, further disintegration (both of the "freezing" and "boiling" types) is predictable. For the same reason, political conflicts that are settled by the grant of communal rights to an insurgent cultural identity group must be considered, in a real sense, merely "settled" rather than "resolved."[36]

Compared with the settlements achieved through war and power-based negotiations, agreements that satisfy even a partial sense of identity have a stability that suggests final resolution. But appreciating the relative falsity of all identities that stop short of species-identity forces us to relativize the notion of conflict resolution itself. Genuine conflict resolution takes place only when basic human needs are satisfied. In the case of identity needs, this means recognition of all of one's true identities, from unique individual to self-conscious *homo sapiens.* It follows from this that human needs theory has a transformative implication: it is only through liberating struggle that humans discover what their true needs are, and how they may truly be satisfied.

THE NEED FOR IDENTITY AND CLASS CONSCIOUSNESS

With this said, we can turn briefly to the question of class struggle that, together with ethnic, national and religious conflicts generates much of the political violence that now wracks world society. Conflict between social classes produces a wide range of violent phenomena ranging from crime and other forms of anti-social behavior to rioting, terrorism, civil war, and interstate war.[37] Indeed, certain forms of violent conflict (e.g., industrial violence and social revolution) are specific to class struggle while many of the most intense, protracted conflicts afflicting the world at present are simultaneously ethnic, cultural, national, or religious identity group struggles and class struggles. Few analysts would dispute Ted Gurr's recent statement that:

rebellions are likely to be more numerous and intense in societies that have sharp class stratification and ethnolinguistic cleavages, and are likely to be greatest of all where dominant groups are distinguished from others by both class and ethnicity.[38]

Given the prevalence of class-based political violence, it is striking that human needs theory at its present state of development does not have more to say about the relationship of human needs to social class. Some theorists appear to consider conflict between social classes to be "materialistic" in the vulgar sense as if the dispute were simply about which group gets the largest piece of pie. But a social class is not an economic "interest group;" it is a group whose relationship to the total system of production generates, over time, a common frame of meaning and a political culture. As a result, social revolutions pose more clearly than any other form of political conflict the question of total human development. They raise the issue of property because modes of production that limit society's productive potential, misdirect environmental transformation, and maldistribute the social surplus, stand as absolute barriers to the satisfaction of genuine needs both "material" and "immaterial."

The view that social classes are economic groupings in the narrow sense (and the associated view that conflicts between them are "zero-sum" games resolvable only through violence or power-based bargaining) is the bitter fruit of both liberal and Stalinist social thinking. Liberal praxis resolves social classes into fragmented interest groups whose relations are managed by a neutral state. Class consciousness, in this context, is nothing more than trade union, occupational (or management association) consciousness.[39] Stalinist praxis, both in its Second and Third World varieties, dispossesses the bourgeoisie and proclaims an end to class struggle, while constituting a national bureaucracy the permanent "trustee" of the proletariat's interests. Class consciousness, in this context, is resolved into office-consciousness on the part of the elite and nation-consciousness ("socialism in one country") on the part of the masses.[40]

What is missing in both cases is the concept of social class as a group of humans occupying a common relationship to the means of production, existing *across* ethnic, cultural, religious and national boundaries, and destined to become a self-conscious identity group. Rather, the definitions of class accepted and institutionalized by capitalist and state managed systems represent what Marx would surely have considered *false identities* – false, that is, not in the sense of being utterly divorced from reality, but in the sense of being premature stopping points in the development of a more complete identity. Of course, class consciousness is not a stopping point either; it is an indispensable (because factually rooted) step on the road to the development of species-identity. Without it, basic human needs, including the need for identity, must remain unfulfilled. Without it, that is, we remain "alienated."

Reading again Johan Galtung's interesting typology of basic human needs and their satisfiers, one finds, opposite the need "for self-expression, creativity, praxis, work," the satisfier, "jobs."[41] Two comments about this may be appropriate. First, Galtung has the wisdom to consider this an identity rather than a welfare need: he groups it under the heading of "Identity needs (needs for closeness) – to avoid alienation." Nevertheless, I would argue that the need for identity is not merely a need for closeness; members of Ku Klux Klan "Klaverns" are "close," and, in this purely subjective sense, non-alienated. The need can be satisfied only if affective bonds are rooted in an evolving social reality. We cannot discuss the need for identity without doing a social analysis that distinguishes between efficient and inefficient satisfiers. The identity constructed on the basis of racial bonds – or, indeed, on the basis of any purely ideological commonality – requires increasingly costly defense against the hammer blows of social evolution. If needs theory is to be founded on human nature, it must transcend the purely subjective, egoistic, non-developmental view of humanity bequeathed us by the natural law philosophers. It must put *homo faber* in his proper place.

Second, once the identity need is properly defined, it becomes apparent that "jobs" (i.e., tasks defined by an existing market for labor power) are a false satisfier. Just as tribal identity, say, satisfies a genuine identity need partially (and, to the extent that it represents a stopping point, creates a "false need"), jobs satisfy a genuine need for creative associated work partially. The latter creates a false need for what bourgeois and state managed societies define as "work" (i.e., toil). The "ethic of work," which vainly attempts to make a virtue of necessity, and unmistakable signs of disintegration in the workplace – for example, massive use of narcotic drugs by workers attempting to make intolerable jobs tolerable – reveal how false this need is.

In general, there is increasing evidence that the labor incentive systems operated by both capitalist and state-managed societies are breaking down in the face of humans' irrepressible need for pleasurable, autonomous work.

The normal kind of work (socially useful occupational activity) in the prevailing division of labor is such that the individual, in working, does *not* satisfy *his* own impulses, needs, and faculties but performs a pre-established function.[42]

The basic need denied by current class dominated work relations is the need to replace alienated labor with "a system of expanding and enduring libidinal relations, which are in themselves work relations."[43] To cope with the disintegration caused by this unsatisfied need, state changed systems have restored features of the private market while capitalist enterprises experiment with "self-management" and other attempts to humanize the work process; but we may well doubt whether such partial and manipulative attempts to satisfy a basic human need will succeed.

Liberating human needs theory from the assumptions of Natural Law philosophy requires that we recognize social production as the field within which human nature is progressively shaped and revealed. Human needs that are ontological and universal cannot be satisfied within the limitations imposed by *any* class-based productive system. Such needs are rooted in the present with its desiccated social landscape. They are watered fitfully by "satisfiers" which, under present circumstances, do not and cannot satisfy fully and whose partiality continuously creates false stopping points in the development of human nature. They can flower only in a future which permits men and women to become masters of production, of the state, and of themselves.

In the present epoch, the domination of material conditions over individuals, and the suppression of individuality by chance, has assumed its sharpest and most universal form, thereby setting existing individuals a very definite task. It has set them the task of replacing the domination of circumstances and of chance over individuals by the domination of individuals over chance and circumstances.[44]

NOTES AND REFERENCES

1. See, for example, Abraham H. Maslow, *Toward a Psychology of Being* (Princeton: Van Nostrand, 1962).
2. Johan Galtung, "The Basic Needs Approach", in Katrin Lederer (ed.) with Johan Galtung and David Antal, *Human Needs: A Contribution to the Current Debate* (Cambridge, MA, Oelgeschlager, Gunn & Hain, 1980.
3. Galtung: "The Basic Needs Approach": 61.
4. Galtung makes it clear, and I agree, that social movements involving either violence or withdrawal are not necessarily "diseased" but may represent attempts to restore social "health."
5. See John W. Burton, *Deviance, Terrorism, and War: The Process of Solving Unsolved Social and Political Problems* (New York: St Martin's Press, 1979).
6. See Peter Gay, *Freud: A Life for Our Time* (New York: W. W. Norton, 1988): esp. 244 et seq.
7. A. P. d'Entrèves, *Natural Law* (London: Hutchinson University Library, 1970) rev. edn.
8. According to Cicero, natural law is "right reason in agreement with nature." This theme is adopted by Thomas Aquinas and has become a consistent feature of Natural Law theory down to the present time.
9. Anton G. Pegis (ed.), *Introduction to Saint Thomas Aquinas* (New York: Modern Library, 1948): 609.
10. An excellent illustration of this point is the problem confronted by the U.S. court in a case holding that torture of political prisoners was contrary to customary International Law notwithstanding that it was still a fairly common practice. See *Filartiga v. Pena-Irala*, 630 F. 2d 876 (2d Cir. Court of Appeals, 1982).
11. Pegis, *Thomas Aquinas*: 643–4.
12. See *Griswold v. Connecticut*, 14 L.Ed. (2d Series) 510 (Sup. Ct., 1965).
13. In most contested cases, of course, the "plain meaning" of a statute or other legal rule cannot be easily determined, and the court is compelled to discover the rule's "purpose." Still, the typical rule in a system of Positive Law is a statute, and most statutes are specific enough to limit interpretation in ways natural lawyers would find unduly confining.
14. See Georg Lukacs, *History and Class Consciousness* (Cambridge, MA: MIT Press, 1971); C. B. MacPherson, *The Political Theory of Possessive Individualism* (Oxford: Oxford University Press, 1962).
15. R. D. Laing, *The Divided Self* (Harmondsworth: Penguin, 1966): 39 ff.
16. Galtung, "The Basic Needs Approach": 67–71.
17. Pegis, *Thomas Aquinas*: 643–4.
18. Galtung, "The Basic Needs Approach": 59–60.
19. Among sophisticated needs theorists there is a tendency to hedge this point by asserting that there may be non-universalizable basic needs but that, if so, we may simply note and ignore them. If warranted, however, this concession eviscerates basic needs theory (as it does Natural Law) by returning to us the "war of each against all."
20. See, for example, Ted Robert Gurr, *Why Men Rebel* (Princeton:

Princeton University Press, 1970).

21. See Burton, *Deviance, Terrorism and War.*

22. Richard E. Rubenstein, *Rebels in Eden: Mass Political Violence in the United States* (Boston: Little, Brown, 1970); *Alchemists of Revolution: Terrorism in the Modern World* (New York: Basic Books, 1987). See also Albert Camus, *The Rebel: An Essay on Man in Revolt* (New York: Vintage, 1956); Hannah Arendt, *On Violence* (New York: Harcourt, Brace, 1969); Joe R. Feagin and Harlan Hahn, *Ghetto Revolts: The Politics of Violence in American Cities* (New York: Macmillan, 1973).

23. Eric J. Hobsbawm, *Social Bandits and Primitive Rebels: Studies in Archaic Forms of Social Movement in the 19th and 20th Centuries* (New York: Free Press, 1959).

24. Paul Chevigny, *Police Power: Police Abuses in New York City* (New York: Pantheon, 1969).

25. H. Jon Rosenbaum and Peter C. Sederberg (eds), *Vigilante Politics* (University of Pennsylvania Press, 1976).

26. Rubenstein, *Alchemists of Revolution.* See also Walter Laqueur, *Terrorism* (Boston: Little, Brown, 1977) rev. edn. (1988).

27. Burton, *Deviance, Terrorism and War.* Considering the enormous toll that communal violence has taken in this century – and considering that state terror is often a form of communal violence which ensues after one culture group has taken state power against the wishes of others, the paucity of literature on this subject is remarkable. But see Irving Louis Horowitz, *Taking Lives: Genocide and State Power* (New Brunswick, N.J.: Transaction Books, 1980); Lucy Dawidowicz, *The War Against The Jews. 1933–1945* (New York: Holt, Rinehart & Winston, 1975); and Michael Stohl and George A. Lopez (eds.), *Government Violence and Repression: An Agenda for Research* (Greenwood Press, 1986).

28. Rubenstein, *Rebels in Eden.*

29. Noam Chomsky's work on the Middle East is a good example: see, for example, *The Fateful Triangle: The United States, Israel, and the Palestinians* (Boston: South End Press, 1983).

30. Erik H. Erikson, *Identity: Youth and Crisis* (New York: W. W. Norton, 1967). See also his *Young Man Luther: A Study in Psychoanalysis and History* (1958), and *Ghandi's Truth: On the Origins of Militant Nonviolence* (1969).

31. See the cases discussed in Diane B. Bendahmane and John W. McDonald, Jr. (eds.), *Perspectives on Negotiation: Four Case Studies and Interpretations* (Foreign Service Institute, U.S. Department of State, 1986).

32. Karl Marx and Frederick Engels, *The German Ideology*, reprinted in David McLellan, *Karl Marx: Selected Writings* (Oxford: Oxford University Press, 1977): 166 et seq.

33. Galtung, "The Basic Needs Approach": 67–71.

34. Kurt Vonnegut, *Breakfast of Champions* (New York: Delacorte Press, 1973).

35. Indeed, the assumption that there is a natural, coherent individual identity unrelated to social evolution is dubious. There is evidence that what we consider individual identity is the result of the integration of

partial identities over time and in relationship to the development of society. See, for example, Herbert Marcuse, *Eros and Civilization* (Boston: Beacon, 1966); Laing, *The Divided Self*; Gregory Bateson, *Steps to an Ecology of Mind* (San Francisco: Chandler, 1972).

36. The distinction between settlement and resolution has been stated with great force by John W. Burton in "Conflict Resolution as a Political System," Working Paper 1, Center for Conflict Analysis and Resolution, George Mason University. I am not sure that Dr Burton will agree with this application of it.

37. The literature on class conflict is voluminous, although one would wish for more syncretic work. An important book is Eric Wolf, *Peasant Wars of the Twentieth Century* (New York: Harper & Row, 1969). See also Charles Tilley, *From Mobilization to Revolution* (Reading, MA: Addison-Wesley, 1978): Theda Skocpol, *States and Social Revolutions* (Cambridge: Cambridge University press, 1979).

38. Ted Robert Gurr, "Persisting Patterns of Repression and Rebellion: Foundations for a General Theory of Political Coercion", in Margaret P. Karns (ed.), *Persistent Patterns and Emergent Structures in a Waning Century* (New York: Praeger Special Studies, 1986): 159.

39. V. I. Lenin, *What Is To Be Done? Burning Questions of Our Movement* (New York: International Publishers, 1960). See also Rosa Luxemberg, *Reform or Revolution?* (New York: Pathfinder, 1970). I have offered a description of this phenomenon in the United States in *Left Turn: Origins of the Next American Revolution* (Boston: Little, Brown, 1973).

40. The classic exposition of this development is by Leon Trotsky in *The Revolution Betrayed* (New York: Pathfinder, 1965). See also his *Problems of the Chinese Revolution* (New York: Beacon, 1972).

41. Galtung, "The Basic Needs Approach": 66.

42. Marcuse, *Eros and Civilization*: 220.

43. Marcuse, *Eros and Civilization*: 212.

44. Marx and Engels, *The German Ideology*: 179.

Name Index